WF

VCPPP

The gift of this book was made possible by the generous support of the Waters Foundation of Massachusetts, United States of America, to the Vermont Conference on Primary Prevention, Inc., Department of Psychology, University of Vermont, Burlington, Vermont 05401, United States of America.

power, the liberation of women, and the restoration of dignity to the elderly. Running through many of the papers is the argument that social and political powerlessness is a principal source of current emotional disturbances. The great variety of viewpoints and blueprints for suggested changes make this book a valuable aid to all those concerned with bringing about conditions that will both reduce psychopathology and enhance positive mental health.

"The best single source of up-to-date information on research and conceptualization in the field of primary prevention in the country, and, insofar as I know, in the English-speaking world."— BERNARD L. BLOOM, *University of Colorado*

"The Vermont Conferences have been an annual shot-in-the-arm promoting responsible thinking about national issues of mental health, and the published volumes are a national resource for professionals and other citizens concerned with the promotion of psychological well-being and the prevention of mental disorder, ineffectiveness, and misery."— M. BREWSTER SMITH, *University of California, Santa Cruz*

"In the field of primary prevention, the Vermont Conference and the volumes proceeding from it are first-rate, and of primary importance."—EDWARD ZIGLER, *Yale University*

"These conferences and the publications that have resulted have had a major influence in advancing current research and practice in the field of primary prevention. They are essential reading for every serious worker in population-oriented mental health. The books record in a sophisticated and highly readable form the cutting edge of innovative ideas in Prevention."—GERALD CAPLAN, M.D., *Hadassah University Hospital, Jerusalem*

Prevention through
Political Action
and Social Change

Primary Prevention of Psychopathology
George W. Albee and Justin M. Joffe, *General Editors*

Prevention through Political Action and Social Change

**Justin M. Joffe and
George W. Albee, editors**

Published for the Vermont Conference on
the Primary Prevention of Psychopathology
by University Press of New England
Hanover and London, 1981

University Press of New England

Brandeis University
Brown University
Clark University
Dartmouth College
University of New Hampshire
University of Rhode Island
Tufts University
University of Vermont

Copyright © 1981 by the Vermont Conference
on the Primary Prevention of Psychopathology

All Rights Reserved

Library of Congress Catalog Card Number 80-51504
International Standard Book Number 0-87451-187-9

Printed in the United States of America

Grateful acknowledgment is made for the excerpt from "Two Tramps in Mud Time" from *The Poetry of Robert Frost*, edited by Edward Connery Lathem. Copyright 1936 by Robert Frost. Copyright © 1964 by Lesley Frost Ballantine. Copyright © 1969 by Holt, Rinehart and Winston. Reprinted by permission of Holt, Rinehart and Winston, Publishers.

Library of Congress Cataloging in Publication data will be found on the last printed page of this book.

Contents

vi   Contents

Preface

In the summer of 1975 we held a Conference on the Primary Prevention of Psychopathology on the campus of the University of Vermont. The idea of such a conference had been developed in conversations with James and Faith Waters of the Waters' Foundation. The foundation was seeking a way to invest in an activity or program that would enhance the emotional stability of children. The Waters responded positively to our suggestion that the emerging field of primary prevention desperately needed support, visibility, and encouragement. We found that although efforts at primary prevention were occurring in a number of separate and diverse fields spanning education and the social and biological sciences, little effort had been made to bring together people from these diverse fields to present their research. So far as we have been able to ascertain the 1975 conference was the first such effort.

The response to our announcement of the conference far exceeded our expectations. Nearly 300 persons journeyed to Vermont to listen to and discuss the papers presented. The response was so encouraging that the Waters' Foundation readily agreed with our proposal to hold further conferences to deal with more specific aspects of primary prevention.

The second year's conference focused on environmental factors and psychopathology, the third conference was concerned with ways of building competence and coping skills in children, which led to a fourth conference that dealt with building competence and coping skills in adolescents and adults.

Our decision to focus on the field of primary prevention was either prescient or fortunate. Clearly, primary prevention is an idea whose time has come. Conferences dealing with various aspects of the subject are now common, and eleven states have established separate offices concerned with prevention programs. When the President's Commission on Mental Health was established in 1977, soon after President Carter's election, it was decided to include a Task Panel on Prevention among the various study groups reporting to the commission. The Final Report of the President's Commission on Mental Health paid important attention to primary prevention and made a number of recommendations focusing on this area. The director of the Alcohol, Drug Abuse and Mental Health Administration added prevention as a fourth area of major focus for program planning and development.

Clearly the Vermont Conferences can not claim major responsibility for increasing attention to prevention, but we like to think that we have had a significant influence by providing a sound theoretical and knowledge-based review of important aspects of this developing field. We have focused attention on research and theory. This has sometimes led to frustration and criticism from some of the people attending our annual meetings, who want more discussion of and emphasis on programming and practice. Our response has been that there are many other meetings and workshops that emphasize practice. Our belief is that the permanent published record of each of our conferences is its most important product. In addition, thanks to the generosity of the Waters' Foundation we have been able each year to send a copy of the resulting book to a large number of university libraries in developing countries around the world. The foundation has also donated copies to colleges primarily serving minority students in the United States.

The more immersed we have become in the field of primary prevention of mental and emotional disturbance and the enhancement of competence and coping skills, the more we have become aware of the strong resistance to efforts at prevention. It took us some time to see and understand that resources invested in prevention often must be diverted from efforts at individual treatment, and this requires a redistribution of power as it is reflected in budgets. Even more important, efforts at prevention often suggest social and political changes that involve further significant redistribution of power. Our fifth conference, reported in this volume, resulted from our decision to confront these issues directly. Clearly it will be the most controversial of the series. While we made an effort to have different points of view represented, many of the papers clearly are critical of the old established ways that emphasize individual treatment and rehabilitation. We are pleased with the quality of the papers and delighted to be able to share them with a wide audience.

Burlington, Vermont   Justin M. Joffe
July 1980   George W. Albee

PART I

Society and Psychopathology

Introductory Notes

George Albee, in his keynote address, sets the stage for later papers that examine the effects of social conditions on psychopathology and that describe the effects of sociopolitical systems on mental health. He outlines the differences of opinion between those who believe that societal change can ameliorate and prevent psychopathology and those who believe that biological rather than social factors are of paramount importance in the etiology of psychopathology. Albee, unequivocally taking his stand on the side of those who attribute deviant behavior and unhappiness primarily to factors outside the individual, argues that stressful and damaging environmental conditions are almost invariably linked with excessive imbalances in power. In addition, he suggests a more subtle (and in some ways frightening) side to the relationship between social structure and psychopathology. Not only does the socioeconomic system that breeds poverty, racism, sexism, and ageism create psychopathology but the system feeds on itself: it causes or encourages an ethos supportive of the view that people's problems and unhappiness are due to their own defects; the economic system makes necessary the belief in individual internal causes. In other words, our models of causation provide "scientific" justification for the varied conditions that create the problem the models are designed to address.

In the course of examining alternatives, Albee discusses Rawls's analysis of social justice and also touches on the themes of liberty and coercion that are discussed by Thomas Szasz in his midwinter lecture.* In examining the links between the nature of mental illness and the nature of liberty, Szasz poses the question of the individual's right to behave "undesirably." His concern with the issue of *who is to decide* what constitutes undesirable behavior parallels Albee's. If "mental illness" is indeed only

---

*Szasz gave the midwinter Waters' Lecture; he was invited to talk on the theme of the forthcoming Fifth Conference—prevention through political action and social change. His talk was recorded (he spoke from notes); we transcribed it, and sent it to him for editing. He has kindly agreed to it being included in this volume.

undesirable behavior, can it be prevented without destroying liberty? Szasz's discussion of this issue is complex and provocative.

On an initial reading, both authors appear to agree in arguing against coercion and for individual liberty. Clearly Albee and Szasz are at one in opposing involuntary hospitalization and/or treatment in the cause of mental health and in their belief that the psychiatric notion of mental illness is inextricably linked with coercion. But at another level there are profound differences in their views. Can power be redistributed equitably in a Jeffersonian framework of individual liberties? Is it sufficient to provide free individuals with accurate information on dangers (of drugs, or pollution, or racism), or is it necessary somehow to control people's access or exposure to dangerous substances or the dangerous behavior of others toward them? To protect individuals from the consequences of abuses of power, do we have to infringe on their liberties? Must society set limits on the damaging uses of power? To ameliorate the social factors implicated in producing psychopathology do we have the right to use coercion? From their papers it seems likely that Albee and Szasz would give very different answers to these questions and to others of a similar sort—and in these different answers is reflected one of the dilemmas of those who would set about preventing psychopathology by political action and social change.

Most of the papers in this volume do not call for extensive comment. Szasz's paper is an exception, principally because he comes to a conclusion more or less opposite to everyone else's represented at the conference. The Szaszian reasoning goes something like this: There can be no such a thing as the prevention of mental illness because behavioral disturbances are not illnesses. Prevention programs can be shown to prevent genuine diseases, but since the conditions called "mental illnesses" are really moral and political judgments it is folly to talk about preventing them.

One can agree with Szasz that on the basis of present evidence the functional mental disorders are not real diseases. One can also agree that psychiatric coercion involving forced incarceration, forced treatment, and stigmatizing diagnoses is not justified and should be abandoned. But even if we agree with him on these issues, it does not follow that we must agree when he argues against programs to prevent psychopathology.

When these conferences began five years ago, we chose the term *psychopathology* because we wanted a neutral term that would avoid the use of the words "mental illness." *Psychopathology* means twisted, or disordered, mind. It does not require the discovery of any physical or organic causation. Perhaps the term has the disadvantage of possibly being associated with the medical specialty of pathology that studies tissues and other bodily components for evidence of disease. But the word also has other acceptable connotations—like the pathology of Nazism, the pathology of war, the pathology of prejudice—in which no organicity is suggested.

We would argue that behavioral abnormalities and serious emotional disturbances do exist, and that they often follow from pathological social experiences and dehumanizing conditions. Children of psychotic parents, for example, are at very high risk of becoming emotionally disturbed adults. Babies reared in orphanages very often grew up to be cold and affectionless adults. They have many of the same kind of social problems that Harry Harlow's motherless monkeys showed as adults. Babies born to very young unmarried women are at high risk. Marital disruption often leads to depression, suicide, and hypertension.

Szasz says that he prefers "to let people make their own decisions about matters that do not injure others rather than coerce them by means of religious, penal, or psychiatric sanctions." It is obvious, he concludes, that adherence to these libertarian principles would require "scuttling pathology." A key to his position is his statement that people should be left alone in "matters that do not injure others." But by saying this, Szasz undermines a significant part of his argument against attempts at the prevention of psychopathology. It is quite clear that large numbers of children and adults *are* victimized by a wide range of brutalizing, exploitative forces in society. It is also clear that such brutalization and exploitation produce serious emotional damage. Szasz does not consider the evidence that orphanages all but destroy warmth and spontaneity in children; that meaningless, underpaid, repetitive labor is dehumanizing; that physical and sexual abuse of children produces emotionally crippled adults; that the endless depiction by the mass media of women and minorities as inferior creatures and the disenfranchisement and enforced powerlessness of the elderly lead to higher risk of serious emotional distress.

Szasz picks his arguments carefully. People should have the right, he says, to smoke marijuana, to snort cocaine, and to kill themselves. But no libertarian, including Szasz, would support the freedom to kill, torture, or enslave others. Nor would Szasz be likely to defend the maiming of innocent children, the mutilation of women, the torment of the elderly. Yet all of these barbarisms exist in society and they result in serious psychological damage to the victims. John Stuart Mill argued that over one's own body one is sovereign—but *not* that one can be free to harm others. For twenty years Szasz has railed with passion and with reason against psychiatric coercion. To be consistent he should oppose with equal fervor the coercion of the weak and of the powerless by the powerful. Such is the key to the prevention of psychopathology.

We agree with Szasz when he argues against the medicalization of problems in living. The new Diagnostic and Statistical Manual of the American Psychiatric Association (DSM III) offers many examples of the nonsense of psychiatric "medical" diagnosis. But we disagree that human emotional distress ("the scope of psychopathology" Szasz calls it) would shrink to "near-nothingness" if psychiatric coercion were eliminated. We are far less concerned with the folly of the medical diagnosis of victims than with the prevention of victimization in the first place—the prevention of psychopathology.

Politics, Power, Prevention, and Social Change

George W. Albee

Back in the days when the world was a much simpler place, a great many of us held firmly to the belief that scientific judgments were based on facts, and that social policy changed with accumulating scientific findings, and that theories were held only so long as they were supported by objective evidence. Those who thought of themselves as politically liberal held to the conviction that the world was slowly and steadily changing for the better, and that with improved education, more scientific research, new evidence, and practice society would eventually reach a condition of universal justice and fairness.

I am a slow learner. I no longer believe these things to be true. I now believe that the thirst for power is an addiction, far more dangerous than any other addiction. When Baron Acton (1907) said "Power tends to corrupt, and absolute power corrupts absolutely" (p. 504), he was stating a fundamental human law. Power needs override the tempering consequences of human empathy and blind the addict to considerations of justice and fairness.

After reviewing the literature on primary prevention, Marc Kessler and I (1975) said:

Everywhere we looked, every social research study we examined suggested that major sources of human stress and distress generally involve some form of excessive power. The pollutants of a power-consuming industrial society; the exploitation of the weak by the powerful; the overdependence of the automotive culture on powerful engines—power-consuming symbols of potency; the degradation of the environment with the debris of a comfort-loving impulse-yielding society; the power struggle between the rich consuming nations and the exploited third world; the angry retaliation of the impoverished and the exploited; on a more personal level the exploitation of women by men, of children by adults, of the elderly by a youth-worshiping society—it is enough to suggest the hypothesis that a dramatic reduction and control of power might improve the mental health of people. (pp. 577–78)

Marx and Engels (1936) pointed out many years ago that "the ruling ideas of each age have ever been the ideas of its ruling class" (p. 225).

Twenty years ago I wrote *Manpower Trends in the Mental Health Professions* (Albee, 1959). After a careful review of the literature I concluded that the dominant model used to explain human emotional problems— an illness model that finds causes *inside* the person, causes that are labeled sicknesses, defects—failed to account for a wide range of empirical facts. Further, this model that demands one-to-one treatment of the victims was a hopeless effort both because it did nothing to change the social forces producing victimization and because it was largely ineffective in reaching the vast numbers of people damaged by the social and economic system. A social learning model seems much more accurate, and prevention makes more sense than treatment. But the defect model endures. It has powerful defenders. For 20 years a number of us have been marching around the walls of Rockville, Maryland, sounding the trumpet call of truth, but the walls have not come tumbling down! Indeed, they seem as invulnerable as ever. The entrenched defenders of the defect model support treatment and oppose primary prevention for ideological reasons. The ideology supports the status quo.

For the past five years we have brought the best thinkers and scholars in the field to this Conference on Primary Prevention of Psychopathology. The published record of these conferences is a continuing account of effective approaches to primary prevention. Further, last year a group of us prepared a summary account on primary prevention for the President's Commission on Mental Health. The Task Group on Prevention (1978) included some of the most knowledgeable people in the field, and our final report was a relatively dispassionate examination of the compelling research evidence for primary prevention efforts. Our report was written soberly and simply. But unlike other reports to the commission, ours was referred for special evaluation, comment, and criticism to one of the Establishment figures in psychiatry, Albert Stunkard, of the University of Pennsylvania, who damned it. According to Herbert (1979), the report of the Task Group on Prevention had not pleased Daniel X. Freedman, the psychiatrist who "captained the Research Task Panel," and he had nudged the commission into asking for another opinion. Stunkard came down heavily on the side of early treatment (secondary prevention) and suggested more research on high-risk groups and on basic brain research to get at the "causes of specific disorders." No other task force report was subject to this kind of second guessing.

Because of the interest of a couple of steadfast friends of prevention who were members of the President's Commission on Mental Health, our report was accepted and it received a hearing. The commission did make recommendations that included efforts at primary prevention, and it recommended that a special Center on Prevention be established at the

National Institute of Mental Health (President's Commission on Mental Health, 1978).

Recently, in frustration, I wrote an article entitled "The Prevention of Prevention" (Albee, 1979) that reported on the effective strategies to kill prevention efforts used by the moles buried within the mental health bureaucracy and on how they have succeeded in keeping the Center on Prevention from being established. The ten million dollars proposed for the center is a fly speck on the federal budget. One would think that the fly speck was deadly plutonium, given the efforts made to contain it and get rid of it. Why is prevention anathema to the field?

During the past few years there has been a spate of articles in the psychiatric literature expressing fervent opposition to efforts at primary prevention. These may give us a clue.

Two prominent psychiatrists (Lamb and Zusman, 1979) writing in the *American Journal of Psychiatry*, the official journal of the American Psychiatric Association, sharply attacked the growing interest in efforts at primary prevention. They criticized the "fuzziness of the concepts" and the "assumption—which is yet unproved—that difficult life circumstances lead to mental illness" (p. 12). They went on to try to establish a distinction between preventing mental illness and preventing emotional distress. Making the flat statement that "the cause and effect relationship between social conditions and mental illness is extremely questionable," they argue that primary prevention is impossible without a knowledge of specific causes. Though they credit medical research with making progress in discovering some of the genetic and biochemical factors responsible for mental illness, they express concern that primary prevention is largely in the dangerous hands of those who want to make social changes. They make the bald statement that "There is *no evidence* [emphasis added] that it is possible to strengthen 'mental health' and thereby increase resistance to mental illness by general preventive activities" (p. 13).

Lamb and Zusman go on to argue: "Mental illness is probably in large part genetically determined and it is probably therefore not preventable, at most only modifiable. Even that it can be modified is questioned by many and there is little hard evidence one way or the other" (p. 13). If the President's Commission on Mental Health (1978) is correct in its estimate that 35 million Americans suffer from serious emotional problems, then we may have a real genetic disaster on our hands! Lamb and Zusman assess the research that finds relationships between social disintegration and high rates of psychopathology and argue that such studies "fail to demonstrate that there is a *causal* relationship between the particular stressful environmental factors under consideration and the occurrence of mental illness" (p. 14). They also shrug off the relationship between poverty and high rates of mental disturbance as a correlation that does not prove causation.

The bottom line of their argument concludes that since there is not enough mental health money to go around, it is dangerous and foolish to divert funds that can be used for one-to-one treatment into prevention programs.

One of the ironic aspects of this frontal attack on primary prevention is the insistent demand for high-quality research efforts before any programs in prevention are initiated. In the same issue of the journal in which their article appeared, there are a number of articles, research notes and brief communications, as well as a special section reporting a major clinical research effort on depression. None of these other studies meets the quality standards demanded for research in primary prevention. Indeed the long report of the major cooperative program on depression sponsored by the National Institute of Mental Health (NIMH) contains apologetic comments about the inadequacies of the research design (NIMH, Clinical Research Branch Collaborative Program, 1979). Similarly, a number of the reports on drug therapy and on psychotherapy are intellectually tattered and torn. A double standard prevails—research on primary prevention must be significantly better than the research on secondary prevention!

I have not searched out and quoted the Lamb and Zusman article in particular to prove a point. There have been many articles from other leading figures in psychiatry in the last few years cautioning against the growing enthusiasm for primary prevention. Leon Eisenberg (1975), one of the best known figures in psychiatry, cautioned against deemphasizing secondary prevention, which he regards as the field of major progress in psychiatry for the past twenty years. Once again he sounds the familiar theme: "There are a variety of psychiatric disorders, each with causes, mechanisms and outcomes. The task for primary prevention is to devise specific methods for each" (p. 119). Again we hear about the "strong evidence for genetic predisposition" and a vote from Eisenberg for the importance of genetic counseling. Also, once again, he joins the chorus proclaiming that there is "accumulating evidence that biochemical defects underly the schizophrenic psychosis." He comes out in favor of individual treatment, "because we possess powerful methods of secondary prevention" (p. 123).

Eisenberg is growing conservative as he grows older. Back in 1962 he was more oriented toward social action. As president of the American Orthopsychiatric Association he was foursquare for prevention: "As citizens, we bear a moral responsibility, because of our specialized knowledge, for political action to prevent socially induced psychiatric illness. This implies fighting for decent subsistence levels in public assistance programs; good housing, health care, education, and the right to work for all" (Eisenberg, 1962, p. 790). Since then he seems to have weakened his stand on the social origins of "psychiatric illness" and on the importance of political action. Not everyone would agree with his support of a dictum by Virchow: "Physicians are the natural attorneys of the poor; social problems fall to a larger extent within their jurisdiction" (Eisenberg, 1975, p. 127).

A third attack on primary prevention is contained in an article by Henderson (1975) in the *Bulletin of the Menninger Clinic*. He attacks the "destructiveness of social psychiatry" and the "magical notion of 'primary prevention'" (pp. 234–235). Henderson argues that only a very few (organic) conditions (like syphilitic brain disease and phenylketonuria) can be prevented. Once again we hear an old familiar theme:

Since human suffering is prevalent if not universal the role of the mental health professional is not so much to venture into the community with ill-reasoned, ill-tested, and sometime naive claims of preventing that which is *innate* [emphasis added] to human existence, but rather to get on with the job of helping his fellow man. That help, of course, is therapy, not prevention. Early therapy by all means, thorough therapy if at all possible, but above all, *therapy*. To do otherwise is a neurotic and ineffectual compromise. (p. 243)

Welcome, fellow neurotics! We are in good company.

Nearly half a century ago Harry Stack Sullivan (1931), one of the few true giants in American psychiatry, sounded the opposite theme:

Either you believe that mental disorders are acts of God, predestined, inexorably fixed, arising from a constitutional or some other irremediable substratum, the victims of which are to be helped through an innocuous life to a more or less euthanistic [*sic*] exit . . . *or* you believe that mental disorder is largely preventable and somewhat remediable by control of psychosociological factors. (See Bloom, 1977, p. 70)

Why is primary prevention such an aversive and frightening concept, such an apparent threat, to the mental health establishment? The kinds of arguments advanced to delay or avoid preventive efforts may give us clues. Among the most common arguments are: (1) we do not yet know enough about the specific cause of the specific mental illnesses to allow us to do anything significant about prevention; (2) there is no evidence that efforts strengthening people's mental health have ever succeeded in reducing the incidence of specific mental illnesses; and (3) while there clearly is a correlation between poverty (and other forms of human distress like racism and sexism) and rates of mental disorder, there is no proof that poverty, racism, and sexism *cause* the disturbances.

The defect model—genetic predisposition and biochemical imbal-

ance—is advanced to explain all mental disorder. This approach is seen
by many as part of the growing "medicalization of psychiatry" which is
occurring simultaneously with the improving prospects for national
health insurance and reimbursement for medical care. Finding a defect
(or a conflict) inside the person to account for disturbed behavior, or for
social deviance, has been called "blaming the victim." Ryan (1971) has
written a book describing in clear detail how "every important social
problem—crime, mental illness, civil disorder, unemployment—has
been analyzed within the framework of the victim-blaming ideology" (p.
6). The defect explanation provides powerful support for those who oppose social change. There is no need to change society if the cause of the
disturbance is inside the victim!

These arguments are fallacious, but, as is often the case, weak arguments expressed by powerful people have a way of taking on the aura
and credibility of the speaker. To argue that there are a number of separate and discrete mental illnesses obscures or blocks consideration of the
possibility that emotional disturbance is a result of dehumanization and
victimization by social cruelty.

Actually there *is* good evidence that the incidence of emotional distress
and the severity of emotional disturbance can be reduced by teaching
coping skills, by identifying and establishing support groups, by raising
self-esteem, and by reducing particular forms of social stress. A major
form of stress involves, for example, the feeling of powerlessness that is
part of our social order. Powerlessness is associated in our society with
being poor, with being female, with being a member of a minority group,
with being forced into endless and dehumanizing jobs, with being unemployed. Clearly efforts at changing these situations involve a redistribution of power. Social efforts and political movements aimed at the redistribution of power immediately threaten the status quo and stir up
strong resistance from those who have a stake in continuing things the
way they are. Evidence supporting the effectiveness of social factors in
prevention has been presented in this hall. (See the published volumes
based on these conferences: Albee and Joffe, 1977; Forgays, 1978; Kent
and Rolf, 1979; Bond and Rosen, 1980.)

The defect model is often justified and illustrated by the examples of
psychosis with brain syphilis, pellagral psychosis, and schizophrenia.
The first and second conditions were shown early in this century to result
from organic damage. Evidence about schizophrenia is still ambiguous,
but the organicists take comfort from scattered reports of a genetic predisposition and from the allegation that schizophrenics respond to heavy
psychotropic medication. Thus, they conclude, it must be an organic illness and not preventable through social change.

Rimland (1969) says: "I predict that research will ultimately show psychosocial influences to have minor—if any—relevance in causing the limited disorders called 'neuroses' and even less relevance in causing the severe disorders known as 'psychoses'" (p. 704).

There are several logical defects to these arguments. First, the overwhelming bulk of psychiatric practice is not with schizophrenics, nor with other obviously organic mental conditions, but with people who have the interpersonal problems in living that are dramatized so well in the films of Woody Allen. And in spite of what Gerald Klerman (1977a), head of the Alcohol, Drug Abuse, and Mental Health Administration (ADAMHA), says about the growing value of drug treatment, there is no evidence that the drugs cure anything.

Klerman is the nation's chief psychiatrist; as head of ADAMHA his voice carries major authority. Klerman strongly endorses drug treatment and lends his support to the shaky argument that the decrease in population in our public mental hospitals has resulted from the effectiveness of drugs. Before he became head of ADAMHA, Klerman (1977b) acknowledged that the decrease in population of our mental hospitals had resulted in part from the transfer of thousands of elderly "patients" from the hospitals to nursing homes and also from the discharge into the community of a great many ambulatory schizophrenics, undertakings which resulted in major saving of tax expenditures to the states. The truth is that the reduction in hospital census is largely economically motivated and it began in England and the United States *before* the psychotropic drugs were widely used. This latter fact is well documented by Scull (1977) and Mechanic (1969).

Klerman (1972) frightens some of us when he suggests that much of what we have regarded as social deviance—and have always defined in legal language—can now be included under the rubric of mental health and mental illness. He says, for example: "Hopefully, psychopharmacologic agents will prove useful in altering behavior deviance such as alcoholism, drug addiction, and perhaps even crime and delinquency" (p. 1). I wonder which criminals and delinquents Klerman has in mind in suggesting treatment with drugs? Would he include Nixon and the Watergate gang? And what about the vice-presidents in charge of disposal of chemicals and atomic wastes? Or does he have in mind only those criminals in our prisons and reformatories who happen, very largely, to be members of minority groups? Two other respected psychiatrists (Brill and Patton, 1966) see the need for "a mass therapy for conduct and personality disorder, social incapacity, economic dependence, unemployability and vagabondage," conditions that indicate "psychiatric casualties whose primary symptoms are those of gross economic and social incapacity." They observe that "the problems of these people clearly lie within the field of psychopharmacology" (p. 294).

To argue, as does Klerman (1977a), that a reduction of symptoms in schizophrenics in response to psychotropic drugs be counted as evidence in favor of the illness model is a very weak position. Himwich (1955), an acknowledged authority on drugs, has made it clear that these powerful chemicals do not cure, but only make the person so drugged more passive and perhaps more receptive to other forms of therapy. Further, there is growing evidence of devastating damage (tardive dyskinesia) accompanying the prolonged use of the heavy tranquilizers. Irreversible effects involving serious neurological symptoms is the fate of many individuals maintained for long periods on the drugs.

Joel Greenberg (1979) summarizes a number of reports on the damaging effects of long, continued use of various psychotropic drugs. He reports on studies of the reduction in height, weight, and growth of children who have been receiving psychotropic medication for a period of three or more years. He reports on other studies that revealed some unfavorable organic consequences of lithium and summarizes another study reporting that 40 percent of medical and surgical patients in a Boston hospital were given at least one psychotropic drug during their hospital stay that could produce severe side effects.

If we explain poverty, or emotional disorders, or crime and delinquency, or alcoholism, or even unemployment, as resulting from personal, internal, individual defects (like bad genes, bad chemistry, bad constitution), or as a consequence of membership in an ethnic group, a racial group, a sex group, all the members of which are *defective*, then there simply is not much we can do about prevention. We can dose these people with drugs, even use brain surgery; or we can exclude them from our society or from our psychological world. It is as though these people are regarded as *predestined* to be mentally ill. Indeed, there is a flavor of predestination to the current position of the establishment in the mental health field.

For the past few years I have been increasingly intrigued with the power and influence of the Protestant ethic on our Western thinking about human social problems. The Protestant ethic world view fitted beautifully into the development of industrial capitalism (Weber, 1904–05/1958); it also provided a fertile nurturing ground for the development of Western science. Merton (1938/1970) wrote insightfully about the growth of science in England, the establishment of the British Royal Society, and the special affinity that existed between the Puritans and science. I do not want to make too much of this, but I do want to make something of it. The Puritans were interested in science partly because they were so obsessive and partly because it was an individualistic enterprise through which the mysteries of the natural universe, expressing God's handiwork, might be revealed.

The Puritans, like the earlier Calvinists, were a self-centered group who were convinced of their own special place in God's plan. I will not belabor the obvious, except to point out that there is considerable consistency between the Calvinist's view that much of humanity is doomed to damnation and hellfire and the view of the Protestants in British (and American) science who were convinced of the inferiority, the constitutional defect, of the non-Nordics. Darwin and his cousin Francis Galton, together with Spearman, were the intellectual forebears of the genetic theories of Yerkes, Terman, Goddard, Burt, and Jensen.

If you think that I may be overstating the case, I recommend to your reading Leon Kamin's (1974) *The Science and Politics of IQ* for a history of the incredible racism and ethnocentrism of the early intelligence testers in the United States and of their advocacy of sterilization, eugenics measures, and immigration law reform.

Yerkes was active in the eugenics movement and supported sterilization laws. Goddard went to Ellis Island with his Binet kit under his arm and tested a "representative sample" of immigrants. He reported that "83% of the Jews, 80% of Hungarians, 79% of the Italians and 87% of the Russians were 'feeble-minded'" (see Kamin, 1974, p. 16).

Following World War I, during which one and three-quarter million Army recruits were tested by psychologists, Brigham, at Princeton University, summarized the Army's test findings and concluded that persons of Nordic origin were superior to persons of Alpine origin who in turn were superior to persons of Mediterranean origin. And, of course, blacks were regarded as a subhuman species. Brigham (1923) says:

We must face the possibility of racial admixture here that is infinitely worse than that favored by any European country today, for we are incorporating the negro [*sic*] into our racial stock, while all of Europe is comparatively free from this taint . . . the decline of American intelligence will be more rapid . . . owing to the presence here of the negro. (pp. 209–210)

Madison Grant (1919), then chair of the New York Zoological Society and trustee of the American Museum of Natural History, favored eugenic solutions and suggested massive sterilization. He said:

This is a practical, merciful and inevitable solution of the whole problem and can be applied to an ever widening circle of social discards, beginning always with the criminal, the diseased, and the insane and extending gradually to types which may be called weaklings rather than defectives and perhaps ultimately to worthless race types. (pp. 50–51)

Sarason and Doris (1969) have written an incisive history of the degeneration model (sometimes called taint theory) used to explain mental "illness," mental deficiency, prostitution, pauperism, and poverty. As I read these historical accounts of the powerful influence of *taint* and *defect* to explain human misery and distress, I find myself again flashing back to theological ideas of the Calvinists and the Puritans. Last year, almost by chance, I discovered a series of insightful articles, and more recently a book, by Mordechai Rotenberg of the School of Social Work at Hebrew University in Israel, on Calvinism and deviance.

Rotenberg (1978) traces the Western European and American insistence on discovering or inventing an internal defect supporting the concept of mental illness. He suggests the powerful influence of Calvin in this model. Predestination is a pervasive influence in the social sciences in Western industrial countries. Lombroso's (1912) "discovery" of the "born criminal" and Herbert Spencer's writings about natural selection, social Darwinism, and the "dangerous classes" are all ascribed to the influence of Calvinism. What exactly did Calvin have to say? Here is a typical statement: "It is a notion commonly entertained that God adopts as His children such as He foreknows will be deserving of His Grace, and devotes to the damnation of death others, whose disposition He sees will be inclined to wickedness" (*A Compend of the Institutes of the Christian Religion* by John Calvin, quoted by Rotenberg, 1978, p. 1).

Rotenberg (1978) agrees with Merton (1938/70) and others (see Albee, 1977) that Calvinism, and its subsequent expression in Puritanism, gave rise to science in its modern form, and he shows how deeply rooted is the Puritan belief that though nature is changeable and investigable by science, the human being is unchangeable. Much of human behavior is still viewed through this doctrine of predestination and immutability.

How do we know who is a member of the *elect* and who a member of the *damned*? The Protestant ethic gives a clear answer. If one is *successful* in one's calling, it is a pretty positive sign; if one is a *failure*, a pauper, or of course, especially if one is obviously a sinner, then one is to be classed among the *damned*.

Most historians in the field of psychopathology claim for the concept of mental illness an historic advance over earlier notions that insanity resulted from possession by demons. Klerman (1977a), our nation's First Psychiatrist, says: "While there may be some residual stigmatizing elements in the current use of the label of mental illness, seen in historical perspective these uses are far less stigmatizing than the pre-Enlightenment labels of 'possessed'" (p. 229).

Rotenberg (1978, p. 3) suggests that the notion of spirits possessing a person, as well as of demons infesting one, is a much more *hopeful* hypothesis than the notion of foreordained, inescapable evil. (Indeed, we could entertain the notion of developing ways leading to the primary prevention of demons or of repelling the Devil—perhaps bags of garlic worn around the neck!) Demons can be cast out, and evil spirits can be frightened off. In such instances of possession the victim is not personally responsible, and external agents may find effective methods of removing or preventing the evil. In the case of the Calvinistic model, however, nothing can be done. The afflicted person, or group, has been damned in advance and can be treated by heartless incarceration or punitive intervention—what does it matter *when* their punishment begins if they are doomed anyway?

The defect model did not begin with Calvin, of course. Persecution of women was evident early in the Christian era (and existed before), but it became even more intense during the period of renewed enlightenment—the Renaissance.

The support for social Darwinism (elimination of the incompetent) appeared with the rise of science during the 19th century in England and America. Mental illness was seen as a way that Nature had of eliminating the unfit from the population. If the mentally ill and the criminals were treated harshly by the Puritans, and their spiritual descendants, it was no great matter. As Erikson (1966) points out: "If a culprit standing before the bench is scheduled to spend eternity in hell, it does not matter very much how severely the judges treat him" (p. 190).

There is an important point to be underscored. If the Calvinist view is a dominant influence in the mythology of a society—the view that persons are rigidly programmed from before their birth to play out a predetermined and predestined role—then nothing much really can be done to prevent insanity, or poverty, or criminality. Indeed, it may be sacrilegious to attempt to interfere with God's plan for these unfortunates. (Protestant theology has had a hard time with the paradoxical fact that people are not responsible for their behavior because it is preordained, but also are sentenced to spend eternity being punished for the behavior that they did not freely choose. This problem has also perplexed the psychoanalysts who, following Freud, have accepted a rigidly deterministic model.) Fromm (1960) points out that in the Protestant system there can be no such notion as "the equality of mankind" (p. 76). Nor, we could add, equality of the sexes, nor equality of justice.

Foucault (1965) reported in detail the gradual separation of the insane, their segregation and incarceration, specifically in Western societies. Other observers (Edgerton, 1969; Kitano, 1969) report that both in preindustrial, and in Western industrial cultures not affected by the Protestant ethic, the label *mentally ill* and rejecting attitudes, are surprisingly absent.

The Calvinist doctrine of predestination has served very well as the religiously supported ideological excuse for slavery, social discrimination, racism, sexism, and eugenic solutions like sterilization of the defective. Rotenberg (1978) summarizes his argument:

If Puritanism may indeed be conceived as the cradle of American–Western culture, or as "the origins of the American self" . . . then it is in the historically and culturally relativistic sense . . . that one should examine the claim that the Western single "medical model" of deviance casts people in irreversible, degrading, deviant roles. (pp. 39–40)

A great deal of British and American science during the 19th and early 20th century emphasized and stressed physical defect and degeneration as major causes of poverty, insanity, and mental deficiency. Galton (1869) "established" the hereditary nature of genius, and he and others were convinced, and convinced others, that pauperism was hereditary and a sign of degeneracy. Alcoholism, too, was explained as resulting from degenerative heredity. Many early eugenicists proposed strict segregation, or even sterilization, to eliminate the degenerative germ plasm and thereby save the human race.

Among those who had major influence in establishing a taint theory for mental and emotional problems were Gray and later Rosanoff (1905) in psychiatry and Goddard in psychology. Gray became editor of the *American Journal of Insanity* in 1854 and argued over many years for a brain degeneration model of insanity. Rosanoff wrote an influential early textbook where "polymorphous neuropathology" explained most forms of mental disorder. Goddard (1912) wrote about the Kallikaks, long familiar to most of you I am sure. The feebleminded side of the Kallikak family could never escape their heredity taint. Goddard said:

No amount of work in the slums or removing the slums from our cities, will ever be successful until we take care of those who make the slums what they are . . . not until we take care of this class and see to it that their lives are guided by intelligent people, shall we remove these sores from our social life. (pp. 70–71)

The defects of the "research" supporting these views are so obvious, the methodology so poor, the analysis so sloppy, it is hard for us to understand how these conclusions could have been so widely accepted by other scientists and by the public. Obviously, they fit a prevailing *zeitgeist*.

Conant (1947, p. 36) has argued, quite convincingly, that theories do not get abandoned on the basis of new facts, but only because they are replaced by better theories. And, it might be argued, there is a significant interaction between the climate of the society and the theories that will be judged to be "better."

The American Psychiatric Association (1979) has recently unveiled its latest version of the Diagnostic and Statistical Manual. DSM III extends the concept of mental disease into entirely new areas of problems in living not claimed before by psychiatry. One of the many distressing things about this expansion of the medical model is the new diagnostic responsibilities claimed as psychiatric in the areas of childhood and adolescence adjustment problems. The world is soon to be informed that problems involving speech difficulties, shyness, childhood fears, and adolescent rebellion, to name just a few, are now to be regarded as *mental illnesses*. Even so conservative and solid a citizen as Norman Garmezy (1978) has written a brutally critical article about these DSM III categories that he regards as a "wasteland that can only evoke concern in all those involved in the betterment of the mental health of children." Joseph Zubin (1977–78), another scientist whose credibility is above reproach, says: "Scientific values were bent to suit the needs of psychiatry, third party payments, certification and economic exigencies of one sort or another including territorial rights" (p. 7).

Seymour S. Kety (1975) one of the world's best known research psychiatrists warns against classification systems that encourage inferences about causation. "If psychiatry recognizes, at the fundamental level of nosology, that the great problems with which it wrestles, such as schizophrenia or depression, are simply phenomenological clusters with little demonstrated etiological or pathogenic meaning, it may keep itself from a premature adoption of whatever etiological hypotheses happen to be in vogue" (p. 13). Kety's warning has gone unheeded in the development of the new Diagnostic and Statistical Manual III, which appears to be far more a political document than a scientific one.

When the defenders of the illness model argue against efforts at primary prevention they use *schizophrenia* as their example of a "mental illness" for which there is little encouraging prevention evidence. So, the argument goes, let us not waste time and money on prevention. But DSM III actually calls *adolescent rebellion* a mental illness; so is *shyness* in children; so is *dyslexia* (reading problems). Are we to be led to believe that all these problems of children are mental illnesses (DSM III says yes) that cannot be prevented? Can we really let them have it both ways—every problem an illness and nothing preventable? The illogic is assailable!

The illness model is not grounded in logic, nor supported by empirical evidence.

There must be deeper reasons for the extension and expansion of the model. In saying this I want to be clear that I do not subscribe to a *conspiracy* theory. No secret agreements have been reached between the leaders of the military-industrial complex and the mental health establishment. The interlocking ideology is supported by more subtle and effective connections. The careful selection of professional neophytes for training, the careful control of grants and research funds, the constant

presentation of illness and taint models by the mass media, the generous
professional financial support of politicians with a conservative ideology,
the domination of political office by wealthy WASP males, and the insidious and pervasive patriarchy throughout our culture—all these and a
hundred other arrangements support the prevailing ideology. And the
support is reciprocal.

A key to our understanding the source of opposing theoretical explanations of the origins of psychopathology is suggested by the research of
Pastore (1949). Pastore hypothesized that scientists' views about the relative influence of heredity and environment would be reflected in their
views on social, political, and economic matters. Pastore selected widely
respected scientists from England and America and grouped them according to their views toward social and political issues. Conservative
scientists were found strongly to favor a hereditary position, while liberal and radical scientists emphasized environmental origins of behavior.
Of course Pastore's study does not establish the direction of causal relations, although I suspect that most of us would believe that the social and
political values influence explanatory choice rather than vice versa. Sarason and Doris (1969) after reviewing the Pastore study say:

We must strenuously resist assuming, implicitly or explicitly, that our practices
are the result of cold logic and scientific fact unmediated by the knotty problems
of values. As we pointed out earlier, social action and practices are not derivable
directly from scientific facts; at some point there has been an explicit or implicit
acceptance of certain values" . . . (p. 274) Facts and theories never lead to social
action programs—it is only when expert knowledge interacts with a meaningful
value system that programs involving social action occur. (pp. 251–252)

If we are to consider seriously programs for social change and political
action that are to improve the mental health of large numbers of people,
we had better make clear what our values are. I hope the papers and discussions of this conference will help us formulate a clear position on the
values required and the ways we must act to move toward effective political change.

In thinking about these questions I have been reading social and political philosophy. I have discovered that, like many psychologists, I am
largely ignorant of important material in other fields of scholarship. I
also learned that there are other ways to knowledge besides the collection
of empirical data. While I am still relatively illiterate in social philosophy
and in social history, I have found in the last few months a great deal in
these fields that has influenced my view about the future of psychological
study.

First of all, most science, and clearly most psychology, is a bourgeois
phenomenon, studying subjects useful to the Establishment and avoiding

subjects dangerous or threatening to the status quo. Most of the scientific ideas in a given time in history are those that support the ideology of those in power. Occasionally, however, intellectual breakthroughs occur.

One of the most important books of this decade (and probably of a great many decades) is John Rawls's *A Theory of Justice* (1971). Rawls's view on justice has had a great impact on social philosophy and the law. I have not yet found many mental health professionals who have read Rawls, yet most of us believe in social justice as a prerequisite to positive mental health. The problem is to translate this belief into active opposition to the many forces that lead to injustice in our society. Reading Rawls helps.

Rawls begins with "justice as fairness" and in a complex series of intellectual steps, he arrives at two principles he believes essential to a just society. He argues that these principles would be developed by a group of "parties in the original position," each "with a veil of ignorance" about their own sex, their age, social class, and talents. Under these imaginary conditions rational people, Rawls argues, could arrive at agreement about conditions epitomizing fairness in the society.

His first principle is: "Each person is to have an equal right to the most extensive basic liberty compatible with a similar liberty for others." And his second: "Social and economic inequalities are to be arranged so that they are both a) to the greatest benefit of the least advantaged and b) attached to offices and positions open to all under conditions of fair equality of opportunity" (Rawls, p. 83).

This formulation of a system of justice, if applied to contemporary society, would guarantee, according to Rawls, "political liberty (the right to vote and to be eligible for public office) together with freedom of speech and assembly; liberty of conscience and freedom of thought; freedom of the person along with the right to hold (personal) property; and freedom from arbitrary arrest and seizure as defined by the concept of the rule of law" (p. 61). These liberties are all required to be equal by the first principle, since citizens of a just society are to have the same basic rights. Rawls's second principle is in opposition to the traditional conservative and liberal conception. The dominant view in present-day society allows for status and income to be determined by individual abilities and talents. Rawls argues: "There is no more reason to permit the distribution of income and wealth to be settled by the distribution of natural assets than by historical and social fortune" (p. 74). In Rawls's theory of justice, in order to provide real equality of opportunity, society must make every attempt to redress the social inequalities that have led to disadvantage. This means more attention and effort to those in less favorable social positions. This might roughly be translated into programs we call affirmative action. Rawls's view is very close to that of Justice Brandeis,

(1953) who said: "The measure of a civilization is not its lifeless art but its living solicitude for the most vulnerable."

Clearly women and minorities and the poor have been denied equal opportunity and basic liberty for centuries. If justice is fairness, as Rawls argues, it demands maximum social efforts to compensate for these historical injustices.

Nielsen (1978, p. 226) goes beyond Rawls. He argues for a socialist view of justice where liberty and equality *must* be seen as indivisible. He argues that the deep class divisions in capitalist societies make equality impossible and therefore liberty impossible. Corporate, multinational capitalism means human exploitation. He quotes approvingly Engels's claim that: "The real content of the proletarian demand for equality is a demand for the *abolition* of classes" (see Nielsen, p. 238). Meaningful work is the origin of self-respect and meaningful work must be autonomous (though it can be cooperative); this is only possible where everyone shares in the ownership of the means of production.

Feinberg (1975) in discussing economic justice states the standard clearly:

> Let us consider why we all agree . . . in rejecting the view that differences in race, sex, IQ or social "rank" are the grounds of just differences in welfare income. Part of the answer seems obvious. People cannot by their own solitary choices determine what skin color, sex, or IQ they shall have, or which hereditary caste they shall enter. To make such properties the basis of discrimination between individuals in the distribution of social benefits would be to treat people differently in ways that profoundly affect their lives because of differences for which they have no responsibility. Differences in a given respect are relevant for the aims of distributive justice, then, only if they are differences for which their possessors can be held responsible; properties can be the grounds of just discrimination between persons only if those persons had a *fair opportunity* to acquire or avoid them. (p. 421)

If we are to reduce stress, encourage competence, and strengthen support systems we must work towards the establishment of a just society. We *must* examine the reasoning of the social philosophers and make some conscious moral choices about the uses of psychological knowledge and the causes it serves.

If we are serious about the role of our professions in the promotion of human welfare we may find ourselves engaging in political and social action in roles and in places where we least expect to be. Carnoy (1976) points out that a society that is truly oriented toward *human* welfare rather than toward the ever-increasing output of goods, or the maximization of returns on capital, needs to change the structure and content of its educational system. He goes so far as to suggest that schools would have to promote values and attitudes that would ultimately lead to the dismantling of our current system, and "to the creation of a humanistic democratic socialism governed primarily from the local level and pervading all aspects of economic and social life" (p. 276).

Carnoy and Levin (1976), and other educational philosophers, have argued in sharp and searing detail the role that schools play in maintaining the exploitative economic system. Carnoy (1976, p. 277) points out that teachers are selected carefully from the urban working class or lower middle class and that they aspire to move upward socially through this white-collar intellectual work. They are subject to the scrutiny of principals, superintendents, and school boards, which have been carefully selected to maintain the economic status quo. Teachers who threaten or violate the established patterns are quickly dismissed. Censorship of school libraries, firing of teachers for using such radical books as *Brave New World*, the purging of libraries of seditious and salacious material, all serve to warn teachers of the dangers of threatening the system.

In a similar way, I contend, the models we are required to use to explain mental and emotional problems are formulated to protect and support the system.

One of the most powerful reasons for the support of the illness or defect model, or *taint theory*, is the protection it offers to those power forces that control and exploit the world's natural and human resources. Taint theory rationalizes the enslavement of people, the exploitation of the Third World, and the subjugation of women by a subtle process that portrays all of these groups as naturally inferior and therefore beyond empathy or help. The old Calvinism is discernible in the ideology. (Both Baltzell [1964] and Domhoff [1967] have provided data, if data are required, to show how clearly our society is dominated and controlled by the economic and political values of a white male protestant sexist elite.)

There are three interwoven advantages to the illness model. First, social forces are not held responsible for individual pathology because it is an individual, internal, defect; secondly, there is no need, no reason, for social change as a form of primary prevention because social forces are not involved in creating "mental illness"; and thirdly, there is no point in trying to treat the social failures and misfits because they are incurable— they can be drugged, or surgically altered, in order to pose less of a threat to the social order. Thus psychiatry, insofar as it supports a taint theory, supports the Establishment.

Psychiatrist Seymour Halleck (1971) provides a thoughtful analysis of *The Politics of Therapy*.

There is no way in which the psychiatrist can deal with behavior that is partly generated by a social system without either strengthening or altering that sys-

tem. Every encounter with a psychiatrist, therefore, has political implications. (p. 36)
Any treatment that removes symptoms without simultaneously increasing the patient's awareness of his environment is potentially repressive. (p. 80)

I want to warn that we must take great care not to fall into the trap of trying to formulate a new *patriarchal* revolution. One of the most widespread and serious forms of psychopathology is *sexism*, which has its origins in patriarchy. Sexism is a clear prototype of the defect model I have been discussing. It is subtle, it is pervasive, it is supported in many ways by the Establishment and especially by religion.

Until the consciousness of a significant number of white male psychologists was raised in the late 60s about the sexist nature of our research, about the "old boy" system of academic hiring and promotion, about the widespread discrimination against women in graduate admissions, about the masculist language used in our journals, the sexist bias of our concepts of adult mental health, the sexist discrimination against women authors of scientific articles, we largely were unaware of the damaging effects of our value system.

Clark (1974) wrote: "Any form of rejection, cruelty, and injustice inflicted on any group of human beings by any other group of human beings dehumanizes the victims overtly and in more subtle ways dehumanizes the perpetrators" (p. 144). For me, Clark's statement *is* the keynote message. It applies to the whole range of human injustice. But it means that to reduce or eliminate injustice some enormously powerful sources of injustice must be our targets.

Not only must we examine the dehumanizing consequences of the exploitative economic system, but we must confront the unbelievable emotional damage done to half the human race by organized religion. I had planned to talk at some length about sexism and religion, but time precludes any detailed consideration. I have been working for some weeks on a paper on the primary prevention of sexism and reading the incisive scholarly work of Mary Daly (1968/75) and Elizabeth Gould Davis (1971). My consciousness has been raised to the point where I am a born-again atheist! I am convinced that the sexist orientation of much of religion—Catholic, Protestant, Jewish, Islamic—have I left anyone out?—is at least as destructive a source of dehumanization and distress as the economic system.

What is the alternative to destructive models? I suggest we may spend the next several days working out in detail the answer to this question. The very fact that there have assembled here so many people interested in hearing about and talking about social change and political action as methods of primary prevention suggests that (1) we believe social forces cause psychopathology; (2) social change may well reduce or eliminate human distress; and (3) the road to successful social change is dangerous and we will become a mutual support group.

What is it that we seek to prevent and by what means? I have spent a lot of time trying to think through and formulate an appropriate answer to this question. I suggest that we seek to change damaging social conditions and restrictions that limit people's freedom of choice. We want to ensure that people can maximize their potential in a context that respects the rights of others to do likewise. Is there a simpler way to say this? I suggest that in primary prevention we attempt to *prevent* the arbitrary use of power in ways that damage others or reduce their opportunities. And that we use our resources to help those who are most disadvantaged.

We have brought together at this conference a number of speakers chosen because they have something significant to say about the political and social changes necessary to improve the human condition. Each of them in her or his own way has already established a high degree of credibility as an insightful thinker about the problems of society and about ways we might approach them. Let us begin.

References

Acton, J. *Historical essays and studies.* London: Macmillan and Co., 1907.

Albee, G. W. *Mental health manpower trends.* New York: Basic Books, 1959.

Albee, G. W. The Protestant ethic, sex, and psychotherapy. *American Psychologist,* 1977, *32,* 150–161.

Albee, G. W. The prevention of prevention. *Physician East,* 1979, *4,* 28–30.

Albee, G. W., and Joffe, J. M. (Eds.). *The issues: An overview of primary prevention,* Primary Prevention of Psychopathology, vol. 1. Hanover, N.H.: University Press of New England, 1977.

American Psychiatric Association. *Diagnostic and statistical manual of mental disorders* (3rd ed.). Washington, D.C.: 1979.

Baltzell, E. D. *The Protestant establishment: Aristocracy and caste in America.* New York: Random House, 1964.

Bloom, B. L. *Community mental health: A general introduction.* Monterey, Calif.: Brooks/Cole, 1977.

Bond, L., and Rosen, J. (Eds.), *Competence and coping during adulthood,* Primary Prevention of Psychopathology, vol. 4. Hanover, N.H.: University Press of New England, 1980.

Brandeis, L. D. In S. Goldman (Ed.), *The words of Justice Brandeis.* New York: H. Schuman, 1953.

Brigham, C. C. *A study of American intelligence.* Princeton, N.J.: Princeton University Press, 1923.

Brill, H., and Patton, R. E. Psychopharmacology and the current revolution in mental health services. *Proceedings of the Fourth World Congress of Psychiatry. Part One.* Amsterdam: Experta Medica Foundation, 1966, 288–295.

Calvin, J. *A compend of the institutes of the Christian religion.* Quoted in Rotenberg,

M. *Damnation and deviance: The Protestant ethic and the spirit of failure.* New York: Free Press, 1978.

Carnoy, M. Educational reform and social control in the United States, 1830–1970. In M. Carnoy and H. M. Levin (Eds.), *The limits of educational reform.* New York: David McKay, 1976.

Carnoy, M., and Levin, H. M. (Eds.). *The limits of educational reform.* New York: David McKay, 1976.

Clark, K. B. *The pathos of power.* New York: Harper and Row, 1974.

Conant, J. B. *On understanding science.* New Haven: Yale University Press, 1947.

Daly, M. *The church and the second sex.* With a new feminist post-Christian introduction by the author. New York: Harper and Row, Colophon Books, 1975. (Originally published 1968).

Davis, E. G. *The first sex.* New York: Penguin Books, 1972 (first published in the United States by G. W. Putnam's Sons, 1971).

Domhoff, W. *Who rules America?* Englewood Cliffs, N.J.: Prentice-Hall, 1967.

Edgerton, R. B. On the recognition of mental illness. In S. C. Plog and R. B. Edgerton (Eds.), *Changing perspectives in mental illness.* New York: Holt, Rinehart and Winston, 1969.

Eisenberg, L. Primary prevention and early detection in mental illness. *Bulletin of the New York Academy of Medicine*, 1975, *51*, 118–129.

Eisenberg, L. If not now, when? *American Journal of Orthopsychiatry*, 1962, *32*, 781–793.

Erikson, K. *Wayward Puritans.* New York: John Wiley, 1966.

Feinberg, J. Economic justice. In K. J. Stouhl and P. E. Stouhl (Eds.), *Ethics in perspective.* New York: Random House, 1975.

Forgays, D. (Ed.). *Environmental influences*, Primary Prevention of Psychopathology, vol. 2. Hanover, N.H.: University Press of New England, 1978.

Foucault, M. *Madness and civilization.* New York: Random House, 1965.

Fromm, E. *The fear of freedom.* London: Routledge and Kegan Paul, 1960.

Galton, F. *Hereditary genius.* London: Macmillan, 1869.

Garmezy, N. DSM III: Never mind the psychologists; is it good for the children? *The Clinical Psychologist*, 1978, *31*, 3 & 4, 1, 4–6.

Goddard, H. H. *The Kallikak family: A study in the heredity of feeblemindedness.* New York: Macmillan, 1912.

Grant, M. *The passing of the great race* (Rev. ed.). New York: Scribner, 1919.

Gray, John P. The study of mind (Editorial). *American Journal of Insanity*, 1856, *17*, 233–249.

Greenberg, J. Behavior page. *Science News*, May 26, 1979, *115*, 345.

Halleck, S. *The politics of therapy.* New York: Science House, 1971.

Henderson, J. Object relations and a new social psychiatry: The illusion of primary prevention. *Bulletin of the Menninger Clinic*, 1975, *39*, 233–245.

Herbert, W. The politics of prevention. *APA Monitor*, 1979, *10*, 5, 7, 8, 9.

Himwich, H. H. The new psychiatric drugs. *Scientific American*, 1955, *192*, 2–6.

Kamin, L. *The science and politics of I.Q.* Potomac, Md.: Lawrence Erlbaum Associates, Inc., 1974.

Kent, M. W., and Rolf, J. E. (Eds.). *Social competence in children*, Primary Prevention of Psychopathology, vol. 3. Hanover, N.H.: University Press of New England, 1979.

Kessler, M., and Albee, G. W. Primary prevention. *Annual Review of Psychology*, 1975, *26*, 557–591.

Kety, S. Classification in science. In *Report of the Task Force on Behavioral Classification*, Board of Professional Affairs, American Psychological Association, August, 1975 (mimeographed) 8–14.
Kitano, H. H. L. Japanese-American mental illness. In S. C. Plog and R. B. Edgerton (Eds.), *Changing perspectives in mental illness*. New York: Holt, Rinehart and Winston, 1969.
Klerman, G. Psychotropic hedonism *vs.* pharmacological Calvinism. *The Hastings Center Report*, 1972, *2*, 1–3.
Klerman, G. Mental illness, the medical model, and psychiatry. *The Journal of Medicine and Philosophy*, 1977, *2*, 220–243(a).
Klerman, G. Better but not well: Social and ethical issues in the deinstitutionalization of the mentally ill. *Schizophrenia Bulletin*, 1977, *3*, 617–630(b).
Lamb, H. R., and Zusman, J. Primary prevention in perspective. *American Journal of Psychiatry*, 1979, *136*, 12–17.
Lombroso, C. *Crime: Its causes and remedies*. Montclair, N.J.: Montclair, 1912. (Originally published, 1876).
Marx, K., and Engels, F. Manifesto of the communist party. Section II. In Karl Marx, *Selected works* (Vol. 1). New York: International Publishers, 1936.
Mechanic, D. *Mental health and social policy*. Englewood Cliffs, N.J.: Prentice-Hall, 1969.
Merton, R. K. *Science, technology and society in seventeenth-century England*. New York: Harper and Row, 1970. (Originally published, 1938).
Nielsen, K. Class and justice. In J. Arthur and W. H. Shaw (Eds.), *Justice and economic distribution*. Englewood Cliffs, N.J.: Prentice-Hall, 1978.
NIMH–Clinical Research Branch Collaborative Program. Special section. *American Journal of Psychiatry*, 1979, *136*, 49–70.
Pastore, N. *The nature–nurture controversy*. New York: Columbia University Press, 1949.
President's Commission on Mental Health. *Report to the President*. Washington, D.C.: U.S. Government Printing Office, 1978.
Rawls, J. *A theory of justice*. Cambridge, Mass.: Harvard University Press, 1971.
Rimland, B. Psychogenesis versus biogenesis: The issues and the evidence. In S. C. Plog and W. B. Edgerton (Eds.), *Changing perspectives in mental illness*. New York: Holt, Rinehart, and Winston, 1969.
Rosanoff, A. *Manual of Psychiatry*. New York: John Wiley & Sons, 1905.
Rotenberg, M. *Damnation and deviance: The Protestant ethic and the spirit of failure*. New York: Free Press, 1978.
Ryan, W. *Blaming the victim*. New York: Random House, 1971.
Sarason, S. B., and Doris, J. *Psychological problems in mental deficiency* (4th ed.). New York: Harper and Row, 1969.
Scull, A. *Decarceration*. Englewood Cliffs, N.J.: Prentice-Hall, 1977.
Sullivan, H. S. Quoted in B. L. Bloom, *Community mental health: A general introduction*. Monterey, Calif.: Brooks/Cole, 1977.
Task Group on Prevention. President's Commission on Mental Health. *Report on Primary Prevention*. Washington, D.C.: U.S. Government Printing Office, 1978.
Weber, M. [*The Protestant ethic and the spirit of capitalism*] (T. Parsons, trans.). New York: Scribner's, 1958. (Originally published, 1904–05).
Zubin, J. But is it good for science? *The Clinical Psychologist*, 1977–78, *31–32*, 1, 5–7.

On "Preventing Psychopathology"
A Libertarian Analysis

Thomas Szasz

Before turning to a consideration of the subject of "preventing psychopathology," I should like to offer some remarks about two basic issues with which I have tried to wrestle for a good many years. One is the nature of so-called mental illness—lunacy, madness, psychosis, psychopathology, call it what you like. The other issue, which now seems quite separate from psychopathology, but which was very much a part of it in the early nineteenth century, is the nature of liberty—freedom, autonomy, choice, responsibility, call it, again, what you will. In the course of the last century or so, these two concepts and the social problems to which they point have become separated. My contention is that unless we reunite them, we can make no sense out of the riddle "mental illness"—and are likely to injure the cause of liberty.

For a quarter of a century, I have maintained that there is no such thing as mental illness (see Szasz, 1961). To many people this has seemed—and still seems—a very exciting and daring thing to do. Why? Actually, my assertion is no more daring than declaring (to a secular audience) that there is no God. Today, a lot of people no longer believe in God—at least not in the Hebrew, Christian, or Islamic version of a God that made the world in six days and gave mankind rules about what to eat and drink, how to have sex, and so forth.

This sort of disbelief in revealed religion does not mean that one must go out into the streets and tear down synagogues, churches, or mosques, kill the priests, burn the Bible or the Koran. It means only that we recognized these religions as culturally evolved conventions; and that we realize that moral codes—ethical systems—may exist and operate without a belief in God or revealed religion. In fact, the Constitution of the United States guarantees our right to believe or not believe in religion.

This paper was adapted from a lecture delivered at the University of Vermont, Burlington, January 25, 1979.

Not so with mental illness. Mental illness, authorities now assert, is a fact, just like physical illness is. Saying that there is no mental illness thus sounds like saying that there is no cancer of the colon—which would indeed be a stupid thing to say. The point (which I have made in several of my early books) is that bodily illnesses are literal diseases, whereas mental illnesses are metaphorical diseases. This follows from the fact that we are human beings who *have* bodies and *display* behavior. Bodily abnormalities are physical, or literal, diseases. Behavioral "abnormalities" are mental, or metaphorical, diseases. For thousands of years, such "abnormalities" were viewed as religious problems. Then they were viewed as moral and philosophical problems. Only in the last two hundred years or so have some of these phenomena been viewed as "mental diseases." The fashionable contemporary contention that "mental diseases" are, or are due to, as yet undetected lesions in the brain need not detain us here. Perhaps some are; those that are, are real, bodily diseases (similar to neurosyphilis or brain tumor). The fact remains that the term "mental illness" is used to identify undesirable behaviors, an identification whose primary significance is perforce moral and political.

If a behavioral act is deemed undesirable, two questions about it arise immediately: 1) Who is the actor, and who judges his behavior? 2) Undesirable or not, should the behavior be allowed or should it be prohibited? Suicide is a good example. A person—say Ernest Hemingway—wants to kill himself. Psychiatrists say that that proves he is mentally ill, restrain him as insane, and "treat" him with electric shock against his will. The underlying question—which the psychiatric imagery and strategy helps to avoid and evade—is whether a person has a right to kill himself. That, briefly, is how the concept of mental illness connects with the concept of liberty.

It is generally believed that liberty—individual self-determination—is a much-treasured value in our society. That is both true and not true. Let us remember that most societies throughout history were based on the assumption that individuals have no rights. Ancient societies were tribal societies. The individual existed only as a member of a group. I cannot here trace the development of the idea of individual freedom. Suffice it to say that the idea is relatively recent, and, with a few exceptions, has not taken real root outside of English-speaking countries. The belief that individuals possess "inalienable rights" that the state has no "right" to take away from them is, of course, quintessentially American.

What, you might ask, has all this to do with the prevention of psychopathology? Just this: The enterprise we now call psychiatry rests on two major pillars—mental illness and coercion. "Mental illness," as I indicated, supplies the rhetoric for the so-called "medical model"; that is, it supplies the mechanism for medicalizing everyday human problems—problems of growing up, sexual and marital relations, bringing up children, adjusting to illness and old age, and so forth. Coercion, masquerading under the euphemism of "mental hospitalization" (which is classically involuntary), is the political intervention by means of which deviance is implicitly authenticated as disease. Coercion is essential to psychiatry. This is why there is an inexorable conflict between psychiatry and liberty. If psychiatric diagnoses could be attached only to individuals who ask for and consent to them; if, in other words, psychiatric interventions were restricted to consenting adults—the scope of psychopathology would shrink to near-nothingness, and psychiatry, as we know it, would disappear.

How, then, can we talk about the "primary prevention of psychopathology" if I am right that there is no such thing as psychopathology? If psychopathology is simply a misleading term—psychopathologizing, as it were, moral, legal, political, social problems? What now follows is my effort to address this problem—without getting entangled in the implications entailed by the vocabulary of psychopathology.

You know the proverbial wisdom that one man's meat is another man's poison. It seems to me obvious that, similarly, one man's psychopathology is another man's psychological normality—or, indeed, psychotherapy. The importance of this simple fact can hardly be exaggerated. It explains why all efforts to prevent psychopathology have been such utter failures—in free societies. It also explains why such efforts have been (or at least have officially been declared to be) such glorious successes—in totalitarian societies.

Free societies are characterized by their toleration of contradictory moral and political philosophies and hence by the existence, within their borders, of individuals and groups holding widely differing values. These differences affect attitudes toward both physical and (so-called) mental illness. For example, there are people in America who believe it is better to die of a hemorrhage than to receive a blood transfusion. Others believe that it is better to give birth to unwanted children than to practice contraception or resort to abortion.

When we turn to "mental illness" and look at it as a euphemism for personal conduct of which the psychodiagnostician disapproves, then it becomes immediately obvious that this is a matter to which the maxim about one man's meat being another man's poison applies quite literally. Did not Freud insist that religion was a mass psychosis? This was a crucial modification of Marx's condemnation of religion as the "opiate of the people," since Marx's phrase, unlike Freud's, was couched in terms that did not (yet) impart to the opinion the status of a scientific fact. Freud's imagery and terminology implied nothing less than that—which is why I think he was not just a genius but an evil genius. (I have touched on this subject in several of my recent books; see Szasz, 1976, 1978.) Suffice it to say now that the idea that Freud's great achievement was, so to speak, religious, and that, depending on our values, he was a genius for good or evil, has occurred to a number of persons long before I espoused this idea. For example, Arnold Zweig, who was in sympathy with Freud's moral and political aspirations, put it this way (in a letter to Freud):

To me it seems that you have achieved everything that Nietzsche intuitively felt to be his task, without his really being able to achieve it. . . . He longed for a world beyond Good and Evil; by means of analysis you have discovered a world to which this phrase actually applies. Analysis has reversed all values, it has conquered Christianity, disclosed the true Antichrist, and liberated the spirit of resurgent life from the ascetic ideal. (December 2, 1930; in E. L. Freud, 1970, p. 23)

But the "true Antichrist" cannot be "disclosed." "He" can only be attributed. Such reflections bring us right back to my earlier remark about the prevention of mental illness. Although it is possible to believe that psychopathology is something objective, like a falling stone obeying the laws of gravity, or that psychiatric diagnoses of depression can be correct or incorrect like medical diagnoses of diabetes or leukemia can be—indeed, probably many of you believe something like this—only in totalitarian societies can one impose one's beliefs about psychopathology on an entire population by making the political system itself the agent of prevention and therapy. It may be useful to recall, in this connection, that while approximately one-half of American servicemen who received medical discharges during the Second World War were discharged for psychiatric reasons, there were no such discharges at all from the Russian armed forces. The Russians had no battle fatigue, no combat neurosis, no psychopathology of war at all. Of course, this was no great surprise for those who knew that already before the war the Soviets had managed to eradicate such troublesome civilian psychopathologies as alcoholism and crime. Today, China experts tell us that there are no neuroses in that country. Please do not scoff and say that these are ridiculous claims for which there is no evidence. What evidence is there for the claim that God gave the Jews the Promised Land, or that Jesus was the son of God, or that psychoanalysis is a science? In our everyday life we are awash with claims of all sorts. Our moral, religious, and political character is thus shaped and defined in large part by the claims we accept as valid and reject as invalid. Let me illustrate this point by means of some brief remarks about ancient Judaism and early Christianity as codes of conduct resting, ultimately, on certain unproved and indeed unprovable claims (about gods and their desires).

To the Israelites of antiquity, the supreme value was procreation. Accordingly, marriage was, in effect, compulsory and heterosexual behavior between husband and wife was approved and even prescribed. Early Christianity was, in my opinion a sort of libertarian revolt against this form of mandatory matrimony and copulation. Instead of marriage and procreation, the supreme Christian values were celibacy and chastity. Clearly, each of these religions has had a powerful effect in shaping the behavior of its members. However, it would be awkward, and indeed self-stupefying, to view Judaism as a method for the "primary prevention" of celibacy, or Christianity as a method for the "primary prevention" of matrimony.

Let us now jump two thousand years and look at the spectacle of another great religious-political metamorphosis and the convulsions occurring at its inception. For the past quarter of a century, the Shah of Iran was supposedly engaged in trying to "Westernize" his country. What did he actually do? Did he encourage individual liberty and responsibility through a limited, constitutional government? Freedom of the press? The free market? Not exactly. He did encourage alcoholism, pornography, and the destruction of the nation's traditional religion. That is not merely my opinion, it is the way many Iranians see what happened. I mention this example of the religious-political nature of what is now often smugly called psychopathology because it struck me, a good many years ago, that one of the things the Shah was trying to do was to "alcoholize" his people. I have borrowed and modified this phrase from Krafft-Ebing who spoke of "civilization and syphilization" to describe, nearly a century ago, the cultural impact of western colonists on primitive people. In my book *Ceremonial Chemistry*, I give a detailed account of the Shah's veritable program against opium (Szasz, 1974, pp. 49–51). Briefly put, the story is that until the 1950s, the cultivation and use of opium were legal in Iran. There was a special lounge in the Iranian Parliament set aside for the deputies to smoke opium. With the stroke of a pen, the Shah declared opium smoking an illness as well as a crime, and introduced draconian punishments for the cultivation, sale, and use of opium. At the same time the Shah permitted, and indeed tacitly promoted, the use of alcohol, which is prohibited by the Koran. One writer put it this way: "Prohibition [of opium] was motivated largely by prestige reasons. At a time of modernization, which in most developing countries means imitation of Western models, the use of opium was considered a shameful hangover of a dark Oriental past. It did not fit with the image of an awakening, Westernizing Iran that the Shah was creating" (Szasz, 1974, p. 51). As a result of such "reforms," swinging Iranian youngsters took to proving their westernization by drinking whisky and soda, forbidden by the Koran. During the riots in Iran in December, 1978, the protestors singled out movie theaters, symbols of Western decadence, as their special targets. After a few days of disturbances, all but 8 of nearly 200 theaters in Teheran lay in ruins. Evidently, the revolt was fanned, at least in part, by the fact that to many people the Shah's meat was poison, and his poison was meat: in other words, many people—even well-educated people—saw virtue in traditional Moslem dogma, and wickedness in modern Western doctrines. In Teheran, it was reported that "where most females wear Western dress, many college women these days are donning the chador, a traditional all-enveloping robe, as a gesture of defiance and explaining their actions in words that to some Western ears sound quaint." Their words may sound quaint to the reporters, but they do not sound quaint to me:

Nahid, a sociology major at Pahlavi University who wears slacks and drapes her head in a brown scarf so that no skin shows except for her face and hands, recalled: "When I first started college, my professors were telling us that we should kiss a boy if we like him, even sleep with a man if we wanted to. But inside we were confused. We knew that it was spiritual love that matters. Now we feel more secure because Islam tells us that it is the right way to feel. It tells us how to live." (Gage, 1978, p. 2)

Precisely!

The Koran tells people how to live.

The Bible tells people how to live.

Moses, Jesus, Marx, Lenin, Hitler, Stalin, and the Reverend Jim Jones tell people how to live.

The idea of "preventing psychopathology" thus comes down to this. First, we must examine the contents of various moral codes and the specific behavioral repertoires they promote and prohibit. Second, we must decide whether or not using coercion to enforce such codes is desirable, and if so under what circumstances and in what ways. Each of these issues must be dealt with separately. I shall indicate, briefly, the principal options we have with respect to these complex, age-old problems—and my own preferences.

Let us first consider coercion. The three classic Western religions are—and I prefer to be clear and candid about such things—authoritarian systems. Each prescribes a particular code of conduct and compels adherence to it by means of various sanctions. It is precisely their demand for submission to authority, their moral certitudes, and their communalism that make such (and similar) religions appealing to some people and unappealing to others. I dislike such authoritarian systems of external controls, especially when they rest their legitimacy on their alleged familiarity with the desires of divinities. I prefer a moral order in which self-control is valued more highly than external coercion, which envisions the peaceful co-existence of a multiplicity of legitimate human life styles rather than the eventual triumph and universality of a single—theologically or scientifically rationalized—code of conduct.

Turning to the behavioral content of various moral codes or "life styles," I would stress that this subject does not lend itself to summary analysis. The only generalization I would hazard is that such systems display an ends-means character, making efforts to alter the means without attending to the ends inefficient or worse. Furthermore, behind all such systems lurks the question of the ultimate aim of life, now often concealed or repressed by concentrating on the "technical fixing" or "problems." Matrimony versus celibacy, heterosexuality versus homosexuality, drinking alcohol versus smoking opium, and countless other human options are now promoted or prohibited without any effort to fit the option into the means-ends context of the individuals (or the society) for whom such behaviors are advocated.

The implications of this analysis for the prevention of psychopathology are obvious. I shall use a single example—the problem of what is now called "drug abuse"—as an illustration. Scrutinizing the pertinent behavioral repertoire, we might ask: Is smoking marijuana better or worse than smoking cigarettes? Is chewing coca leaves better or worse than drinking coffee or alcohol? Such questions imply, of course, the further necessity of choosing between making truthful statements about the chemical effects of certain substances or lying about them for the sake of one cause or another. Next, we must consider the question of coercion: Should we use politically legitimized coercion to prohibit (or promote) this or that substance, depending on its effect (or regardless of its effect)?

My own preferences are these. I would rather know the truth than be beguiled by lies. I would rather know that penicillin is more effective against pneumonia than prayer, that heroin is a better pain-killer than aspirin. And I would rather let people make their own decisions about matters that do not injure others than coerce them by means of religious, penal, or psychiatric sanctions. It is obvious, however, that adherence to these principles would require scuttling the vast majority of present-day programs devoted to preventing psychopathology.

References

Freud, E. L. (Ed.). *The letters of Sigmund Freud and Arnold Zweig*, trans. by E. and W. Robson-Scott. New York: Harcourt, Brace, Jovanovich, 1970.

Gage, N. Many Iran women seek return to Islam practice. *The International Herald Tribune*, December 19, 1978.

Szasz, T. S. *The myth of mental illness: Foundations of a theory of personal conduct.* New York: Harper & Row, 1961.

Szasz, T. S. *Ceremonial chemistry: The ritual persecution of drugs, addicts, and pushers.* Garden City, N.Y.: Doubleday, 1974.

Szasz, T. S. *Karl Kraus and the soul-doctors: A pioneer critic and his criticism of psychiatry and psychoanalysis.* Baton Rouge, La.: Louisiana State University Press, 1976.

Szasz, T. S. *The myth of psychotherapy: Mental healing as religion, rhetoric and repression.* Garden City, N.Y.: Doubleday Anchor, 1978.

PART II

Some of the Victims

Introductory Notes

In this section the papers do not deal with *all* the victims of an unjust society; instead the authors discuss the plight of *some* of the powerless—the retarded, the old, and children. A few figures in the shadowy arena of injustice and discrimination are made visible, and we see that some can stand for many.

Burton Blatt has long painted eloquent pictures of the abuse in our society of those labeled mentally retarded. Here he deals critically with what many regard as great progress in the treatment of retarded people. The provision of the retarded with the "least restrictive" living conditions, education, and workplaces has been widely heralded as a victory for progressive forces. Blatt, while granting that Public Law 94–142 (the federal legislation that gives force to the concept of "least restrictive environment") is a step in the right direction, raises serious doubts about how much progress it truly represents. Is a "least restrictive environment" one we would choose for ourselves? If not, why do we feel it is adequate for others? He makes it clear that the important distinction between a least restrictive environment and a free or even privileged environment does not lie in the physical characteristics but in its less tangible features—and that the distinction has to do with human freedom, including the freedom to take risks and to expose ourselves to danger. Blatt, in his discussion of these issues, echoes something of Szasz's concern about reducing freedoms in the name of protecting ourselves and our environments. Blatt also introduces a theme that occurs in later papers in this volume: namely, there is more useful guidance toward human happiness in the writings of poets than in the regulations of bureaucrats.

To a large degree Robert Binstock's analysis of the plight of older citizens in our society reinforces Blatt's point about the risk of bureaucratic solutions. Binstock provides the startling information that more than one quarter of the fiscal 1980 federal budget will be spent on programs on aging—and despite this $132.2 billion expenditure, most of the elderly's severest problems will not be alleviated. Binstock's outline of the pressing problems of the old—economic insecurity, inadequate and costly health care, and inadequate social services and facilities—is a devastating indictment of our social system. Binstock argues that the media-promoted image of "senior power" is not a political reality upon which older citizens can count to bring about change. The old vote in large numbers but not as a block; they are not a homogeneous political group. But this does not mean that the old lack political power. Binstock delineates the sources of their power, but he is not hopeful that the goals of organizations of older people will help them solve their fundamental economic, biomedical, and social problems. Even the imminent, substantial increase in the proportion of citizens over 65 will have little effect on American politics. Indeed, since the perception exists that the old have political power, the rest of society may be convinced that the elderly have obtained what they need. In this light, "senior power" may be "more of a danger than a hope."

Binstock argues that we must do several things if we are to make real progress. He recommends that we begin to state issues in terms that transcend interest group politics in order to form effective coalitions and that we pick a few problems to solve rather than try to deal with every imaginable problem of the aged. As he points out, severe deprivation transcends age, race, and other categorizations, and the problems and causes of the old are the problems and causes of most of society's victims. The injustices and indignities suffered by our older citizens are more difficult for us to ignore than the abuses we allow to be inflicted on other victims of our society, since in the case of the old we cannot as easily pretend that our own eventual fate is not linked with theirs. Binstock emphasizes the need to attempt to deal with the conditions that inflict deprivation on people of all ages and argues for direct militant action in local communities as a way to improve conditions for all victims.

In looking at a third group of victims, our children, Thomas Cottle does with individual children what this section of the report does with groups of victims: he lets one stand for many. Cottle's approach is very different from Binstock's in style but very similar in substance. In three "life studies" Cottle lets the children speak for themselves and in his discussion he places these lives in context. The context is a familiar one: children are victims of the same societal injustices that deprive the retarded and the old of economic and political power and thus diminish their freedom. Cottle's children's stories give these abstractions a human face. They show what poverty means in human terms, how social systems hurt real people, and how economic forces destroy them. They display the awful boredom and the nearly total hopelessness of those trapped in poverty. If any hope emerges from reading these personal encounters with deprivation, it lies in the realization that these victims are fully conscious of what is happening to them, a realization that at the same time makes their stories more painful. But the clarity of their perceptions and the courage with which they confront the intolerable bear witness to the extraordinary strength of the human spirit. It is easier to turn away than to hear them describe their pain, and Cottle does us a service in directing our attention towards their plight. He explains articulately how our system not only destroys them but does so in a way that is evil—by changing them so that they destroy themselves.

Bureaucratizing Values

Burton Blatt

Since the beginning of human experience, people have behaved as if freedom meant more to them than their lives. Yet, even more important to them has been the need to belong to a community, to be part of a fabric larger and more enduring than their fragile selves. This is why among the ancient Greeks to be banished was a punishment more severe than death. Only recently have we come to realize that many recipients of our human services have been punished by *both* banishment and loss of freedom in socially and often physically restrictive environments. As a result, uncounted commissions and agencies, bureaus and bureaucrats are today engaged in righting the wrong under the flag of the "least restrictive alternative."

I too have grieved for those we punished in the name of kindness; and I am glad that at last some of our official bureaus have taken human rights as an official concern. Yet the term "least restrictive alternative" is one I have misgivings about. Though better than outright banishment or imprisonment, it nevertheless implies an environment and conditions that I would not want for myself. So long as we speak of "least restrictive," we are speaking of "restrictive," and no "alternative" could be my "first choice." Certainly, we must work at minimizing the harm our society does, but in this chapter I would also like to look past this task to a society that maximizes good.

There is, however, a more immediate, less utopian concern I wish to explore in this chapter. The issue we confront in human services is one of very fundamental human values—freedom and community. Yet, our hopes and plans for securing these values for everyone are invested in government agencies and public laws, in an approach that codifies and mechanizes the "delivery" of values. In holding to our hopes we have seriously overestimated the power of bureaucracy. That is why, in the last

Parts of this paper were also presented at the annual meeting of the American Association for the Education of the Severely/Profoundly Handicapped (October 26, 1978, Baltimore, Maryland) and at the annual meeting of the American Association on Mental Deficiency (May 28, 1979, Miami Beach, Florida).

The writer is in debt to Andrejs Ozolins who helped to do something about improving this chapter, which was even more needed then than now.

analysis, the concept of "least restrictive alternative" will remain, even in its most precise definition, no better than an exactly specified degree of banishment.

Understanding Transitions

In the past 30 years, the mission of the mental retardation field has changed in crucial ways. In the 1950s, its purpose was to provide expertise and professional treatment to those afflicted with retardation. Then, our plea was to the nation, but our focus was clinical. To the extent that we addressed society at large, it was only to ask for support of our professional efforts—that is, to provide funding. Today, our primary work seems to be that of transforming not mentally retarded people but the society in which they live. Certainly we are still concerned with special applications of, for example, medicine and education, but the pivotal concerns of our field are now societal—gaining community acceptance of mentally retarded people, changing the attitudes of typical children toward handicapped children, securing for mentally retarded people the legal and human rights that the rest of us enjoy. Our major benchmark of this century was reached with the passage by Congress of Public Law 94–142, providing for the "least restrictive alternative." As reflected by this achievement, our activities have assumed a significant political thrust.

One of the characteristics of political activity is that it can seldom expect to succeed by openly seeking its final goal. A program must be presented, rather than as a totally realized whole, in politically feasible steps. This is necessary, in part, because society would repel any attempt at wholesale change—it must be urged and lured by small, often circuitous, steps toward the larger goal. But in still larger part, this is necessary because the goals of social change are invariably unclear. Not only is it difficult to specify what we would wish to happen, it is usually impossible to anticipate what the achievement of our wish would bring about in actual practice. History is replete with political visions turned to nightmare by success; and even "successful" social experiments more often than not turn out rather different from what their authors initially had set as their objectives. For example, today's "bad guys,"—those who wish to segregate special needs individuals—were our heroes of the 40s, the 50s, and the 60s, and could well be heroes again if society says it has had its fill of mainstreaming, normalization, and Public Law 94–142. And who knows, psychoanalysis could make a comeback, behavior modification could be declared unworkable, and the trains could again be made to run on time. Almost anything tried with enthusiasm works well for a while;

then there are unexpected consequences, then disillusionment, then nothing seems to work.

Although our goals may be unclear, we know enough about them to specify some essential elements for the future we have in mind. Mentally retarded persons will have to have certain legal rights that have been denied them—public education, public standards of health care, a fair chance at economic self-support, and the incidental rewards of self-support. Because most of us do not have serious doubts that a society which grants these and other basic rights to everyone will be a better society, we do not worry about what that society will be like in detail. But it should be apparent to us that, although we need not worry, we *really do not* know what that society will be like—except that it will be different and that there will be many points of great strain for all of us in the change. Whatever the price may be, we are committed to pay it for the sake of a better world.

However, not only is the future obscure, the present as well is often hard to assess. The rights of handicapped people emerged as a social issue with a suddenness that revealed to us how unaware we had been of the social implications of labeling, institutional segregation, and devaluing stereotypes. Most of us would have acted quite differently 15 or 20 or 30 years ago if we had understood some of the side-effects of our programs. Thus, the political and social process (in which PL 94–142 is but one step) is a powerful thrust from a world we do not understand very well toward a world we cannot predict, and, quite probably, will not ever understand well.

This is certainly not to say we should not continue that thrust. In the real world, the "facts" are never all in, and analyses and understandings are always imperfect. This is why action has to be based on judgment rather than deduction and why there is often so much disagreement among people who share similar goals: Their *judgments* of what should be the next step toward the goal can vary widely. But though we all know these things—that our understanding is imperfect, that the consequences of what we passionately advocate today may be unanticipated or even undesirable tomorrow—nevertheless, we must act as though there were no doubt about what we do. The success of any program of social reform depends too much on decisiveness and confidence to permit the awareness of our human condition to dampen it. Thus, PL 94–142 has its enthusiastic advocates not because the law is "the" answer, but because it is perceived to be an important step in the right direction. Those who feel that the next urgent order of business is to create jobs for handicapped adults have their eyes on the immediate benefits to the economic and social status of handicapped people rather than on global economic factors. Obviously, these and other programs have merit. Each nudges us closer to a good society. But equally obviously, each of them is in a sense irrelevant to what we want as a goal. PL 94–142 is quite clearly a transitional device; no one could suppose that its reimbursements, incentives, and formulas should constitute a lasting form of justice for all citizens. Like affirmative action, it can be justified, if at all, only as a part of the remedy, not as a state of health. And providing jobs for handicapped people is also important as a step, but hardly begins to address the factors that have heretofore oppressed mentally retarded people. At this time, when the mentally retarded are excluded almost entirely from job opportunities, we are justified in demanding the creation of those opportunities. Yet in the long run, this demand will have to be reconciled with the fact of widespread unemployment in society as a whole, and even with our nation's uncertain fortune in the economy of the world.

It would be foolish of me to offer solutions to such complicated and long-range problems. But neither can I bring myself to concentrate solely on the daily business of our current programs. Just like those we were enthusiastically "promoting" 20 years ago, these programs too will probably contain new prejudices and misunderstandings. We should begin to look for them and clarify them now, before they become too firmly established in our thinking, our practice, and even in our laws— that is, before they become a new set of intransigent institutions for us to evacuate.

The temptation is to take the easy way and to discuss the various ingredients of PL 94–142: individual educational plan, mainstreaming, zero reject, and of course the topic of the day, least restrictive alternative. The problem with these terms and others like them is that, at present, they are little more than shibboleths and slogans. We simply do not have an adequate understanding of what they mean. That may be a harsh conclusion but there are not many people around who would deny that there are lots of different definitions for each of these concepts, some of them in conflict with one another. So I will take the hard road—for me the easy way out—which is to get to ideas that go beyond the current law or, indeed, beyond the issue of the handicapped themselves. If we are going to offer mentally retarded people the freedoms and benefits of our society, we should look at what it is we have to offer. To protect people in spite of themselves is sometimes to protect them from living. To avoid potential dangers is sometimes to avoid life. Even for the retarded—possibly especially for the retarded—the rule should not be to reduce risk taking. Rather, it should be to encourage certain reasonable risk taking. Risk taking is unavoidable for those who would develop well. To legally prohibit virtually any potential hazard is also to inhibit one's opportunity to mature. As educators, we must be committed to the belief that people can learn and mature in their judgment and that, when all is said and done, this is the only protection from the dangers of life.

What Is a Least Restrictive Environment?

What is going on in the United States? How free are we? Never mind the mentally retarded—how free are you? Let us take a look at a few aspects of life in the United States today. The Talmudists have the luxury—indeed, the divine responsibility—to read word by word, letter by letter, and to compare a tiny mark to an even tinier mark. Because they no longer have legal power over the people, they can be legalists of the narrowest variety. Contrast them with the founding fathers of this country who needed a Supreme Court to interpret the law in the context of the times. To appreciate the concept of "least restrictiveness" requires, I think, an overview of a couple of society's institutions and not the Talmudist's, nor the scientist's nor the compulsive's special talents. That is, I think that "least restrictiveness" should be understood as a whole and not by its parts. Of course, the catch is that the concept is too complex to be understood that way. And, of course, there is too much to know about all of those institutions to get it all down here. But you live in our society as well as I do, and you know what is happening as well as I do. Consequently, these remarks are intended to do no more than to make us want to think about what we already know.

First of all, it seems to be as true today as it was when Calvin Coolidge said it years ago, that "the business of America is business." That is why we need stock exchanges and antitrust laws. That is why we need law schools, corporations, and Madison Avenue, and much of what is on television, and much of what is on people's minds. That is why General Electric claims "Progress is our most important product," though nobody believes them. And it is in the name of business that DuPont can bellow from today to doomsday that chemistry makes better things for better living, but nobody will believe DuPont. Because it is good for business, Nestlés can get away with promoting in Third World countries powdered milk that may be as lethal to babies there as uncontrolled asbestos plants are here.

It seems impossible to conjure up the march of American business without its accompaniment of nonsense and outright hazard. Our system and its freedoms have been designed to foster the creation of wealth and power, not to control them when they are used or pursued irresponsibly. That is why Ralph Nader is now inevitable and necessary, though terribly wrong. He is incontestably right that "they" are bastards. "They" could not be anything else because the profit motive and the free market are utterly indifferent to human values—unless those values affect sales. However, Nader is mistaken when he suggests that what "they" are doing, from price-fixing to manufacturing gas tanks that explode, represents some sort of aberration that could be corrected without attacking the business of America at its heart. And Nader is quite wrong in his avalanche of proposed laws for us to control the bastards. The effect of those regulations is likely to be as destructive as "their" lawlessness. We betray the human race and, in the final accounting, the individual as well, when we deny that the world must necessarily be a dangerous place. Most of us would pay high prices for our freedom; I am claiming now that Nader wants to exact a higher price for my safety than I am willing to pay.

American business has given us the possibility of the four-day work week and the two-home and three-car family at the same time that it has given us the choice of destroying either our health or our freedoms. Seizing upon the wonders of American technology, big business has made us free, but within narrower confines than ever before. It has given us the time to pursue virtually any hobby or interest we have, but it has also enticed us to sit in drugged stupors watching a lighted box. In America, only the truly brave, strong-willed, innovative person can exploit the genius of the American system and reject the damaging side-effects that accompany progress and that make us less well off than our grandparents.

Why is it so difficult for a parent to gain permission to teach a child at home or to help the teacher teach the child in school? Schools seem to be unnecessarily restrictive. Most parents once accepted it as their parental responsibility to teach their young. Even while schools have become necessary, there remain important things for parents to teach. But today parents are excluded from sharing that responsibility. Of course, teachers are not what they used to be, but that is not my point—they never were what they used to be. What I am getting at is that almost everybody today has the time and the potential competence to teach something to somebody. One would think that most people would enjoy the opportunity to teach if they could·believe in themselves sufficiently to enter into such activity. Teaching could be like jury duty. But if it were like jury duty practically everyone would ask to be excused. Most people would feel they had nothing to teach. Today even teachers ask to be excused. They too have nothing to teach, except in their areas of specialization. Everybody seems to have excuses when it comes to teaching something outside of his or her narrow ranges of interest and preparation. All of this is another way of saying that, with the exception of a few "genuine" teachers, virtually everybody in America lives in a very restricted intellectual environment. Furthermore, virtually everyone seems to be content with this situation.

Things could be different. A friend of mine insists that a person should learn the names of trees in his neighborhood, that when he walks to work it is good to be able to distinguish the sycamore maple from the sycamore. It helps one know better where one is going, and even why. This friend of mine also keeps bees. He knows what most of us forget, that bees are absolutely essential for our lives to continue, and that in no sense are they in competition with humans. As we shoo bees away, we shoo life away. There are millions and millions of potentially excellent teachers around, people who could interest us in trees, and bees, and aerodynamics, or how the body works, how to make a kite, or bait a hook. And yet, in spite of this knowledge, our "best minds" have come to the conclusion that the only people who may teach must be certified and degreed. There is more to this problem before us than what is the least restrictive environment for the mentally retarded.

There was once a time—admittedly a dangerous time—when learning and living were not governed by certification and regulation and legislation. It was the time when our idea of freedom started its development toward its present shape. From "Sweet Land of Liberty" to "Born Free," from Tchaikovsky to Tin Pan Alley, we have been sung to, entranced, and bombarded with cannons in the name of liberty. If musicians today thought like lawyers and spoke like legislators, they would serenade us in the names of least restrictive environment, zero reject, and mainstreaming. And if the prophets and the psalmists had thought like bureaucrats, they too would have told stories about zero reject rather than about strangers in the land of Canaan. But what was once one—religion and the law—is now, by law, separate. And so what was once the predominating influence, our religion, today predominates only on Sunday, and even then for a minority of our society. Today, the law prevails over all beings and institutions, over religion itself, and our freedom must live between its lines.

The law is concerned with who is and who is not restricted. There are forced restrictions and voluntary restrictions. There are those restricted by prejudice, those restricted by regulations. In our "let-it-all-hang-out" culture today, least is best. The Puritans, on the other hand, thought differently. The mode today is that the less restriction the better, the mode today is concerned more with the body than with the soul. Today, the mode is about what we do rather than about what we think. It seems that most people today would be satisfied with being physically unrestricted though mentally enchained. So today, what looks like an almost completely unrestricted, free, unfettered, unhampered, "doing-your-own-thing" society is, in another view, a culture that works by rote response and by communication through intermediaries. It may be fair to say that ours is at once the most unrestricted and restricted society ever created. *So what is a least restrictive environment?*

Privileged Extensions of Freedom

Least restrictive alternatives cannot be understood out of the context of the particular culture under examination. Whether an environment is restricted or free depends on where that environment is, who is in it, and how we look at it. Certainly, the least restrictive alternative in Nazi Germany was not at all the same as the least restrictive alternative in the present-day United States. And the least restrictive alternative in the United States of 1800 was not at all the same as the least restrictive alternative in the United States today.

Within the context of any setting, moreover, we find privileged extensions of freedom, the unchallenged special considerations that certain people or groups enjoy. Certainly, Nixon not only wanted the privileges awarded to the president of the United States, but he took for himself privileges that earlier office holders did not have. Certainly, a Rockefeller, a United States senator, a "super star," and other individuals and groups (such as priests and rabbis) enjoy special privileges. Such privileges as those that are the right of clergy and celebrities are not what we have in mind when we advocate the least restrictive alternative for mentally retarded people, but they are part of the context in which our definition will have to work.

On leave once from my university responsibilities in order to direct a new Division of Mental Retardation in a State Department of Mental Health, it was my responsibility to oversee all of the state's institutional programs for the mentally retarded, which were many, as well as their community programs, which at that time consisted of a handful of nursery school classes. Soon after assuming this position, I visited one of the state schools and, accompanied by the superintendent, toured the entire facility. It was payday and people were queued up at the cashier. Off to the side was a large table on which were piled hundreds of dozens of eggs. As the workers left the cashier's cage, many of them stopped at the egg stand and purchased one or more boxes of eggs from a man who seemed to be very familiar with the situation. I went over to ask him how much the jumbo eggs cost. "Twenty cents a dozen," was the reply. I identified myself and expressed surprise that the state was selling its eggs in this manner and at such a low price. He informed me that these were not the state's eggs, but his. He also informed me that he was the manager of the state school's farm and that the chickens who laid these eggs were his chickens. After probing, I learned that the state indeed owned thousands of chickens, but so did he. I also learned that this man had the unusual ability to know for sure which were the state's chickens and which were his. And he repeated that these, indeed, were his eggs, laid by his chickens.

Anyone who can look at a field of thousands of chickens and know which are his and, furthermore, know for sure that his chickens would not eat the state's feed, is indeed a special person. But I think it is not coincidental to find such special people, who enjoy omnipotent characteristics and unusual privileges, in places where most of the other people are exempt from virtually all privilege. And certainly, a home for the mentally retarded is just the place for a bright state employee to learn to be better than most other people; not only better, but different, possessed with rare powers.

People lust for privileges, for more than their share. Why a person wants more than he or she deserves is perhaps mainly due to a rotten memory. People who do not remember that they are going to die seem to engage in more than their share of silly business as they take more than their share of the common wealth. Perhaps the most prominent recent example of forgetful and silly greed is Nixon. Why would he buy a million dollar house here and another one there, while all the time he had a big free White House in Washington and a free camp in Maryland?

There are infinite anomalies in our thinking and not thinking about death, perhaps because we tend to think about death only in terms of human beings. We assume animals are not concerned with their impending deaths. But it is the human being who is anomalous and not death. As everyone really knows, death is the most invariant of phenomena, one to which there is no less restrictive alternative. But how do the mentally retarded think about death? They do, of course, but do *we* remember that they do? It seems that it is difficult enough to remember our own deaths, much less whether the mentally retarded remember theirs. Of course, we think a lot about what will happen when we go, and what will happen to Billy or Mary, our retarded son or daughter. Or that Billy is one of God's innocents and will therefore surely go to heaven. But do we ever think about whether Billy thinks about his death? Of course not! In the same way that we do not think (or is it care?) about what our pet canary thinks about his death, it is difficult for us to think that retarded people have the same thoughts and worries that we have. As a matter of fact, in all the years I have been in this work, I have found but one article in the literature that deals with this question; and that 40-year-old report restricts itself to the mildly retarded, those who are most nearly like the rest of us.

What does death have to do with privileged extensions of freedom? Maybe almost everything. The privileged "need" a million dollar estate to counteract the often dim but always disquieting knowledge of their fate. Mentally retarded people are not even thought about as people who know they are going to die. As an extension of this attitude, little attention is paid to what else the mentally retarded may be thinking about, what they may like to have in terms of the world's extras. After all, *we* deserve that car, that cruise, that cashmere, that special privilege. *We* have something to worry about. Not the retards! They get life's subsistence rations, not merely because they have not earned more, but because they will not appreciate more, and because they will not suffer the way we suffer during our mortal lives. They do not need diversions to make them forget their mortality.

Well, it may not be true. Mentally retarded people may know an awful lot more than we think they know. The mentally retarded person may know more about the underprivileged than almost anyone around, even those who live in the ghetto. They are experts on the most restrictive environment. The mentally retarded person and Mr. Nixon should write the definitive book on the least restrictive environment. They represent the range and the expertise.

Loopholes

Perhaps the most important point I want to make is that the issues and solutions in our field can appear clear and simple only as long as we wear the blinders of specialization. It is not hard to think we know exactly what a least restrictive environment is if we think of it as a contrast to a dreary, segregated, and educationally counterproductive special class. It is even easier to think we know what it means in contrast to the locked back ward of an antiquated institution. Yet, life does not derive its meaning or dignity from contrasts; people do not remain cheerful from being told that things could be, or used to be, worse. Although in the end we may be unable to articulate precise definitions, we must try to provide mentally retarded people with opportunities that are not merely better but good. It should be a sobering reminder to us that when the pioneers in our field undertook this task, despite the greatest good will and thoughtful deliberation, their efforts led to the development of modern institutional settings. In offering enormous benefits, their work led to the loss of everything important to their beneficiaries.

If the line between love and hate is at times indistinct, the line between privilege and restriction may at times be nonexistent. How can we distinguish between people who are very rich and people in the most restrictive institutions? To be provided with all possible services, to have them at hand and receive them free is to enjoy enormous privilege. The very rich can have tutors instruct them or their children in their own homes. So can the mentally retarded—although their homes are called state schools. The very rich and the mentally retarded have swimming pools, parks, playgrounds on the premises where they live; doctors make house calls; paid staff cook meals, wash clothes, clean and straighten up their rooms.

And the difference between the very rich and the mentally retarded is not to be found in the attitudes of the public. Both are viewed in stereotyped, often dehumanizing, ways by "typical" members of society. They are frequently assumed to be unable and unwilling to perform meaningful work. They are assumed to prefer to be "with their own kind," apart from general society. Members of neither group are supposed to have an understanding of "real life" sufficient to make them independent and viable members of society. And finally, both the very rich and the mentally retarded are often regarded as unpredictable and potentially dangerous.

Of course in making these comparisons, which could be extended even further, I am not uncertain about which structure is the mansion and which is the state school. I have constructed the ridiculous parallel only in order to point out that, in practice, we distinguish between the conditions of wealth and mental retardation not on the basis of the objective criteria—in which they are similar—but by means of an intuitive grasp of countless unspecified subtleties. Precise criteria only work in these matters when we know the conclusion ahead of time. We know that despite the restrictiveness of the trappings of wealth, the life of the wealthy is the freest possible; and that despite the privileges of institutionalized life, the life of the mentally retarded is restricted to the point of extinction.

In the past, when policy was guided by the supposedly dangerous mechanism of judgment, this intuitive understanding of differences was enough. Today, because we have grown impatient with our history of cruelly mistaken judgments, our policy must be in the precise and objective form of a federal law. So, what *is* a restrictive environment today?

Quasi-Legal Practices

Part of the reason we are now in need of legal definitions for the field is that so much of what has been reprehensible in the past has been quasi-legal. I am no lawyer, and a good lawyer would surely discuss this less clumsily than I am about to, but most good lawyers probably do not know as much about the quasi-legal practices in the field of mental retardation as I do. So you will have to settle for the inevitable trade-off. Discussing quasi-anything usually requires one to walk a fine line. While there may not be a law or regulation allowing a given practice, there does not seem to be very much precedent forbidding it. Or conversely, while there may not be something on the books forbidding a practice, it does not seem to be in good taste. Some examples of quasi-legal practices in the field of mental retardation must certainly include the continued approval of sterilization, inmate employment without compensation, and assignment of the recently deceased as medical school cadavers.

For many years, I have written about all of this and more. Indeed, I have spent the last 20 years cataloging virtually every type of legal, illegal, and quasi-legal abuse perpetrated on the mentally retarded. I have described the work of the cadaver committee in a New England city, sterilization practices at various state schools; the pulling of teeth of inmates who bite themselves or others; the pulling of plugs at distinguished medical centers; other premature or strange deaths, even stranger autopsy investigations; peonage in its almost infinite forms; a severe spastic choking to death on a whole hard boiled egg; a severely retarded bed patient nearly bleeding to death after his groin was ripped open by an assailant in the night and he was not seen by a doctor until morning infirmary call; inmates involuntarily volunteered for dangerous experiments at Ivy League medical schools; children raped by older inmates; and older inmates brutalized by marauding adolescents. And of course, although many of these atrocities could have been classified as illegal and the perpetraters could have been prosecuted, they hardly ever were; there is hardly a disruption of institutional routine when such situations occur.

I rummaged through my files, but there seemed nothing new to say about quasi-legal practices. Yet, I knew that I must say something. The very idea of "least restrictive environment" was born out of a history of quasi-legal practices applied to people. I then went to my diary, which is used, if anything, as a last resort. I knew exactly what I was looking for, the raw notes and description that provided the background for a book I started alone in late 1975 and, luckily for me, finished in 1978 with Andrejs Ozolins and Joe McNally.

Now I have read all of those pages and I want to tell you about Sophie, who was a resident of the state school for the retarded and died at a local hospital, and may have died of neglect. To this day, the only consequence of Sophie's quasi-legal demise was the withdrawal of medical services to the state school by the group of physicians in the community who had then been serving that place. There have been other inadequately explained deaths since Sophie's, and there have been other medical groups attending residents of the state school.

I am sure that somebody somewhere in America today has just seen an inmate die needlessly, or has just learned that a medical group is withdrawing its favors from the state's bughouse, or has just attended a meeting where promises were made to finally fix up the state school, or is right now reading in the evening paper that the state has finally found a way to serve the residential needs of the mentally retarded. But the deaths continue, nearly unnoticed and sufficiently legal. I am not surprised. If everything about Sophie's life was legal, why should not everything about her death be legal?

What follows was written at the time it happened in late 1975.

This has been a strange week, very strange indeed. My mind wanders to thoughts about last evening's meeting of our Advocacy Board. I could kick myself for getting so angry, for showing my anger. Why can't these good people realize, as I realize, that case-by-case advocacy will consume us, will play into the hands of those who want to maintain the status quo or regress further toward a segregated and bureaucraticized society? We "win" victory after victory on behalf of this family or that one—no mean achievements—and I am not knocking those accomplishments. However, while we win those skirmishes, the city breaks ground for a new segregated facility, this one to contain the so-called "trainables." Case by case, we advocate for children and their families. Some we win, some we lose; the record is fairly impressive. But, we are losing too many; too many children are still denied educations; too many people sit in back rooms receiving little or nothing of society's interest or services; too many are in locked institutions, not because they must be locked up but, rather, because there is no other "place" to be, because the (only) "place" was created for them. The debate wore me out, driving me eventually to leave the meeting, not because of my anger—though I was angry—but because I was weary, and wanted to go home, and remove those stale clothes and drive out of my head the morbid thoughts of practical people.

Indeed, it has been a strange week. I forced myself to think about Sophie, but not to cheer myself up. Last Monday was scheduled to be a low-keyed, routine day. Nobody knew very much earlier than Monday—therefore nobody told me—that Sophie was to be buried on Monday. And, even had they known it would happen that she needed to be buried on Monday, nobody would have suspected earlier that I would have been asked to attend the funeral, or that I would have accepted the invitation had the offer come. You see, the very first time I ever laid eyes on Sophie was this past Monday at the Garfield Funeral Home. I saw her, but she didn't see me.

Sophie was a resident at the State Developmental Center, near the State School, near the Asylum for Idiots. She had been there for many, many years, leading what I was told was an uneventful and unhappy life. She became ill, very ill, so ill that she was removed to the Community General Hospital. There she died, approximately one week later.

What was interesting about all this, quite inflammatory in this community, concerned the allegation that Sophie did not die of natural causes. There were charges, confused and contradictory but strong charges, that—as we have lately learned to say—the plugs were pulled. Sophie was euthanized; she was rewarded with a dignified death. A big cheer for Death With Dignity, and the Happy Angel that supervises it all. Rejoice, some told us. Sophie has left this vale of misery to an eternal peace and happiness that she did not find on earth. So we gathered together at the funeral home, the priest gave his blessings and read from the Scriptures, some said their Hail Mary's or Hail whatevers, we signed the guest book—guests!—and went on our own ways.

The Death With Dignity Society, and there is one here, should be pleased. The crazy thing about it all is that, in the Cosmos, there may be some explanation for all of this; and, it would not surprise me if such an explanation agreed with the death wishers. Yet, there is also something evil here, something that would tell a human being that it is time for her to die; but if we were in your shoes, sister, we would live! It's best that you die now, first because you're sick. If you were not sick, we would not kill you. Yet, not only are you sick, you are old (is 63 really that old) and, not only are you sick and old, you are defective. Sickness, we sometimes tolerate if it's not too much sickness. And, even the defectives need not be marked early or, especially, with the Terrible Decree. But, Sophie, even you must agree that you gave us no choice. Being sick, old, and defective necessarily must strip you of the rights other people have guaranteed to them. Don't blame us, Sophie, this is all your fault. Besides, you'll be happier up there than down here. It's all over for you, and we have yet to face the terror that is now behind you. What we have done for you is the stuff that causes ordinary people to become true humanitarians.

It is the day after Sophie's funeral. It is 8:00 P.M., then 9, then the hour approaches midnight. We are in Room 407 of the County Courthouse. The County Legislative Commission to Investigate Mental Health and Mental Retardation is holding its last formal hearing prior to its report to the citizens. I am a member of the Commission and, just before termination of the long evening's discussions, I ask the superintendent of the State Developmental Center to reflect upon the future: "In the best of all possible worlds, what do you envision for the Developmental Center in ten years?"

He responded: "In ten years things will not be very much different than they are today. Can I speculate about the world in 50 years?"

"Will the people wait 50 years? There are people who desperately need help, not even in 10 years, tomorrow," I said.

"Don't misunderstand me. If I had my way," he replied, "we would evacuate the Developmental Center in 10 years, five years, or sooner if we could. We would give it to the State, or to your university to use as a dormitory, or for some other educational purpose."

I do not misunderstand. I am embarrassed for him. I think about those times six years ago when it might not have been too late to stop the construction of this $25,000,000 monstrosity. I attempt to avoid remembering the pleadings and arguments, even the threats we made, anything to block construction of the new State School. I remember too much.

Quite early the next morning, I am back in my office . . . The phone rings. It's the Executive Director of the President's Committee on Mental Retardation. Not any president's committee, *The President's*! Would I do a study for them! Would I visit the institutions that continue to defy extinction? Would I expose the rottenness, the abuse, the mismanagement, the inhuman treatment?

"Sure" I reply, "what else do I have to do? As a matter of fact, I was just thinking about those problems today. I'll study these state schools for you. I hope you don't think I've been sitting by this phone all morning waiting for you to call, though. You just happened to catch me in, between assignments, so to speak. Between life and death. You caught me just as I was beginning to believe that Sophie was the lucky one."

I have been arguing that, as Robert Frost might have said if he had been a poet of the human service industry. Something there is that doesn't love a definition. No sooner do we build a row of definitions— definitions of restrictiveness or abuse, freedom or dignity—than it begins to crumble into loopholes, exceptions, and quasi-legal rubble. I have been trying to show that this is not so much because we do not build good definitions, but because life simply will not be captured in definitions.

Yet even as I describe our failure to define things better, even as I read my notes on Sophie whose life slipped away over the edge of a definition of human rights, I too have to agree that we need better definitions. Perhaps, to burden Robert Frost a little more: Good definitions make good neighbors. And though they fall down in the winter of our inattentiveness, each spring we must build them anew, as though they would stay.

Variations on the Definition of Restrictiveness

All of those who have tried have had difficulty defining restrictiveness. Consequently, I need not preface my suggestions with any elaborate disclaimer: I too will not provide the definitive statement. But for whatever it is worth, I think about a "restrictive environment" as one in which, if placed there him or herself, the superintendent of a state mental institution would feel insulted and threatened. Conversely, I think about a "least restrictive environment" as one in which, if placed there, the inmate of a state mental hospital would sense that he or she was now living somewhere that is quite different from, and much more pleasant than, the hospital. Certainly, these definitions will not escape the need for revision. And certainly, they only shape our thinking for purposes of developing a continuum. But in some situations, they may offer useful analogies, and analogies may be the strongest definitions we can get.

Suppose "least restrictive environment" were understood to mean "what I demand as rights," and suppose "restrictiveness" were understood as "that which is contemptible and inhumane"; would not the mentally retarded and the mentally ill and the elderly and other modern-day pariahs be better represented than they are now? If we thought about restrictiveness in terms of the Golden Rule, would we be defining small institutions as relatively less restrictive and, consequently, more acceptable? If we remembered the Golden Rule—"Do unto others as you would have them do unto you"—would we need to remember all of this folderol about per capita floor space, staff/patient ratios, standards for state and federal reimbursements, or accreditation?

A big deal is made about the technical aspects of environments for the unwanted because, first, people do not want to admit they are dealing with the unwanted and, secondly, people do not want to put themselves in the same category as these unwanted. I know that no loving child or parent could ever easily place a parent or child in one of our traditional state institutions, be it designated most restrictive or least restrictive. I also know that the term "least restrictive environment" ought to be reserved for places that, by definition, fall outside of the state's traditional mental institutions. A truly least restrictive environment would have nothing to do with state departments of mental health or with clients placed in their facilities *because* of mental incapacitation. In the world of mental health and mental retardation, people live either in large institutions or small institutions. People who are caught in the mental health–mental retardation net, by definition should not be thought of as living in a least restrictive environment.

I can envision many variations of the definition of restrictiveness. How can we be satisfied with one-dimensional definitions? Is that really what science is all about? Or is it really what blind professionalism is all about? I am dissatisfied with the official definitions, so dissatisfied that I am unable even to note them here for the record.

Maybe it is my idiosyncrasy, but I think I would better understand the situation a person is in if I knew how many mistakes he or she was entitled to make before being yanked from the game. Robert Frost defined my idea of the least restrictive life very satisfactorily when he wrote in "Two Tramps in Mudtime":

> But yield who will to their separation,
> My object in living is to unite
> My avocation and my vocation
> As my two eyes make one in sight.

To be yanked after one mistake or two might occur in a terribly restrictive situation. And to be in a position in which one's job and interests are integrated, in which one wants to do what one has to do is an example of what a least restrictive environment might be.

Why is it that artists seem to describe life so much better than the rest of us? Then why is it that the rest of us do not turn more to artists to explain what we are unable to explain for ourselves? It has not always been this way. In the old days, artists rendered reality in a descriptive manner, from Victorian painters who described street urchins and fallen women, to Dickens who wrote about them, to journalists who reported it all. Artists were once society's definers. What got in the way were the universities and their professors, and the professionals they eventually trained, and the disciples of the professionals, the gullible public. Unnecessary science became a mischievous nuisance.

The discourse sounds more conspiratorial and menacing than I want it to be. To be sure, professionalism in America was not created to close out the artist and to do in the consumer. To be sure, the country had its fill of barber surgeons, patent medicines laced with dope; and not only quack doctors and quack patients, but quack ministers, teachers, and scientists. Abraham Flexner had a point to make just as Ralph Nader had virtually the same point to make half a century later. Flexner's point was that amateurs were running things, and it was time for professionals to become organized and monitor the world. Nader's point is that we had better beware of the professionals who are greedy louts running things for their own benefit. Abraham Flexner once saw the enemy embedded within the suspicion, the prejudice, and ignorance of the 19th century. Ralph Nader sees the enemy embedded within the firm pillars of status and respectability created out of the Flexner Revolution. And while it is not difficult to find many among us today who see the shortsightedness of Flexner's vision, there are too few here who see the catastrophe of Nader's "revolution." Flexner created a professionalized society. Nader seems to want to overcome that evil by a bureaucratized society, one to be controlled by the people to be sure but, nevertheless, people who would weigh everything, test everything, define everything, and be suspicious of everything. Possibly, at this time what is needed more than either Flexner or Nader is a good poet who would give us some hints on how to live better with each other. Maybe we once needed Flexner. Maybe we needed Nader when he came along. But I will take Frost.

Conclusion

In the real world, people die for their freedoms. In the field of mental retardation, they hold conventions or invite each other to conferences. In the real world, people learn from each other, help each other, and protect each other. In the field of mental retardation, one must be licensed to teach, certified to treat, and commissioned to protect. That which is considered to be good about the real world naturally unfolds. That which is considered to be good about the field of mental retardation is professionally controlled. What is least restrictive about the real world derives from thousands of years of human discourse under such diverse leaders as Attila and Lincoln, Pharaoh and Moses, George III and George Washington, Martin Luther and Martin Luther King. What is most restrictive about the world of mental retardation derives from 200 years of professional interest in the pathology rather than in the universality of people. Professionals have created much of the need to do something about the problem of too-restrictive environments forced upon the mentally retarded. We have created or have been much of the problem, and now we seem anxious to do something about our unholy work. Indeed, we must do something, but less to rescue the mentally retarded than to redeem ourselves; less to obtain their freedoms than to establish ours; less because they need us than because we need them.

When I was a little boy, I would jump out of bed most mornings barely able to wait for what lay ahead. And there were days when I could not sleep because of eagerness to push aside the darkness to reach a time when people were allowed to take advantage of all the wonders there. Frost said he had "a lover's quarrel with the world." I did not know about Frost then, and I surely did not know the world on those terms. But I too have had an affair with the world, with the air and the birds, but also with the movement of people on hot steamy sidewalks, and even with the institutions, with everything we think of as life. From the start, I felt lucky to be born and to live as a free person. I never had to learn what it is to be alone in an alien land. I never had to know what it is to be without advocates, what it means to need advocates. I never needed protection against my brothers. I never needed protection against my government. I never needed protection against God. What harm befell me, I usually did to myself. What grief occurred was the grief done to any fragile human being, usually more by accident than by design. Thank God I was born free and now live free. But I am very sad that not everyone shares such good fortune.

We have listened to neither the inner heart nor the call for the common good, not to God nor fellow man. We have made swords into guns. We will believe only the poets who confirm what we have believed. We want to believe that literal fences do indeed make good neighbors, and that tough attitudes characterize practical and wise men of the world. Our faith is more in ourselves than in mankind, but little in ourselves. We have created an unnecessarily restricted society. To free ourselves, we must free the old, the weak, and the handicapped because, in truth, they *are* us. Yet we resist that kind of world. Our problem is not one of merely defining what represents the least restrictive environment in an unjust society, but rather one of changing that society for everyone. This is not a local or professional issue, but a world issue. We should stop confusing ourselves. We should try to better understand that we are not dealing here only with the problem of the mentally retarded, but with our common problem, the problem of facing our lives as if they will end, and in believing in the hereafter as if it might be there.

Perhaps the reason I kept returning to poets in this paper, the reason I believe they can give us better guidance in life than bureaucrats or scientists, is that when we read poetry we *know* that we are dealing with metaphors, analogies, ways of thinking—rather than lists of facts. Surely there can be no doubt that if the Golden Rule were a federal regulation, it would become meaningless and useless. Emerson nailed down one part of our common problem when he said: "All our science lacks is a human side." A serious part of our common problem is that too much of humanism has gone scientific. And too much of our science makes it easier to banish our brothers and sisters from our lives.

The Politics of Aging
Dilemmas and Opportunities

Robert H. Binstock

The contemporary politics of aging do, indeed, present many dilemmas and opportunities. My basic message with respect to the opportunities is that they lie, ironically, in discarding the notion that the aging are a monolithic constituency. We thereby enable ourselves to focus on policy issues and political actions dealing with those subgroups within the aging population that are most seriously disadvantaged. I will consider the opportunities that can be presented through such a focus, shortly, after outlining some of the major dilemmas in American policies toward the elderly and then briefly reviewing the politics of aging which shapes them.

The Dilemmas of Our Policies on Aging

The contemporary dilemmas of American public policy toward aging have been shaped by four major factors.

The first, which has been termed "the graying of the budget" (Hudson, 1978), is that our national government's existing policy commitments toward the elderly currently lead it to spend one-fourth of the annual federal budget on programs for the aging. This is slightly less than the proportion spent on defense programs. The estimated total for federal expenditures in Fiscal Year (FY) 1980 is $531.6 billion; of that, $132.2 billion will go for programs on aging.

Second, the present policies do not substantially alleviate the severest problems—poverty, ill health, and inadequate services—experienced by millions of the most disadvantaged elderly.

Third, if present policies are maintained, the mere demographic increase in the number of older persons in America would lead federal expenditures on aging to more than triple in real dollars early in the next century and thus comprise 40 percent of total federal outlays (Califano, 1978, p. 1576). Today we have 24.4 million persons who are 65 and older; in the year 2000 we will have 30.6 million (Siegel, 1976, p. 3).

And fourth, there are no foreseeable elements in the future of the

American economy or in the characteristics of the emerging elderly population that will eradicate the severest problems of old age. Today's policies will cost even more in the future, but millions of older persons will
still experience severe deprivation.

The central dilemma posed by these factors would seem to be whether
to retrench collective responsibility for alleviating some of the dire hardships experienced by older persons or to carry forward, even increase,
our responsibilities to the aging at the cost of other national goals. Before
considering how the politics of aging may bear on the resolution of this
issue, let us examine how this broad dilemma of policy toward the aging
is expressed in more specific forms for several sectors of social policy
concern.

ECONOMIC SECURITY

The need for adequate income is perhaps the most critical problem confronting the aging population of the United States. To be sure, the federal
government is spending a great deal on income programs for the elderly;
in FY 1980 it will provide more than $96 billion in direct cash benefits and
$33 billion in health care benefits to older persons. Additional tens of bil-
lions will be paid out through state and local governments and private
pension plans. But the fact remains that a substantial percentage of older
persons experience severe poverty.

The government's official poverty index, widely criticized with respect
to the adequacy of its components, records some 3.3 million older persons, or 14 percent of the elderly, as below the "poverty line" (Brotman,
1978, p. 1625). This widely used scale for judging income adequacy was
adopted by the federal government in 1969 and is updated annually to
reflect changes in the Consumer Price Index (CPI). Though widely used,
it imposes an exceedingly harsh judgment. It is constructed on the basis
of an "economy food plan" defined by the Department of Agriculture as
providing a "minimally nutritious diet for emergency or temporary use";
according to the Department of Agriculture only 10 percent of the persons actually spending the daily amount that it postulates for food expenditures in the economy food plan would be able to receive a nutritionally
adequate diet (U.S. House of Representatives, 1978, p. 84). Moreover, it
should be noted that the annual adjustment of the poverty index in accordance with the CPI inadequately reflects the expenditure patterns and
consumption necessities of the poor. The CPI includes the costs of many
goods and services that are not used by the elderly poor, but which are
subject to relatively slow rates of inflation.

The harsh measure imposed by the poverty line may be appreciated by
considering the actual dollars involved. The poverty level for a "non-

farm" elderly couple in 1977, for example, was $3,637. If one shared the Department of Agriculture's assumption that one-third of this sum would be expended for food, then a couple that had *reached* the poverty line would have a budget something like this. One-third of the budget, or $1,212 would be available for food; this comes to $1.66 a day for each person, or $11.62 a week. If another third were available for housing, this would allow the couple to spend $101 a month for rent, or for property taxes, maintenance costs, and mortgage payments (if any). A remaining $50.50 per month per person would be available for clothing, utilities, transportation, medical and dental care, furniture, personal and property insurance, and all other expenses.

Since this is the budget for older persons who have *made it* up to the poverty line, small wonder that the poverty index is sharply challenged as a standard for measuring economic security among the aging. Indeed, the person who initially developed that index has recently revamped it. She estimates that 8.7 million elderly, or 36 percent of the aged, have inadequate incomes for the essentials of daily living (U.S. House of Representatives, 1978, p. 203).

Wherever the poverty line is drawn, it is clear that millions of older persons are clustered just above it. For them, in addition to the millions who are below the line, economic insecurity is a problem that permeates all other dimensions of existence. Beyond the day-by-day challenges of subsistence—food, clothing, shelter, and heat—lie the costs of health care and social services, the expense involved in gaining access to those services, and the financial demands for participation in family life and social networks. It is probably not too much to say that economic security or insecurity is the fundamental element in determining an older person's prospects for well-being.

Both the short-term and longer-term outlooks for improvement in the economic situation of current and future older persons are at best problematic. Double-digit inflation seems to be with us. The nation's rate of economic growth has slowed markedly and seems likely to decline further before it recovers. The changing demographic profile of the nation will yield a larger number of older persons, and they will be a greater proportion of the population than at present. And private pensions, in their present form, do not seem likely to become a universal panacea for the income difficulties of the elderly.

HEALTH

Receiving less attention than economic security in the past few years, and probably far more difficult to deal with in the long run, are issues concerning the improvement of older persons' health. Older persons are subject to more disability than younger persons, see physicians 50 percent more often, have about twice as many hospital stays and, once hospitalized, will stay there twice as long (Brotman, 1978, p. 1624).

The Medicare and Medicaid programs enacted in 1965 have helped to defray the costs of seeing doctors, staying in hospitals, and obtaining several additional specific health services and goods. But these programs do not seem to have had much impact on the health status of older persons. Shanas (1978), for example, conducted a national probability survey on the health status and health care activities of the American older population in 1962 and again in 1975. The only change she found in this 13-year period was that the percentage of older persons who had not seen a doctor in over a year had dropped from 32 percent to 19 percent. But she did not find any change in the health status of older persons, whether aggregated for all persons 65 and older or disaggregated for different age groups within that population.

The contemporary challenges of providing adequate health care to the elderly are enormous. The probability of any person being institutionalized at some time after the 65th birthday is 25 percent or one in four (Kastenbaum and Candy, 1973). And we are much too familiar with the uneven, often scandalous nature of institutional care, as well as the feckless pattern through which our national and state governments deal with abuses in nursing homes and other long-term care institutions. We have seen often enough the cycle through which media exposure of nursing home conditions engenders a sense of public outrage. A commission is appointed to investigate conditions and to recommend legislation to deal with them, and reasonably strong regulatory standards are enacted. Nonetheless, the nursing home industry is able to remain remarkably immune to regulation by neutralizing or capturing the machinery of regulatory implementation (see Mendelsohn and Hapgood, 1975).

The highly touted alternatives to institutional care—home health care and homemaker services—are still touted, but not implemented on a substantial scale. One major reason they have not been fully developed is because neither Medicare nor Medicaid provides for most elements of home service that do not involve a skilled nursing component (U.S. Comptroller General, 1979). Consequently, a great many of the theoretically viable alternatives to institutional care remain financially impracticable.

Whether or not institutionalization is required, the social implications of ill health are significant and wide ranging. It is well established by now that an individual's health status affects his or her: self-esteem, social status, capacity for work, level of income, range of social contacts, and overall life style. We also know that the health status of an aging individual has a direct impact on the total family: on each member's own physical health; on the nature of family relationships; on the number of contacts within the family; on its living arrangements; on its economic status; and on its social and instrumental activities (Brody, 1980). This clearly emerging picture of the social implication of health is why we have come to speak of a "continuum of health and social services" or a "continuum of care" in which we recognize the need for support throughout the range of these overlapping areas of concern.

If we consider the current situation regarding the provision of the continuum of supportive care that is required for older persons, we can see why the future need for provision may be overwhelming. Let us focus, for example, on Califano's (1978, p. 1581) estimate that 70 to 80 percent of the supportive care that is now given to persons 55 and older is provided by their adult children. Unfortunately, there are major trends in American society which indicate that family and kinship sources of care will not be available to this extent in the very near future.

Statistics that show increasing numbers and proportions of women entering the labor force suggest that the adult daughter care-givers, who have been providing most of the family care, will be otherwise occupied in the decades ahead (Brody, 1979, p. 15). Other changing social practices and population trends also indicate that the family is unlikely to be a major source of supportive care. As British historian Peter Laslett (1980) has pointed out, patterns of family support do not seem to change in relation to a nation's degree of industrialization. Rather, they seem to weaken with the aging of populations and in relation to such cultural variables as rates of divorce, rates of remarriage, rates of adoption, and so on. The American trends for all of these factors are currently in a direction that indicates weakening of family supports for the aging. In short, even our current patterns of providing supportive care, which we recognize as inadequate, and which are largely family-based, seem unlikely to continue at their current levels.

Can we look to biomedical research to help reduce the challenges of providing supportive care? Not very likely. Biomedical research may make some progress in prolonging life by eliminating cancer, heart disease, and stroke; but if so, this would lead to more survivors at later ages, adding to the number of persons who might be expected to have disabling physical and mental health conditions (see Hayflick, 1976, and Pfeiffer, 1976). We can hope that research will lead to elimination of organic brain syndromes and other disabling conditions, but this seems even less likely at the moment than progress in eliminating the major fatal diseases. It is for this reason that many forums have begun to address issues concerning the quality of an extended life span.

SOCIAL SERVICES AND FACILITIES

With all the attention that is being directed to the costs of income security and health care programs, other federal programs among the total of 134 benefiting the aging (U.S. House of Representatives, 1976) have hardly been noticed, probably because their budgets are comparatively negligible. Nonetheless, the problems that such programs are supposed to be alleviating are of considerable importance to many older persons and their families.

Perhaps the most useful example is provided by the Older Americans Act of 1965, a legislative omnibus administered by HEW's Administration on Aging (AOA) and currently costing just under $600 million a year. The range of programs initiated and supported through this act, which was reauthorized and expanded in 1978, has set forth an extensive agenda of American society's responsibilities toward its older citizens. Through nearly 15 years of legislation and implementation, the Older Americans Act has brought to the fore as legitimate public concerns the need for: home care services, transportation, nutrition, leisure programs, protection against crime, legal services, home repair, regulatory ombudsmen, research and career training in aging, and a variety of other supportive services. In order to implement programs aimed at these concerns, AOA has elaborated a so-called "national network on aging" anchored by nearly 600 Area Agencies on Aging. The network also includes 1,100 senior centers, 9,000 nutrition program sites where congregate meals are served, and hundreds of public and voluntary service and planning organizations, as well as research and education programs devoted to concerns of older persons. Without sustenance from the Older Americans Act, most of these operations would not exist or would be devoting their attention and efforts to matters other than aging.

There is no doubt that the programs of the Older Americans Act directly help many older persons through the provision of a variety of health and social services, free meals, and opportunities to make useful contributions to community life. And there is little question that AOA's nationwide bureaucratic network generates ongoing support for the act and its programs. Almost every congressional district is served by an area agency and has within it some older persons who are benefiting from specific services provided through AOA's programs.

Unfortunately, these positive features of the Older Americans Act go hand-in-hand with a series of weaknesses.

First, the extensive range of programmatic responsibilities has been elaborated without much sense of priority. Consequently, the small amount of available funds is distributed relatively thinly among many objectives and is far from sufficient to make a substantial impact on any given problem.

A second and related weakness is that the programmatic agenda and the bureaucratic network have been developed with sufficient fanfare to create a cruel illusion that a variety of problems can eventually be solved through funding and implementation under the Older Americans Act. We can appreciate the extent to which this is an illusion if we consider that no one problem (of the many toward which the act's programs are directed) could be solved through the present patterns even if funding were drastically increased. For example, it is estimated that the act's Nutrition Program is currently meeting about one percent of the national need (see U.S. Senate Subcommittee on Aging, 1979, pp. 305–306). Are we looking toward an appropriation of over $20 billion that would be required to fund an adequate number of nutrition programs throughout the country? And tens of billions for each of the other programmatic needs?

A third weakness is that the bureaucratic components of the network—the public and voluntary service agencies and the universities and colleges—have quite understandably become preoccupied with sustaining and expanding the different, thinly funded program elements with which they are directly involved. Each program element has a corresponding set of bureaucratic or educational mechanisms, and each of these sets has developed its own professional organization or association. As a consequence, one finds a great deal of attention given to the apportionment of Older Americans Act funds earmarked for each of the bureaucratic domains in the network, but little, if any, attention to how a given problem confronting older persons is to be solved. In many states and in Washington there has been continuing conflict among associations for area agencies, for nutrition projects, for home care corporations, for senior centers, for gerontological research and education, for municipal councils on aging, and the like. From time to time these associations attempt to straighten out their bureaucratic and trade differences and come to some settlements about their division of the territory and its resources. But these settlements are not made with an eye to solving the problems of older persons so much as with an eye to entrenching firmly the role of the bureaucratic and trade components of the network (see U.S. Senate Subcommittee on Aging, 1979, p. 306).

In effect, the Administration on Aging and a number of other agencies scattered throughout the federal government—Department of Agriculture, Labor, Transportation, HEW, HUD, the Community Services Administration, the Veterans Administration—are doing what they can to deal with an extensive agenda of social service and facility needs of older persons, an agenda which Congress and the executive branch have officially established. But the number of people these agencies can help is very limited, given their meager funding, lack of priorities, and cumbersome mechanisms for program implementation.

The Politics of Aging

In briefly reviewing the results of federal programs for the aging, I have applied what some persons may regard as a severe or unrealistic standard of judgment—namely, whether those programs solve or substantially alleviate problems that our national government is officially committed to solving. But when we are allocating a quarter of our federal budget to combat those problems it may not seem an unrealistic criterion, and certainly should be an instructive one. By spending $132 billion on the elderly we are helping a great many people in a great many ways. Yet about nine million older persons, well over one-third of the elderly pouplation, are in severe financial distress. We have not improved the health status of the aged population since the introduction of Medicare and Medicaid. And a great many other problems of aging have only been met by token responses.

Many advocates for the severely disadvantaged aging, recognizing the limited effectiveness of our current policies, have comforted themselves with the notion that "senior power" will sharply increase federal expenditures and administrative efforts to improve the income security, health, and social problems of older persons. Looking to the ever-growing proportion of older voters in the population, they cling to images of the aging as a powerful or soon-to-be powerful voting bloc and organized interest.

Journalists and scholars of subjects other than politics have reinforced this image of a powerful, nationwide older persons' vote. Noting increased programs and expenditures for the aging, they portray politicians as being bullied by senior power. Inspired by demographic trends, the American Association for the Advancement of Science went so far as to sponsor a symposium in 1974 to address, seriously, the issue of whether the United States would become a gerontocracy in the 1990s or in the early 21st century.

Can we, in fact, expect that senior power will augment and/or redirect our expenditures of collective resources in a fashion that will redress the problems of the severely disadvantaged aged? If we heed the conventional wisdom the answer would seem to be yes. But if we carefully examine the political attitudes and behavior of individuals as they age, and the political behavior of aging-based organizations, we find that the popular images of senior power are inaccurate. The politics of aging is hardly likely to become focused on the problems of the severely disadvantaged.

Both those who cherish the image of senior power and those who fear it have been misled. Although older persons do cast 15 percent or more of the vote in national elections, they do not all vote the same. The population of older persons is politically heterogeneous, just as it is economically and socially heterogeneous (Hudson and Binstock, 1976).

Even if we accept the problematic assumption that voters are swayed by issues favoring their self-interest, most older voters do not primarily identify themselves, and hence their self-interest, in terms of aging. When a person reaches 65 or enters retirement status, he or she does not suddenly lose all prior self identities—sex, race, education, peer group and community ties—and the self interests that can be derived from them. Take the case of a 73-year-old Caucasian, Catholic widow in Chicago, living comfortably on income from capital gains and dividends, who is deeply involved in advocacy for children's programs. Given a candidate who takes positions on race relations, abortion, urban affairs, tax reform, day care for children, and on senior issues, which self-interests are decisive in influencing the vote of this senior citizen?

In short, the notion that the elderly are a homogeneous political constituency is an artificial and simplistic construct. Analyses of age as a variable in political attitudes and voting patterns have consistently shown that the differences within age groups are greater than the differences between age groups (Campbell, 1971). No sound evidence has been assembled showing an instance in which an "old-age interest" or an "old-age candidate" can be presumed to have shifted older persons' votes as a cohesive force.

Although the commonly purveyed images of the aging as a political force are inaccurate, the images, in themselves, provide resources for some limited forms of power. The image of an aged voting bloc leads many politicians to support propositions that seem favorable to older persons, and to attend sizable meetings that involve older persons and their presumed interests. They do not wish to be listed among the missing, when the rolls of supporters of the aging are compiled. On the other hand, the image of the aging as a voting bloc is not sufficiently powerful to evoke more than moderate, incremental, and symbolic support.

The relatively few politicians who make a heavy investment (even a symbolic one) in support for the aging, relative to their support for other constituencies, learn regretfully about the inaccurate image of the aging voting bloc. Most sophisticated politicians make sure that they are counted as sympathetic to the aging, but give relatively low priority to the elderly among the constituencies from which they seek votes. For example, in the 1976 Carter campaign for the presidency of the United States, the "seniors desk" had the lowest budget and least number of paid personnel among the eleven desks established by the Democratic Presidential Campaign Committee (Riemer and Binstock, 1978).

The image of bloc voting tendencies among the elderly is nurtured, however, by several dozen national organizations that are more or less exclusively preoccupied with issues related to aging. These might be termed aging-based organizations in that they depend in large measure for their activities upon the existence of older persons: as mass membership for the organization (e.g., the American Association of Retired Persons); as consumers of goods and services offered by organization's members (e.g., the American Association of Homes for the Aging); as clients for the practitioners who belong to the organization (e.g., the American Geriatrics Society); as subjects for study by educators and researchers who comprise the organization's membership (e.g., the Gerontological Society); or as a population subgroup for advocacy attention by reformers concerned with issues affecting minority groups (e.g., Asociacion Nacional Pro Personas Mayores).

None of the several dozen aging-based organizations is able to swing blocs of older persons in elections. None provides financial campaign contributions to public officials. And to date, none of them has been known to provide bribes or material forms of patronage to politicians (see Pratt, 1976).

To the extent that these organizations have power it is derived from the political legitimacy provided by the existence of more than 24 million older Americans. In the classic pattern of American interest group politics, public officials and other politicians feel it incumbent upon themselves to invite these groups to participate in most policy activities related to aging. Moreover, the organizations provide a ready means for public officials to be in touch, symbolically, with millions of constituents. Through a brief meeting with the leaders of the aging-based groups, an official can claim he has obtained the represented views of a mass constituency. Though the inherent distortions of such forms of representation are well known (Lowi, 1974), the normative role that interest groups have achieved in modern democratic societies readily legitimizes the actions and inactions of officials who have consulted with them. In this context, a working relationship with aging-based membership organizations is indispensable for the public officials. Because of this legitimacy the organizations have essentially three forms of power available to them.

First, they have ready, informal access to public officials—to congressmen and their staffs, to career bureaucrats, to agency and department heads, and occasionally to the White House. As a consequence, they can put forward their own proposals and work to block the proposals of others. To be sure, their audiences or targets may often be unresponsive; but access provides some measure of opportunity.

Second, their legitimacy as aging interest groups enables them to obtain public platforms in the national media, in congressional hearings, and at pseudo-events such as the decennial White House Conferences on Aging. From these platforms they can exercise power by initiating and framing issues for public debate. They can bring attention to conditions in nursing homes, point up the double jeopardy to which black older persons are exposed, or ask whether biomedical breakthroughs in the prolongation of human life are desirable given the qualitative problems of existence for the aging in the United States. And of course, they can use such platforms to register public support or opposition on any issues that have already been framed.

A third form of power available to these groups, particularly the mass membership organizations, might be termed "the electoral bluff." As indicated earlier, the votes of aging persons cannot be swung in a cohesive block through an age-based interest appeal. Most politicians (certainly national politicians) recognize this, and do not develop special appeals to the aged as the central issues of their electoral campaigns. Nonetheless, they wish to avoid offending the aged and therefore are disposed to favor proposals for providing incremental benefits to older persons. The aging-based interest groups, with their access to politicians and their platforms for framing issues, are in a key position to interpret the interests of the millions of aging voters whom politicians do not wish to offend. By virtue of their symbolic role in "representing" millions of aging citizens, the mass membership organizations are particularly credible in interpreting the interests of the aging. Whether the interpretations are accurate is never politically tested. Within moderate limits, the public officials are responsive to the interpretations of the interest groups; and the interest groups keep their interpretations within these moderate limits, never putting forward radical proposals that might force the politicians to call the bluff of the aging vote.

Given these forms of power, what do the interest groups do with it? The activities of the aging organizations in national politics are hardly militant or radical. They do articulate and support many issues that are favorable to the interests of elderly persons, and clearly maintain themselves as organizations. But their efforts do not reflect a vigorous pursuit of major policies that could bring about substantial changes in the fundamental status of the aged in American society. The goals articulated and sought by these organizations are not of a kind suitable to redress fundamentally the economic, biomedical, and social problems of the severely disadvantaged aged (Binstock, 1972). While they probably would not have sufficient power to achieve such goals even if they sought them, the very incentive systems that create and sustain their organizational viability—the interests of their members, and the pursuit of their trades and professions—preclude them from testing the extent of their power to achieve fundamental changes for the aging. In short, these organizations are similar to those in many other arenas of interest group activity that have been examined by students of American politics (see Truman, 1951).

Will the emergence of greater numbers and new cohorts of older persons change these patterns of individual and organizational behavior? As I have argued at length elsewhere (Binstock, 1974), this is not very likely. All of the generational cohorts that will reach 65 years old between now and the year 2025 have already displayed their political heterogeneity, so the chances of cohesive voting behavior are slim. Even if the aging proportion of Americans were to double, the most powerful consequence one can reasonably imagine is that politicians might woo the aging vote as assiduously as they now woo the vote of organized labor. But even this is most unlikely. The organizational structure of unions provides a far stronger (though hardly reliable) mechanism for swinging the votes of laborers than any aging-based interest groups are likely to develop.

The aging-based organizations may develop credentials to participate in a broader range of interest group political arenas. Currently they are only legitimated for invitation and access to arenas that are clearly labeled as relevant to the aging or to some category of disabled adult. But with substantial increases in the number of citizens they symbolically "represent," they may find the door of more general policy forums thrown open to them. Even as the 1981 White House Conference on Aging will not be conducted without prominent representation of business and labor interest groups, the aging interests may become welcome and sought after guests at major forums dealing with issues central to business and labor.

To suggest these possibilities is to intimate that a substantial increase in the proportion of aging persons will have little basic impact on the nature of American politics. To be sure, some roles in the system will have changed if aging voters are wooed a bit more than some other category of voters, and if aging groups take some other interest's seat at the many bargaining tables of interest group politics. And some aging citizens as well as the aging organizations will achieve incremental gains in the playing out of what Theodore Lowi (1969) has characterized as Interest-Group Liberalism.

The Opportunities for Social Change

Because of the contrast between the images and facts concerning the aging as a political force, continuing attention to the notion of senior power may very well be a source of danger to disadvantaged older persons rather than a source of opportunities for change. In the years ahead the aging-based organizations will strive to maintain their resources and political legitimacy by claiming as large a constituency as they can. In doing so they will undoubtedly suggest that incredible number of citizens, tens of millions of older persons, can be mobilized by them as a cohesive voting bloc in response to old-age issues. The media will disseminate the suggestion because it will make good—that is, dramatic—copy. But, in fact there will be no such bloc.

It is not at all improbable that within the next decade or two older persons will come to be viewed as a controlling or decisive electoral force, despite their diverse voting behavior. And as slower rates of economic growth force us to reconsider explicitly many of the allocative decisions our nation has made, our frustrations will mount and could very well be displaced onto the mythical power of seniors. We have already seen a number of articles about the "social security ripoff" and other exercises in hyperbolic castigation of politicians for being "bullied" by the aging. One hopes that these are not portents of an era in which the aging will become a collective scapegoat for economic and political frustrations. But even if they are not, a serious danger lies ahead.

Simply put, the danger is that the people of our nation will find it convenient to assume that an imaginary political force of older persons has obtained all that is needed, perhaps more than a fair share, of public resources and assistance for the aging. As a consequence, those older persons who are in fact helplessly subject to severe deprivations will not be likely to receive significant attention from our government. Several journalists, for example, have discovered that 25 percent of the federal budget is currently spent on benefits for the aging. They have already begun to suggest that the country cannot afford to carry forward its social policy commitments to older persons; yet, they do not address, for example, the issue of how nearly 9 million poor among 24 million older Americans are to have minimally adequate incomes.

If the notion of senior power is more of a danger than a hope, where do the opportunities lie for redressing the economic, health, and social problems of the severely disadvantaged aging? A first step is the need to frame issues that will disaggregate the political, economic, and social images of aging, so as to focus on policies that can affect specific subgroups of older persons. To be sure, this will require a measure of political courage. We prefer to view the world in terms of the distortions purveyed by aggregate images because they are convenient and comforting. They help us to live with complex matters by making them seem simple. They allow us to evade issues of scarce resource allocation by redefining them as issues of economic growth. They enable us to measure health and income in terms of averages, and thereby to ignore the difficult cases.

Our society has probably gone far enough in recognizing that the phenomena of aging, in general, are worthy of considerable attention. It is not too soon to begin reframing public issues in terms that cut across age groupings and other convenient aggregate categories of citizens, and to start generating public policies that deal with severe deprivations that can be readily identified within the human condition.

The political history of this nation seems to indicate that we enact and implement public policies for the purpose of solving social problems rather than the problems of politicians only in those rare instances when a sense of crisis has been engendered. Sometimes that sense of crisis has been engendered by economic, social, and technological forces, sometimes through the moral leadership of politicians and other public figures, sometimes through a coalition of persons who experience a deeply shared form of severe deprivation, and occasionally through the impact of extreme changes in local conditions. To which of these crisis sources might we look for a change in the patterns of policy response to the trends of aging? I believe that our best hopes lie with the possibilities of coalition among the severely deprived, and in the impacts that can be engendered through direct action in local communities.

Since the Age of Enlightenment, a classical Western device for generating optimism has been to rely passively upon the unfolding of economic, social, and technological trends as vehicles for amelioration. But those trends we have considered at the outset of this discussion, as well as many others that we might consider, are likely to have negative rather than ameliorative implications for older persons. Even if the impact of such major forces may in the long run prove to be positive, passive anticipation of them will do little to improve the quality of life for many millions of persons who will suffer in the interim.

To rely on moral leadership from politicians and other public figures is also a problematic and passive basis for hope. To be sure, there is an important job that could be done by leaders. The capacity to frame issues for social intervention, and to convey them effectively as crisis issues, is an important source of power. Those aging persons who are and will be substantially disadvantaged could benefit greatly from leadership that would frame issues dealing directly with conditions of severe deprivation experienced by specific subgroups of older persons who can be readily identified. But this would require a measure of political courage that we have rarely witnessed. Our leaders prefer to view the world in terms of the distortions purveyed by aggregate images. The emergence of courageous leadership that would dare to penetrate the politically functional cover of aggregate indices and images is a prospect too unpredictable to serve as a basis for hope.

The most optimistic prospects would seem to lie in the crises that exist in the lives of individuals and that are felt profoundly in local communities. For these are crises that provide unmistakable incentives to those who can undertake to solve them, namely, the people who are affected by them. It was the randomization of disaster throughout almost all the strata of our society that provided a coalition for the political leverage leading to the Social Security Act and other ameliorative measures of the New Deal. And it was the extreme impact of sudden and large waves of immigration in the latter half of the 19th century had led to the development of genuinely effective public services—police services, fire protection services, and public health services—designed to solve extreme local crises. I believe that, similarly, it is through national political crises engendered by coalitions of the severely deprived that we will achieve adequate income transfers and adequate public regulation to meet the challenges of aging. And it is through local crises resulting from the absence of local service support systems, that we will achieve adequate services to meet the challenges of aging. Both prospects—national coalition and local service crises—are unlikely unless active efforts are undertaken to bring them about. But the active efforts required do not have to await the accidental emergence of a political leader or the impact of larger economic, social, and technological forces. The prospects lie among us and in our hands.

The forging of an effective coalition requires us to abandon the boundaries of artificial constituencies—such as "the aging," "the poor," "the handicapped," "the unemployed," "the minorities,"—which hide the heterogeneous conditions within all these categories, including many persons who are quite comfortable and many who are moderately comfortable. The very heterogeneity found within each of these categories precludes any one of them from serving as a foundation for the vigorous political organization and goal pursuit that is necessary to solve social problems. In their places we must build coalitions formed on common conditions of severe deprivation that transcend age, race, and other conventional categorizations. Effective advocacy through political organizations is built upon constituencies that are held together through a common set of incentives (see Wilson, 1973). The chronologically aged are not such a constituency. It is true that our focus to date on this large but

72   ROBERT H. BINSTOCK

artificial category has brought attention to aging as a social issue. But if we are to meet the priority needs generated by the trends of aging, it is time for us to shift gears and to focus attention on the commonalities of deprivation experienced by persons of all ages.

To the extent that such a coalition of the severely disadvantaged could be successful in engendering a political crisis at the national level, it might be effective in shaping federal income and regulatory policies that can solve priority problems. But given the fragmentation of power and authority in our political system, it is most unlikely that any comprehensive, coordinated health and social service delivery systems can be launched at the national level and effectively implemented at the local level (see Binstock and Levin, 1976). Any services that have developed effectively in our nation have begun in single communities as responses to local crises.

Again, I suggest that it is our own direct actions that can meet the challenge of developing effective service policies. If we wait for the crises of absent supportive services to emerge through natural evolution we will witness an enormity of human suffering. But we do not have to wait if we are willing to abandon our conventional approaches and undertake direct, militant action in our local communities. Our political history is replete with numerous models of effective political protest strategies that create a sense of crisis in local communities and elicit satisfactory responses from local governments. We can look to the tactics of Saul Alinsky (1971), the strategies of Martin Luther King, Jr. (1963), and to rent strikes and welfare sit-ins (Lipsky, 1968).

We hardly lack effective models for success in local political action. What we seem to lack is the motivation and commitment to undertake the onerous tasks required. Even as it is convenient for our public officials to hide behind aggregate indices and symbolic policies, it is convenient for us to simply blame them or to reassure ourselves that some form of technology, or coordination, or senior power will magically bring forth what is needed. In my view, the policies that are needed to cope with the trends of aging in America will not be forthcoming unless great numbers of us undertake direct political action to make them come forth.

References

Alinsky, S. D. *Rules for radicals: A pragmatic primer for realistic radicals.* New York: Random House, 1971.
Binstock, R. H. Interest-group liberalism and the politics of aging. *Gerontologist,* 1972, *12*, 265–280.

Binstock, R. H. Aging and the future of American politics. *The Annals of the American Academy of Political and Social Science*, 1974, *415*, 199–212.
Binstock, R. H., and Levin, M. A. The political dilemmas of intervention policies. In R. H. Binstock and E. Shanas (Eds.), *Handbook of aging and the social sciences*. New York: Van Nostrand Reinhold, 1976.
Brody, E. M. Women's changing roles, and care of the aging family. In *Aging: Agenda for the eighties*. Washington, D.C.: National Journal Issues Book, 1979.
Brody, E. M. Health and its social implications. In M. Marois (Ed.), *Aging: A challenge to science and social policy*. London: Oxford University Press, 1980.
Brotman, H. D. The aging of America: A demographic profile. *National Journal*, 1978, *10*, 1622–1627.
Califano, J. A., Jr. U.S. policy for the aging—a commitment to ourselves. *National Journal*, 1978, *10*, 1575–1581.
Campbell, A. Politics through the life cycle. *Gerontologist*, 1971, *11*, 112–117.
Hayflick, L. Human aging in 2025 A.D.: A prospective analysis. In *2025 A.D.: Aging in America's future*. Somerville, N.J.: Hoechst-Roussel Pharmaceuticals, Inc., 1976.
Hudson, R. B. The "graying" of the federal budget and its consequences for old-age policy. *Gerontologist*, 1978, *18*, 428–440.
Hudson, R. B., and Binstock, R. H. Political systems and aging. In R. H. Binstock and E. Shanas (Eds.), *Handbook of aging and the social sciences*. New York: Van Nostrand Reinhold, 1976.
Kastenbaum, R., and Candy, S. E. The 4% fallacy, a methodological and empirical critique of extended care facility population statistics. *International Journal of Aging and Human Development*, 1973, *4*, 15–21.
King, M. L., Jr. *Why we can't wait*. New York: Harper and Row, 1963.
Laslett, P. The comparative history of aging and the aged: With particular reference to the household position of aged persons. In M. Marois (Ed.), *Aging: A challenge to science and social policy*. London: Oxford University Press, 1980.
Lipsky, M. Protest as a political resource. *American Political Science Review*, 1968, *62*, 1144–1158.
Lowi, T. J. *The end of liberalism*. New York: W. W. Norton & Company, 1969.
Lowi, T. J. Interest groups and the consent to govern. *The Annals of the American Academy of Political and Social Science*, 1974, *413*, 86–100.
Mendelsohn, M. A., and Hapgood, D. The political economy of nursing homes. *The Annals of the American Academy of Political and Social Science*, 1974, *415*, 95–105.
Pfeiffer, E. Health care and well-being of older Americans in the year 2025. In *2025 A.D.: Aging in America's future*. Somerville, N.J.: Hoechst-Roussel Pharmaceuticals, Inc., 1976.
Pratt, H. *The gray lobby*. Chicago: University of Chicago Press, 1976.
Riemer, Y., and Binstock, R. H. Campaigning for "the senior vote": A case study of Carter's 1976 Campaign. *Gerontologist*, 1978, *18*, 517–524.
Shanas, E. *Final report: National survey of the aged*. Washington, D.C.: DHEW, OHD-90A-369, August, 1978.
Siegel, J. S. Demographic aspects of aging and the older population in the United States. *Current population reports* (special studies series p. 23, No. 29). Washington, D.C.: U.S. Department of Commerce, Bureau of the Census, 1976.
Truman, D. B. *The governmental process: Political interests and public opinion*. New York: Alfred A. Knopf, 1951.

U.S. Comptroller General. *Entering a nursing home—costly implications for Medicaid and the elderly.* (Pad-80-12.) Washington, D.C.: U.S. General Accounting Office, November 26, 1979.

U.S. House of Representatives Select Committee on Aging. *Federal responsibility to the elderly: Executive programs and legislative jurisdiction.* Washington, D.C.: U.S. Government Printing Office, 1976.

U.S. House of Representatives Select Committee on Aging. *Poverty among America's aged.* Washington, D.C.: U.S. Government Printing Office, Comm. Pub. 95–154, 1978.

U.S. Senate Subcommittee on Aging of the Committee on Human Resources. *Older Americans Act of 1978.* Washington, D.C.: U.S. Government Printing Office, 1979.

Wilson, J. Q. *Political organizations.* New York: Basic Books, 1973.

Talking to Your Children's Souls

Portraits of Deprivation

Thomas J. Cottle

One could very appropriately call the last few decades in America the period of self-consciousness. The term, of course, is a complicated, almost mischievous one. To be self-conscious can connote self-interest to the point of wasteful vanity. On the other hand, it may connote a careful, cautious, discerning approach to all matters, private as well as public. Surely the last years have revealed Americans—or some of them—reveling in excessive, narcissistic behavior. Self-interest has been glorified, and whether or not we admit to it, there is not a great deal of incentive across the society for generous, much less openly altruistic, behavior.

Consonant with this philosophy, or overriding life style, the most needy people in our country have seen very little progress in the state of their well-being. Governmental policies at state and federal levels come and go, but whatever the effects, planned or unplanned, of these programs, a sizable group of poor people remains. Moreover, given the way contemporary programs are run, a sizable population of poor people will continue to exist. There is no longer need to recapitulate the familiar statistics nor human scenes of poverty. Indeed even as I write these words I recognize their familiar ring and the normal response made to them. Yet, a rather intriguing aspect of America's so-called needy classes now presents itself. For if one looks across the social and economic boundaries of the culture, one finds a truly extraordinary panoply of variegated peoples, all of them having one thing in common: The belief that their respective group, if not they themselves as individuals, has been deprived. Surely the very poor of the land feel this, but quite remarkably, one hears the same refrains of deprivation among families of all social classes. They have been excluded from some prized resource or something. They are out of touch with some liberal agency or seat of power, or they feel, somehow, separated from mystical, magical powers. Again, people of all classes and circumstances seem to feel they have lost out, or are lost in the pursuit of their real and imagined life goals. Or perhaps they harbor some actual or primitive competitive sense and have determined that given the society's standards of accomplishment or worth, they have lost. The loss, moreover, is irrevocable and puts them in the difficult position of being separated from successful people, truly affluent or comfortable people.

Driving this sense of loss and separation is the belief that one is legitimately entitled to, well, something, or more than one has. Politics, social history, one's origins, the degree of one's loyalty to country, years of hard and thankless work, anything and everything may be invoked to justify one's sense of entitlement, a sense not so incidentally, born from the public virtue of individualism or individually based achievement. One man, one vote, quickly becomes transliterated to: I am, therefore I am entitled. As a result of this clamoring for what one believes one is entitled to, the entire structure of political action, seemingly, has been transformed. National mass movements of a voluntary nature are far more difficult and treacherous to establish than they were even a decade or so ago. Now, as Theodore Roszak (1978) points out, we seem to have an endless chain of voluntary associates, each with his or her own special political concern and focus, each feeling his or her rights have been jeopardized or compromised, and each feeling his or her own political claim is utterly legitimate, whether or not it touches upon the political legitimacy or claims of the next in line.

To be sure, many of these political associates transact their business as if they were merely calling attention to themselves, which, I suppose, is a first step of political reform. Some, moreover, act as if the look-at-me aspect of their work constituted the entirety of their politics. But whatever their claims and strategies, it cannot be denied that they all are claiming they have been victimized by large-scale, planned, and systematic deprivation. In a word, they lack something, usually some fundamental right, and in many cases, when one examines their situation, one can feel sympathetic to their cause. In many cases, furthermore, one is impressed by the leaders of these voluntary associates, whose number and variety would have surprised even Alexis de Tocqueville, who saw in America's voluntary associations the genuine strength of America's political energy. Indeed, the string of voluntary associations is extraordinarily impressive, despite the selfish, or highly self-interested, or even solipsistic nature of individual political struggles.

No one, clearly, can set forth with objectivity and disinterest, a hierarchy of America's political needs or list America's most deprived populations. Self-interest dominates our culture to uncontrollable degrees. We are, in many respects, a culture reeling out of control, partly because of the irreconcilable nature of our excesses and deprivations. We reel from the bureaucratic neutrality foisted upon us, from institutions that literally revel in dehumanizing processes and policies, and from still unsolved matters of racism, poverty, and colonialism. In a sense, America has not found itself and has not yet determined just what age it would like to be, much less what it believes it ought to be when it grows up.

Still, on the subject of deprivation, it is my impression that the various political voluntary associations, or even the innumerable political and social groupings, have recently tended to act much like siblings competing with each other for some real or imagined parental attention. No, this is not precisely the case. In fact, the very poor of the country and a certain portion of the country's minority families have now passed through an era—as short lived as most American eras—where it seemed as if they were receiving, not only the attention, but the benefits all people covet. Against the background of an omnipresent racism and a generalized disgust for and with poverty, most Americans could tolerate popular political movements aimed at redressing the inequities of poor and minority people. But only up to a point. After a time, the country responded in a sense to the antipoverty and black movements with a resounding "We want it, too." A reaction to the poverty programs was set in motion. If some groups were getting special attention and additional resources, then why could other groups not enjoy a commensurate amount of attention and resources. The majority of Americans resented poor and minority populations before our brief period of attention to these families, and they resented them even more intensely as they saw them actually having some of their demands met. Compounding the problem was the belief, sometimes legitimate, sometimes invalid, that benefits were accruing to some populations at the direct expense to other populations. In many cases, however, the resentment of another person receiving some minimal attention only exacerbated many people's contention that they were the truly overlooked souls of the earth, the genuinely dispossessed people.

What follows are three brief portraits of children. I have selected these children from a group of children with whom I have worked over the last 15 years because I felt their particular stories spoke most powerfully to the issue of deprivation.

The first life study is that of a young American boy and it addresses the matter, the business really, of medical care, or the lack of it.

The second story is of a young West Indian girl who lives in London. Though some might automatically assume that we perhaps "contaminate" our data and exegesis by focusing on a foreign case, I think in fact just the opposite holds true: The account of Doreen Grainger just may sum up the spiritual pain of economic deprivation in the most universal of terms. Besides, an occasional glance at Europe, a glance that may burgeon into what we call cross-cultural research, can only inform us and give us a perspective on our own lives, as well as provide us with a sense of how extensive and rapacious is this thing called poverty.

Finally, the story of Jeremiah Kelser provides, if nothing more, an ending to the story of human deprivation. It is hardly the only ending; nor is it the one we might desire. Still, it reminds us of the extraordinary politicizing power that the economic and social order has on the solitary individual or family attempting to go about the business of leading a life. It reminds us, too, as do the other life studies, of the exquisite need for systematic change. For the culture, as I suggested earlier, has relied too long now on a source of evolution that is downright antipathetic to human life.

Wilson Diver is the smallest, thinnest, and most frail-looking of the nine Diver children. At 12, he looks younger than his 11-year-old sister Theresa and his 10-year-old brother Curtiss. On meeting Wilson for the first time, everyone believes he is either on his way to a hospital or has just come out of one. His mother, Mrs. Claudia Diver, claims the boy eats as much as his brothers and sisters and has the energy of his brothers and sisters, but that he just looks sickly most of the time. It does not help young Wilson's condition that he and his family are among the poorest families in Massachusetts.

It was very clear to Claudia Diver that her eighth baby, even at birth, was not as strong as the others. Wilson had a fine disposition and seemed to walk and talk at the normal time, but he was, somehow, an unwell child. The first sign of illness came when he was two, when for weeks at a time he would lie in his crib whimpering, unable to breathe, and running high temperatures. As he grew up, these bouts of asthmatic bronchitis—as they later were diagnosed—came more frequently, eight, nine times a year. Wilson would show the beginning signs of a cold. He would cough and sneeze and find his nose running. Then, usually at night, the coughing became unbearable. He would cough without respite until his chest would sag and deep rings lined his eyes. He could not talk, and by flaring his nostrils and opening his mouth, he barely got sufficient air into his lungs. The cold weather made his life miserable, particularly at night when there was no heat in the Diver apartment. There was no way to keep him warm or provide him with any relief. His mother would prop him up in bed and hold him while she and his sleepy brothers and sisters would stare at him, expecting him, surely, to die at any moment. No one could believe how sick Wilson could become in such a short time. One day he was fine, the next morning he would show symptoms of a cold, and by that night he would look to be on the brink of death.

Wilson was examined once by a medical student in the large hospital six miles from the Diver house. The doctor said that he heard nothing in Wilson's chest to indicate a chronic problem. "Some kids," he told Mrs. Diver, "are just susceptible to pulmonary and bronchial complications when they get sick." He prescribed medicine to use the next time Wilson became ill. The medicine seemed to help; at least it gave Wilson relief in breathing. Strangely though, it also seemed to stimulate him so that he was unable to sleep. Mrs. Diver had to decide which was more important, relief in breathing or sleep.

By his 12th year, Wilson was more than used to his periodic illnesses. He did his best to avoid catching colds, but he simply was more susceptible to them than anyone he knew. No matter how warmly he dressed or wisely he ate, the infections got to him. Claudia Diver kept promising she would move the family to a warmer climate, for she had relatives in Birmingham, Alabama, but her shortage of money never allowed for this. There was no way she could find a job as good as the one she held in the small wool factory near her home. "Wilson has survived this long," she said, "and he's getting bigger and stronger. He'll survive the rest of the way. Has to."

In February, two months before Wilson's 13th birthday, he became sick again. All the usual signs appeared; the unstoppable coughing at night, the runny nose and eyes, the pains in the sinus areas behind his cheeks and forehead, chest aching from strain and fatigue. This time, however, the infection seemed to hang on longer than ever before, and a new symptom was present. Early one morning, Wilson grew nauseated and began to vomit violently. Even when he had rid his stomach of its contents, a muscular reflex continued, and he gagged until he felt he would expel his lungs. Blood appeared in the vomit.

Awakened by the sounds of Wilson retching and crying, McCay, his older brother, found him in the bathroom and promptly woke his mother. At six o'clock in the morning the family decided that, as difficult as it would be, they had to take Wilson to the hospital. A portion of the hospital trip was described by Wilson himself several months later:

"First we called the police, you know, and they said they couldn't send nobody 'round to our house 'less we could prove it was an emergency. McCay said I should get on the phone and cough for 'em. He wasn't joking neither. But they wouldn't come out, so we went down to the corner and waited for the bus. It was so cold out there we might as well froze together. Everybody was standing around me, trying to keep me warm, you know. Must have had ten coats and jackets on me. And I kept up this gagging and choking I was doing. So after half an hour, the bus comes, and we get on.

"Then we had to transfer to another bus, and finally we got there. We were real early too, but this waiting room they got there was crowded with people, it was like we were going to a bus station or something. Every chair was filled up. Some old man, you know, gave his seat to my mother, but McCay and me, we sat on the floor. Place was cold too, man, and there wasn't nothing to eat. They had a real nice water fountain, I remember.

"Now here's the truth: we must have got there by eight o'clock, and we didn't talk to no one, no one, man, 'til eleven, or maybe later. And that was this woman who took our names and stuff like that, you know. She wasn't even a nurse! She was just taking our names. And the place was getting more crowded every minute. You should have seen the people coming in there too, man. Broken legs, and bleeding. They brought this one guy in on a table and they said he died. Man died there after the doctors saw him.

"So then, like at twelve, maybe, the woman calls our name and we go up to this desk, and she tells my mother we don't have the right kind of insurance. She needed to prove where she worked or something, but anyway, McCay has to go all the way home and get this card, like, that proves she can come to the hospital, that we live in the neighborhood. And 'cause we don't have no telephone we can't call up at home, and anyway no one was home 'cause they was all at school.

"So McCay goes and he comes back, this time with the police. He just went there and told him his problem and this cop gave him a ride all the way. Now it's like one thirty and I ain't seen no doctor yet. Finally they get all the stuff straightened out on the papers. Oh, here's what it was. They thought it would be better for my mother to say she was on welfare than to say she had a job. It worked out better for me and them if they did it like that. So they did. She didn't care none, she just wanted me to see the doctor 'cause I wasn't getting no better. Finally, they call my name and I see this doctor. He tells me to take off my shirt and lie on a table, one of those tables like that guy died on, only this one had a clean sheet. So I get on the table and I'm thinking to myself, this doctor looks too young. And it's cold in this hall they got me in too, 'cause it's not a room, it's just a hall with a sheet hanging down from the ceiling to kind of hide me, you know what I mean. Then the doctor goes out and he don't come back. I'm lying there with my shirt off freezing. So finally I get up and walk out and ask somebody, can I put my shirt on and this man there he say, 'you can put your hat on for all I care. If you can walk and ask questions you ain't sick enough to be in no emergency room.' So

I get disgusted and go back to my little sheet room in the hall, you know, and get dressed.

"While all this is going on, McCay goes home 'cause he's so hungry he can't stand it no more. But he asked someone before he left, how come no one's helping *me*, and the woman tells him it's her job to choose which people coming into the room look sickest. I guess since I didn't look that sick to her she kept me waiting. So then I go out again and tell someone I'm really hungry, man. This time it's a doctor, and he looks at this little piece of paper they had me carrying with me and he say, 'You've been vomiting, so you better not eat.' When I went back again to my sheet room I saw the clock said five thirty. Still nobody had come to see me.

"You ain't going to believe that nobody came until six thirty. Then this other doctor comes, not the first one, but a different one, and he's looking so tired, and he's talking to so many people he looks sick himself. So he say, 'Take your shirt off Mr. Wilson.' I say, 'My *first* name's Wilson.' He don't hear me. He's got that thing in his ears already and he's starting to listen on my chest and on my back. Then he lays me down and pushes his hands so hard on my stomach I thought he was going to kill me 'stead of cure me. Then he asks if I'm hungry. I say I ought to be, haven't eaten since last night. So he gives me this hard candy he's got in his pocket, and he tells me where he buys it and pats my face. Nice guy.

"'How you feel?' he say. I tell him I want to go home. 'You're going to be fine, Wilson my boy,' he say. 'You're going to be good as new. You just got to eat my special candy.' Man, did I feel good after that. I ask him, 'Can I go, doc?' 'Hold still a bit longer,' he say. All this time he's writing on a sheet of paper. 'You got a phone number?' he say. 'No.' 'What's your address?' I tell him. 'Now can I go?' 'Hold still,' he say. Tough too. So now I have to wait some more. But when he leaves he promises me he'll come right back. 'Don't worry.' Then he leaves and I hear him tell this nurse there's a boy in there who's very sick. We got to find him a bed. I didn't know what he meant. Then I figured maybe they want me to go to the hospital 'cause I wasn't fine, and I started to cry. Real soft 'cause I didn't want no one to find me. When nobody came back I put my shirt on for like the tenth time and went out to get my mother, but she was gone. The room wasn't crowded no more, neither. Then I really got scared. But there was this new woman there and she had a note saying my mother would come back and I shouldn't worry. Shouldn't worry, why not? They wanted to put me in the hospital, which meant I was real sick. I'd been there all day and only one person saw me and he only was there a couple minutes. 'Course he gave me that candy which was my breakfast, lunch and dinner. They did give me *that*! So then I waited some more.

"Then, like about ten o'clock in the night, a nurse comes in the room where they got the television to say a policeman's outside waiting to take me home. She says I should be in the hospital and they've been waiting for a bed to open up, but since they had no room they was sending me home. Before I left she had to take some blood from me which hurt, man, like out-of-sight pain! 'You going to drink it?' I say. 'I been here all day, lady,' I told her. 'Me, too,' she say. Angry old bitch. Anyway, the cop took me home! I fell asleep and the cop had to carry me into the house. Everybody was asleep 'cept my mother and McCay. They tried to get back to the hospital, but the buses wasn't running no more. That was the longest day of my life, man. Started out with me vomiting up my lungs, ended with a policeman carrying me home. I knew I had to go back to the hospital. I told my mother, couldn't she find a better hospital? She say they were all the same, and anyway, this one had my records. I was doomed, man. I told McCay: 'If I go back there I'm going to die, man. Hospital's going to kill me off just by all that waiting.' My mother told me not to talk that way, but McCay, he say 'Wilson's right. What about that man we saw who died on the table like the one they put Wilson on!' My mother told him to shut up, but he was right. Only I didn't want nobody to talk about it like he did. He didn't have to go back there like I did."

Ten days after Wilson Diver's examination, the hospital sent a letter to Mrs. Diver saying that the results of his blood tests indicated that Wilson should enter the hospital for further tests. The hospital would notify the Divers when a bed was free, but it would be helpful if they could return to the hospital before that time for a chest X ray. It was three weeks before the X ray was taken.

"This time," Wilson said, "I only waited three hours, only I was by myself. But it was all right 'cause I didn't have to go to school all that day. People were nice to me too. The woman remembered me from before. 'Bout a week later they wrote to my mother saying they had a record of me coming in for X rays but no record of the X rays. So I had to go back all over again. And you got to remember that each trip to the hospital, man, takes about two hours, if you don't have to wait too long for the buses. Each time you got to wait outside in the cold, you know what I mean, and you're getting so cold you don't know whether to go on or go back. One time I went back and told my mother I went. Then I had to cut school another day so I could go for real. So they did the same X ray all over. I was feeling how my chest seemed to be getting smaller. For a while I was thinking so much about going to the hospital and worrying about if I was sick, I didn't even think about *being* sick. But I never vomited again like I did that one night. I just couldn't shake my cold, you know. It was stuck to me, like I was going to have it forever. I don't know. Maybe I will."

Four months after his first examination and the decision to hospitalize him, Wilson Diver was admitted to the hospital. He was placed in a room with five other boys. New doctors examined him this time; he rarely saw the same doctor twice. A third chest X ray was taken and a variety of medical tests performed. On the third afternoon of his hospitalization, Mrs. Diver was called into the doctor's office on the second floor for consultation. Her son was suffering with pulmonary problems, she was told. But there was more. The X rays had revealed a spot on his right lung which indicated tuberculosis. Furthermore, while the doctors were not certain, several tests suggested the possibility of his also having leukemia, although it was, hopefully, a treatable form. He also was malnourished. As Claudia Diver reports it, the doctor was stern but helpful. He was about to remonstrate with her for the way she had failed to provide her son proper medical attention. But after looking at her, he had stopped himself. She did not have to explain Wilson's circumstances, or her own.

No one could rightly argue that Doreen Grainger is a dreamy child, a child who fantasizes more than she approaches life realistically. To be sure, Doreen, 11 years old, one of six children living in a three-and-a-half-room flat in Clapham, spends a great deal of time by herself, just sitting and thinking. Her family reports that she does; she admits she does. But when I ask her if she is willing to share some of her feelings and thoughts of these private moments with me, we both can see there is nothing dreamy or fantasy-like about them. One could say that much of what she contemplates is fantastic. I have told her this on numerous occasions, but she doubts my words.

No, she tells me again and again, her interest lies in the study of history. She is fascinated with the events of long ago and the people who preceded her in time. She reads history books for children, mainly ones on the history of England, and one of her most common expressions is "in the olden days." In the olden days, she will begin a sentence, sounding very much like a school teacher, the people carried their goods to the market place on animals. Then, misinterpreting the expression of fascination and delight on my face as doubt, she will invariably add, "It's true. Really. It's true. They used animals, like donkeys." All of this is said in the calm, placid, but hardly emotionless manner that is so characteristic of her.

Her brothers and sisters as well as her parents are well aware of her placid way and the sense of inner peace that emanates from her. Everybody notices it. She is a placid child, not passive, retiring, without feeling, merely calm. One relaxes in her presence and feels òne's own irritabilities and anxieties receding. There is always time with Doreen Grainger, always enough hours in the day to do what has to be done. The single day seems to be long enough for one to fulfill one's projects and dreams, not that Doreen is wholly optimistic about all the outcomes. No one living in the poor circumstances she has always known could be wholly optimistic. It is simply that at this point in her life, she rarely reveals impatience or despair, or even intense personal frustration. If she does not reveal enormous displays of energy, it just may be that she is storing up her strength for use sometime in the future. And, while it may seem ironic that a child fascinated with history should be storing up her reserves for future use, Doreen herself would not think so. She would say: I am certain, that no one can plan for the future, much less attempt to catch glimpses of it, without concentrating long and hard on the past. So her involvement with time, and history in particular, seems perfectly right for her, and perfectly natural.

As is always the case when one offers only samples, snippets really, of what a person has said in many conversations, much of the richness of thought and language is lost. Not only that, but even by presenting extended passages of speech, a person still may come across in a somewhat thin or unfinished way. Speaking with some people causes me to feel this reservation intensely; one of these people is Doreen. In recalling what she has said, I often fear I have omitted too much or not caught precisely enough the delicacies of her associations and combinations of thoughts. Perhaps this is because she has a peculiarly acute sense of time, which means a special alertness to the sequence of events and possible causation. It is not bending the truth to say that the large majority of our conversations focus on matters of time, however implicitly they may be drawn. But her awareness of and concern with the predicaments of England's black communities is never far from the surface of these conversations. We share many interests in common, Doreen and I, and while she describes feelings and attitudes for me which she believes are what *I* am looking for—as if I always knew what I was looking for—she is also eager to tell me what matters most to *her*. Here then is a sample of what this child, my friend of two years, has told me.

The words that follow are taken from a recent conversation in which Doreen's normal calmness seemed more brittle than ever before. It seemed to me that anger was trying to break through her usually peaceful nature.

"I was thinking," she said that afternoon, "about what it must be like when people die. I keep thinking—probably they put you in a grave and you don't feel anything. At least that's what people say, you don't feel anything. But what if you do? What if dying means feeling everything, but you can't get anything to move, like your eyes and your mouth, so you can't say, stop putting me in the grave. I can hear you, just don't bury me. What if too, when people die with their eyes open, they can see? Only nobody knows they can because their eyes never move and they can't tell anybody what they're seeing. If people can't talk when they're dead, how do we know what dying is? Maybe people are lying in their graves still thinking about things. It could be, nobody knows for sure. Even my mother said it *could* be true. I was thinking, maybe I like to read history so when I die, if I can still think, I can think about all the things that went on before I was born and after I was born, too.

"Some children are afraid to die, but I'm not afraid. They think it's awful to die, so they never think about people long ago dying, or think of themselves getting older and older and pretty soon dying. I don't think about it all that much but sometimes I'm afraid of getting older and not just because when you get old you get sick, and your body gets stiff. And you cough a lot. What I worry about is that, like, I have many things I want to do with my life, many people I would like to be, you know. Then I get worried, maybe there won't be enough time. Maybe I'll start too many things too late, then I'll run out of time. My mother laughs at me when I talk this way. She says, there's enough time; children should never worry about things like that. But all I ever hear *her* talking about is how there's never enough time and she'll be dead before she knows it. So she tells me one thing and herself something different. And she isn't *that* old. She thinks she is, but she isn't. People, I hear, they always tell each other, oh, you aren't that old. Then the other person says, I don't care how old I am, I *feel* old and that's all that matters. Well, I feel old lots of the time. People think children only think about getting old but never that they're old. But everybody is only as old as they are, so they feel *that* old. Children can die too. Adults forget this.

"You know what I think? I think families that don't have lots of money always feel older than they really are. Maybe it's like no one gives them a chance to be children. They pretend they're children, and everybody pretends to treat them like children, but everybody knows they aren't regular children. In the old days they made children work. Then they had laws that said they couldn't work that way any more. But the children who live around here, they do all the same things other children do, except the rich children who have their own houses and things like that; but I don't think they're really children, like children are supposed to be. You remember before when I told you I think sometimes there isn't going to be enough time for me to do all the things I want to do? Well, children like us, we're afraid too many things are going to happen that are going to make it bad for us. So that's what we worry about some of the time. Most children, though they don't think like that. They do whatever they want or whatever they have to do, and don't care about what happens to them all that much. But we can't do that. We have to worry about it or pretend there's nothing to worry about.

"So we act like we're children, which *is* what we are, but we don't always feel like children because we're worrying about those other things. I think maybe I like history because I'm afraid to find out what's going to happen to me. Or maybe something even worse; maybe I already know what's going to happen to me.

"See what's important about history is that you can sort of be alive when you weren't really alive. That's why teachers should tell you about the people who were alive then, and not just the *things* that happened. Because then you can pretend that you were alive too, when they were alive, or you'll pretend that you will be alive when you know you won't be alive any more. You can pretend that what's going to happen when you're not here is what happened to people a long time ago when you weren't here either. That way, learning about history is like making believe you could live three different lives instead of just one life: The life you have, the life people had before you were born, and the life people are going to have after you die. So you can know about things and pretend about things too. Maybe things have always been the same; I don't think so, but maybe for some people they are. But people don't look like they did millions of years ago, so how could other things be the same?

"I was just thinking, maybe what I want to know about history is whether everything will be for my family like it is now. I mean, it's fun to know about other people, but I want to know whether it will always be like this for me and my family. And then how will it be when I get older, and then very old. Nobody can see the future, but they can see what history was like, only not the kings. The kings don't tell me anything about me, or anybody I know. They only tell what it's like for the important people, like in government. Maybe that's why we study them, because the rich people in government like the kings, they tell the rest of us how we have to be. One thing that isn't fair is just reading about the rich people who lived long, long ago. They, for sure, don't tell me anything about me or people like us. All you have to do is figure out a little what happened to your own family long, long ago, and you know *that's* never going to happen. I guess history makes me sad sometimes.

"My mother says, you never know what tomorrow will bring. That's the wonderful thing about going to sleep every night. But why does she say that when we all know what tomorrow's going to bring? Tomorrow's going to bring another day like today, and yesterday. So who she trying to kid? She gets me wound up when she talks like that. She must know she is too, and there she is always telling us, no matter what we do or say, we must never lie to anybody and especially to people in our family. But she's doing it. She's lying, and it's not because she wants us to go to bed on time. She could tell us a million other things to get us into bed. My father does. He tells my brother Frederick every night: If you don't get into that bed in one minute I'm going to pull down your pajamas and whack your backside. It gets him in bed all right.

"So why does my mother lie? I'll tell you why. Because no matter what she tells us, she knows nothing is ever going to get better for us. She pretends by saying you never know what tomorrow will bring that maybe she won't know, but she knows. She tells us how nothing will ever be better for her, which would be all right if she knew it was going to be better for us. But she thinks she's going to die with the world being just as bad for us as it is for her now and when she was a child. All she's doing is telling us a fairy story so she can get us into bed, but the rest of the time she'll tell her friends, how is it ever going to be better.

"So maybe that's why I worry a lot of the time. If she says it's going to be tomorrow and tomorrow and tomorrow like it is today, then why should I grow up at all? Or if it's going to be the same when I'm an adult like it is now, then it's like I'm already an adult, and that means I'm an adult and a child—a little adult, that's all. Now that kind of thinking is much more scary than wondering what it's like to die. I can't even figure out what it's like to be alive. You could tell me all children think like I do, but I wouldn't believe it. I know they don't, especially rich children. You ask them if they think tomorrow, or when they grow up, they're going to be living just like they're living now? They'll say, oh no, I'm not. I'm going to be living here, or I'm going to be going there and doing this. Maybe I'll keep changing where I live and what I do. That's the kind of thing they'll tell you. But the kids that live near me, they might tell you those same things, but they know they're only making up those words because that's the way children *like* to think. That's how we're different from them. When I'm pretending, I *know* I'm pretending. I could tell you when I grow up I'll have lots of houses and travel all over the world like the Queen, but I know I'm telling you a big lie. And I can't really be all that happy when I know I'm telling you a lie, even if you asked me to tell you what I'm going to do when I get older. Or, I could say, well, I don't know, come back and see me in twenty years, and you and I will both know what I did, or what I'm doing then. But you don't need to come and see me in twenty years. Because if I'm alive I'll know where I'll be and what I'm doing. I won't be able to leave England. Where could I go? Maybe they'll make us go somewhere, but I hope not, because this is where I come from and this is where I should be. I bet if you come to see me in twenty years you won't have any trouble finding me because I bet I'll be living where I live right now. Nobody I know moves away. Some new people come in and live near us, but nobody moves away. My father always says, if people like us are moving away, it means either they're giving up for good, or they're foolish enough to think there's a better chance for them somewhere else. They pretend maybe there's a good thing waiting for them somewhere, but all they're doing is pretending so they can feel better about themselves. I say if they're pretending, then they're acting more like children than we are.

"I know everything about the future because I find out about history. I don't think the world changes so much. That's another thing people want to pretend about, that everything is changing, getting worse, or getting better. It stays the same, that's why I know for sure what's going to be. When you live around here, the most exciting thing sometimes is to wonder whether this might be the day when you're going to die. I know that sounds like a horrible thing to say, but it isn't. It's true.

"We see the same people everyday, and the same places, and most of us keep thinking the same things and saying the same things. I know people who read, and all they do is read the same thing over and over again. The newspapers are always the same, and the telly is always the same. People get so cross when they change shows on the telly. They want to know that every Monday is the same as every other Monday. They change shows and people get upset. But you know when they get excited? When someone dies, like in a fire, or a little baby, or some old person. That's the only thing that gets people even a little interested. They come running into the streets, and they talk louder and make a lot of noise which is different from the way they usually are. Maybe they don't *want* people to die, although it sure looks like they do when you see how they act when someone's been killed, like in an accident. That's all everybody talks about. And that's because their lives are so boring.

"Sometimes I hope something horrible will happen, too. I mean, I don't wish it, but I say to myself, it's about time for something exciting to happen. I mean, I don't *want* anybody to get hurt, but I know if they do we can all get excited about it. You see all these people sitting in front of the windows, you know. They have their tellys on, but they rather look out the window, just in case something happens they wouldn't want to miss it. It might be the most exciting thing that ever happened to them. I wouldn't want to miss it either. When I get to be my mother's age, I'll probably *really* feel this way. I don't want you to think the people 'round here are mean. It's just they don't have anything else to be interested in. They never go anywhere, they never do much of anything except be at home and go to work. I don't blame them. Maybe I wish they were different, but I don't see how they could be. No one lets them do what they want to do, so what else *can* they do? They don't *want* to be the way they are; they just are. They know they're never going to be any different, even if there was excitement in the streets every day of their lives. All it is is a little excitement; it doesn't make anyone change."

I would like to present one more voice in this brief and personal exploration of the concept of deprivation. It is, I suppose, the voice one associates most readily with the issues we have been addressing.

The notion that children have only the barest notion of deprivation is all too quickly disconfirmed by talking to them. One wishes that systematic, or even wholly idiosyncratic, deprivations would escape the eye of the child, but clearly facts speak for themselves. Adults are just as adept at knowing when they have been taken in, or outrightly deprived. Yet detection of deprivation is hardly the significant matter. More to the point is that deprivation wounds the child and influences the child's own assessment of himself or herself, not to mention other people's assessments of the child. This last point, incidentally, should not be dismissed. People are what they are, or what they think they are. Their self-assessments are in part a product of other assessments of them. I am speaking here not only of the psychological concept known as the self-concept, but more generally, more philosophically, if you will. Our very self-knowledge is lodged in our cultural, societal, political, economic and linguistic patterns and styles. At some level, we recognize these "other factors," yet the dynamics of that which we seem to agree should be called our identity, fights against these "other factors." We would like, in other words, to be known as unique beings, products of nothing but our own efforts, initiatives, and capacities. But let me amend this slightly: Young people seem to fight more strenuously, and at times rather dogmatically, against the idea of a sociological, cultural, or political determinism. I am me, they contend, my good parts combined with my less good parts. Most significantly, however, they would contend, I am the sponsor of all the parts; indeed they constitute my singular identity.

These are not mere words. The foregoing philosophy has surfaced in one form or another in myriad conversations with America's economically poorer children. In the words of a 13-year-old black boy from the Washington, D.C. area: "I believe black people are oppressed. I believe racism makes it hard for me to get to where I want to go. But in the end, like my Daddy says, the only thing going to hold me back from getting *anywhere* is me. And I believe that too!"

The speaker is Jeremiah Kelser, whose mother has been on welfare for as long as he can remember. He speaks often of his father, but in truth he sees his father infrequently, less than a half dozen times a year. Jeremiah's older brother, Lamar, is one of his school's extraordinary athletes; his two younger sisters do outstanding work in school. Though he has never been in serious trouble, it is Jeremiah, a small, handsome boy, who has always been his mother's greatest worry. Somehow, she just does not feel the boy has what it takes to make out all right. Maybe, too, she feels that although in a broader sense the whole family has known their share of deprivation, Jeremiah has had some additional burden to bear. I must confess, while I admire Mrs. Kelser and trust in her deep knowledge of her children, I have never seen anything in Jeremiah that would confirm her apprehension. Granted, I have heard all too often her argument about the deprivations experienced by poor families and her belief that only the special child can escape the destiny shaped by these deprivations. I still remain unconvinced by her assessment of Jeremiah. More significantly, I have heard her assessments in the beliefs and attitudes of the boy himself:

"My mother thinks I'm not as good as my brother and sisters, which may be right. There's nothing I do as good as they do—sports and school work—but I still don't think that means I can't do as well as they do. Let's face it, you don't grow up black in this country and expect to make it as easily as all the rest of those folks. You're always going to be one step behind, least in their eyes. Even when you go do something extra good, folks look at you like maybe they're surprised you could so something sort of all right—you know what I'm talking about. Even my mother, she feels that way every once in a while. She may not mean to, but that's what she makes me think she's thinking. Hell, I don't know for sure.

"Fact is, I don't know nothing for sure, except if you work hard enough at something, chances are you gotta make out all right. Sure I have to go without lots of stuff other kids have, or all those products they advertise on television. Half of them, all they have 'em for is to remind you what you don't have and what you're supposed to have if you want to call yourself a big success. But I can live with that. So I don't have this, or that, a big yard or lots of trees, or a new baseball mitt every year. I can make out. I can make out with what I got just being me, you know what I mean. I got the right number of eyes and ears and arms and legs, don't I? I got a brain that works, don't I? So, what's the big deal! Maybe I got a little farther to go than a lot of these other folks, but in the long run all it depends on is little ol' me. Sure I come from what they call a deprived family. Fact is, that's all my mother talks about half the time, how we've been deprived this and deprived that. My father used to tell her she'd do better getting down to work, on no matter what, 'stead of limping around the house complaining all the time about this and that. How many times you think folks have to hear all that before they have it stuck in their minds for good that, like, something's supposed to be the matter with them. You don't have to keep throwing out the same message every day, you know.

"Trouble with my mother is that she believes I'm the only one who's got to fail. She thinks my brother's going to make it with sports, and my sisters with school work. But then there's me, and she can't figure how I'll do it. I think she's got a big excuse all ready just in case. She'll tell folks, hey, what chance you think kids like mine got. Growing up the way we did they got to be twice as good and twice as smart as anyone else. That's right. Got to be better than better! We're different from all these other folks. Nobody gives us a break. Nobody helps us. Nobody even believes we can make it even when we're right in the middle of making it. My mother's got so many lines, you can't tell which way she's going.

"Way I see it, a person goes just as far as he can go by himself. If you're a sixty-mile-an-hour man, you go sixty. If you're only a twenty, then you go twenty. Now, it's true you got half the society trying to keep you going sixty. But what you going to do if they're trying to keep you from going sixty? You just work harder, push your engine so damn hard there's no way folks going to stomp on you, keep you from moving. Now these other kids, if they worked as hard as I'll probably have to, they'd be going seventy and eighty miles per hour. But nobody works harder than they have to. If all you have to do is spit in the engine to turn it up to sixty, then all you're ever going to do is spit. No one makes it harder on himself. Things go smooth, you take it easy. Things go tough, you push harder. That's all you can do. That's all anybody can do. My mother, see, she's got herself believing I don't have a chance 'cause there's nothing I can do that comes real easy to me. Okay, that's fine. But just 'cause I got to work hard for it don't mean I ain't going to get it, no matter who wants to keep me from getting it. But she don't want to see it that way. She thinks 'cause of welfare and all these other programs that we're already out of it, or I am anyway. And I haven't even done nothing yet to make her think that way. Nothing at all. I ain't in no trouble. I do my work in school like I'm supposed to. I ain't so happy about the way we have to live doing all the things we gotta do in order to keep getting what we get from the government, but she doesn't hear me complain. I don't say nothing to no one. I don't understand where she gets all her ideas. Living in a housing project ain't what you would call being a big time millionaire, but just 'cause you live in one doesn't mean you can't change things. Hey, I could become a millionaire myself and end up buying some great big house for all the rest of the people in my family, which means especially my mother. Could happen, you know. Just

92   THOMAS J. COTTLE

'cause all these conditions you gotta grow up in are supposed to mean you sort of end up just where you started from doesn't mean it has to happen to everyone.

" 'Course I'm not so sure I'm the one who's going to make it. I mean, I don't want to seem like I'm bragging. I ain't sure about nothing. I might do it, and I might not. Nobody knows for sure. You can't tell what's going to happen. My mother thinks you can, but you can't tell nothing! I could be higher than high tomorrow, or in two years, how's anybody going to know. I could be a bum too. I could be way up one part of my life and just that far down another part. That happens too. Pushing eighty per one second, and stalled, man, 'til the motor burns out the next second. How you going to tell. How you going to know how anybody or anything's going to deprive you. And if I'm so *deprived*, like my mother always tells all of us are, but especially me, then how come I know all about these things? How come I understand about life and she doesn't even know how I think about any of this stuff? If you're really deprived, like she tells me, then you wouldn't even know it. Fact that you know already means you're pushing twenty, maybe even thirty per. Has to, man!"

As I noted, this bit of conversation took place with Jeremiah Kelser when he was 13 years old. That was seven years ago. Now, three months short of his 21st birthday, Jeremiah Kelser is in prison, serving a three- to five-year sentence for his role in the robbery of a grocery store.

References

Cottle, T. J. *Busing*. Boston: Beacon Press, 1976.
Cottle, T. J. *Barred from school*. Washington, D.C.: The New Republic Book Co., 1976.
Cottle, T. J. *Children in jail*. Boston: Beacon Press, 1977.
Cottle, T. J. *Black testimony*. London: Wildwood House, 1978.
Roszak, T. *Person/planet*. New York: Anchor Press, Doubleday, 1978.

PART III

Obstacles to Change

Introductory Notes

The papers in this section link the papers in Part II (Some of the Victims) with those in Part IV (Strategies for Social Change). One cannot look at the circumstances of the victims without becoming aware of some of the obstacles to change nor devise strategies for change without analyzing obstacles that stand in the way. As a result, allocation of papers to Part II or IV is to some extent arbitrary. For example, Binstock's analysis (Part II) of the plight of the old also identifies obstacles to change and suggests some strategies. Hilliard's discussion (in this intermediary section) of prevention of psychopathology of blacks describes strategies as well as the circumstances of another group of victims. Brodsky and Miller's discussion of the use of the class action suit in prisons and mental hospitals (Part IV) identifies more of the victims. The emphasis in this section, however, is on analyzing the obstacles to change—on identifying the enemy.

Ira Goldenberg's paper introduces a theme that recurs in later papers: The idea that our ability to deal with our problems effectively will be closely related to our ability to conceptualize them differently. The relationship between groups seeking social change depends on their concept of the enemy. To the extent that this concept is shaped by differing ideological vantage points, the enemy is very often seen differently by different groups, a process resulting in disunity. Our realities differ and our identification with a given group—a class, a race, a gender—inclines us to identify other oppressed groups as enemies. This disunity leaves pressure-group politics as one of the few paths open and Goldenberg, like Binstock, sees such an approach as unlikely to produce real change. Instead of ministering to the victims of oppression, we need to direct our attention to dismantling its causes. Timidity has prevented us from conceptualizing our problems adequately and from taking action to deal with the causes. To the extent that we are the products of our system and have difficulty in transcending the timidity it imposes, Goldenberg's message is a stark one: "We have met the enemy—and he is us."

Ira Iscoe, like Goldenberg, expresses concern that the reflections of social forces within individuals—in the case Iscoe presents, professionals
concerned with the alleviation of human suffering—constitute major
barriers to the adoption of preventive strategies. Iscoe believes that we
are unaware of the complex of forces that work against the widespread
adoption of a preventive approach to psychopathology, and he attempts
to open our eyes by describing economic and conceptual factors that
keep our efforts focused on treating the casualties while we demand
changes in the policies that create these casualties. For a variety of reasons, not the least of which is our system of reimbursing health care providers, we respond to demand rather than need. We treat the victims
rather than intervening in a way that prevents their demands from arising. Prevention may be less expensive than treatment, but it is also less
profitable, and we all, personally and professionally, are oriented toward
profit. Iscoe goes on to describe the history of professional training in
clinical and community psychology and in counseling to illustrate how
the neglect of prevention has been entrenched in training programs, primarily because of the values of professionals who control these programs. He suggests a conceptual model of points of intervention, from
which he derives possibilities for training requirements that would prepare persons to become effective in prevention.

Thomas Hilliard's paper expands and further documents Goldenberg's
point about our failure to attack causes. Instead of attempting to deal
with the social, economic, and political dynamics that create so many of
our problems and that are basic causes of psychopathology, we "psychologize" our problems. In victims such as blacks we seek psychodynamic
mechanisms and individual frailties to account for the high incidence of
casualties. This is comparable to a general attempting to explain the casualty rate at Hiroshima by pointing to the lack of vitamins in the victims'
diet. However Hilliard does not simply dismiss psychogenic factors:
Rather, he argues for a recognition of the relationship between politico-
economic and psychological variables and an examination of their interaction in producing psychopathology in oppressed people. Hilliard's
proposal that personality develops in and is shaped by a political and economic framework and is in part determined by social institutions links
the concepts of the authors who deal with political action and social
change to the concepts of those who deal with psychopathology. It also
provides us with an analysis that not only encompasses both the causes
and consequences of oppression, but also suggests where we should direct our interventions if we wish to prevent—rather than treat—casualties. "Simply stated," Hillard says, "unless there is a substantial reduction in . . . political and economically based oppression, there will not be

an overall improvement in mental health." Failure to recognize this is a major barrier to preventing psychopathology, and psychologizing the problem is a major obstacle to change.

David Manning White's paper documents and expands a point made by Hilliard concerning the important role of the media in the socialization process, and its deleterious influence on members of society and on their mental health. In examining their effects on our society, White concerns himself with both the process and the products of the media. The effects of the products are perhaps more familiar to us, and White discusses some of the effects of violence on TV, the amount of time spent watching TV, and the distorted picture of the world that people acquire from TV. He examines the effect this distortion has on people's values and desires and the reasons for the hold that this medium has on the public. As long as we have an economic system that is based on insatiable consumption, thereby making the mass media so profitable (and therefore so powerful), White says that putting blame on the media for their flaws and excesses may be misdirecting us from dealing with the roots of the problem. His survey of the media—records, movies, TV, radio, publishing—leaves us in no doubt of the colossal financial structure of these enterprises and the advertising industry that is so intimately linked with them. His analysis leaves us less likely to underestimate their impact or to doubt that the danger lies not so much in the potential for control of public opinion, but in the way that the very size of the enterprises demands further expansion: "Their dominant motive is to make even more money." White argues that this mindless corporate greed contributes to perpetuating socioeconomic policies that help to create and maintain psychopathology in society. His analysis leaves one in little doubt that the media present an obstacle to change; they are indeed, the major buttress of the present social order and a massive distraction from its noxious effects, to which they themselves contribute. White concludes with suggestions about what we might do, as a society and as individuals, to combat the "mediacracy."

In the final paper in this section, Henry M. Levin examines the interaction between our economic and our educational systems and their relation to the problems we face in attempting to bring about social change. We so often, in Richard de Lone's (1979) words, "defer the dream." * We accept that there are injustices and intolerable inequalities in our society, and, to deal with them, we place the burden of eventual change on our children. To make the world a better place we will feed the children, educate them, equalize their opportunities—and thus, a generation from

*R. de Lone. Small futures: Children, inequality, and the limits of liberal reform. New York: Harcourt, Brace, and Jovanovich, 1979.

now, we will have a just society. Elsewhere de Lone has shown how often this approach has failed, and Levin's paper helps us understand why such failures occur. Our schools—the major institutional agents we have for shaping our children's values—are themselves reflections of the larger society, designed, albeit in a haphazard and nondeliberate fashion, to create citizens who will be compatible with the economic system. Levin documents and analyzes the dialectic between the educational system and the workplace and examines the implications this process has for achieving economic democracy. Through his description of the structure of work and of the workplace and his illustrations of how both the social structure of the schools and the content they teach prepare people for roles in this system—and to acquiesce in its indignities and abuses—we see that our schools are more of an obstacle to social change than a force for bringing it about. Levin argues, however, that contradictions within and between both institutions, the schools and the economic system, will be exacerbated by the ending of a continually expanding economy and will thus provide a dynamic for change. His examination of "career education," "life long learning," and "back to basics" illustrates the way in which educational reforms result from changes in the workplace: "Each of these can only be understood in light of the increasing difficulties in integrating young and relatively educated persons into the workplace." He suggests that none of these approaches will be able to deal with the problems of overeducation in a nonexpanding economy and that, consequently, changes must occur in the workplace itself. The intrinsic unattractiveness of the workplace may be altered through the implementation of economic democracy. If such changes occur in the workplace, corresponding changes will occur in schools to create a new equilibrium. Implicit in Levin's discussion is our failure to focus on changing our schools, a failure that acts as a major obstacle to effectiveness in changing our society. With his demonstration of the likelihood that changes in the workplace will inevitably result in changes in the schools, the discussion of obstacles to change ends on an optimistic note.

Dilemmas of Social Intervention

A Retrospective Analysis of the Politics and Contradictions of Timidity

I. Ira Goldenberg

Popular myth has it that time and distance make for increased clarity. Objectivity, so the guiding fiction goes, is a function of our ability to remove ourselves from events initially perceived as either too ambiguous or complex for balanced analysis. When this distancing is accomplished through conscious effort it is seen as evidence of heroic self-discipline or, at the very least, effective professional training. When it is simply the result of the passage of time, it is perceived as both inevitable and uncontrollable.

More than 15 years have passed since our nation's last foray into its own presumed reconstruction. We now live in a time when the public has seemingly embraced Proposition 13 with a vigor reminiscent of the rhetoric that previously accompanied the skirmish referred to as the War on Poverty. The very same "target population" that was once going to be liberated from the bonds of enforced inequity has now been transformed into the agent of our economic and social ruination.

Is it possible then, within this altered context, to understand the past without succumbing to the lures of nostalgia or self-righteousness? Probably not. Our penchant for alternately romanticizing or denigrating the past is matched only by our ability to rationalize either course of action. We have become masters of the art of writing our own epitaphs.

Nevertheless, we must try, if for no other reason than to provide our heirs with a perspective within which the struggle for liberation retains its meaning in the face of those whose unremitting hostility or insatiable idealism toward all such struggles leads only to resistance, apathy, or cynicism. Let us at least be one with Yevtushenko (1963) when he wrote:

I hate the cynics with their lordly view of history, their scorn for the heroic labors of my countrymen, whom they try to represent as a lost flock of sheep, their skills for lumping the good with the bad and spitting on the whole thing, and their utter inability to offer any constructive alternative. (p. 40)

And if objectivity is beyond our ken, let us surely leave to the next generation a clearer understanding of the contradictions that both limit and define attempts at social intervention in a postindustrialized society bereft of a true revolutionary history. The purpose of this paper is to contribute to that understanding by focusing attention on an issue that has consistently interfered with or undermined our efforts to create a society more worthy of those whose labors built it: It is the issue of our own timidity in the face of contradictions—and the manner in which that timidity has influenced both the ways in which we have conceptualized problems and the actions we have undertaken to deal with them.

On Timidity

According to the venerable Mr. Webster, to be timid is to be lacking in courage, boldness, and determination. But it is much more than that. It is a revulsion over the prospects of dealing directly with the vicissitudes of personal action in an unpredictable and often irrational world. To be timid is to look at the world and purport to see rationality "just around the corner" or a light "at the end of the tunnel." The timid are eternally optimistic about the progress and potential of humankind, and so long as that progress and potential demand taking no personal risks, the timid will be in the forefront of every battle for human dignity and freedom. To be timid is to cultivate a lifestyle in which struggles are forever occurring "out there" in a depersonalized world that could easily be transformed if only the forces of oppression could be tempted, educated, or impressed (often by research results whose findings are either redundant or could have been predicted long before the studies were undertaken) to listen to the muted cries of the disenfranchised and disaffiliated. But the timid will not put themselves "out there," for they have seen what often awaits those who have accepted the responsibility of first being what they want others to become (need we mention again the fate of the Kennedys, Martin Luther King, and Malcolm X?). And so, the timid always seek to fulfill their visions and needs by continually creating two separate worlds for themselves. The first is a world of ongoing concern for a generalized and often abstract humankind, a concern bordering on genuine passion for both the oppressed and their oppressors. The second, however, is a world so constructed as to prevent themselves from ever having to change or give anything up, a world in which the timid do not risk exposing themselves or their own interests to the very same society from which they demand a commitment to self-reflection and renewal.

More than anything else, however, being timid is being unable to free oneself from one's own conditioning; it is being unwilling, even in the face of the most obvious of contradictions, to scale the walls of our own personal and professional prisons; it is being incapable of forging an identity between our own sense of incompleteness and the social, economic, and institutional imperfections that currently define the conditions under which most of our brothers and sisters struggle to survive.

Any serious attempt at a retrospective analysis of the events of the past 15 years must begin with an appreciation of the consequences of our collective timidity. Perhaps a few examples will suffice.

The War on Poverty

For all its accomplishments (some of them unintended), the War on Poverty remains the single best example of the sacrifice of impact on the altar of consensus. In retrospect we can see that the late-lamented War on Poverty was never intended to be a war at all. At its very best it was a painfully timid and overly self-conscious assault on the consequences, rather than the causes, of human misery. It was the kind of program whose philanthropic appeal was from the very beginning basically devoid of the threat that would have accompanied it had its creators touted it as a crusade against the social, economic, and institutional foundations of our society. Consequently, the initial consensus that surrounded the War on Poverty was one of the unthreatened and the unembittered. They saw their lives, not as indictments of the "American dream," but rather as testaments to its validity. Unlike the "target populations" for whom it was intended, the War on Poverty was created by people whose faith in America and its institutions was as unshaken as their belief that poverty could be eliminated through the development of a massive program of individual remediation.

And that is the key: "individual remediation." The War on Poverty was both an expression of and, more important, a vehicle for the perpetuation of the view that poverty was basically traceable to individual shortcomings on the part of poor people themselves. Thus, whatever limited resources the War on Poverty had at its disposal were almost entirely devoted to "fixing up" individuals. Poverty was to be eradicated through more personalized forms of counseling, training, and education, through programs specifically aimed at "Pygmalionizing the poor," however varied and lofty the accompanying rhetoric. What was not stated was the obvious: that people were poor because they had no money, goods, or power in a society that judged human worth specifically in those terms. What was not acted upon was equally obvious: that the barriers to possessing either goods or power were not created by the victimized, but by the institutional sources of their victimization. And so the War on Poverty, whatever its accomplishments, actually served to extend and reinforce the doctrine of personal culpability. As Cloward (1965) put it in his testimony before the Senate Select Subcommittee on Poverty:

The chief target of the federal anti-poverty program is the victim of poverty, not the sources of victimization.

If fundamental institutional change is not the primary object of the anti-poverty program, massive individual remediation is, and this is the sense in which the program does not constitute a plan to attack longstanding social and economic inequalities in our society.

Nothing being said should be taken to mean that casualty programs are not needed. No humane society can abandon those who have already experienced the ravages of prolonged deprivation. The point is, however, that low-income people as a class cannot expect to benefit from the anti-poverty program as it is currently conceived. But if we fail to make a broad spectrum of institutional changes, new casualties will steadily fill the vacuum left by individuals who are helped by the anti-poverty program, for the causes of economic deprivation will continue to be at work.

The broad consensus favoring the current anti-poverty program is hardly proof of a national determination to wipe out economic deprivation. The very breadth of this consensus, however, merely lays bare the fact that no vital institutional interests are threatened by the program. (p. 231)

Were we timid in settling for a not-so-massive program of individual remediation? Of course. Was it politic, good sense, and expedient to settle for so much less than was needed? Probably. Were we ignorant or naive about the consequences of accepting programs whose ultimate intent was to perpetuate a blaming the victim mentality? Absolutely not. We chose, for whatever reason, to disregard or, by our very muteness, to weaken Cloward's argument and position.

The Social Technicians

Timidity takes many forms. In the case of the War on Poverty it manifested itself as a willingness to accept and work within a conceptual and programmatic framework of unquestioned mischief-making potential. At other times it has surfaced in the form of tolerating reactionary practices within the helping profession itself, practices parading under the umbrella of "social change agentry," but clearly oriented toward systems maintenance.

During the past 15 years (as has probably been the case throughout recorded history), we have seen similar symbols and rhetoric employed by people with apparently opposing social intentions. Both Richard Nixon and Huey Newton spoke of "power to the people," but they surely meant different kinds of power for different groups of people. Even today, living as we are in a period of obvious retrenchment, it is stylish for almost anyone, independent of how directly or indirectly he or she may be involved in the basic issues of change, to refer to him or herself as "social change agents." Thus, we now find change agents tilling the soil on organic farming communes in Vermont, "Rolfing" each other at the Esalen Institute in California, or just plain trying to "make it through the night." They all proclaim that "my life is a political statement" and profess a deep and unabating kinship with various movements for human liberation. So be it. But at some point we must begin to call into question those individuals and practices whose rhetoric, however appealing, serve to mask a set of patently reactionary motives.

We have not done so in the past, more than likely because of a misguided and conditioned reluctance to expose our own profession (and colleagues) to the judgment of social history. Nowhere has this been clearer than in our unwillingness to publicly disavow ourselves from the "social technicians" masquerading as change agents, who have enriched themselves at the expense of the people.

Unlike social interventionists, social technicians function as guardians of the system. The results of their work generally show up as systems' maintenance rather than systems' change, regardless of the rhetoric that usually accompanies their styles or techniques. Social technicians appear in many forms, maintain that their orientation and skills are "value-free," and often claim to be solely interested in increasing the sense of well-being and overall competence of those who inhabit the setting to which they are ministering. In fact, the results of their efforts are to mute discontent, "cool out" the situation, or otherwise inhibit the transfer of power and resources from those who control them to those who are controlled by them. The social technician identifies strongly with the employing institution's values, sees little need for any basic change, and encourages the adaptation of low-status/low-income members to the system's needs through the application of a variety of techniques derived from research in the social and behavioral sciences.

A few instances. Following the ghetto riots of the late 1960s, many mental health professionals undertook (with NIMH and HEW support monies) the training of so-called nonprofessionals in the application of individual and group techniques for use in instances of "community crisis intervention." Upon closer examination, especially by local community groups, such projects often were revealed to be rather elaborate attempts to employ inner-city people as defusers of community discontent in their own neighborhoods (CRRC, 1971). In the field of organizational behavior, much of Argyris's (1967) work, particularly with the State Department during the American military buildup in Vietnam, could be viewed as consistent with a social technician's orientation. Finally, in the fields of education and criminal correction, one cannot help but be frighteningly impressed with the upsurge in the use of mental health professionals to either isolate and remove troublesome students/inmates or to run longterm training programs designed to better equip school/prison line personnel and administrators to deal more efficiently with problems of discipline. These activities are geared to focus attention away from the broader and more basic ideological and political issues which are at the root of much of the current unrest in our public educational and correctional institutions (Goldenberg, 1973; McArthur, 1974). Have we really arrived at a point where we seriously equate the implementation of token economies and behavior modification programs with the requirements for social justice?

Let us finally be clear about the fact that the social technician, whatever his or her status and presumed membership in the helping professions, is no ally in the struggle for a more equitable society. The social technician is generally called into a situation when there is a problem as defined by those who control the setting. Such problems usually involve decreasing profits and efficiency, client or consumer unrest, or an increased questioning of the setting's values by those, usually the majority, who are most directly and adversely affected by the setting's policies. The social technician's job is to check the problem as quickly as possible. Like his or her employers who control the setting, the social technician is fundamentally afraid of basic change, perhaps for two reasons: first, because his or her own social and economic interests would be endangered; and second, because at some deep level he or she views the masses as inherently violent and destructive in nature, as in need of being controlled by a class more benignly virtuous and stable by disposition, and as being incapable of handling the responsibility for determining the direction of their own lives. With the social technicians as our comrades, we need never want for enemies.

"Separate-But-Equal" Formulations of Oppression

Any retrospective analysis of the past, especially one that finally enables us to uncover and expose the reactionary influences that reside within our own profession, should not delude us into thinking that we have been less timid in confronting the contradictions that exist among those with whom social interventionists have historically identified themselves.

We have recently been witness to revelations and have felt revulsion for a crypto-fascist clique in the White House that attempted to further subvert the quality of our national life. In its aftermath, beyond the time covered by the predictable euphoria that accompanies any exorcism, we have seen passivity, resignation, and even a newfound fearfulness take hold of the American people. But even more than this, we seem to be caught at a particular moment when poor people, minorities, and women—the groups historically most systematically excluded from the body politic—are more separated from each other and more fragmented than ever before. At a time when our country might once again be moved, however grudgingly and hesitantly, toward a reexamination of its collective consciousness, those whose unity is so crucial in that struggle appear newly estranged from each other's pain. To accept this situation without attempting to change it would be nothing less than a reaffirmation of our timidity, this time with respect to those with whom our own dreams and destinies have always been bound.

The problem is clear, and it is important that we recognize it for what it is: There is no semblance of a "united front" to pool the efforts and resources of those whose only real leverage lies in the weight of their numbers. The reason for this state of affairs is equally clear: Oppressed peoples hold mutually exclusive and antagonistic views on the nature and origin of their oppression. There are different realities, and the failure to acknowledge these distinctive realities is to succumb to fantasy. But even more so, the inability or unwillingness to transcend these realities is an exercise in stupidity, however conflict-ridden the process of transcendence might be.

Take the present author as an example. My own approach to the problems of oppression and social intervention is essentially a class-based approach. What that means, of course, is that the concept of economic class is the fundamental dimension around which I seek to understand both the original nature as well as the subsequent historical development of the exploitative process. But what that also means is that, since class is conceived as the unifying superordinate theme, questions of race and sex (not to mention age and sexual preference) are necessarily relegated to a subordinate position within the analytical framework. In short, issues of racism and sexism are both contained and subsumed below the imperatives of a class perspective. But that is my reality, and no matter how much I am committed to its essential validity, it is currently not the functional reality of other minorities and of women. For black people there is an incontestable experiential legitimacy that makes for a racial view of the world, a perspective within which questions of class and sex become subordinated to issues of race. For feminists, on the other hand, the essence of the oppressive experience is sexual in nature, with class and race assuming a secondary analytical role. While poor people, Third World peoples, and women are all oppressed, each group can separately and with compelling justification define the genesis of the oppressive experience in such a manner as to transform members of the other two oppressed groups into residents of the enemy camp.

Even among members of the "same" group there is tension and conflict that can only be understood as the result of multiple group identity. Describing the plight of politically active black females, Beal (1970) wrote:

Since the advent of Black Power, the black male has exerted a more prominent leadership role in our struggle for justice in this country. He sees the System for what it really is, for the most part, but where he rejects its values and mores on many issues, when it comes to women, he seems to take his guidelines from the pages of the *Ladies Home Journal.* (pp. 342–343)

The movement for women's liberation is a struggle whose most recent phase was largely initiated by middle and upper-class white women, but it seeks the active involvement of poor white and Third World women. It also functionally excludes (perhaps even views or speaks of as part of the "enemy camp") poor males, both black and white. Thus, of course, it presents low-income women, both Third World and white, with the problem of choosing between their economic class and their social caste, a choice as divisive and uninspiring as it is unfortunate. And the situation is not discernibly different with respect to struggles involving the self-determination of Third World peoples (both rich and poor) and poor people (both black and white). In each instance, because of the nature of the superordinate imperative around which the social order is analyzed, class versus race versus sex, members of one or another oppressed group will find themselves at best, left out or, at worst, identified as part of the oppressive process.

If we have learned nothing else from the history of liberation movements, we should at least appreciate the degree to which existing social orders have benefited from a disorganized and divided citizenry. When that disorganization is imposed from without it can be dealt with comparatively easily as an expected manipulation emanating from those whose vested interests are being threatened. When, on the other hand, the disunity has its origins among the oppressed themselves, the situation fast approaches the level of a catastrophe. We are currently at that point, and the "separate-but-equal" formulations of oppression should no longer be tolerated because of some misguided sense of symbolic loyalty to a nonexistent alliance.

The Consequences of Our Own Socialization in a Goods and Power Oriented Society

Thus far we have focused attention on the consequences of knowingly accepting limited definitions of the nature of longstanding social and economic inequities, of the need to finally purge our profession of systems-perpetuating practices, and the necessity of openly challenging our brothers and sisters in struggle to forge a new unity of purpose founded upon a collective analysis that transcends self-defeating parochialism. Having reviewed these issues, it is time that we point to a final variable in the change process, a variable that has too long gone unexamined: ourselves.

Let us begin by recognizing that we live (and have been socialized) in a society dominated by an ethos revolving around the acquisition and retention of Goods and Power. Let us also understand that the American ethos is predicated on the existence of three critical assumptions about Goods and Power. Simply put, these assumptions are that:

(1) Goods and power are not, either by definition or by their nature, limitless; (2) whatever goods and power exist at a particular point will, under no conditions, be shared equally among the people; and (3) it is the individual who is the major referent for any and all analyses concerning the manner in which goods and power are both acquired or not acquired and used or misused.

In a very real sense the assumptions given above, especially when taken together, provide the intellectual and perhaps the spiritual basis for the development of a socioeconomic system which, of necessity, must be exploitative in nature and competitive in design. It is a system in which one person's advantage ultimately depends on another's disadvantage, in which one person's success must be predicated on another's failure, and in which one person's rise must occur at the expense of another's decline. Add to this scenario the perpetuation of inequity across generations, and one can begin to appreciate the power of a system to both create the past and negate the future.

Given the above, it is much easier to become philosophically and even politically opposed to the assumptions underlying the social order than it is to be free of the effects of having been processed by that order. The years of socialization, of learning and internalizing the myths and cultural imperatives that come to govern one's life, are not easily overcome; they leave in their wake a powerful legacy of experiential and behavioral predispositions. These predispositions may well be at variance with the goals of social intervention. At their very best they can impede the process of social change; at their very worst they can disable it permanently.

For the social interventionist, the problem of transcending one's own socialization involves a great deal of unlearning, particularly in those areas having to do with status, security, and control needs. It can only be accomplished to the degree that one's capacity to be self-critical about one's own needs (and the social genesis of those needs) match one's commitment to the legitimate aspirations of those with whom one is working. However distasteful one may find the historical consequences of a system predicated on an exploitative individualism, one must acknowledge its subtle impact on one's life, particularly as that impact manifests itself in the manner in which one relates to the struggles of others.

Are we prepared to acknowledge the impact of having grown up, of even having "made it," in a social order we now need to change? I think we are, for we have seen and lived too long with the contradictions of not doing so. It is, I suspect, much less frightening to demystify our own existence than to continue to bear witness to the consequences of our own timidity.

Summary and Conclusions

The human drama continually unfolds, almost as if guided by the momentum of its own incompleteness. Its possibilities assume their meaning through struggle. Both the noblest and meanest moments of our collective history as a species have emerged through the struggles to alter the conditions of bondage. Indeed, the whole of humankind is the unfinished story of oppression and the attempts to undo its obscenities to the human spirit (Goldenberg, 1978).

The need for a radical reconstruction of American society is no longer a matter worthy of serious or extended debate. It will not be accomplished through a reenactment of predictably timid and overly self-conscious thrusts at the consequences, rather than the causes, of suffering. And it will certainly not be satisfied by equating social change with the momentary relief that may accompany the exorcism of Richard Nixon from the body politic.

What is required, at least as a beginning, is a thoroughgoing analysis of the contradictions and possibilities of a superindustrialized technocracy whose very power and existence depend on the perpetuation of the powerlessness and expendability of those whose labors built it. The historically oppressive character of the "American experience" is its own demon. It is not just our leaders who require the exorcist's touch, but also our institutions and ourselves. It is this that Otto Rene Castillo was telling us in his poem "Apolitical Intellectuals."

One day
the apolitical

intellectuals
of my country
will be interrogated
by the simplest
of our people.

They will be asked
what they did
when their nation died out
slowly,
like a sweet fire,
small and alone.

No one will ask them
about their dress
their long siestas
after lunch,
No one will want to know
about their sterile combats
with "the idea
of the nothing."

No one will care about
their higher financial learning.
They won't be questioned
on Greek mythology,
or regarding their self-disgust
when someone within them
begins to die
the coward's death.

They'll be asked nothing
about their absurd justification,
born in the shadow
of the total lie.

On that day,
the simple men will come.

Those who had no place
in the books and poems
of the apolitical intellectuals,
but daily delivered
their bread and milk,
their tortillas and eggs,
those who mended their clothes,
those who drove their cars,
who cared for their dogs and gardens
and worked for them, and they'll ask:

"What did you do when the poor
suffered, when tenderness
and life
burned out in them?"

Apolitical intellectuals
of my sweet country
you will not be able to answer.

A vulture of silence
will eat your gut.

Your own misery
will pick at your soul.

And you will be mute in your shame.

If there has been an overall theme to this paper, it has certainly been a
simple one: that the reconstruction of our society (or any society) carries
with it a very fundamental belief, not only that the dehumanizing aspects
of a social order can indeed be changed, but also that the very process of
changing the social order can be as ennobling of the human spirit as it is
cleansing of the human condition. It is this belief—call it a guiding fiction if you will—that enables us, even in the face of our sometimes meager accomplishments, to recommit ourselves to the struggles that lie before us, to the "unfinished business" entrusted to us by our predecessors.
It also enables us to reach out for the fabric that joins people together, to
pursue the human chorus whose song will never be captured or
contained.

As finite beings caught somewhere in the midpassage of civilization,
we are a part of an evolutionary process whose beginning and end will
never be a part of our direct experience. We were neither present at our
inception as a species, nor will we hopefully be in attendance at our collective demise. It is through struggle that we come into contact with the
meaning of our existential passage.

By their very nature, the problems of oppression and social intervention cut across the usual and often comfortable distinctions we seek to
make between our public–professional roles and our private–personal
missions. We cannot claim immunity from ourselves. This, I should like
to believe, is what Alinsky (1971) meant when he wrote: "A major revolution to be won in the immediate future is the dissipation of our illusion
that our own welfare can be separate from the welfare of all others" (p.
23).

References

Alinsky, S. D. *Rules for radicals.* New York: Vintage Books, 1971.

Argyris, C. How effective is the State Department? *Yale Alumni Magazine,* May 1967, 38–41.

Beal, R. M. Double jeopardy: To be black and female. In R. Morgan (Ed.), *Sisterhood is powerful.* New York: Vintage Books, 1970.

Castillo, O. R. Apolitical intellectuals. From *Let's go.* Translated and with an introduction by M. Randall ©. London: Cape, Golliard Press in association with Grossman Inc., New York, 1971.

Cloward, R. A. Poverty, power and the involvement of the poor. *Testimony before the U.S. Senate Select Subcommittee on Poverty.* Washington, D.C., June 29, 1965.

Community Research Review Committee of the Black United Front. *Review of the Laue Project entitled Community Crisis Intervention.* Boston: May, 1971.

Goldenberg, I. I. The problem of safety in our inner-city school: A view from the bottom. *Testimony before the U.S. House of Representatives General Subcommittee on Education.* Washington, D.C., February 26, 1973.

Goldenberg, I. I. *Oppression and social intervention: Essays on the human condition and the problems of change.* Chicago: Nelson-Hall, 1978.

McArthur, A. V. *Coming out cold.* Lexington, Mass.: D.C. Heath & Co., 1974.

Yevtushenko, Y. *A precious autobiography.* New York: E. P. Dutton, 1963.

Conceptual Barriers to Training for the Primary Prevention of Psychopathology

Ira Iscoe

The great French scientist Flourens remarked in the late 1860s that everything in science depends on the viewpoint and that a new approach brings different results, often transforming a difficult task into an easy one. While there has been a steady increase in the number of persons in various disciplines who recognize the need for preventive and intervention activities designed to eliminate or significantly reduce various types of maladaptive behavior, there is presently not much vigor among mental health professionals as far as the primary prevention of psychopathology is concerned. On the surface what could be more logical than to espouse, support, and promulgate a doctrine of prevention? Psychopathology is not good for human beings or their welfare. It is responsible for the majority of hospital beds in the United States; it precludes human beings from approaching their full potential; *it interferes* with creativity; and psychopathology feeds the great reservoir of emotional handicaps. It is expensive, counterproductive; it is dangerous not only to individuals, families, and groups but to the nation as a whole. Statistics abound, indicating the incidence and prevalence of psychosis, educational failure, psychophysiological disorders, juvenile delinquency, crime, unhappiness, and depression.

There are acknowledged shortages of skilled persons to deal with observable psychopathology, yet there is little emphasis on preventing these conditions even though we are at a point where we can take a new look at old problems and make significant progress in preventing them. The concept of prevention is certainly not a new one, and the need for increased attention arises from a variety of sources including new concepts about the origins and continuation of mental illness, as opposed to mental health; the enormous costs of treating diagnosed mental illness; and the general draining, weakening, or loss of human resources to the nation.

We are in the midst of a knowledge explosion that forces us to look hard and fast at old problems. This approach is harmonious with the true purposes of research, that is, to examine again and again those conceptions and beliefs that we hold most strongly. If they stand up under our most critical and continuous scrutiny, they are strengthened and prolonged. If they do not, then they have to be changed or discarded in the light of new knowledge. Failure to recognize reality and truth results in the psychopathology of a system or a discipline, and the system or discipline becomes less able to cope effectively with the problems it is supposed to deal with. This is the situation in the mental health fields today. We are confronted with enormous problems in the design, delivery, and evaluation of mental health services and the success rate of these services is far from spectacular. Mental health planners, including economists and politicians, have written many promissory notes, and the public, as well as legislative bodies, are calling in these notes and finding that there is little cash on hand to honor them. Though 15 years of community mental health activities have clearly brought about a change in the locus of treatment of emotional disturbances from hospital-based to community-based, the most difficult problems such as the severely mentally ill, the aged, children, and minority populations have not been dealt with effectively. The hope that community mental health centers would gradually be taken over and funded adequately at local and state levels remains largely unfulfilled. Community mental health centers have a shaky financial future, and we are belatedly recognizing some of the cynicism, rather than altruism, that prompted the move towards deinstitutionalization and the naivete with which mental health planners (including psychologists), almost totally divorced from community realities, assume that mentally ill people—many after long years of institutionalization, devoid of family or friends, without job or social skills—can be treated and retained in community settings. The enormous complexity of dealing with problems of mental illness and mental health in community settings has encouraged an outpouring of publications, some of them research-based, others more philosophical. Representative of these studies are the writings of Regester (1974); Musto (1975); Bassuk and Gerson (1978); Snow and Newton (1976); Wolkon, Karmen, and Tanaka (1971); Becker and Schulberg (1976); and Arnhoff (1975).

The recently published four volumes of the President's Commission on Mental Health (1978) reexamine many of the difficulties previously noted. While it is not appropriate in this chapter to review the various studies, volume 4, the report of the Task Force on Prevention, points out many of the problems and barriers to carrying out a genuine prevention program. Among the recommendations of the task force is a call for much more vigorous action on the part of the National Institute of Mental Health to institute preventive activities, including research and training. In a publication entitled "Primary Prevention: An Idea Whose Time Has Come," Klein and Goldston (1977) have written about and compiled definitional and procedural strategies in the area of primary prevention activities. Several studies supporting at least the feasibility of primary prevention are in existence, and the recent publications of Cowen (1977) and Dohrenwend (1978), among others, detail procedural and conceptual possibilities in the primary prevention of psychopathology and advancement of the goals of prevention.

My purpose here is to examine in depth some of the barriers to training for the prevention of primary psychopathology and to focus on some of the conceptual difficulties that have to be addressed and surmounted before training can take place. The emphasis will be on the field of psychology, although it is quite clear that psychiatry, social work, and psychiatric nursing share some of the same conceptual difficulties. Though it would seem that we have accumulated sufficient, valid knowledge to at least emphasize the potential and actual benefits of a preventive approach, this is not presently the case. The failure to implement and support prevention, albeit frustrating, can be explained by concepts that are firmly rooted in our culture. I firmly believe that unless we understand the origin and workings of certain forces we are doomed to failure. Kurt Lewin (1947), the eminent social psychologist, emphasized the need for an understanding of the context of social actions and pointed out that "nothing stands alone in space and time." Things "happen" because of the meeting of certain forces, and for Lewin one of the most important tasks of social psychology was the determination of the interaction of various forces. Failure to do so results in "local determinism" rather than a sophisticated recognition of what is causing what, in Lewin's terms, "field determinism."

It is unfortunately characteristic of psychologists and mental health professionals that they are largely unaware of the political social forces that shape their professions nor are they sensitive to the subtle interplay of trade-offs underlying social movements or legislation. For a community psychologist this knowledge is all important. The politics of training for prevention have yet to be worked out, and until they are worked out, it is doubtful whether there will be much push for training in prevention. If we take a field force approach and ask why is it that presently we have very little emphasis on training in prevention, we can identify a number of factors, but it is not possible to fix the blame on any one group, profession, or discipline. If we ask is it the fault of those who deliver services, those who train mental health professionals, administrators of programs, providers of funds, consumers of services, the state of the art, etc., no one clear culprit emerges. This is frustrating indeed. The mental health field, like human service fields generally, is caught up in a web of forces. It is worthwhile to examine some of these forces, keeping in mind that even if we conclude that present directions in the delivery of human services are counterproductive, there is no guarantee that these directions can be changed simply by identification or censure. A number of changes at the individual, group, organizational, institutional, and social policy levels will be necessary before a direction in favor of prevention will emerge.

Prevention and the Concept of Direct versus Indirect Costs

Our society is production oriented. Presently we are on a quantitative kick and the accountant mentality is becoming more influential in universities and human service agencies. There are buzz words, such as cost effectiveness, zero-based budgeting, goal-attainment scaling, planning and evaluation; all of these in my estimation are really mechanisms for avoidance and expressions of frustration. The pursuit of these ends occupies an enormous amount of time, thus serving the purpose of diverting persons away from more serious issues. Beneath the jargon are, however, easily quantifiable goals and objectives couched in a language understood by budget and accounting types and, of course, legislators at all levels. Measurement becomes especially important when our country faces serious inflation, an energy shortage, and a taxpayer rebellion. It would seem that the selling of a preventive approach should be easy at this particular juncture.

Why not save money by prevention? The evidence is certainly clear but the paths are not. It is at this point that the notion of direct versus indirect costs becomes a factor. This economic concept was first introduced by Fein (1958) as one of the inquiries sponsored by the Joint Commission on Mental Illness (Ewalt, 1960). Direct costs are those incurred in dealing with mental illness directly. These include treatment, residential care, outpatient care, follow-up, and rehabilitation. Indirect costs are those exacted from society by lack of productivity, unemployment, revenue loss, and so forth. It should be noted that no estimate is made of the human indirect costs of mental illness. The terms are strongly financial, and they belie the untold misery and suffering, not only of the victims of psychopathology, but of their families and society.

We have not yet developed units for measuring human suffering, although somewhat facetiously I suggest that it might be a rewarding enterprise. In a production-oriented society, it is understandable that elected officials and administrators usually prefer to keep direct costs as low as possible and either postpone the indirect costs for the future (when they most likely will be out of office) or ignore them entirely. Thus, the wanton utilization of natural resources reduces direct costs now, but for later generations it raises enormous indirect costs. Failure to develop human resources, neglecting to teach children to read, for example, keeps direct costs low or contained but later raises further direct cost obligations as well as indirect costs. Direct costs are visible or temporal, and the more direct costs can be lowered, the better a program looks. From this approach an ounce of prevention is really not worth a pound of cure, because cure is tangible, reimbursable, and most likely profitable.

Prevention, on the other hand, is presently for the most part a nonreimbursable expense. One of the real barriers to the setting up of prevention programs is that their potential beneficiaries are not visible, while those already suffering from mental illness are. The great majority of mental health services delivered today are defended on the basis that they help people in distress or strengthen their coping process, so that they will not be mentally ill later on (secondary prevention). If a person is ill and is cured or helped, it is a visible statistic required in a production-oriented society. While the true heroes of any profession are the genuine researchers, those more likely to pick up the financial rewards are those who "deliver" services. If a water treatment plant results in the reduction of dysentery, typhoid, or other diseases, it is not possible to indicate by name and address the persons who were helped. Preventive programs generally are actuarial and not person specific, and they are difficult to fund because the populations at risk may not be clearly defined.

It is appropriate to point out that some of the major contagious diseases were contained by preventive activities resulting from research. The answer may be that there is little or no profit in the treatment of epidemics of typhoid, diphtheria, polio, smallpox, and the like. Their contagious aspects threaten wide segments of the population, and they were worth preventing on a humanitarian and economic basis. Now, preventive activities have become part of the value system of our culture, and, in fact, a physician who fails to offer appropriate immunization to a patient would be found guilty of malpractice. This type of situation has not yet arrived in the mental health fields, although there does seem to be mounting evidence that failure to institute certain preventive and interventive regimens could be the basis of malpractice if we could find the appropriate person or persons to blame. This brings us into the area of social policy and prevention.

Social Policy and Prevention

Mechanic (1973) among others has detailed the relationships between social policy and mental illness. There is an understandable temptation to attribute malevolence, greed, stupidity, and rigidity to those forces or professions that deemphasize or devalue primary prevention. There is little to be gained by this approach. It is appropriate, however, to ask what stands in the way of training persons in the prevention of psychopathology?

There is much to be gained by an analysis of the prevailing field forces that presently mitigate against the training of persons in the prevention of psychopathology even though there exists enough data to encourage preventive and interventive activities. If we were to inquire both at an academic and community level about the feasibility of training persons in the primary prevention of psychopathology, the most likely answer would be further queries: Are there jobs for such persons, at what level, at what pay, and under what type of working conditions. This is an economic reality in a production- and status-oriented society.

One of the main thrusts of this paper is to emphasize that social policy in terms of the reality of monetary support is the key element affecting the adoption of one particular approach over another. Money determines policy, and there is a saying in community psychology: A community gets what it pays for and people perform the work that is really expected of them. Attempts to have prison guards become rehabilitation resources are doomed to failure. Prison guards are paid to guard prisoners, and until we are willing to change their job descriptions and reward them for rehabilitation efforts we have no right to expect them to be anything else but prison guards. They get paid for "guarding," not for rehabilitating. Attendants in mental hospitals attend the mentally ill. They make sure that no one "escapes," that medications are given on time, that sexual activity is not overt, and that certain types of "appropriate" behavior are observed. The job description of attendants seldom includes therapeutic or interactive work with patients; and even if the job description does include these activities, other demands on an attendant preclude socializing. There are roles assigned to mental health professionals and mental health workers, both paraprofessional and professional, and the pay varies according to the presumed importance of the position.

In a materialistically oriented, capitalist society such as ours, the salary determines the status and the importance of the work. Parenthetically, the medical model against which psychologists so bitterly complain is less criticized by psychologists in independent practice where incomes are more equal to those of psychiatrists. Similar analogies no doubt come to mind. The point to be made is that the delivery of any service or any activities occurs in context, and unless that context is understood, there is danger of attributing failures (and successes) to inappropriate sources or perhaps to persons who really are only doing their jobs in the way they understood that the job should be performed. Thus it is inappropriate and unfair to blame community mental health center directors, mental hospital superintendents, private practitioners, administrators of nursing homes, to mention a few, for the current lack of emphasis on prevention. If these people have built up vested interests in maintaining the status quo, are they much different from other persons in other positions who also have investments in certain approaches to problems? Without encouragement and a certain amount of reward it is doubtful that persons can be made to change their approaches, nor does there seem to be much possibility of those devoted to primary prevention storming the Bastille, as it were, and changing current procedures. I once asked a border guard between Texas and Mexico what would happen if the flow of illegals were cut off or reduced to a trickle because of the rising prosperity of Mexico or other factors like effective deterrents to illegal crossings. He said it could not happen; and then when he was pushed to imagine that it might happen, he said almost plaintively, "Then what the hell would we do?" He recognized that his job depended upon a steady supply of illegal aliens. Total success was the last thing the border guards wanted. The same holds for the deinstitutionalization of the mentally ill, for outpatient treatment, or for welfare programs. The examples are referred to because unless we understand where we are, we will not be sure about what directions to take in order to alleviate the situation.

The "More of the Same" Philosophy

In a production-oriented society, if four mental health workers are doing a job and are obviously overworked, the present tendency is to add more personnel. The danger in the "more of the same" philosophy is that it does not force those in charge to examine better ways to use personnel instead of adding to the personnel roster. The director of a mental hospital or clinic that has 70 employees is more powerful than one that has 20. Similar observations apply to the addition of money. We have calls for more attendants, more mental health workers, more personnel, more of the same of everything. If a person is not improving in once-a-week therapy, then double the therapy sessions. If a hyperactive child is not settling down, boost the medication dosage. Despite clear evidence of the failure of the "more of the same" approach, professionals and nonprofessionals alike are apt to fall back on it. We do so because in most cases the climate does not allow a more careful consideration of the definition of the situation. A different definition brings different approaches.

From 1945 to about 1975, the National Institute of Mental Health spent about $1¼ billion on the training of mental health personnel, one-half billion of which was for psychiatrists and one-quarter billion each for psychologists, social workers, psychiatric nurses, and paraprofessionals. We would think that such an outpouring of funds would make significant inroads on the treatment of mental illness, but according to the President's Commission findings, this is not the case. Large populations remain underserved or unserved, and the severely mentally ill and distressed children are perhaps the worst off of all. The plea for mental health personnel should go unanswered since there is no evidence that increased personnel will significantly reduce the incidence and prevalence of diagnosed mental illness. The cure lies in changing approaches rather than in numbers of staff persons. Boston has perhaps the largest concentration of mental health personnel in the United States, yet there is no evidence that the mental health of the city's people is any better than in other locations in the United States. The "more of the same" philosophy is one that has to be changed if we are to institute effective primary preventive programs.

Need versus Demand

Closely related to the "more of the same" philosophy is the "need versus demand" dilemma. It is an understandable outgrowth of a production-oriented society and in some ways also an indication of an affluent culture. Can we afford to ignore the severely mentally ill and persons in need of help while we look around for preventive measures? There is the old adage that when one is knee-deep in alligators, it is no time to drain the swamp. There is also the response that unless one drains the swamp one will always be knee-deep in alligators. There is, too, more than the suspicion that being knee-deep in alligators is where the action is and where the rewards are. What better time to talk of peace than while a war is being fought? Analogous is "the starving children approach," where on the surface the demand is to feed the starving children, when, in fact, the need is for starving children not to occur; and in order for starving children not to occur, a host of antecedent conditions are necessary, most of them rooted in social policy and prevention. Failure to make the distinction between need and demand is one of the barriers to appropriate training in prevention. The realities of political support are based on demand, not need, but the realities of prevention lie in finding ways to stop certain situations from occurring. The economics of the delivery of mental health services are no different from the economics of the delivery of human services in general. Persons in reasonably comfortable positions understandably defend their turf, their beliefs, and the status quo, or perhaps improvement, and a person that threatens the status quo may be met with hostility and derision. This is why, incidentally, changes come about so slowly in training centers, and as will be pointed out later, this is one of the chief obstacles to training persons in preventive activities. It is instructive to note that as far as disciplines are concerned, changes in field forces in the last few years are bringing about changes in the "truce" between psychology and psychiatry and that the resumption of open hostilities is a distinct possibility, if it has not already started.

Intradisciplinary warfare is also increasing. Psychiatry is being attacked by behavioral medicine and family practice procedures. Clinical psychology is under fire from community psychology and threatened by outpouring of graduates from the professional schools. Traditional social work is faced with schisms in its ranks and new breeds are emerging, such as social psychotherapists, The New Professionals (Paraprofessionals United), and nontraditionally trained counselors.

Reiff (1974) has rendered a distinct service to the human service field by pointing out that the purpose of professionalism is not to improve services but to hoard knowledge. It is clear that containment is not working. The democratization of knowledge makes it increasingly more difficult for one profession or one discipline to control information. These factors have to be considered as we go into an in-depth consideration about barriers to training and prevention. In so doing it should be pointed out that an activity such as primary prevention does not stand alone but should be considered as a special case of a general case. If we currently do not emphasize the training of specialists for the prevention of primary psychopathology, it is only a special situation in which the preventing of problems of human beings in their personal and social environments is not much emphasized. The mental health professions have generally espoused a deficit or "sick" model. Although this model is generally attributed to medicine it really has wider roots. It is a posture to be assumed by persons seeking help and we are basically in a casualty-oriented society. Health insurance has adopted a "fee-for-service" approach. It is instructive to note that most larger health insurance carriers emphasize the casualty approach such as going to the hospital rather than outpatient treatment or paying for persons being well. Although in recent years Health Maintenance Organizations are beginning to adopt a preventive approach, the great bulk of the delivery of medical services to the United States is demand oriented. The same can be said for social work and psychological services.

It is worthwhile to point out here that society gets what it pays for. If the legislation or the orientation is towards production of cases, that is what society will carry out. We should bear in mind that presently prevention in mental health is generally a nonreimbursable expenditure and that preventive activities in medicine such as inoculation are not highly paid procedures. Though some writers, like Klerman (1977), call for a renegotiation of responsibilities for the care of the mentally ill with other professions and with society on the whole, they end up defending the sickness model. Translated this means that the overall trend is to deal with the demand and train accordingly.

Lack of Prevention Emphasis in Professional Training Programs

A brief overview of the history and content of training programs in clinical, school, counseling, and community psychology is helpful in assessing the current situation. Emphasis is on training in clinical psychology, inasmuch as this area is where the major expenditure of funds has taken place and where research has been apparently emphasized the most. In all, some five conferences have been held on training in clinical psychology since its inception after World War II. A brief examination of the focus of each conference may help clarify the reasons for the relative lack of attention to prevention in mental health training programs for psychologists. (It is my understanding that the content of training in psychiatry, social work, and psychiatric nursing is similarly demand- and casualty-oriented.) The conceptual differences between incidence and prevalence, necessary versus sufficient causes, receive as little emphasis as they do in training for clinical psychologists.

The Boulder Conference in 1949 was the first national conference on graduate education in clinical psychology (Ramey, 1950). It concerned itself with meeting the increased demands for clinical services during the immediate post–World War II era and with the many issues that a developing field had to face. The two-week conference considered some 15 general issues, such as core curriculum, the selection and evaluation of students, accreditation, licensing, and the problems faced by a fledgling profession. The scientist practitioner model, with emphasis on both professional training and research skills, was articulated at Boulder, and until the Vail Conference in 1973, was, on paper at least, the guiding force of orientation for university-based clinical psychology training programs. It was at Boulder also that the planning for the training and support of clinical psychologists was discussed in detail. First the Veterans Administration and later on the U.S. Public Health Service developed huge programs to subsidize training in clinical psychology. There was no discussion of prevention; the emphasis was on treating mental illness. There was a good number of psychiatric casualties from World War II. Employment opportunities for psychologists were abundant, and at the time of the Boulder Conference the hope of the psychologist as an *independent* practitioner was still only a hope. The psychologist would offer, under medical supervision, diagnosis, treatment, and research skills, a triple-threat product that was later to materialize.

Some 6 years after Boulder, the Stanford Conference (1955) on "Psychology and Mental Health" (Strouther, 1956) recognized the rapid growth of mental health movements in the early 1950s and the need to follow up on training developments. The Conference also reflected broadening views about the role of clinical psychologists and along with psychotherapy, dealt with alternate methods to producing behavior change. At the Stanford Conference the question of therapeutic environments and a possibility of preventive intervention to deal with negative environmental influences was discussed in some detail, but no action was taken. Demand for mental health services was high and academically based psychologists were not about to get involved with the problems of human beings on any large scale.

About 3 years after the Stanford Conference, a third national meeting was held in Miami in 1958 to deal with "Graduate Education in Psychology" (Roe, Gustad, Moore, Ross and Skodak, 1959). There was less emphasis on clinical psychology. There was much discussion on emerging new roles for psychologists and on issues with regard to their certification and licensing. While there was recognition of the need for some changes in the training of clinical psychologists, the demand for psychologists of all types was very strong, and this demand tended to mitigate against any radical changes in the training. Why talk of prevention when there was a mandate to train psychologists to deal with pressing problems?

The Chicago Conference in 1965 addressed the professional preparation of clinical psychologists (Hoch, Ross, and Winder, 1966). It was openly admitted that the clinical psychologists who had been trained over the past 20 years were abandoning research and that the scientist practitioner model had not held up. Despite the recognition of new challenges for psychology to deal with pressing social problems such as increased college unrest, crime, school failure, burgeoning institutionalized populations, most of the Chicago Conference recommendations were never implemented, including those dealing with environmental influences and possible preventive interventions. Clinical psychology programs were prospering. The demand for clinical psychologists was high and the illness model was clearly dominant. Employment possibilities were for persons who could deal with patients and clients. An increasing number of states had passed psychologist licensing laws and the private independent practice of psychology was becoming more evident. In retrospect, Chicago also marked a clear division between academia and the clinic. Departments of Psychology were at their zenith. There were many other sources of support for graduate students other than clinical psychology training programs. Colleges were bursting at their seams. This was clearly not a time to pay much attention to such nebulous concepts as prevention. Although the reports of the Joint Commission had already been out 5 years, little attention was paid to its recommendations, especially as far as institutionalized populations were concerned.

Some other events concomitant with the Fourth (Chicago) Conference are worth mentioning. In 1965 community mental health centers were emerging. Staffing demands were enormous and could not be met from existing resources. Albee's prediction (Albee, 1959) about personnel shortages was clearly coming to pass, and his appeal for new approaches to the problem and for a departure from the one-on-one emphasis was unheeded. Mental health association training programs were being started, and the country was beginning to face problems of alcohol and drug abuse, areas, incidentally, that clinical psychologists had by and large not been exposed to. To the credit of American psychology, the profession developed its first position paper entitled "The Community and Community Mental Health Center" (Smith and Hobbs, 1966), in which the challenges to psychology were pointed out and pleas were made for careful assessment of the *needs* of a particular community before starting a community mental health center in it. The position paper also advocated that 50 percent of every community mental health center's budget be allocated for work with children and families, and they also stressed consultation and education as important forces in community settings. It is most unfortunate that clinical psychologists, community mental health planners, and the National Institute of Mental Health paid very little attention to this highly significant position paper. We know that to a great extent work with children and families was not and is not stressed in community mental health centers and that of the five services mandated in 1966, namely, outpatient, day care, emergency, inpatient, and consultation and education, the latter was never really given parity with the others. Several studies produced evidence that only about 5 percent of community mental health center funds were devoted to consultation and education activities. Thus, the one possibility of spreading a preventive, interventive orientation and enlisting such institutions as schools in planning preventive activities did not succeed.

Another event that took place in 1965 is of historical and current interest. A national conference on "The Education of Psychologists for Community Mental Health" was held in Boston (Swampscott), Massachusetts. Known as the Boston Conference (Bennett, Anderson, Cooper, Hassol, Klein and Rosenblum, 1966), it emphasized the need for study and treatment of individuals within a community context. It proposed several different training models and agreed that the medical model was no longer adequate for the task at hand. The conference sanctioned and encouraged interdisciplinary training experiences and psychology. As a result of this conference, the term community psychology was given preference over community mental health. Within the context of community psychology certain areas of needed research were identified:

1. The study of man in the community, including the effects of varying physical and social environments upon his functioning both as an individual and as a member of social organization.

2. Assessment of the individual's reaction to planned change by varying methods of social intervention in a wide variety of human problems and concerns.

3. Basic research on the relationship between social-cultural conditions and personality functioning in order to add knowledge about the positive mastery of stress.

4. Examination of the effects of social organizations upon the individual, particularly those creating high-risk populations, and alternative social patterns which may serve to reduce their creation.

5. Facilitation of social-organizational change through modification of motivational and personality factors in the individual.

6. Evaluative research on consultation and other social change processes. (p. 23)

These research suggestions have direct bearing on training for prevention. It is unfortunate, too, that community psychology became identified with community mental health and still has not yet completed its separation.

The Vail Conference in 1973 (Korman, 1974) was the fifth national conference, and it dealt with levels and patterns of professional training in psychology. The deficiencies in academic training programs that had been identified some 8 years earlier at the Chicago Conference were all the more evident. The main area of dissatisfaction was the "lack of fit" between existing doctoral programs and the demands of employment situations. It was pointed out that some of this dissatisfaction had led to the formation of the National Council of Graduate Education in Psychology and was finding expression in new training ventures such as Psy. D. Programs and the founding of Schools of Professional Psychology. It was at the Vail Conference that the professional practice model was explicitly put forth. In promulgating this model the emphasis was on the application of findings from research and practice and there was encouragement for certain training programs to move out of the traditional academic settings into a variety of other locations. While Vail spoke boldly of the needs of ethnic minorities, women, and special populations, it did not to any large extent emphasize prevention. The conference also recognized levels and patterns in the delivery of mental health services and supported a masters-level degree. Very few of the Vail recommendations were implemented in training programs. Demand rather than need was once more stressed. Prevention, it should again be emphasized, is mainly a nonreimbursable expense with no one discipline responsible for carrying it out.

In 1975, in commemoration of 10 years of community psychology, a national conference on training in community psychology was held in Austin, Texas. Referred to as the Austin Conference (Iscoe, Bloom, and Spielberger, 1977), it examined models for doctoral training in community psychology and attempted to clarify future directions in training. There was much stress on intervention and prevention, with most of the participants being interested in preventive intervention systems analysis, social intervention, social ecology, and applied social psychology. It was noted then, as it should be noted now, that there were few genuine community psychology training programs and as Bloom noted, community psychology had not made a qualitative break from community mental health. There were no positions specifically entitled community psychologists, and it was doubtful whether such titles would arise except in academic settings. We should bear in mind that in contrast, up until very recently, there were abundant employment situations for clinical psychologists either in independent practice, community mental health centers, hospitals, or clinics. A variety of skills were demanded, most of which could be acquired in existing training programs. Very few employment notices, if any, even made mention of prevention.

In summarizing studies that examined how well training and practice in the fields of community psychology and community mental health mesh with their articulated ideologies, Bloom (1977) pointed out a discrepancy between reality and rhetoric: "Staff members in community mental health centers, including psychologists, continue to spend the bulk of their time in activities directly or indirectly related to clinical practice and their interests in the development of additional skills are concentrated in clinical topics. Directors of graduate training programs in community psychology and community mental health continue to place major emphasis on the development of clinical skills and the use of clinical field settings" (p. 241). Bloom pointed out that while graduate students were more interested in carrying out prevention, there were really no resources within graduate programs for them to obtain training in prevention. The primary emphasis on training in 1965 was on the technology of community mental health and the emerging field of community psychology. The 1975 Austin Conference produced about seven models, among which intervention and prevention and social ecology received the most attention and support. To date little change is evident in the content of training programs. Most continue in a clinical mold and advertised positions for community psychologists usually bear the prefix or suffix of clinical. There are only a few out-and-out community psychology training programs, that is, a program that does not emphasize or include clinical training. This is another example of demand versus need.

A review of national conferences on training in counseling and school psychology shows little or no emphasis on training and prevention. The 1952 Northwestern Conference was to counseling psychology what the Boulder Conference was to clinical psychology. A second conference in 1964 (Thompson and Super, 1964) recognized the limitations of traditional one-to-one counseling and the increasing social demands for a wide variety of indirect counseling services but few changes were made in training programs. School psychology, which superficially at least would appear the most logical place to emphasize prevention, has unfortunately been caught in a web of jurisdictional disputes about level and patterns of training, and currently it is certainly not heavily involved in planning or carrying out primary prevention activities.

From this brief review of major training programs in psychology, it is clear that the lack of emphasis on prevention stems from several forces, including the value system of those who direct programs as well as those who control intern and practicum settings. While positions labeled clinical psychologists, school psychologists, counseling psychologists appear frequently in the employment bulletins, the title Interventive and Preventive Planner rarely emerges. Though there is some mention in the job description of intervention and prevention, they are clearly not primary, and there are clear implications that prevention is carried on if and when we have time. And based on present demand, there is no time. We turn now to a consideration of field forces that produce barriers to training in primary prevention.

Where and How to Intervene?

In attempting to investigate the combination of field forces that currently act against programs for training in primary prevention, it is useful to examine conceptions of human service delivery systems. There are many such systems extant depending on the discipline involved. A scheme proposed by Glidewell (1977) conceptualizes the matrix of professional practice and is presented in Table 1. In this approach Glidewell takes four foci

Conceptual Barriers to Training   125

Table 1. A Scheme for Conceptualizing the Matrix of Professional Practice

Cultural Preoccupation	Psychosocial Phenomenon	Client	Practitioner	Point of Intervention
Life enhancement	Dreaming, Planning, Inventing, Affluence	Participant-developer	Planner, Designer, Evaluator	Policy-making
Social conflict	Resolute, Contention, Struggle, Deviation	Misfit, Deviate, Subordinate culture	Consultant, Negotiator, Conciliator	Conflict arena (on site— off site)
Distributive justice	Poverty, Discrimination, Neglect	Have-not, Discriminated against, Neglected	Advocate, Organizer, Agent	Local exchange point— mass media
Pain-distress	Illness, Injury	Sufferer, Patient	Healer, Therapist, Counselor	Private life- Institution

In J. C. Glidewell, Competence and Conflict in Community Psychology. In I. Iscoe, B. Bloom, C. D. Spielberger, (Eds.), *Community Psychology in Transition*, Washington, D.C.: Hemisphere Publishing Corp., 1977.

of intervention or planning. He terms these the cultural preoccupations, and as can be seen from Table 1, they range from pain-distress, distributive justice, social conflict, and life enhancement. Each of these preoccupations has its own psychosocial phenomena, its primary clients, its practitioners, and its points of intervention. This is a factor worth noting because the constellation of forces for the relief of pain and distress involves different clients compared with, for example, the relief of social conflict. Likewise the practitioner plays a different role. In the relief of pain-distress we have healers, therapists, counselors, persons in direct contact with the sufferer or the patient or people labeled mentally ill, or persons that generally fall into the categories embraced by the medical model. As concern moves away from immediate pain and distress (observable psychopathology) to other concerns (cultural preoccupations), such as social conflict and life enhancement, less personal contact occurs, and there are different types of consumers of the services, different practitioners, and different points of intervention.

In the late 60s and early 70s there was a shifting away from the sufferer to the clients who would be involved in a cultural preoccupation dealing with distributive justice and social conflict. There was concern about ethnic minorities, the distribution of power, the rights of subordinate counselors, and persons who generally did not fit into the clinical mold. It is instructive, however, to note that many explanations of the motivations of persons using drugs, of urban riots, of demonstrations on university campuses were cast into clinical molds; thus concepts like mass insanity, acting out behavior, and unresolved hostility towards authority were invoked to explain social movements and, of course, failed to do so. The needs of the clients in a subordinate culture could not be met by healers and counselors; they could best be met by negotiations between contending forces and by reparative actions to existing social systems. From a community psychology standpoint these would be explained by shifting and sharing of power within community settings.

It is not difficult to see that many of the present efforts in mental health, including clinical psychology, social work, and psychiatry (and the medical model generally) deal with the cultural preoccupation of pain and distress. There are, of course, advantages to the deliverers of services at this level: the clients are defined, they are ill, they are hurting, they need our help. The role of the practitioner is one of high status—healers, therapists, counselors, gurus, persons of power and sagacity. The level of intervention is in the private life of the person, perhaps in family or group therapy, with little attention paid to organizations or social systems. One accepts "reality" and the reality is that things are as they are. One does not fight a social system, and though perhaps the therapist and the clients could wish for a better world, they must be realistic and accept what is. From the practitioner's point of view, what could be a more noble endeavor—healing the sick, having status in society, and being paid well for it. It is no wonder therefore that the private practitioner in the mental health fields has highest status and is most resistant to change, or for that matter, resistant to the application of research findings. Why bother when there really is no necessity to do so? What matter if psychotherapy is effective or not effective when there are sufficient clients. We can only predict that if national health insurance provides broadly defined mental health services, then the pain-distress dimension and all it entails will be expanded, and life enhancement as reflected in policy making and prevention will not be emphasized. We are, after all, in many ways an action-oriented society. As has been stated before, prevention is presently a nonreimbursable expense (and unless there is a policy decision that makes preventive intervention activities reimbursable we can be very sure that they will decline).

It is at the policy-making level and perhaps in the conflict arena that preventive activities can best be implemented, although we should not turn our backs on effective intervention at any level. There is the question of efficiency and resources. Lead poisoning is best dealt with by lead poisoning not occurring, and the way of avoiding lead poisoning is not to have lead in paint. There are a variety of activities at the policy level that clearly influence mental health and mental illness. Family solidarity is certainly not advanced by policies concerning aid to dependent children. A change in policy could very well bring about changes in family structure. We know enough about separation of children from their parents in times of stress to support the concept that provision should be made for hospitalized children to have a parent or relative with them as much as possible. There is sufficient knowledge about mental retardation and birth weight to know that the best way to prevent mental retardation and birth anomalies is to raise the weight of the fetus. In order for this to be accomplished, changes in social policy with regard to nutrition, availability of services, and the delivery of pre- and postnatal care are required.

Evidence with regard to smoking and its relationship to circulatory diseases and cancer is abundantly clear, yet the most alarming increase in cigarette smoking is currently in females, especially young females. Social policy changes with regard to advertising, education, and practices about indoctrination and social sanction are called for. Perhaps more directly related to the primary prevention of psychopathology are the questions of the effect of smoking and drinking on the fetus. Here, too, while the demand may be for the treatment of casualties, the need is for social policy changes.

Last, but certainly not least, there is clear evidence about the relationship of reading disability, juvenile delinquency, and crime, including lack of self-esteem and the clear manifestations of psychopathology. A number of effective interventions are available. The price is right, yet the social policy is not there. Intervening at the sufferer level keeps remedial programs in existence but does little or nothing to cut down on the incidence of reading disability, illiteracy, and school failure. Having delineated a scheme for levels of intervention, we now turn to a conceptualization of training and the difficulties involved.

A Conceptualization of Training

In moving from pain–distress towards life enhancement and prevention, differences in goals and levels of intervention were pointed out. These differences call for different approaches to training, and Table 2 attempts to delineate these different foci and tries to pinpoint some of the existing difficulties in training of persons for primary prevention activities. It is not the lack of positions alone but also the blurring of professional identities. It is not easy to risk the disapprobation of one's colleagues, and it is extremely uncomfortable to be in a field where a viable social support system is currently lacking or at best weak.

In Table 2 we focus on training in psychology, although it seems reasonable that other mental health professions experience the same problems and the same difficulties in training. In order to be effective in pre-

Table 2. Integrative Schema—The Clinical and Community Continuum

	Clinical	Clinical/Community	Community/Clinical	Community
Goals	Ameliorate symptoms of identified patients	Remedy family work, living, group problems	Improved mental health in total community	Better quality of life for community
Approaches	Psychodiagnosis, psychotherapy	Family, group therapy systems intervention, mental health consultation	Early case finding (secondary prevention), education, consultation and planning re social class and ethnic group influences	Conceptualizing, planning, managing evaluations re community systems development
Working Bases	Hospitals, mental health clinics, private practice	Community mental health centers, health departments, rehabilitation centers, group private practice	Judicial, health educational, governmental and manpower systems, private corporations as mental health professionals	Community systems as community development psychologists
Early Doctoral Education	Personality abnormal, social development-psychology, psychopathology, neuropathology	Epidemiology of mental illness, systems theory, family-work group theory	Community health, judicial, educational, governing systems, social class, ethnic status	Interdisciplinary-based sociology, anthropology, community psychology theories of political development
Later Doctoral, Post Graduate Education	Psychodiagnostics and psychotherapies, individual clinical studies and experimentation	Family, group therapy, mental health consultation	Systems intervention through community organization, advocacy, broad consultation	Community systems, conceptualizing, planning managing, politicking, evaluating, writing
Funding for Education and Work	NIMH, State Mental Health, private insurance and NHI	Specialty social problem groups—NIAAA, drug administration, rehabilitation, LEE, health foundations and HMOs	Agency budget contracts, private nonprofit corporations	Agency budgets, universities, professional psychology research centers

Nurse, Rodney. Preconference Materials, Austin Conference on the Training of Community Psychologists, Austin, Texas, 1975.

vention, one must have a broad educational base and have a variety of training experiences, experiences not available in any predoctoral programs in the United States. If we take a continuum (Table 2) of Clinical Psychology through Clinical/Community through Community Psychology, and if we consider the six variables (left-hand column, Table 2)—

Goals, Approaches, Working Bases, Doctoral Education, Later Doctoral, and Postgraduate Education and Funding—clear differences can be seen. While the goal of a Clinical approach is the amelioration of symptoms of identified patients (the pain-distress continuum of Table 1), the goal of a Community Psychology approach would be better quality of life for the community as a whole. A Community/Clinical approach would be to improve mental health in the total community. While a Clinical approach would emphasize psychodiagnosis and psychotherapy, Community/Clinical and Community approaches deal less with the "laying on of hands" and more with designing, planning, and evaluating. It is in the early Doctoral Education that very clear differences can be seen with Community/Clinical and Community differing markedly from the concentration in Clinical and Clinical/Community.

As we move away from direct contact, we get into content areas that are not taught within discreet departments and involve considerable interdisciplinary interactions. While academia is very fond of talking about interdisciplinary cooperation, the reality is that one leaves one's discipline only at great peril. Interdisciplinary programs are not in vogue and as a matter of fact, they have never been in vogue. The amount of communication on a university campus between sociology, anthropology, psychology, political science is small at best, usually confined to personal friendships or carried out within an institute or a study center. The main identification is with one's own discipline (and that is where the rewards are, especially for younger faculty).

Field training also differs greatly in these approaches. In order to learn prevention one has to be exposed to such concepts as systems intervention, consultation, intervention, evaluation, incidence versus prevalence, necessary versus sufficient conditions, primary, secondary and tertiary prevention, and concepts that are perhaps best dealt with in a public health approach and in schools of public health. In most instances schools of public health do not have high status nor do public health practitioners. It seems pretty clear that for psychologists seeking training in prevention the predoctoral level is currently not the place to get it. It is in the area of where the money comes from (funding for education and work) that the biggest crunch occurs. From Table 2 it can be seen that the relief from symptoms of pain and distress comes from a variety of sources, including state mental health programs, insurance, and the National Institute of Mental Health. Planning, conceptualizing, evaluating, and carrying out preventive activities are supposed to arrive from agency budgets, universities, and professional psychology research centers; perhaps also from private nonprofit corporations. This type of support is hardly sufficient to attract, train, and maintain persons in careers in the prevention of primary psychopathology. The current rising opposition to research is another barrier. It is clear that budgetary support for training in prevention is not available, nor is there much emphasis on the fundamentals of prevention. In retrospect, most of the persons who are presently strong advocates of primary prevention did not receive this training in predoctoral education. The majority of psychologists who are important forces in the training of primary prevention seem to have received all or most of their prevention orientation from schools of public health at the postdoctoral level. This may well be a path for the future.

Directions for the Future

The foregoing has been an attempt to describe some of the barriers that lie in the way of training personnel to carry out primary prevention activities. The emphasis has been on the recognition of a cultural preoccupation with casualties and "production," the source and amount of rewards, and the relatively low status of persons in the prevention field. While there is evidence to support the need for preventive actions and policies, most of the prevailing funding sources and forces today are aimed in the opposite direction. There is a tendency to denigrate preventive interventions, and those who advance the concepts of prevention may be called impractical dreamers acting without evidence or just tilting at windmills. Typical of this approach are statements such as: "Until we know how to prevent schizophrenia we should devote our efforts to treating the diagnosed schizophrenics and stop wasting our time and money;" or "If we don't know what causes something how can we prevent it?" The reality is that only by continuous research and questioning will we find the means to overcome opposition. Arguments against the prevention of psychopathology also largely ignore the legitimate questions about the efficacy of current treatment of mental illness, the overwhelming evidence about the mounting financial burden, the human misery involved, and the chaotic state of the mental health delivery system. It is not necessary to know the precise causes to carry on effective prevention or at least reduce high incidence. The British Navy served limes to its sailors for over 100 years as an effective way to prevent scurvy; yellow fever was first brought under control by the draining of swamps. It was not until many many years later that the precise connection between vitamin C and scurvy was discovered, and the transmission cycle of yellow fever fully understood. Lack of such precise understanding did not interfere with preventing deaths from scurvy or yellow fever, nor should it today in the field of prevention. There are certain things we can do, certain environments and styles of life which we can encourage that can help reduce the incidence of primary psychopathology. Understanding the precise underlying mechanisms will take more time, and our approaches will have to be constantly modified with increasing knowledge. The impatience of persons in power with any other approach is a clear threat to first-class primary prevention activities and related research. Currently, given a "practical" orientation, I see a mounting danger to research on prevention, with such research receiving less emphasis than at present, and the demand function receiving more prominence in the future. If this "more of the same" philosophy prevails, we can, I fear, look forward to less attention being paid to types of prevention and more money being spent on treatment. The proliferation of special classes for deviant children, the mushrooming of homes for the aged, and increased funds for the treatment of substance abusers are examples of this "more of the same" trend.

This is the time to ask what can be done or what can those who believe in the prevention of primary psychopathology do? From the point of view of a community psychologist, clear changes in public policy are called for. How can this be accomplished? How can the existing situation be changed in the face of strong opposition? First of all persons who advocate primary prevention cannot be summer soldiers. They must be prepared for a long haul, ready to take on formidable oppositions, and they must have information resources and facts lined up clearly. Evangelical zeal must be backed with valid information. There is a need to be low on rhetoric and high on the facts. In order for this to occur we must know the field of prevention thoroughly—its risks and its possibilities. Here are some specific recommendations:

1. The American Psychological Association should appoint a task force on prevention and this task force should come up with a position paper on the primary prevention of psychopathology.

2. All training programs under the purview of the American Psychological Association should have a prevention input as part of their course work. Just as a certain number of courses in psychotherapy, experimental design, and theory are required for an approved program, so each APA approved predoctoral program should have a prevention component.

3. National organizations such as the Mental Health Association should seriously reexamine their present posture with regard to prevention, and via their national networks educate staff and boards about the realities of primary prevention.

4. The National Institute of Mental Health should be one of the leading advocates for prevention. While there are some signs that NIMH is moving in this direction, it is largely dominated by a treatment-delivery philosophy. There should be a clear designation and budget for pri-

mary prevention activities manifested by NIMH support of training programs at the pre- and postdoctoral levels in the areas of prevention of psychopathology. It is a truism that trainees go where the money is, and if more funds are put into primary prevention training, then the personnel to carry on these activities will emerge.

5. At the policy-making level Congress should stipulate that a certain percentage of funds given to human service programs are involved in research on and evaluation of primary prevention. Further, in making grants to State Departments of Mental Health and State Departments of Health, Congress should attach a primary prevention stipulation.

6. The average citizen as well as the expert should stand ready to testify on funding of mental health programs, armed with facts, and pushing for more funds to be devoted to public policies designed to prevent primary psychopathology.

7. Finally, at the professional agency, volunteer, and citizen levels, well-armed with facts, we should make a continuous assault on the present mental health delivery system and its casualty orientation. Clinical psychologists, social workers, psychiatrists, and psychiatric nurses should not be allowed to forget the casualty orientation. If there is a hearing, for example, at a community mental health center interested citizens should ask about prevention. A Prevention Fact Book (it might be slim at first) should be available for circulation, preferably put out by the American Psychological Association or the National Institute of Mental Health, provided of course that it espouses genuine prevention. If informed citizens, academics, and professionals abandon their continued advocacy for prevention, we can only look forward to increased bureaucratic activities oriented towards "more of the same." It may very well be that the increased costs of delivering mental health services, plus the none-too-outstanding record of treatment effects to date, will incline policymakers towards a more sympathetic approach to primary prevention. This is a distinct possibility and possibilities are enhanced by working on them. There is no substitute for knowledge.

References

Albee, G. W. *Mental health manpower problems.* New York: Basic Books, 1959.

Arnhoff, F. N. Social consequences of policy toward mental illness. *Science,* 1975, *188*, 1277–1281.

Bassuk, E. L., and Gerson, S. Deinstitutionalization and mental health services. *Scientific American,* 1978, *238* (2), 46–53.

Becker, A., and Schulberg, H. C. Phasing out state hospitals: A psychiatric dilemma. *The New England Journal of Medicine,* 1976, *294*, 255–261.

Bennett, C. C., Anderson, L. S., Cooper, S., Hassol, L., Klein, D. C., and Rosenblum, G. *Community psychology: A report of the Boston Conference on the Education of Psychologists for Community Mental Health.* Boston: Boston University, 1966.

Bloom, B. The rhetoric and some views of reality. In I. Iscoe, B. Bloom, and C. D. Spielberger (Eds.), *Community psychology in transition: Proceedings of the National Conference on Training in Community Psychology.* Washington, D.C.: Hemisphere Publishing Corp., 1977.

Cowen, E. Baby-steps toward primary prevention. *American Journal of Community Psychology*, 1977, 5, 1–22.

Dohrenwend, B. S. Social stress and community psychology. *American Journal of Community Psychology*, 1978, 6, 1–13.

Ewalt, J. *Action for mental health.* New York: Basic Books, 1960.

Fein, R. *The economics of mental illness.* New York: Basic Books, 1958.

Glidewell, J. C. Competence and conflict in community psychology. In I. Iscoe, B. Bloom, and C. D. Spielberger (Eds.), *Community psychology in transition: Proceedings of the National Conference on Training in Community Psychology.* Washington, D.C.: Hemisphere Publishing Corp., 1977.

Hoch, L., Ross, A., and Winder, C. L. *Professional preparation of clinical psychologists.* Washington, D.C.: American Psychological Association, 1966.

Iscoe, I., Bloom, B., and Spielberger, C. D. (Eds.), *Community psychology in transition: Proceedings of the National Conference on Training in Community Psychology.* Washington, D.C.: Hemisphere Publishing Corp., 1977.

Klein, D. C., and Goldston, S. E. (Eds.), *Primary prevention: An idea whose time has come.* DHEW Publication No. (ADM) 77–447, 1977.

Klerman, G. L. Mental illness, the medical model, and psychiatry. *Journal of Medicine and Philosophy*, 1977, 2, 220–243.

Korman, M. National conference on levels and patterns of training in psychology: The major themes. *American Psychologist*, 1974, 29, 441–449.

Lewin, K. *Principles of topological and vector psychology.* New York: McGraw-Hill, 1947.

Mechanic, D. *Social policy and mental health.* Englewood Cliffs, N.J.: Prentice-Hall, 1973.

Mechanic, D. Sociocultural and social-psychological factors affecting personal responses to psychological disorder. *Journal of Health and Social Behavior*, 1975, 16, 393–404.

Musto, D. F. Whatever happened to "community mental health?" *Public Interest*, No. 39, Spring, 1975, 53–65.

President's commission on mental health reports: Task panel reports, (Vol. 4), 1978. Available from No. PCMH/P-78/21, National Technical Information Service, U.S. Dept. of Commerce, 5285 Port Royal Road, Springfield, Va., 22161.

Ramey, V. C. *Training in clinical psychology.* Englewood Cliffs, N.J.: Prentice-Hall, 1950.

Regester, D. C. Community mental health—For whose community? *American Journal of Public Health*, September, 1974, 64, No. 9, 886–893.

Reiff, R. The control of knowledge: The power of the helping professions. *Journal of Applied Behavioral Sciences*, 1974, 10, 451–461.

Roe, A., Gustad, J. W., Moore, B. V., Ross, S., and Skodak, M. (Eds.). *Graduate education in psychology* (Miami Conference). Washington, D.C.: American Psychological Association, 1959.

134   IRA ISCOE

Smith, M. B., and Hobbs, N. The community and the community mental health center. *American Psychologist*, June, 1966, *21*, 499–509.
Snow, D. L., and Newton, P. M. Task, social structure and social process in the community mental health center movement. *American Psychologist*, August, 1976, *31*, 582–594.
Strouther, C. R. *Psychology and mental health* (Stanford Conference). Washington, D.C.: American Psychological Association, 1956.
Thompson, A. S., and Super, D. C. (Eds.). *The professional preparation of counseling psychologists.* Report of the 1964 Greystone Conference, New York Teachers College, Columbia University, 1964.
Wolkon, G. W., Karmen, M., and Tanaka, H. Evaluation of a social rehabilitation program for recently released psychiatric patients. *Community Mental Health Journal*, 1971, *7*, 312–322.

Political and Social Action in the Prevention of Psychopathology of Blacks

A Mental Health Strategy for Oppressed People

Thomas O. Hilliard

Those who profess to favor freedom and yet deprecate agitation are men who want crops without plowing up the ground, they want rain without thunder and lightning. They want the ocean without the awful roar of its waters.

—Frederick Douglass

An effort should be made to attenuate the viciousness of a system of which the doctrinal foundations are a daily defiance of an authentically human outlook. . . . The function of a social structure is to set up institutions to serve man's needs. A society that drives its members to desperate solutions is a non-viable society, a society to be replaced.

—Franz Fanon

The colonial condition cannot be adjusted to: like an iron collar, it can only be broken.

—Albert Memmi

During the past 15 years, coincident with the community mental health movement, there has been a rapid acceleration of interest in preventive mental health, although elements of prevention concepts found expression much earlier in the "child guidance" and "mental hygiene" movements. However, apart from the current wave of interest in prevention, the mental health field has been overwhelmingly adult and rehabilitation oriented in its theory and intervention strategies. The renewed interest in a preventive approach as a more efficient strategy for attacking society's mental health problems stems from a recognition of the limitation in the traditional medical or "disease" model and reflects an awareness of the inadequacies of the current deployment of the mental health professional resources to provide sufficiently for the current and projected mental health needs of the American population (Albee, 1967; Joint Commission on Mental Illness and Mental Health, 1961).

Although there have been a wide variety of intervention techniques employed to implement primary prevention efforts (Kessler and Albee, 1975), these interventions may be dichotomized into two major strategies or approaches. One approach, frequently characterized as "the promotion of mental health," results in mental health activities directed toward a "population at risk" or "the host" in order to develop skills, competencies, or resistance that would allow them to withstand future stresses or cope more effectively with traumas. On a more sociological level, this approach involves facilitating and strengthening support systems for "at risk populations." The other major preventive approach encompasses activities or interventions that focus on ameliorating or reducing the deleterious environmental factors or noxious stimuli that produce the mental dysfunction. Thus, when the focus of the preventive efforts are directed towad eliminating functional psychological disorders, the preventive efforts are focused on the milieu, social conditions, or the social system. The type of intervention strategy explicated in this paper falls into the latter category.

The subject matter of the present paper—the role of political and social action in preventive mental health and the discipline of Black psychology—reflects an interface of two fields, in each of which the ignorance would seem to far exceed the understanding of the phenomenon in American psychology. Nevertheless, the present paper is focused on a beginning or preliminary formulation of prevention theory and intervention with Blacks and, by implication, other oppressed people. However, in my opinion, it is not feasible to formulate effective social or political intervention strategies without an implicit or explicit conception of the dynamics and development or etiology of the dysfunction. The relationship between a theory of psychopathology and the corresponding intervention is crucial. For instance, if you conceptualize the cause of psychological disorder in Blacks as resulting from the lack of congruence between ideal/self perceptions, then techniques such as clarification and reflection of feelings are appropriate therapeutic responses; or if you adopt a more psychoanalytic notion involving neurotic defenses organized around the repression of sex and aggression impulses stemming from unresolved oedipal conflicts, then therapeutic strategies such as the interpretation of defenses and conflicts, and the manipulation of transference relationships are logical sequelae.

In appreciating the theoretical limitations of the prevailing views of personality development or psychopathology with Blacks and other oppressed people, it is significant that the major theorists developed their theories of personality development and psychopathology with White, middle-class and upper-middle-class clientele. Freud's psychoanalytic theory, as is widely acknowledged, grew out of his psychotherapeutic experiences with "transference neurotics" in 19th century Vienna, Carl Rogers's self-theory stemmed largely from counseling experiences with college students, and Harry Stack Sullivan's from work with hospitalized schizophrenics as clients (Roth, Berenbaum and Hershenson, 1967). Similarly, Maslow's theory of self-actualization was based largely on a study of persons such as Walt Whitman, Henry David Thoreau, and Abraham Lincoln. The psychologists mentioned, consistent with their clinical and professional experiences, failed in their formulations to provide even a cursory treatment of the relationship of variables such as poverty, racism, and other forms of political and economic oppression to personality development and psychopathology. Thus, as might be expected, the application of their theories to Blacks and other oppressed people is constrained by both class and racial biases. In fact, there is an abundance of literature that documents the ineffectiveness of treatment approaches derived from traditional theories of personality and psychopathology with Blacks and low-income clients. Excellent critical reviews of the impact of socioeconomic class and racial variables on the psychotherapeutic process are provided by Jones (1974) and Griffin (1977), respectively.

In striking contrast to the void in most prevailing theories of personality, psychopathology, or psychotherapy, clinicians who work with personal problems of Blacks, particularly low-income clients, are acutely aware of the failings of the social system and its contribution to the stress and psychopathology of Black people. Similarly, another important source of contemporary work on mental health relevant to Blacks and other oppressed people is the cross-cultural work of Franz Fanon (1963, 1967), Albert Memmi (1965), and Joseph Howard III (1972), who have written poignantly about the "social psychology of colonialism." Each has described the social processes of colonialism as a form of oppression and the impact of its social processes on colonized or oppressed people.

Thus my attention will focus on problems or impediments to an appropriate frame of reference for Black psychology, my conception of a preliminary conceptual framework for Black psychology, and an identification of the political and social action implications that flow from such a "world view."

The overriding point of view of this paper, based on my clinical experiences and personal observations, is that the nature and cause of severe

Black dysfunctions, particularly with low-income people, stem less from psychogenic factors and more from political and social oppression, although psychogenic explanations and political/economic analyses need not operate independently of each other. Despite the considerable controversy over the role and potency of political/economic and psychogenic explanations, the issue seems not to be a choice between psychogenic and political/economic variables, since in many cases, both classes of variables operate, and in fact, interact. The critical issue, from the point of view of mental health strategy, may be at what point or level should the intervention be directed. Nevertheless, the focus of the present social analysis is on the properties of the social order or social system and its relationship to human suffering, pain, and dysfunction. This social analysis need not discount the role of the family in child development, nor does it assume that all faulty child-rearing practices or other deleterious experiences can be attributed to the sociopolitical conditions. Rather, in my opinion, it demonstrates the substantial explanatory potency of a sociopolitical perspective that operates in conjunction with an analysis of individuals. The importance of a sociopolitical perspective is reflected in the recurrence of studies, based on an ecological model, which consistently demonstrate socioeconomic correlates of the incidence and prevalence of severe psychopathology (Faris and Dunham, 1939; Hollingshead and Redlich, 1958; Langer and Michael, 1963; Srole, Langer, Michael and Rennie, 1962), rates of chronic alcoholism (Faris and Dunham, 1939; Harper, 1976), and drug addiction (Drug Abuse Survey Project, 1972). In addition, there are countless other works that describe the role of racism, poverty, and other forms of sociopolitical oppression on the quality of life of Blacks in this country (Willie, Kramer, and Brown, 1973; Jones, 1972).

Nevertheless, despite the obvious association between poverty and racism and the psychological functioning of Blacks, there has been only a limited amount of work on oppression and its role in the development, precipitation, and maintenance of psychopathology. In fact, when discussions of the role of political and economic phenomena are approached, they are disguised by the use of euphemistic and more palatable terminology that refers to "disadvantaged populations," "inner city problems," and "cultural deprivation." The prominence of such terminology as a replacement for a more appropriate delineation of the details of the oppressive experiences is more than semantic. Rather, such confused terminology avoids depicting the core causes of social problems and in fact distorts the reality of Black life. This jargon or terminology shifts the cause of the problem from societal conditions to properties or traits of the "casualties" or "victims."

The "scholarly" treatment of the Black family by behavioral scientists represents a prime example of how victims and their institutions and milieus are viewed as the causes of their own problems. Scientific studies, from this vantage point, provide an endless recitation of data and statistics to describe the deteriorating family structure, high crime rates, number of welfare recipients, problems of illegitimacy, and so forth. This proclivity to focus almost exclusively on social pathology of Blacks caused Benjamin Quarles (1967), a Black historian, to note:

When we pick up a social science book, we look in the index under "Negro," it will read "see slavery," "see crime," "see juvenile delinquency," perhaps "see Commission on Civil Disorders"; perhaps see anything except the Negro. So when we try to get a perspective on the Negro, we get a distorted perspective. (p. 29)

The classic example of this social orientation is the so-called "tangle of pathology" thesis by Moynihan (1965), which utilizes correlational data to infer that there are causal relationships between the instability of the Black family and the social conditions of Blacks. Although paying "lip service" to the relationship of oppression to the social pathology in Black communities, this view implies that a kind of "culture of poverty" occurs in which certain destructive aspects of poverty become self-perpetuating and, in a sense, are functionally autonomous of external forces that spawned them and have a momentum of their own. Similarly, Albert Memmi (1965), in his study of colonialism in North Africa, describes the "mythical portrait of the colonized" which distorts the characteristics of the colonized and thereby provides rationalizations for the continued existence of colonialism as a system of oppression. More recently, William Ryan's *Blaming the Victim* (1971) provides a systematic explication of the nature and role of "victim analysis" in American thought. He concludes that "the logical outcome of an analysis of social problems in terms of the deficiencies of the victims is the development of programs aimed at correcting these deficiencies" (p. 4). For instance, the present emphasis on child abuse and neglect has been criticized for its almost exclusive emphasis on parental abuse without a corresponding concern with eliminating institutional or other forms of child abuse (Gil, 1971; Hilliard, 1978a). Thus, this myopic view of social problems causes a critical defect in the philosophy, content, and objectives of intervention programs.

Impediments to an Appropriate Conceptual Framework for Black Behavior

Assuming the appropriateness of a theoretical perspective that includes political and economic phenomena for Black psychology, some of the major impediments to such a view are the following:

I. AN OVEREMPHASIS ON PSYCHOGENIC/PSYCHODYNAMIC EXPLANATIONS OF BEHAVIOR

Consistent with the nature of education and training in mental health, and the attendant compartmentalization of the study of human behavior, prevailing mental health theory and practice have maintained a narrow psychogenic orientation, which excludes political phenomena. Thus mental health professionals have relied almost exclusively on variables such as self-concept, ego strength, impulse control, locus of control, passivity, the nature and adequacy of defense mechanisms as explanations for Black behavior. Joseph Howard (1972), for instance, in criticizing the apolitical orientation of mental health, noted the failure of traditional theories of dreams, dream symbolism, and dream interpretation, with their overemphasis on latent libidinal impulses, to account for the political content of dreams of oppressed people, particularly activists. As an example, he reports a dream of a Black college student in psychotherapy, at a large midwestern university during the campus protests and student rebellions in the 1960s, who was grappling with identity issues as a Black in a predominantly White university. The following scenario unfolds in her dream. In therapy the student recalled being enclosed in an all white mass or tent, of trying vainly to escape from the tent and, yet, of being afraid of breaking out. Finally, after considerable vacillation and anxiety, she burst her way out of the white mass that surrounded and engulfed her. As she burst out of the white mass, she recalls that the first things that she saw were the colors red, black, and green. She then woke up. Obviously, these colors must be interpreted as representing the liberation colors of Marcus Garvey and symbolizing her assertiveness and personal liberation as a Black.

Another political limitation in clinical theory is reflected in the psychodynamic treatment of "superego" issues focusing narrowly on morality associated with sexual and aggressive impulses. However, few theorists describe the "political superego" or morality issues that are associated with group identification and system challenging or other political behavior presented by young Black and other minority clients.

More broadly, there is a paucity of work that systematically assesses the relationship between the sociopolitical system, situational stresses, and the resulting personality issues. An exception is *The Politics of Therapy* by Seymour Halleck (1971), which outlines how political phenomena impact on personality and the consequences for psychotherapeutic intervention.

2. LIMITATIONS OF THE CLINICAL ROLE

Psychiatry and the other traditional mental health fields that followed and emulated its tradition started as service oriented approaches with the responsibility for ministering to the problems of individuals. Thus, the focus of the therapy has been the intrapsychological deficiencies of "sick" individuals. This model, largely for practical reasons, has implicitly discounted or minimized other variables that are perceived as inessential to the treatment process. In its most traditional form, it has been widely criticized as an adjustment model, designed to preserve the status quo. In fact, some accounts have suggested that the community mental health system is designed to reduce social conflict (Kenniston, 1968), a role similar to that of the social welfare system in relation to unemployment (Piven and Cloward, 1971). Thus, as an ancillary and supportive service model dealing only peripherally with core issues such as the structure of society, the nature and role of economic resources, the relationship of political power on human relationships, etc., its perspective on human development has been quite limited.

The limitations of the clinical role and its perspective are reflected in the following statements espoused by a former president of the American Psychiatric Association regarding the social role of organized mental health.

It is my opinion that psychiatric services should not be the tool for restructuring society or solving economic problems or for determining new human values. Psychiatric services should be continued as patient oriented activities designed to reduce pain and discomfort and to increase the capacity of the individual to adjust satisfactorily. . . . The purpose of community mental health centers was originally directed toward the prevention of psychiatric disorders and treatment in the community familiar to the patient. Any attempt to dilute or divert the activity of the community mental health center into a non-medical social agency or a political instrument is extremely detrimental to achieving the primary objective of providing adequate psychiatric services for all citizens. (Halleck, 1971, p. 11)

Similarly, Halleck (1971) stated, in response to political activism at a national professional conference:

I would be remiss in my convictions if I did not raise a strong protest to this sort of thing. We are psychiatrists and as such are physicians whose entire level of competency has to do with emotional and mental disorders. . . . Nor do we by virtue of being psychiatrists have any more basis for opinions in the area of politics than would a garbage collector, policeman, lawyer or secretary. Again, it seems to me that our only area of competency is in the framework of medical practice, not social work or social theorizing. (p. 12)

Although these views may be dismissed as representing an extreme position on the social role of the mental health professional, they reflect, in my opinion, a widespread point of view among mental health professionals.

3. PERSONAL FEARS ASSOCIATED WITH CHALLENGING THE POLITICAL AND
ECONOMIC SYSTEM

In addition to the influence of intellectual or cognitive determinants on
the conceptual frameworks and intervention strategies in mental health,
there are, in my opinion, powerful psychological or motivational factors
that impede a proper analysis of the basic political and economic issues
that underlie mental health issues. In fact, at times the limited perspective
of mental health professionals that fails to acknowledge the role of social
and political oppression is merely a device or "security operation" to
avoid the confrontations and personal dilemmas associated with a social
change role. The proclivity to focus almost exclusively on intrapsychic
phenomena results, at times, from what I term a "flight into psycho-
genics." Essentially, this mechanism is interpreted as avoidance behavior
designed to reduce anxiety and minimize the impending personal and
moral dilemmas. Another mechanism utilized to cope with the fears and
insecurities and, in fact, the existential dilemmas associated with confrontations with societal institutions has been referred to by the Reverend
Jessie Jackson as "the paralysis of analysis," an obsessive compulsive defense. The essential feature of this mechanism is the incessant need to collect more data in order to achieve "scientific certainty" about causes before any actions or interventions can be initiated. Again the purpose of
this security maneuver is to immobilize and to prevent any action.

Toward a Frame of Reference for Black Psychology

In an attempt not merely to criticize the prevailing efforts at conceptualizing the behaviors of Blacks, I will outline what are some of the core
principles that may serve as the foundation of a conceptual framework
for Black psychology. Although this frame of reference was designed to
understand Black behavior, it would seem to be especially applicable to
preventive mental health issues with Black people (Butler et al., 1979).
Black psychology, according to this view, may be characterized by the
following principles or guidelines.

1. A set of philosophical assumptions that provide a basis for defining a
   value system that is consistent with the essential nature of Black people and, as such, is consistent with the goal of "liberating" the Black mind.

2. A historical perspective that encompasses both the African heritage of
   Blacks and our unique experiences in this country.

3. A political/economic perspective that permits considerations of the
   relationship between the modal behavior of contemporary Blacks and
   the economic and power dynamics of White society.

4. A broad social/psychological view that facilitates the examination of the role of social institutions in determining Black behavior patterns.

Philosophical/Theoretical Assumptions

During the reexamination of formulations and approaches regarding Blacks, substantial attention is being directed to questions about the validity and appropriateness of the philosophy and the assumptions inherent in the psychological theories and approaches (Butler et al., 1979; King, 1975). At the center of these concerns is the belief that psychological theories reflect the value orientations, cultural perspective, and "world view" of the theorist and that these are responsible for the development of the theories. As an example, recent revelations about the major proponents of the IQ testing movement suggest that political ideologies may greatly influence ideas and theories that may have the trappings of scientifically based conclusions. Yet, these theoretical assumptions and philosophical premises may have far-reaching implications. As Butler et al. (1979) state, in reference to assumptions underlying a discipline:

The nature of these assumptions is critical, for the fundamental premises in which a discipline is grounded determine both the goals and methodologies that the discipline will embrace. . . . Moreover, these premises also delimit the legitimate area of study, the kind of data that will be accepted as valid, and the kinds of principles that will be invoked to explain phenomena of interest. (p. 4)

Although systematic scrutiny of the assumptions and value orientation inherent in American psychology and, indeed, in Western science has only recently begun, there are several concepts that might appropriately serve as good starting points for review. For instance, a major thrust of American psychology has been guided by the notion of "the psychology of individual differences." From this point of view, the superordinate objective of psychological inquiry has been to detect the underlying differences between people or to identify their distinguishing or unique attributes in domains such as intellectual functioning, personality, interests, etc. (that are presumed to exist). But, it would seem that assumptions and related procedures of American psychology are set up to manufacture the expected differences between people. The technology of testing represents perhaps one of the best examples of how "the presumption of individual differences" dictates the approaches that provide data to further support it. For instance, in item analysis related to test development, items are deliberately selected to differentiate between people (confirming preexisting beliefs). Test items that do not differentiate are rejected. This practice and the underlying theory place, in fact, a value on human diversity and differences, and at the same time devalue human commonality.

A corollary concept that seems to provide support for the psychology of individual differences is the normal distribution curve. In fact, although the normal distribution curve is presented as a neutral or value-free concept, it has major political and economic implications. Essentially implicit in the theoretical bell-shaped curve in which the majority of people cluster in the center, with a small percentage at each end of the curve, is a hierarchical social arrangement that influences the distribution of resources and opportunities. One of the most blatant examples of its use to order society is in the use of the normal distribution curve as the basis for distributing grades in educational settings (that is, grading on the curves). In other situations, the "curve" determines the relative place of individuals in terms of a given attribute. For instance, often the "intellectually gifted" in public education are determined not by qualitative features of intellectual performance, but by their relative position on the theoretical normal distribution curve (that is, the top 5 percent on IQ).

Nobles (1972) has similarly criticized the theoretical limitation inherent in western definitions of "self" for the emphasis on the "I" rather than the "we" as reflective of a more individualistic orientation. In contrast, he describes the extended self-concept—or the "we"—as reflecting a more collective orientation, which he sees as more compatible with the ethos of African people.

In summary, the view expressed is that in order to develop a psychology appropriate for the study of Blacks, the underlying philosophical and theoretical premises must be compatible with the nature and social condition of Black people. The assumption and approaches of scientific inquiry must likewise be reexamined in order to insure their appropriateness.

HISTORICAL ANALYSIS

An axiomatic principle of psychology is the notion that in addition to the role of contemporary forces, human behavior is shaped by prior experiences and events. In fact, a historical perspective is as essential to an understanding of a people as a longitudinal developmental analysis is to the understanding of individual Blacks. Yet psychologists have traditionally ignored the historical context within which Black behavior is situated, which would provide critical information and data relative to Blacks and Whites. A proper historical analysis, while outlining the critical and potent role of slavery in determining contemporary Black behavior, must involve a treatment of African history prior to slavery in the United States. Clark (1972) criticizes others' objections to the study of Black historical events as having happened "too long ago" to have contemporary relevance. Nevertheless, a number of accounts have identified, for instance, African retentions in the language patterns of Blacks in the United States (Turner, 1949; Smith, 1978), while others have described the philosophical and religious orientation and patterns of family life as African in origin (Nobles, 1972, 1974).

Numerous other historical accounts have described in great detail the brutalizing nature of slavery and racism and its impact on individual Blacks and institutions. In fact, Nobles (1977), in *A Formative and Empirical Study of Black Families: Final Report*, found that the second most prevalent theme of stories that the Black families reported being told by their parents as children was the impact of slavery on the ancestors of Black people. This empirical study, then, provides quantitative documentation of the saliency of memories of slavery in the present.

A companion clinical study that similarly points out the force of historical experiences in influencing contemporary Black behaviors examined the military trials of the Black Marines involved in confrontations with the White Marines who were self-avowed Ku Klux Klansmen (Hilliard, 1978b). Using extensive clinical data from examinations of the Black defendants, 10 of the 14 of whom were from the deep South, a "collective consciousness" of Blacks was identified, which was amplified by the Black Marines' own personal experiences of racism and bigotry in growing up and in the military. These unique historical and cultural factors that Blacks share as a group combined with situational and personal factors to determine their response. Again, these studies suggest the need to examine historical factors systematically in order to understand the behavior of Blacks.

POLITICAL/ECONOMIC PERSPECTIVE

As stated previously, there is a particular need to delineate the relationship between Black psychology and political/economic variables. Perhaps, the clearest example of the relationship between political and economic factors and the psychology of Black people is reflected in the history of slavery. That is, slavery in America provides one of the best examples of how an entire society and its institutional practices, including religious, educational, and legal institutions, worked conjointly to support the subjugation of Black people for economic gain. Winthrop Jordan (1968) traces in elaborate detail the changes in attitudes, and the development of well articulated anti-Negro attitudes, as the need for slave labor increased. Similarly, Higgenbotham (1978) describes the process of developing legal doctrine to justify and ensure an effective subjugation of Blacks. These and other studies of slavery in the United States provide a political/economic basis to the development of racism, rather than basing it on primarily psychological motivation. At times, the misreading of the history of slavery has caused the misconception that slavery was as Rhodes and Montrero (1968) state, a relationship "between individual slaves and slaveowners rather than essentially social relations between metropolitan White society and colonial Black society in which the rapid development of the former society occasioned the veritable destruction of the other." Franz Fanon, in his study of colonialism and oppression, has warned that racism should not be considered as an individual trait or "quirk," but rather as the most visible sign of a more systemized oppression. In describing the psychological consequences of this "organized domination," Fanon (1967) states:

The social group, militarily and economically subjugated, is dehumanized in accordance with a polydimensional method. Exploitations, tortures, raids, racism, collective liquidation, rational oppression take turns at different levels to make of the native an object. . . . Because no other solution is left, the racialized group tries to imitate the oppressor and thereby tries to deracialize itself. (p. 35)

Although the writings of Franz Fanon and Albert Memmi draw on their experiences in more well-defined colonial situations in Africa, both writers were well aware of the parallels between the colonial situations and the social conditions of Blacks in the United States.

A more recent body of studies suggests a continuation of direct relationships between political and economic variables and Black psychology, and indeed, Black psychopathology. For instance, Brenner in his book, *Mental Illness and the Economy* (1973), provides empirical data to demonstrate the relationship between the economy and the rate of mental illness. Using admission rates to mental hospitals in New York State as the measure of mental illness, he examines the effect of periods of economic instability, such as the Great Depression in the 1930s and recessions on the incidence of major mental illness. Brenner concludes, in contradiction to previous studies of the relationship of the Great Depression to mental illness by Komora and Clark (1935) and Pollocks (1935), that there is an inverse relationship between the state of the economy and mental illness, which has been stable over the past 127 years.

Brenner's analysis is in agreement with the research of Dohrenwend (1973) on the relationship of social status—or more appropriately, socioeconomic positions—to exposure to stressful life events. Not surprisingly, her research, which indicates that low social status groups experience more stressful life events such as death in the family, marital breakdown, job loss, etc., is consistent with the research of Brown and Birley (1968) on the relationship of stressful events to the presence of schizophrenia, and severe depression, respectively. This study by Dohrenwend (1973) further suggests that Blacks have more exposure to stressful life events than ethnic groups with higher social status.

The foregoing studies strongly suggest the relationship between economic, political and social stresses, and psychopathology, particularly among poor people. The impact of these stresses may be experienced directly by individuals or more directly through undermining or destroying basic social institutions that are responsible for Black development, survival, or support. For instance, variables such as limited economic resources, underemployment, or unemployment, poor housing conditions, meager health and nutritional resources may have a direct impact on the mental health of individuals or groups. However, in addition, political and economic stresses that have an indirect but deleterious influence on primary social institutions such as the family, education, and mass media may be more insidious. Frequently, in fact, social policies are espoused, such as the "best interests of children" or "the least detrimental alternative," which profess commitment to the quality of life of children, without a corresponding emphasis on strengthening the basic social institutions responsible for their nurture and development.

SOCIAL-PSYCHOLOGICAL PERSPECTIVE

A critical aspect of a broad social-psychological perspective in conceptualizing Black psychology is the role of the major social institutions or agents of socialization. Traditionally, the responsibility for socialization of the young has been delegated to institutions such as the family, religion, and education. These institutions have provided permanence and continuity for cultural traditions, mores, norms, and values. At an individual level these institutions have been major determinants of identity, morality, beliefs, attitudes, political awareness, and so forth, and thus, in a real sense, influence personal and personality development. However, although these institutions retain a major responsibility for Black child development, in recent years there has been an apparent rearrangement of the role and potency of the various social institutions in relationship to Blacks. These major changes in social institutions, which have had the net effect of reducing the control of the Black community, particularly the Black family, over the socialization process of children, include the following:

1. The reduction in the role and influence of religion
2. The diminished role of the Black community in policy decisions in public schools largely due to the nature of implementation of desegregation in public education
3. The ascendance of the mass media, particularly television, as a major social institution

Although recognizing the role of the Black family in socialization, and to a lesser extent religion, the focus of this section is primarily on providing a very brief overview of the role of education and the mass media. The rationale underlying this emphasis reflects the belief that in a mechanistic and technologically oriented society, these institutions, over which the Black community has minimal influence, have usurped much of the traditional role of the family in socialization.

The role of education as a social institution is critical at every level for its role is far greater than merely providing technical skills, it also has a major role in transmitting a cultural perspective. As Maulana Ron Karenga (1969) stated: "Education . . . is basically a political thing and it provides identity, purpose, and direction within an American context" (p. 39). This cultural perspective is reflected in curriculum content, books and materials, formal and informal communications by staff, and the role modeling that occurs in relationship to the major personnel that staff the schools. The educational literature contains voluminous evidence of the deleterious consequences of American education for Black children. In commenting on the widespread devaluation of Blacks that occurs in public schools, Butler et al. (1979) warn:

Public schools have traditionally made use of content and practices that rob children of self-esteem and encourage an identification with White mainstream culture and a rejection of Black culture. For example, until recently, primary education programs generally exposed children to readers and fictional literature that contained exclusively White characters acting in predominantly middle-class milieus. Moreover, children's books . . . such as "The Hardy Boys," "The Bobbsey Twins" and "Tom Sawyer" consistently depicted Blacks as lazy, ignorant, and subservient to Whites, and consistently referred to Blacks . . . as "niggers," "darkies" and "coons." (p. 16)

The devaluation of Black children that is experienced in educational institutions ranges from a general contempt toward Black culture and experiences, abuses of standardized testing that culminate in the disproportionate and inappropriate assignments of Blacks to lower tracks, to overt racism. Obviously, the negative impact of these experiences, which have increased with the widespread removal and demotion of Black administrators under current desegregation practices, have major implications for the mental health of Black children.

During the post-1950s period, the mass media—particularly television—have demonstrated a substantial increase in potency as a social institution. The powerful role that television has in the shaping of the informational base and world view, as well as attitudes, beliefs, and identity, particularly of Black children, has been supported by research data. Several studies have concluded that:

1. Black children spend a disproportionate amount of time watching television, in comparison to their White counterparts (Bogart, 1962; Greenberg and Dominick, 1969).

2. In general, the total time spent by Black children watching television is greater than time spent in classrooms (Greenberg and Atkin, 1978).

3. There is a substantial belief by children that what they view on television is real (Greenberg and Reeves, 1976).

These data on the television viewing habits of Black and other minority children must be read in conjunction with other data that indicate the overall exclusion of Black characters, the racism inherent in the images, the low status of Black characters, and so forth (Bay Area Association of Black Psychologists, 1973; Black Efforts for Soul in Television, 1972; Butler et al., 1979; Greenberg and Atkin, 1978). These research studies suggest the potential of television, particularly in the formative years of children, for molding self-concept or identity, level of aspirations, values, and coping styles.

Although limitations of time and space have precluded an overview of the socializing role of other forms of the mass media, such as movies, newspapers, or magazines, suffice it to say that they might be reasonably inferred to present the same problems.

IMPLICATIONS FOR SOCIAL AND POLITICAL ACTION

The point of view expressed throughout the paper is merely that the mental health of Blacks is inextricably tied to the overall economic, political, and social status of Black people. Simply stated: Unless there is a substantial reduction in the political and economically based oppression, there will not be an overall improvement in mental health. From this vantage point, mental illness as a large scale social problem is inherently a political and economic problem requiring political and economic solutions. Thus the present one-to-one model of patient care has no potential for a substantial reduction in the incidence and prevalence of mental illness or human suffering. Societal conditions are manufacturing psychiatric casualties more quickly and in greater numbers than we have the capacity to treat effectively now or in the foreseeable future. Thus, any substantial mental health strategy for Blacks must align itself with the total liberation struggle of Black people.

The starkness or bleakness of this assessment of the one-to-one clinical model should not be interpreted as an evaluation of its social utility, for if it can truly demonstrate that it is a viable modality for bolstering the human spirit, stimulating maximum utilization of psychic resources or relieving psychic pain and suffering, these are not achievements that are easily dismissed. Yet mental health strategy must also be evaluated in terms of its potential for the reduction of mental dysfunction as a social problem rather than merely individual dysfunction.

The purpose of this paper was not to attempt to define the specific political actions or tactics to be utilized in eradicating the social conditions generating mental illness and minimizing growth or mental health. Suffice it to say that the full range of political and social actions utilized for social change are appropriate. The objective of this paper, then, was to provide a theoretical context within which to place mental health theory and practice with Blacks.

References

Albee, G. W. The relation of conceptual models to manpower needs. In E. L. Cowen, E. A. Gardener, and M. Zax (Eds.), *Emergent approaches to mental health problems.* New York: Appleton-Century-Crofts, 1967.

Bay Area Association of Black Psychologists. *The effects of children's television programming in Black children.* Position paper presented by Dr. Carolyn Block to Federal Communications Commission, January 1973, Washington, D.C.

Black efforts for soul in television, Content analysis of Black and minority treatment on children's television. Best, Action for Children's Television, 1972.

Bogart, L. American television: A brief survey of research findings. *Journal of Social Issues,* 1962, *18*(2), 36–42.

Brenner, M. H. *Mental illness and the economy.* Cambridge: Harvard University Press, 1973.

Brown, G., and Birley, I. Crises and life changes and the onset of schizophrenia. *Journal of Health and Social Behavior,* 1968, *9,* 203–214.

Butler, P., Khatib, S., Hilliard, T., Howard, J., Reid, J., Wesson, K., Wage, G., and Williams, O. In R. L. Jones (Ed.), *Sourcebook on teaching in Black psychology: Perspectives and course outlines,* Vol. 1, 1–29. Washington, D.C.: Association of Black Psychologists, 1979.

Clark, C. Black studies or the study of Black people? In R. L. Jones (Ed.), *Black psychology.* New York: Harper & Row, 1972.

Dohrenwend, B. S. Social status and stressful life events. *Journal of Personality and Social Psychology,* 1973, *28,* 225–235.

Douglass, F. West India emancipation speech, August, 1857. In P. S. Foner (Ed.), *Frederick Douglass.* New York: Citadel Press, 1969.

Drug Abuse Survey Project. *Dealing with drug abuse.* New York: Praeger Publishers, 1972.

Fanon, F. *The wretched of the earth.* New York: Grove Press, 1963.

Fanon, F. *Toward the African revolution.* New York: Grove Press, 1967.

Faris, R., and Dunham, H. *Mental disorders in urban areas.* Chicago: University of Chicago Press, 1939.

Gil, D. G. A socio-cultural perspective on physical child abuse. *Child Welfare,* 1971, *50*(7), 389–395.

Greenberg, B. S., and Atkin, C. *Learning about minorities from television: The research agenda.* (Paper prepared for conference.) Television and the Socialization of the Minority Child, Center for Afro-American Studies, University of California, Los Angeles, April 1978.

Greenberg, B., and Dervin, B., with the assistance of J. Dominick and J. Bower. *Use of mass media by the urban poor.* New York: Praeger Publishers, 1972.

Greenberg, B., and Dominick, J. Racial and social class differences in teenagers' use of television. *Journal of Broadcasting*, 1969, *13*, 3331–3344.

Greenberg, B., and Reeves, B. Children and the perceived reality of television. *Journal of Social Issues*, 1976, *32*, 86–97.

Griffin, M. The influence of race on the psychotherapeutic relationship. *Psychiatry*, 1977, *40*, 27–40.

Halleck, S. *The politics of therapy*. New York: Science House, Inc., 1971.

Harper, F. *Alcohol abuse and Black America*. Alexandria, Va.: Douglas Publishers, 1976.

Higgenbotham, L. *In the matter of color*. New York: Oxford University Press, 1978.

Hilliard, T. Psychology, law and the Black community. *Law and Human Behavior*, 1978, *2*, 10–131. (a)

Hilliard, T. *The Ku Klux Klan and the Black Marines*. Unpublished paper, 1978. (b)

Hollingshead, A. B., and Redlich, R. C. *Social class and mental illness*. New York: Wiley & Sons, 1958.

Howard, J. Toward a social psychology of colonialism. In R. L. Jones (Ed.), *Black psychology*. New York: Harper & Row, 1972.

Howard, J. H. *The political socialization of the black community*. (Unpublished paper) Annual Convention of Association of Black Psychologists, San Francisco, Calif., 1972.

Joint Commission on Mental Illness and Mental Health. *Action for mental health*. New York: Basic Books, 1961.

Jones, E. Social class and psychotherapy: A critical review of research. *Psychiatry*, 1974, *37*, 307–320.

Jones, R. L. *Black psychology*. New York: Harper & Row, 1972.

Jones, R. L. *Sourcebook on teaching in Black psychology*. Washington, D.C.: Association of Black Psychologists, 1979.

Jordan, W. *White over Black*. Chapel Hill: University of North Carolina Press, 1968.

Karenga, M. R. The black community and the university: A community organizer's perspective. In A. Robinson, C. Foster, and D. Ogilvie (Eds.), *Black studies in the university*. New Haven: Yale University Press, 1969.

Kenniston, K. How community mental health centers stamped out the riots. *Transactions*, 1968, *5*, 21–29.

Kessler, M., and Albee, G. Primary prevention. *Annual Review of Psychology*, 1975, *26*, 557–591.

King, L. (Ed.). *African philosophy: Assumptions and paradigms for research on Black people*. Proceedings for the First Annual J. Alfred Cannon Research Series Conference, April 1975.

Komora, P., and Clark, M. Mental disease in the crisis. *Mental Hygiene*, 1935, *19*, 289–301.

Langer, T. S., and Michael, S. T. *Life stress and mental health: The midtown Manhattan study*, Vol. 2. New York: Free Press, 1963.

Memmi, A. *The colonizer and the colonized*. Boston: Beacon Press, 1965.

Moynihan, D. *The Negro family: The case for national action*. Office of Policy Planning and Research, United States Department of Labor. U.S. Government Printing Office, March 1965.

Nobles, W. African philosophy: Foundations for Black psychology. In R. L. Jones, *Black psychology*. New York: Harper & Row, 1972.

Nobles, W. African roots and American fruit: The Black family. *The Journal of Social and Behavioral Sciences*, 1974, *20*, 66–77.

Nobles, W. *A formative and empirical study of black families: Final report.* Washington, D.C.: Office of Child Development, 1977.

Piven, F., and Cloward, R. *Regulating the poor.* New York: Vintage, 1971.

Pollocks, H. The depression and mental disease in New York state. *American Journal of Psychiatry*, 1935, *91*, 736–771.

Quarles, B. Quoted in R. Staples, *The Black Family*. Belmont, Calif.: Wadsworth Publishing Co., 1971.

Rhodes, R., and Montrero, A. Papers on colonialism, 1968–69. Unpublished.

Roth, R., Berenbaum, H. L., and Hershenson, D. *The developmental theory of psychotherapy: A systematic eclecticism.* Unpublished paper, Illinois Institute of Technology, 1967.

Ryan, W. *Blaming the victim.* New York: Vintage, 1971.

Smith, E. A. *The retention of the phonological, phonemic, and morphophonemic features of Africa in Afro-American ebonics.* Seminar series paper, Department of Linguistics at California State University (Fullerton), 1978.

Srole, L., Langer, T., Michael, S., and Rennie, T. A. *Mental health in the metropolis: Midtown Manhattan study*, Vol. 1. New York: McGraw-Hill, 1962.

Turner, L. *Africanisms in the Gullah dialect.* Chicago: University of Chicago Press, 1949.

Willie, C., Kramer, B., and Brown, B. *Racism and mental illness.* Pittsburgh: University of Pittsburgh Press, 1973.

"Mediacracy": Mass Media and Psychopathology

David Manning White

> Philosophers apply the term sickness to all disturbances of the soul, and they say that no foolish person is free from such sickness; sufferers from disease are not sound, and the souls of all unwise persons are sick.
>
> Cicero *Tusculanarum Disputatium III.iv.9*

If anyone doubts that the American people are intrigued, mesmerized or maybe simply titillated by accounts of psychopathological behavior, consider the popularity of the 1974 motion picture *The Exorcist*. One of my students (by no means a dullard or externally any more neurotic than his classmates) confided that he had seen the film no less than six times during its eight-month run in Boston. Perhaps he should have shaken hands with the Chicago housewife who claims to have seen Alfred Hitchcock's *Psycho* no less than 14 times.

Why a movie such as *The Exorcist* could and did have such box-office appeal, grossing enough dollars to place it fourth in earnings of the more than 40,000 feature films that have been produced this century, is a question that is central to this paper. This film about a young girl possessed by a demon was prima facie so ridiculous that even the Roman physician, Galen, would have laughed at it 1700 years ago. True witchcraft and demonology dominated medical thought and medieval times, but by the 16th century physicians like Paracelsus were challenging demoniacal explanations. Indeed, Hippocrates a thousand years before had refused to accept the idea that mental disturbances were caused by the intercession of gods or by demons who possessed one's body. Not that Hippocrates, brilliant as he was in recognizing many of the classical symptoms of paranoia, for example, was without his foibles. Although he correctly perceived that hysteria was a mental disease, his cultural prejudices convinced him that it was limited to women. As he viewed it, hysteria was caused by the wandering of the uterus through the body, symbolizing the body's yearning for the production of a baby. His remedy for hysteria: marriage.

154   DAVID MANNING WHITE

That in the 1970s so patently hysterical a motion picture as *The Exorcist* induced the American public to donate nearly $100 million to Warner Brothers is a prime example of the power of exploitation, which is the cornerstone of *mediacracy*.

This term was coined by Kevin Phillips, who is rightly concerned about the concentration of persuasive power in increasingly fewer communications conglomerates. Although I share some of his anxiety about their power, it seems too simplistic to state that even gigantic conglomerates like the Columbia Broadcasting System, Gulf and Western, Time Inc., or the Los Angeles Times-Mirror Co. are the molders per se of something as complex as our political behavior or moral values (Halberstam, 1979). Rather, as I hope to make clear, my argument with the mediacrats is that they are the major collaborators in the demeaning and vulgarizing of America. And although I cannot substantiate my hypothesis with a body of studies from the literature of social science, except inferentially, I firmly believe that the mass media contribute, perhaps unwittingly, in various ways to psychopathological behavior in America.

Having said this, let me make it clear that I am not about to launch an *ad hominem* attack a la Spiro Agnew against the mass media. Since at one time or another during my lifetime I have worked as a newspaper reporter and editorial writer, as editor of several magazines, in radio and television as a news commentator, and in several phases of book publishing, I am not about to have a dramatic conversion en route to Damascus. Although I have many caveats about the mass media, they are not voiced in anger, but I do believe sincerely that the image of America that the mass media reflect, promulgate and, in some cases, instigate and reinforce is inimical to our best mental health. Throughout this century, social critics such as Upton Sinclair and George Seldes have pointed out that the mass media are essentially amoral, but the question of who is injured is seldom raised as long as the corporate ledgers show healthy gains.

Corporate amorality can injure individuals. For example: On September 10, 1974, NBC broadcast a two-hour movie for television called *Born Innocent*, starring Linda Blair as a runaway adolescent committed by her parents to a detention center. During the course of the film Blair is "initiated" into the center's way of life by a gang-rape in a communal shower. The scene was depicted with extremely graphic realism. Suddenly the water stops and a look of fear comes into Blair's face. Four adolescent girls are standing across the shower room. One is carrying a plumber's helper, the sort of plunger that most of us use to unclog stopped-up drains. She is waving the plunger near her hips. The older girls tell Blair to get out of the shower, and she steps out fearfully. Thereupon the four girls violently attack the younger girl, wrestling her to the floor. She is shown naked from the waist up, struggling, as the older girls force her legs apart. Then, the girl with the plunger is shown making intense thrusting motions with the handle until one of the four says, "That's enough."

Four days after the broadcast a violent scuffle occurred on a beach near San Francisco, and before it was over a 9-year-old girl had been sexually assaulted with a beer bottle. The subsequent negligence suit brought by the girl's mother against NBC raises many difficult sociological as well as constitutional questions.

What was the responsibility of the network? Should it not have known that impressionable young viewers might imitate the violent dramatic scene? After legal maneuvering by the highly skillful lawyers NBC could afford to hire, the case narrowed down to whether the movie actually "incited" the real-life attack. Eventually the lawsuit was dismissed when the judge ruled it was necessary to prove that NBC "intended" viewers to imitate the sexual attack depicted on *Born Innocent*. There will be future cases like this, I would venture, for sooner or later we are going to have to come to grips with the effects of TV on human conduct. It is small solace to the victim for some network apologist to express regret but temper it with the reflection there were probably hundreds of thousands of young people watching *Born Innocent* that night and only this small handful of kids in California "acted out" in this pathological manner.

One knows that the network recognized that the film might offend or disturb some viewers because it inserted the usual advisory legend at the beginning of the program: "The following program *Born Innocent* deals in a realistic and forthright manner with the confinement of juvenile offenders and its effect on their lives and personalities. We suggest that you consider whether the program should be viewed by young people or others in your family who might be disturbed by it."

As a matter of fact such disclaimers generally have the opposite effect, and I suspect that any veteran television network official would acknowledge that this is so, unless he or she were on the witness stand in a future case of the same kind. Very few parents monitor what their children are watching, and with two or three sets not uncommon in a home, one of them in the children's bedroom or den, it is becoming increasingly difficult to do so.

The question that we in the larger court of public opinion may have to answer is whether such media fare can be justified if indeed only 1/1000 of one percent of the youngsters who see it could be influenced in this way.

I am not implying that the producer of *Born Innocent* or the network official who scheduled it are villainous scoundrels who need to be publicly flogged. There are, indeed, some critics of the mass media who are sure that the violent, flamboyant quality of many television programs, mass magazines, Hollywood films, or rock music recordings is due to some plot on the part of the media moguls. The gatekeepers of the media, on the other hand, often rationalize such products as *Born Innocent* or *The Exorcist* by insisting that they are giving the Great American Public what it wants.

How do they know what the public wants? That is easy—the proof is in the cash box, and in a country where Mammon is a very influential god, money talks in convincing tones.

Is it spiteful to single out the mass media for their role in reinforcing an economic system that rewards it so munificently? According to Nicholas Johnson, former member of the Federal Communications Commission, the television industry averages an 82 percent return *each year* on depreciated capital. Many of us became irate when the oil industry had one of its best years in 1978, but the percentage of profit in the television industry was three times as great. Yet why pick on the mass media, when as Gossage (1961) once pointed out, the very stability of our economic system seems to rest on a magic device, the good old pyramid club. Are we not locked into a system that demands ever-expanding production, which in turn needs an ever-expanding population with a concomitant ever-expanding consumption? While respectable economists nervously watch the Gross National Product as if it were devised on Mount Sinai, most Americans play a kind of chain-letter pyramid game. There has to be a sounder approach to the economic cycle than endlessly consuming more and more, but if there is, the mass media, which rely on advertising for their life blood, do not want to discover it. In not very subtle ways the mass media continually tell us that if we want an affluent life in this country we must acquire a lot of wealth and material goods. The trouble with this message is that only a few thousand ever acquire enough money to stop the quest for it; for the rest it is an elusive, alluring brass ring that the mass media say is the alpha and omega of life.

Within a few years the Gross National Product of this country may reach two *trillion* dollars. What do we produce of such lasting value that costs 80,000 times more than the Louisiana Purchase? Even today the personal consumption expenditure by Americans is about one and a quarter trillion dollars, and if the not-very-hidden persuaders of Madison Avenue have their way we will spend more and more each year. We had better, they tell us, lest the pyramid crumble and we slide into a recession or God forbid, a repetition of the 1930s depression.

Where do we spend all that money? One major area is our mass communications system and the goods and services it produces. It is not possible to separate economic events and their impact on the mass media, nor to understand the clout of mediacracy without examining a few current trends. For example, take the record industry. Whether you bought an album of Sir Georg Solti leading the Chicago Symphony in Bruckner's Ninth Symphony or Rasputin and the Freaked-Out Monks in their last rock assault on the human ear, the list price on the albums in the last few months went up at least a dollar. That is because oil is used to make phonograph records, and as the OPEC nations dramatically raised the price of crude oil on the world market, the cost was passed on to the consumer. Despite this price increase the record industry is thriving and expects to gross more than $3 billion in 1979. Among these albums is one by a group known as the Bee Gees, the sound track for a film called *Saturday Night Fever*, which since its release in 1977 has grossed nearly $350 million.

When a motion picture such as *Star Wars* earns more than $200 million in domestic rentals alone, topping even the bonanza of a 1975 film *Jaws*, it is quite evident that the big films of the movie industry earn the much-coveted megabucks. In the world of mediacracy, the Radio Corporation of America (which owns NBC, Random House, Modern Library and Hertz Rental Cars) must be the world's leading entertainment company with over $5 billion in sales each year.

In 1896, when Adolph Ochs bought the then ailing *New York Times* for $1 million the price seemed so high that many newspaper aficionados questioned his fiscal sanity. Today the New York Times Co. has yearly sales of nearly $500 million, and in addition to the *Times* owns six dailies and four weeklies in Florida, three dailies in North Carolina, mass circulation magazines such as *Family Circle*, radio stations in New York and Memphis, and three book publishing companies.

There was a time when large newspaper chain owners such as Samuel I. Newhouse expanded their acquisitions by buying up independent newspapers, but the trend today is for the big chains to swallow up the smaller ones. Thus in 1976 Newhouse bought the eight newspapers in the Booth chain, which included *Parade*, the Sunday magazine supplement, for $300 million. An even bigger deal was consummated in June, 1979, when the Gannett chain, which already owned 77 daily newspapers and 19 weeklies in 32 states acquired the Cincinnati *Enquirer*, the Oakland (Calif.) *Tribune*, 7 television and 13 radio stations from Combined Communications Corporation. The price ticket for this merger, a mere $370 million.

In the kingdom of mediacracy the prime minister is advertising. During this decade nearly $300 billion will be spent on advertising in the United States. One is faced with the question: Why has the national yearly advertising budget risen so fast, from about $3 billion in 1945 to more than 10 times that amount today? Even allowing for inflation and a growth in our population this is an unhealthy rise.

Perhaps the consumer has reached a point of commercial saturation. What then follows is a kind of Hegelian thesis, antithesis and synthesis, with the big corporations having to spend more and more money to snag the attention of us consumers. Our antithesis is to build more immunity, and in turn, Proctor and Gamble develops newer and costlier ways to wash our rebellious minds with soap—and thus the triad begins again. I question whether it really takes a $31-billion sledgehammer to drive a 31-cent thumbtack.

But maybe even more important when I read that giant mediacrats like Newhouse or Gannett are willing to pay more than one-third of a billion dollars to augment their media empires I am deeply concerned. Let me reiterate that my concern is not that these media moguls desire to control American public opinion via news or editorials. Not since the heyday of William Randolph Hearst has this approach been prevalent. Rather, my concern is that by the very fact of investing such vast sums of money in acquiring more newspapers, television stations, or magazines, their dominant motive is to make even more money. Thus the cycle of ever-increasing consumption grows and grows. Although I cannot substantiate my convictions with any large-scale study, I firmly believe that this false socioeconomic policy, which the media reinforce in their never-ending quest to look better to their stockholders, contributes significantly to the soil in which psychopathology thrives.

The average American adult spends nearly half of the waking hours of his or her life in some involvement with the mass media. Of the 16 waking hours, 4 are spent in front of a television set, 30 minutes or so reading a newspaper, 15 minutes with one or more of the 10,000 magazines published in this country, and about 2 and a half hours listening to radio (much of this while driving to and from work). Add an occasional excursion to a movie theater, reading a paperback thriller or mystery, playing $3 billion worth of the phonograph records or tapes Americans are buying each year, and the average is just about eight hours a day. Remember there are 60 "free" hours from Friday at 5 P.M. until 7 A.M. on Monday, when one gets ready for another working week (White, 1978).

The mass media are the primary agents of our popular culture, a multifaceted, pervasive process by which most Americans decide what they buy, what style of clothes they wear, what they eat, and certainly how they spend their leisure hours or otherwise acculturate themselves in a mass society. As Shakespeare wrote in *Antony and Cleopatra* (v, i): "When such a spacious mirror's set before him, He needs must see himself." The mass media provide this "spacious mirror," which we enter in some ineluctable way. But as the poet Rainer Marie Rilke (1923) so aptly perceived, we become a part of the mirror even as the mirror simultaneously becomes ingrained in our personal life style.

The average worker in America today has about 2,750 hours of leisure each year (after we subtract the work week, eight hours of sleep each night, eating, bathing, commuting). Why, then, are the mass media so seductive of these hardwon leisure hours? Perhaps because the seductee is getting what he or she has always yearned for, a partial, palatable answer to the questions all people ask themselves, whether they are steel workers in Dannemora or philosophers ambling down Brattle Street on their way to the Yard: Who am I, why am I here in this particular body with eyes that are too set apart and no upper lip, what is the meaning (if any) of my life vis-à-vis the universe?

Throughout recorded history most people have sought anodynes from the deepest anxieties about their existence. Without question, they did so before any aspects of mass culture pervaded their society. Karl Jaspers (1949) quotes an Egyptian chronicler of 4,000 years ago who wrote: "Robbers abound; no one ploughs the land. People are saying: 'We do not know what will happen from day to day.' The country is spinning round and round like a potter's wheel. Great men and small agree in saying: 'Would that I had never been born.' The masses are like timid sheep without a shepherd; impudence is rife" (p. 238).

One wonders how that same Egyptian commentator would react to the national news broadcast by any of our television networks. Almost any day of the year we can hear and see some aspects of the almost insuperable problems of overpopulation, poverty, the rape of the earth's resources, not to mention the ever-present potentiality of atomic apocalypse, whether from some malfunction at another Three Mile Island plant or the paranoid miscalculation of a Dr. Strangelove in Moscow, Washington, or Tripoli. During the six decades of my life more than 50 *million fellow human beings* have died in wars, genocides, and other sundry forms of violence alone.

Most people do not want to contemplate the almost incalculable amount of violence occurring during their lifetime. They seek escape from the terrifying implications of many aspects of contemporary living, and the mass media are only too glad to accommodate them. And I do not mean to exclude myself behind some mask of elitist hauteur. I have indulged in so much media lotus-eating that any supercilious comments about the great, vulgar mass of Americans would make me an insufferable hypocrite.

In the late 1940s the mediacrats quickly surmised the seductive power of the television set. The potential profits were so staggering that they found it hard to believe. But even they could not realize that it would take only a generation to acculturate this country into a nation of videots. The 28-hour a week average that American adults (children under 12 watch a great deal more) spend inertly in front of their sets amounts to

1456 hours a year, or about a quarter of their total waking hours. This means that if the addiction to television continues unabated (and there are no signs that its popularity has waned appreciably) a one-year-old child, whose life expectancy will probably be greater than 75 years, will spend at least 110,000 total hours of his or her life willingly chained to our contemporary version of Plato's cave.

Television is a low-involvement medium that usually requires very little concentration from the viewer. It spews forth an incredible amount of what Steve Allen called "junk food for the mind." When the networks, either in a twinge of conscience, or more likely because they worry that the Federal Communications Commission may license them the way it does individual stations, air an occasional documentary, they invariably get a poor rating. Q.E.D., say the mediacrats, the audience does not care about quality programming. Perhaps they are right, but 30 years of mental pap and aesthetic mush 95 percent of the programmed time is hardly conducive to creating a climate for quality programming.

At a conference on television held at the University of Southern California, Richard Wald (1978), former head of NBC News and now senior vice president of ABC News put it very honestly. "TV harps on a very few themes," he said. "Only those eternal verities—lust, violence, sins and virtues—cut across all lines and make broad waves. These themes have always been with us, and in the past we might have confronted them on occasion, such as when we went to the theater. But now we live in a society where this is rained down upon us all the time. What is this doing to us? How is TV changing the character of modern man?"

There may be another reason for television's enormous hold on the majority of Americans, according to researchers such as Herbert Krugman, Peter Crown, and Sidney Weinstein. Utilizing brain-wave experiments over the past decade they and others have verified that television puts people into a nonthinking alpha state, the condition that occurs when someone is relaxed, passive, and unfocused (Krugman, Crown, and Weinstein, cited in Siegel, 1979).

Most of us at one time or another have slipped into a predominantly alpha state when we are day dreaming or looking at the glowing embers in our fireplace at the end of an arduous day as we start to drift off to sleep. Although our brain is always full of different types of waves, the alpha waves dominate while we watch television. We know that it is almost impossible to remain in an alpha state if one is paying visual attention or actively thinking about something. Perhaps this research only confirms what most of us knew intuitively, that TV like drugs or alcohol is a way to blot out the real world, to retreat into a nonthinking state where worry and anxieties are momentarily displaced.

As Anthony Burgess once pointed out, while hundreds of thousands die all over the world from lack of food, in this country it is a sign of poverty if one does not have a refrigerator. The poverty we individually seem most often to fall victim to is of the emotional or spiritual variety, but most Americans cannot bear to have that pointed out to them. Hence this mass escapism via the media of popular culture, especially television, which most viewers think is free. That, of course, is nonsense, for who do they think is paying the $30 billion each year in advertising but themselves? The world of television is a fantasy world.

Still, allowing a fantasy life to take a tremendous share of one's day does not seem to help those millions of Americans who are predominantly unhappy, bored with life, frustrated, frightened, or who compulsively tune in such programs as "The Price is Right," indulging some obsessive dream that they will win a new car or a trip to Las Vegas. Perhaps they use the fantasy world of the media to compensate for disappointments in their daily lives.

Day after day, year after year of this plastic view of life, of being the ultimate consumer, the sweet target of the Big Sell eventually breaks down the will of millions of Americans to live in any kind of creative way. They turn to the mass media as a magic mirror to tell them, "Oh, yes, you're the fairest one of all (or will be if you use enough Oil of Olay). You're John Travolta and Sophia Loren and tomorrow you'll win $1 million in the lottery." And I say that this is a cruel exploitation of the *anomie* that afflicts millions upon millions of Americans.

Granted that though very few of us go through life without some anxieties, low periods, and a variety of inner struggles, somehow, after a while, most of us manage to "hang in tough" and make a rational detente with the problems that are bothering us. Not so fortunate is that 15 percent of our population whose internal conflicts cause them so overwhelming a sense of turmoil that pathological behavior is almost inevitable, particularly when the source of the difficulty is often quite obscure and the symptoms that help is needed extremely hard to identify.

How do we spot one of the walking wounded who spends his lunch hour at an adult book store perusing the latest shipment of child pornography? The human scum who produce and distribute this particularly noxious form of mass medium are sometimes punished with a misdemeanor fine. But in a lawyer-wise society in which smoke screens about the First Amendment are bandied about with solemn protestations, it should not be forgotten that the $100 million spent on kiddieporn contributes to our vaunted Gross National Product. This helps to pay the wages of a lot of people who work in paper mills or on the assembly lines of a factory that makes offset presses.

Whether the mediacracy is only the mirror for hundreds of thousands of acts each day that are violent, cruel, or pathological enough to interest or titillate the public, or whether they actually instigate such behavior begs the question. That the mass media, particularly television, are a major agent of socialization in the lives of children is beyond debate; that they become a fantasy substitute for reality by these same children when they grow into adulthood must also be considered.

As George Gerbner has shown in his long-range studies at the University of Pennsylvania, the content of television reinforces various cultural beliefs, and, likewise, the social realities of life are modified in the mind of the viewer by the image portrayed on the screen. Thus, Gerbner and Gross (1976) found that heavy viewers see the world in a much more sinister light than individuals who do not watch much television.

It is time now to offer some solutions rather than add detail upon detail to what may already seem too gloomy a jeremiad. Yet, we should recall that more than 50 years ago H. L. Mencken said essentially the same thing and this before radio and television became major factors in our mediacracy. "What ails the newspapers of the United States primarily," he said, "is the fact that their gigantic commercial development compels them to appeal to larger and larger masses of undifferentiated men, and that the truth is a commodity that the masses of undifferentiated men cannot be induced to buy" (Mencken, 1919, p. 104). This pessimistic evaluation of mediacracy was echoed by later critics such as Walter Lippmann and contemporary press critics such as Ben Bagdikian and Edward J. Epstein. If I concur, it is because the future indicates expansion of the basic corporate nature of the mass media with increasing conformity and depersonalization.

What can we do about the negative aspects of mediacracy? One thing seems certain to me: Any major solution will need to involve individuals and small groups, rather than for us to expect meaningful legislative action at the state or federal level. The most significant action would be to educate our citizenry about the patterns and practices of mediacracy. This educational process must begin very early in the child's acculturation, and I propose that the first or second grade in our public schools is not too soon. By the time the student has graduated from high school and watched 15,000 hours of television (as opposed to 12,000 hours total in his or her formal education) the narcotizing pattern of videocy is too well engrained; the mediacrats have them for the rest of their lives. Not every student, of course, but 80 to 90 percent of them.

We need to explore the ways that children can learn to be "critics" of the mass media, so that they can discern the banal and deleterious from those aspects of the media that indeed can be vivifying. With the help of some colleagues from the School of Education at my university who have expertise in primary grade curricula, I am trying to formulate this challenge into a plan of action. The best way not to be "hooked" on television, indiscriminately micturating away the days and nights of your life trying to escape from reality in tubal vassalage is to have a balanced concept of leisure.

There are other, more immediate, ways that we as individuals can show our distaste for mediacratic power. From the National Citizens' Council for Broadcasting in Washington, D.C., one can get the names of local groups in one's area who are equally concerned with the mediocre quality of television, as well as information on how to protest to a sponsor who endorses gratuitously violent programs. A small group of concerned viewers in Newton, Massachusetts, started Action for Children's Television a decade or so ago, and it has become a strong, articulate foe of some of the more amoral practices of the television industry vis-à-vis children. The PTA Action Center in Chicago will send information about its successful campaign for less violence on television programs, and it also maintains a national toll-free hot line to answer questions about the television industry.

The Communications Act of 1934, which created the Federal Communications Commission, empowered the commission to grant licenses to serve the "public convenience, interest, or necessity." A television channel is an enormously lucrative prize worth millions of dollars in profit each year in scores of cities throughout this country. Those who are lucky enough to have secured such a license ought to be regarded not solely as owners of private property with which they can do what they want, but rather as trustees of public property, that is, the air waves, and they should be called on to meet the obligations of public trust.

The Federal Communications Commission is currently engaged in hearings relative to an updating of the 1934 act, which has been obsolescent for years. Some of the questions that might be considered but probably will not be because of the powerful lobby by the three major networks are:

1. Why not license networks as well as individual stations?
2. Why do the networks allow the sponsors and advertising agencies to influence the content of their programs? Should there not be a major stipulation in the networks' license renewal that they must pledge themselves to maintain full control over their programming? There are other media which live off advertisements but do not allow advertising agencies or sponsors to dictate or censor content, but not television. As long as television permits this practice we can expect its mediocre quality to continue.

3. Should not television licenses come up for annual renewal, instead of every three years? Those stations that fail to meet their obligations should have their licenses revoked, but in an agency, which for decades has been the preserve of political hacks, the FCC has, to my knowledge, only revoked one television license in its nearly 50 years of existence.

Do the people of this country want a better system than the present mediacracy? As long as the system relies on mass circulation figures, Nielsen ratings, or corporate earnings as the dominant criteria of success, the great majority of Americans will never know what a better system could be, any more than the people in Plato's cave knew the external realities of the world in which they lived.

It is good to remember that the meaning of the word *psyche* in its Greek origin meant *soul* or *life* itself. So in a larger sense *psychopathology* signifies those elements in modern life which contaminate our spirit, as well as the more scientific meaning of mental illness. And yet that is exactly my point, even though I cannot muster a single chi-square or factor analysis to prove it. I believe that mediacracy in the United States by its lucrative pandering to the escapist tastes of Mencken's "undifferentiated masses" is, in this larger sense, responsible for much of the psychopathology that abounds. Perhaps you recall the myth about Psyche and the god Eros who fell in love with her. Despite the many ordeals inflicted by jealous Aphrodite, Zeus married the two lovers on Mount Olympus amidst great rejoicing. The day when the great power of the mass media is used for something beyond the glorification of Preparation H will be another occasion for joyous dancing on Mount Olympus.

References

Gerbner, G., and Gross, L. The scary world of TV's heavy viewers. *Psychology Today*, April, 1976, 42–43.
Gossage, H. The gilded bough: Magic and advertising. *Harper's Magazine*, May, 1961, 71–75.
Halberstam, D. *The powers that be.* New York: Random House, 1979.
Jaspers, K. *Vöm ursprung und ziel der geschichte.* Munich: R. Piper, 1949.
Mencken, H. L. *Prejudices: First series.* New York: A. A. Knopf, 1919.
Rilke, R. M. Spiegel: Noch nie hat man wissend beschrieben. From *Die sonnette am Orpheus.* Hamburg: Insel Verlag, 1923.
Siegel, B. T.V.'s effect from Alpha to Z-z-z. *Los Angeles Times*, March 11, 1979.
Wald, R. Speech at conference on "Television and Society," University of Southern California, November, 1978.
White, D. M. Popular culture: The multifaceted mirror. In D. M. White and J. Pendleton (Eds.), *Popular culture: Mirror of American life.* Del Mar, Calif.: Publishers Inc., 1978.

Economic Democracy, Education, and Social Change

Henry M. Levin

Next to our jails and the military, the workplace is the least democratic institution in America. Few constitutional protections apply to a worker as any ardent practitioner of free speech would quickly find out if he or she were to use the workplace to test the First Amendment. No Bill of Rights prevails in the workplace, for within a wide latitude the owners of capital and their managers make the basic decisions that affect not only our employment status, remuneration, and possibility of promotions, but the fine detail of our working lives is determined largely by the organization of production and the nature of the work environment. Although all of these matters have a crucial impact on the quality of our daily experiences and our well-being (see House, 1974; Kasl, 1974; and Margolis and Kroes, 1974), they are not based upon a democratic process in which we participate. Rather, they are predicated on the dictates and needs of those who own and manage the workplace (see Tawney, 1931, for a discussion of the prerogatives of private property).

But, if citizens have a right to a participatory role in the political affairs of their societies, why are they refused such a role in the workplace? Most of us have never asked this question, for as the fish is the last to discover the water, so are we the last to question the basic facts of life that have dominated our experiences and formed our consciousness. The major premise underlying this presentation is that the tyranny of the workplace is not legitimate and that every employee ought to have a right as a "citizen" of a workplace to participate in those affairs that impact on his or her life. Economic democracy then, refers to the democratic participation of workers in the decisions that affect their working lives. For illustrations and further discussion see Jenkins (1974), Zwerdling (1978), and *The Annals* (1979). How social change might make this possible is the focus of this paper.

I wish to thank Sharon Carter for her help in preparing the manuscript.

In the following pages, I will attempt to demonstrate the existence of a dialectical relation (see Ollman, 1971, chap. 5) between the educational system and the workplace that both reinforces and—at the same time— undermines the structural relations between employers and employees. Most major social institutions have the properties of both reinforcing the existing social order and at the same time creating the conditions for changing it. Probably in few cases is this as clear as in the historical relation between education and work. The next section provides a picture of the nature of work and of schooling and their connections. Following this presentation I will describe and analyze some of the responses to the present "difficulties" of the workplace that have been raised by young and overeducated workers. Finally, I will address the prospects for economic democracy and their educational implications. The purpose of this paper is to describe a rather unconventional view of social change with respect to a concrete issue, the quest for democracy in the workplace.

A Brief Synopsis of the Relation between Work and Education

For our purposes perhaps the most important single fact about work is that the vast majority (over 90 percent) of the labor force work for corporations, government agencies, and other organizations in exchange for wages and salaries rather than working as their own bosses. That is, most persons are dependent for income primarily on their own labor, which is purchased by those who own the facilities and tools that are needed for production. At the time of the founding of the nation, some four-fifths of the nonslave population worked as self-employed farmers, artisans, or merchants while owning the land, property, or tools needed for their calling. By 1880 this proportion had been reversed with some 80 percent of the population working for firms that owned the means of production and that "hired" their labor.

A second and related aspect of work is the size and centralized nature of the workplace. Rather than the small workshops, farms, and commercial establishments that characterized the late 18th and early 19th centuries, most employment became concentrated in large, bureaucratic firms by the late 19th century (see Nelson, 1975, for details). These entities have come to dominate the markets for their products as well as the demand for labor in the areas where they operate. Thus, most individuals in the labor market do not face a large number of employment opportunities among large numbers of employers, but rather there are relatively limited employment prospects concentrated among relatively few potential employers. Further, the size of these economic entities prevents new competitors from arising, since the former dominate their markets and can practice various types of anticompetitive practices. Moreover, their cozy relationships with both the government regulatory agencies as well as such large government entities as the Pentagon enable them to utilize the power of government for ensuring their profitability (see Baran and Sweezy, 1966).

A third aspect of work is its organization. A historical picture of changes in work organization is provided by Edwards (1978), Braverman (1974), and Marglin (1974). Typically the workplace is organized in a hierarchical fashion with a large number of relatively low-paid workers at the bottom, a smaller number of more highly skilled and supervisory level workers in the middle, and even fewer persons representing the various levels of management at the top. This pyramidal form of organization is based upon an extremely fragmented division of labor, where work tasks have been divided into minute and routinized functions that permit the use of relatively unskilled workers at the bottom where most of the employees are situated. Even at higher levels, there is often such a fragmentation of the productive process, that only at the very top of the organization are a few managers or executives able to relate to the entire production operation. That is, most workers, whether blue collar or white collar, are required to perform repetitive and routinized activities. They are ignorant of the larger production process, and they do not experience the satisfaction of producing a whole product. Further, their activities are highly restricted and regularized by the nature of the job, and there is little opportunity to learn new skills or to make independent judgments. Thus, most workers have very little control over the process of their work activity and have little or no opportunity to express their own ideas, insights, and individuality. While workers at higher levels and managers have increasingly more independence as one moves up the organizational hierarchy, restriction of activity is characteristic even at these levels.

A fourth important aspect of work related to the preceding ones is that given the lack of intrinsic satisfactions, most workers toil for the external rewards. Especially important in this respect is the income that is received and that can be used for consumption of goods. Thus, most workers are forced to relinquish control over the nature of their work activities as part of the wage labor contract, and the wages and salaries become the focus of their work effort. Further, because most employees do not see any possibility of receiving satisfaction from their work activity, they place their hopes in rising levels of consumption of goods and services. Thus, work is looked at as necessary drudgery that must be carried out in order to obtain a meaningful life in the sphere of buying and consumption. In short, it is the prospect of high levels of consumption that provides the major motivation for work rather than factors internal to the work process.

It is little wonder that biographies of workers (see Terkel, 1974; U.S.

Department of Health, Education, and Welfare, 1973, for example) suggest that work is stultifying to personal growth, injurious to the health, and for most persons a very disappointing experience. Most work lacks any intrinsic meaning that makes it worth doing for its own sake. While persons born into such a world must necessarily take this for granted as a requisite for a modern society that is based upon the technology that yields our high "standard of living," a number of sources of evidence argue increasingly in terms of a different interpretation. These studies argue that technology and organizational practices grew to reflect the need for domination of the workplace by its capitalist owners and for extracting profits from the workforce (see Marglin, 1974; Gintis, 1976; and Edwards, 1978). A highly centralized and bureaucratic workplace in which jobs are fragmented into repetitive and routinized tasks simplifies the extraction of labor from workers. Each employee need only follow a specific set of functions at a prescribed speed, which will depend upon the overall rate of production set by the organization and its machinery. Supervision is simplified, since productivity can be readily observed. And the simple nature of the tasks means that workers can be easily replaced if they do not do what is expected. This "efficiency" in production is often associated with the organizational dictates of Weber (1946) and the "scientific management" of F. Taylor, whose approach is analyzed by Haber (1964) and Edwards (1978).

Thus, the internal discipline and control of the workplace by the few at the top of the organization is cemented by both the hierarchy and by the extreme division of labor. Further, the worker is set apart not only from those above and below him or her, but also from fellow workers at the same level. Under conditions of high unemployment, each worker sees himself or herself as fortunate to have a job or to have steady work. Further, the possibility of promotion up the pyramid depends on few rising, so workers are placed in a competitive and antagonistic position to each other. Not only has this mode of organization undermined the establishment of trade unions (where each worker sees his own individual possibilities of employment or promotion depending upon not getting involved in this type of activity), but it has also set groups of workers against each other. Thus, skilled workers are very jealous about maintaining their wage and other advantages over unskilled ones, and other antagonisms according to race and sex are also exploited and exacerbated as individual workers and groups are forced to compete with each other for jobs and benefits.

What is perhaps even more interesting are the recent studies that show that productivity would be higher (although not control of the work force and the extraction of profits through its labor) according to other modes of work organization. The recent study of *Work in America* carried out by a Task Force of the Secretary of Health, Education, and Welfare identified a large number of work experiments and practices that modified traditional work relations and increased productivity (U.S. Department of Health, Education & Welfare, 1973). Studies of industrial worker cooperatives have shown similar results (Carnoy and Levin, 1976a; Johnson and Whyte, 1977). That is, the owners of capital have been able to organize production to meet their needs to control the workplace in behalf of maximizing the rate at which profits could be extracted. While capital accumulation on behalf of the owners of productive property has expanded at a rapid historical rate from this process, the vast majority of workers have been subject to conditions of work that do not permit a healthy personal or social development or productive work experiences.

FUNCTIONS OF SCHOOLS

One can best understand many of the functions of the schools by viewing their roles in terms of preparing workers for the social and skill requirements of the workplace. As the workplace became increasingly centralized and work became fragmented under the practice of scientific management, so did the schools move from a highly decentralized form of lay control to a bureaucratic and centralized institution dominated by professionals (Tyack, 1974; Katz, 1971; Bowles and Gintis, 1976). As work became increasingly subdivided into minute tasks to be allocated to workers according to their capabilities, schools adopted practices for curriculum tracking and for testing students to assign them to tracks. The schools became highly standardized with a system of age-grading and a common set of instructional materials for each grade and curriculum. And many of the "modern" factory practices became embodied in the operations of schools.

Further, schooling became organized into an institution in which rules and regulations dominated educational life. Students learned to work for extrinsic rewards such as grades and promotions and the avoidance of demotions or failures rather than for the intrinsic value of the educational process. And teachers, like the bosses in the workplace, determined which students were following the rules and carrying out their activities in the manner prescribed by the curriculum and the need for maintaining order. Thus, the schools developed in a manner parallel to the workplace with similar modes of organization and values.

The process by which the socialization of the labor force by the educational system tended to follow the transformation of work under monopoly capitalist control is very complex. It has been documented—in part—by a number of researchers (see Bowles and Gintis, 1976; Levin,

1976), and it has been termed the correspondence principle. This principle can be viewed as the tendency for the educational system to follow the organization and content of the workplace as its principle agenda. It can be shown that the inequalities of the workplace are also reproduced by the schools and that the social relationships of capitalist work in its evolving forms were soon emulated by the educational systems. Indeed, the present schools cannot be fully understood without an understanding of the nature of work roles for which the young are being prepared. Alternatively, educational reforms such as those of the War on Poverty that attempted to change these functions have not been successful because of their lack of correspondence with the larger society generally and the workplace specifically. Details of this argument are provided by Carnoy and Levin (1976b) and Levin (1978).

Historically, the relationship of the schools can best be understood by looking at the functions of schools and those of the workplace. The alienating qualities of the work process have been strongly evident in the educational one as well. Students have little control over the process and product of their educational activities, and they are placed in antagonistic relations to one another in the grading and educational selection process. Since those who will do best in school will also do best in the workplace, students see themselves in competition with their fellow students in much the same way that they will experience this relation during their working lives. The concept of correspondence is a very powerful way for integrating an understanding of dominant school practices with those of the workplace.

Threats to the Educational and Work Processes

Although correspondence between educational and work processes is very helpful in understanding the stability of each, the principle is not useful for understanding change. At the present time both the workplace and the school are threatened with disruptions to the existing modes of activity. In this section we will develop briefly some of the dynamics of change that will tend to alter both the workplace and the educational system.

Although the logic of correspondence between education and work and the forces that sustain it are powerful, the reproduction of any social institution that is in contradiction to itself is not smooth. Both the educational system and the system of production and work are characterized by internal contradictions or structural antagonisms such that they operate in ways in which forces that will oppose their smooth operation will arise (see Carter, 1976; Levin, 1978). In the system of work that we described, the owners of the firms and the workers who are hired by the firms have opposing interests. The owners wish to maximize their profits and capital accumulation, while the worker wishes to obtain as large a wage as possible while minimizing his contribution to a labor process that is alien to his personal needs. But maximum profits depend upon the extraction of surplus from the employee, maximizing the amount of labor obtained from him or her while paying the worker only the minimum necessary to reproduce his or her labor power.

As we noted, through the hierarchal division of labor and the development of the educational system to produce socialized workers for the capitalist mode of production, it was possible to mediate these contradictions between the opposing interests of workers and capitalists. Moreover, such conditions as high unemployment further mediate the labor-capital contradiction, for the worker realizes that he or she can be easily replaced by a presently unemployed person if he or she does not do what the capitalist owners and managers require. This is particularly true when there are no alternatives to work for survival.

But over time the success of these mediating forces has tended to decline so that the contradictions have become manifest. In part this is due to the independent dynamics resulting from the internal contradictions in the mediating institutions themselves. For example, the educational system has traditionally provided diplomas and other certificates to reward those who complete particular levels. These certificates could be used, in turn, to obtain jobs at appropriate levels in the economic system. But as students learn to work for rewards external to themselves, such as certificates, rather than for the intrinsic satisfaction of learning and inquiry, the certificates become an end in themselves, and the student will tend to minimize the effort to obtain the reward. Thus, students look for easy teachers, try to guess what the teacher will ask for on exams to minimize studying, and cram for examinations to perform well in the short run while discarding the knowledge after the exam. Obviously, such students have learned behaviors that enable them to minimize work effort in the labor process and that might even provide insights into disrupting that process.

Historically, the correspondence of the schools with the workplace has tended to overshadow the underlying dynamics of the educational system. One of the most important of these is the present tendency of the educational system to provide more educated persons than the economic system can absorb. An important incentive for families and individuals to emphasize more schooling for themselves and their offspring has been the expectation that with additional schooling comes greater life success. The more education that a person attains, the higher the occupational status and earnings that could be obtained. Economists even viewed this process as tantamount to an investment in human capital, where the investment return generally exceeded that for investment in physical capital (Becker, 1964).

As long as the economic system expanded in the aggregate and moved from agriculture to production to the services, there was an expansion of the occupational structure at the levels that could absorb a more and more educated labor force. At each level of education it was possible for workers to view a set of occupational prospects and earnings that was better than the prospects for less-educated persons. And, in general, those with college educations were able to achieve technical, managerial, and professional positions, while those with less education had to settle for lower earnings and less prestigious careers. Thus, the training and socialization provided by the schools at each level also seemed to dovetail relatively well with the eventual demands of the workplace at the appropriate occupational level.

In recent years, though, the rate of economic growth has diminished at a time when there is an unusually large number of persons of college age and when a very high proportion of those entering the labor force have obtained at least some college-level training. The reduction in the rate of economic expansion and the maturation of the structure of the economy have resulted in an inability of the economy to absorb the increase in the number of persons with college training; this is the focus of the work of Freeman (1976) and Rumberger (1978). A more extensive analysis is found in Levin (1978) and Carnoy and Levin (in press). Instead of the economy providing greater opportunities for those with college education, it appears that young persons with college training will increasingly have to accept those jobs that were traditionally filled by persons with much lower educational attainments.

What is evident is that the same incentives that stimulated the expansion of enrollments in the schools for socializing a growing labor force for capitalist and government production will continue to operate even when the opportunities to employ more educated persons do not expand at a commensurate rate. The so-called private returns on educational investment depend not only on the earnings for the additional education, but also on the earnings that would be received without further education. Even if the earnings for college graduates grow slowly over time or decline when adjusted for rises in the price level, a college education may still represent a very good investment if the opportunities for high school graduates decline at an even greater rate. Evidence of this phenomenon is found in Grasso (1977) and Rumberger (1980).

Further, education represents one of the few hopes for most families and individuals for social mobility from generation to generation, so as the ideology of educational attainment continues to persist, the quest for more education as an instrument of status attainment will also persist. The existence of an ideology of education as a path of social mobility—as well as the fact that as opportunities for college graduates decline, there is an even greater deterioration for high school graduates—leads to the following conclusion: The educational system will continue to turn out more and more educated persons regardless of the inability of the economy to absorb them.

On the economic side, there is little on the horizon to suggest that the long-run prospects for economic growth will improve much. First, problems of high energy costs and rising costs of other natural resources run counter to technologies that have been predicated on cheap and unlimited energy and other natural resources. Second, to a large degree the government cannot use either fiscal or monetary policy to increase the economic growth rate without triggering various shortages, bottlenecks in production, and price increases in markets that are dominated by the monopolistic elements characterizing the economic system. Third, the costs of labor and the stability of production in many of the Third World countries promise much greater profits than further investment in the United States. Many countries in Latin America and Asia are characterized by dictatorships that promise enormous profits to foreign investors by preventing their workers from organizing and by refusing to provide child labor laws or meaningful, minimum wage protection for the labor force. While local elites receive substantial rewards from these practices, the majority of the workers are subjected to arduous work at subsistence wages with far greater profits for investors than would be derived in the United States. Accordingly, future economic growth rates in the United States are not likely to approach those of the post–World War II period.

To further aggravate the situation, many existing jobs are being transformed by technology and capital investment into ones that are becoming more and more routinized and devoid of the need for human judgments and talents. Studies of automation have suggested that the critical skills and judgments that are associated with particular jobs are eliminated by greater use of technology and capital (Braverman, 1974; Bright, 1966). Even many traditional professions have become increasingly proletarianized in this way as the expansion of professional opportunities has shifted from self-employment to corporate and government employment. Under the latter forms of organization, the professional is given a much more specialized and routine function, rather than choosing for himself or herself the types of clients, practices, hours, and work methods to be employed.

Thus, not only do the alternatives for the educated person seem to be deteriorating in both quality and quantity, but an analysis for the longer run suggests that the forces that are creating this deterioration will continue to prevail. Thus, young and educated persons are likely to find themselves in situations where their expectation and skills exceed those associated with available jobs. Since most jobs will not have the intrinsic characteristics that would keep such persons engaged, the inadequate nature of the extrinsic rewards will operate to make it more and more difficult to integrate such persons into the labor force. That is, the lack of opportunities for promotion and the limited wage gains in conjunction with the relatively routinized nature of most jobs will tend to create a relatively unstable work force. It is also important to note that the availability of public assistance in the form of food stamps, medical care, and other services, as well as unemployment insurance, tends to cushion the impact of losing employment, so the negative impact of losing or quitting one's job is no longer as powerful a sanction for job conformance.

As the *Work in America* report noted, these phenomena may have rather severe repercussions for labor productivity (U.S. Department of Health, Education, & Welfare, 1973). The dissatisfactions that result from frustrated expectations with respect to the quality of work and its extrinsic rewards can create threats to productivity in a variety of ways. Most notable among these are rising absenteeism, worker turnover, wildcat strikes, alcoholism and drug usage, and deterioration of product quality. Even rising incidences of sabotage are possible responses by young workers who feel that they are overeducated for the opportunities that have been made available to them and who do not see the possibilities of major improvements in their situations.

But the overproduction of educated persons relative to available opportunities is not only creating disruptive potential for the workplace, it is also suggesting difficulties for the educational system. As the exchange values of a college degree and high school diploma have fallen, there are a number of indications of a relaxation of educational standards. For example, there is considerable evidence that average grades have risen at the same time that standardized test scores in basic skill areas have fallen (Wirtz, 1977).

While there are many possible causes for these phenomena, one of the most intriguing is that these are natural responses to the falling commodity value of education. Thus, the educational system seems to be providing higher grades for relatively poorer quality work, and students no longer seem willing to put in the effort to acquire the various cognitive skills. This explanation fits our overall framework in that, to a large degree, existing educational activities will be undertaken for their extrinsic values rather than for their intrinsic worth. As the extrinsic value of education falls in the marketplace, the grades given for any level of effort must rise to ensure a given performance. Moreover, the effort that a student will put in to acquiring an education will also decline as the financial and prestige rewards decline.

A further example of this type of disruptive potential of the schools is reflected in the increasing problem of discipline. To a great extent, the discipline of workers is maintained through the promise of good pay, steady work, and possible promotion for those who conform. Since the work is intrinsically without value to the worker, it is these incentives that must be used to ensure appropriate working behavior. A similar situation has existed in the school, where the fear of failure and of low grades and the attractions of promotion and high grades has helped to maintain discipline among students. These systems of extrinsic rewards have served to ensure that students see it in their best interests to "follow the rules." But, as the job situation and possibilities of social success from education have deteriorated, even the grading system is no longer adequate to hold students in check. In fact, recent Gallup Polls of problems in the schools are consistent in implicating discipline as the most important difficulty (Gallup, 1977).

In summary, there exists a constellation of relations between the schools and the workplace that can provide either reinforcement or disruptive potential. While historically the operations of schools cannot be understood without an examination of their correspondence with the requirements of the capitalist workplace, the independent dynamic of schools and their internal contradictions also represent forces for challenging the institutions of the workplace. The result of these forces is that it is becoming more and more difficult to integrate students into either school life or working life than it has in the past. And the disruptive aspects of this situation are stimulating various responses in both the educational and work setting.

Workplace and Educational Responses

No social institution can continue to function and reproduce itself when the result of its functioning is the creation of obstacles to its further reproduction. This is the present quandary faced by both the workplace and the schools, and substantial efforts are being made in both sectors to create reforms which will avoid the current problems. While I will mention some of the efforts that are being made in the educational sector, I will place most of my emphasis on the changes in the workplace. The reason for this is that our historical analysis suggests that while the educational system can trigger change in the workplace through the workings of its independent dynamics, the changes in the education-work relation will first occur in the workplace. Subsequently, they will be transmitted to the schools in a new pattern of correspondence. That is, the workplace lies at the center of gravity in this interdependent system as reflected in the historical development of the schools.

This means that by looking at present educational reforms we may be observing only a reaction to present educational disruptions rather than a longer-range solution. In contrast, by looking at workplace reforms of a long run and stable nature, we may be seeing the basis for structural changes in the schools that will support the new working relationships. In order to apply this interpretation, it is only necessary to review the three most prominent educational reforms for attempting to improve the articulation of schools and workplaces: career education, life-long learning or recurrent education, and "back to basics." Each of these can only be understood in light of the increasing difficulties in integrating young and relatively educated persons into the workplace.

CAREER EDUCATION

Career education represents a rather diverse set of approaches that seems to focus on integrating more closely the worlds of education and work (Hoyt et al., 1972). Particular strategies include attempts to increase career guidance on the nature of and attributes of existing job positions, to improve the career content of curricula, to intersperse periods of work and schooling as part of the regular educational cycle, and to provide a more "realistic" understanding of the nature of work and available job opportunities. Obviously, an important aspect of this approach is to reduce the "unrealistically high" expectations for high-level careers and to guide students into preparing for more attainable ones. But there is virtually no evidence that such an approach will make students more "realistic" and offset the historic quest for social mobility through the educational system. Without supportive changes in the workplace, it is unlikely that this traditional function of the educational system can be altered by the introduction of career education.

LIFE LONG LEARNING AND RECURRENT EDUCATION

Concurrent with the press for career education has been the movement towards altering traditional educational patterns through life-long or recurrent education (Mushkin, 1974; Peterson et al., 1979). This effort is aimed at reducing the present high social demand for formal education—particularly at the college level—by breaking the traditional educational cycle in favor of one in which students can take instruction at times in their lives when they perceive the need. It is presumed that the young will obtain jobs at existing employment levels, and they will undertake additional instruction only when there is a need to upgrade their skills or when they wish to satisfy some nonvocational curiosity or interest.

The problem with this approach is that there is a dearth of employment positions even at lower levels of educational attainment, including high school graduates. This relative lack of productive work for young persons who leave the educational system will tend to work against their taking the recurrent educational approach seriously. Further, those jobs that are available without college training will rarely permit upward mobility into new careers that will benefit from recurrent education. More specifically, most careers require a minimum educational level for entry to higher positions (see Thurow, 1975; Edwards, Reich, and Gordon, 1975). College-educated executive trainees, engineers, lawyers, and other managerial and professional employees have very high probabilities of maintaining these positions and at least some probability of rising to higher levels. But high-school-educated stock clerks and similar workers have almost no chance of rising to managerial or professional levels through recurrent education. Whatever else their merits, recurrent and lifelong education are not likely to alleviate the problem of overeducated persons in the job market. Again, there is the shortcoming of using an educational strategy to address what is essentially a noneducational problem.

BACK TO BASICS

The back-to-basics movement refers to the attempt by parents, taxpayers, and educators to focus educational institutions on the teaching of basic cognitive skills within a highly structured curriculum. In part, this trend is work oriented in that its advocates assert that the young are unable to do well in the job market because of a failure to learn basic skills and self-discipline. The evidence of declining test scores and rising discipline problems is thought to give testimony to this claim. Even if the dearth of challenging jobs or employment is recognized, it is assumed that a young person with good basic skills and discipline will have an edge over persons without these attributes.

But, again, there is a problem in altering cognitive achievement and discipline through the back-to-basics movement if these problems derive from the falling value of education in job markets themselves. That is, to the degree that students and educators might be more lax with respect to both basic skills and discipline as a result of their declining importance in terms of life opportunities, forces more basic than school curriculum and organization are responsible for the quandary. Thus, it is predicted that career education, recurrent education, and back to basics will not resolve the dilemmas of disruption and breakdown in the traditional functioning of both school and workplace. Unless there are basic alterations in labor markets and the workplace that support changes in the educational setting, the latter are not likely to make much of a difference.

WORK REFORMS AND ECONOMIC DEMOCRACY

Both historical evidence and its extension through our overall approach suggest that the disruptive influences of overeducation in job markets is more likely to be resolved through alterations in the workplace. In particular, the fact that the extrinsic aspects of work can no longer be made attractive enough to fulfill the higher expectations of the more educated job holder means that an emphasis must be placed upon improving the intrinsic qualities of work. The most important class of reforms for enhancing the intrinsic attractiveness of the workplace are those which increase the participation of workers in decisions affecting the work process, that is, attempts to democratize the workplace. Broadly speaking, we refer to these as the implementation of economic democracy, a notion that is discussed by Bernstein (1976), Blumberg (1968), Greenberg (1975), and Jenkins (1974).

The democratizing of the workplace, then, represents an attempt to increase the involvement and commitment of the worker to his or her employer through increasing his or her participation in decision making. It is expected that by increasing involvement and commitment, the traditional rewards of wages, possibilities of promotion, and steady employment will become less important for motivating workers. To a certain degree employees will be willing to trade off these benefits in place of an increased level of satisfaction and participation in the workplace. There are many ways that approaches to economic democracy can be implemented.

Some of the most successful efforts have relied upon the use of work teams or autonomous work groups (Susman, 1976). Instead of dividing the work into fragmented and repetitive tasks that are assigned to individuals, an entire work process or sub-assembly is assigned to a team of workers. Such a process could be the accounting function of a small firm, or the responsibility for a sub-assembly of a large piece of machinery. The work team is given responsibility for most of the work process. That is, the group must schedule the activity, assign particular team members, organize and execute the work activity, and inspect the results for quality control. Thus the team would be responsible, collectively, for its own activities, and these would be determined in a participative fashion.

These approaches have been tried in such diverse enterprises as automobile assembly (Volvo) and the manufacture of pet foods (Gyllenhammar, 1977; Walton, 1975). In almost all cases, the productivity of labor increases as worker turnover and absenteeism decline and product quality rises. In essense, workers relate to a community of colleagues, and they share decision making jointly. To a large degree, the work becomes intrinsically more interesting and meaningful as the worker experiences more of an influence over his or her working life and a greater camaraderie with his or her fellow workers.

While the use of work teams or autonomous work groups represents one form of industrial democracy, there are many other forms. For example, the use of a policy of codetermination in which governing boards of firms are composed of representatives of both capital and labor is prevalent in West Germany and is being considered as part of company policy for the United Kingdom and for the Common Market countries (Jenkins, 1974, Chap. 8). There is some question whether this particular policy will increase participation on the shop floor. A more decentralized approach is the use of worker councils of elected workers who advise management on workers' interests. These functions can also be established through trade unions as in Sweden, where the workers have been given the rights in recent years to share decision making with respect to hiring, firing, distribution of work, and work safety (Schiller, 1977). That is, Swedish managers cannot make these decisions without approval by the workers, and workers are legally entitled to leave their jobs if safety hazards exist.

A more extensive version of industrial democracy is that of worker self-management itself. This mode of control can take many forms, but the Yugoslavian experience is most instructive because of its relatively long establishment in that country (Vanek, 1971). The Yugoslavian model is based upon workers' councils that make the major policy decisions for the firms. In small enterprises (less than 30 employees), all of the workers are members of such councils and in larger enterprises, the councils are elected by the workforce. The council holds all formal power, and it makes decisions regarding hiring and firing, salaries, investment, and other operations of the firm. Under this arrangement, the management is accountable to the workers. Such managers are appointed by the elected representatives of the central board of management. The personal income of the workers is dependent both upon the overall success of the enterprise as well as the contribution of the individual toward that success, although a minimum income is guaranteed to all workers.

While the Yugoslavian approach has particularly broad implications for the democratization of work in public enterprises, its counterpart in the private sector is the producer cooperative. Producer cooperatives are both owned and operated democratically by their members. In these cases, the worker-members exercise control of both the internal organization of work and the levels of remuneration, product planning and development, marketing, pricing, and other functions. Any surplus that is generated is allocated to investment or distributed among the members, so the workers benefit not only from a more democratic form of working life, but also from the financial success of the cooperative. In some cases, firms that might have otherwise closed their doors have been successfully transformed into producer cooperatives by their workforce (Bernstein, 1976; Carnoy and Levin, 1976a).

These examples of increased worker participation and democratization of work or industrial democracy all have one factor in common. By increasing the participation of workers and their intrinsic attachment to the job, it is expected that workers will become better integrated into the workplace. This integration should result in improved productivity through lower worker turnover and absenteeism and higher quality workmanship. A fairly large number of actual cases and experiments have tended to confirm the expectation of higher productivity in the more participative setting (Blumberg, 1968; U.S. Department of Health, Education, and Welfare, 1973).

EDUCATIONAL IMPLICATIONS OF ECONOMIC DEMOCRACY

If these forms of economic democracy will increasingly become evident in the workplace as a means of integrating the "new" worker, surely they will have repercussions for education. Such organizational modes set out rather different educational needs, and if the pattern of correspondence between the school and workplace is to be reestablished there must be changes in the schools. What are some of the new worker requirements that the schools will need to attend to?

Based upon previous analyses (Carnoy and Levin, in press; Levin, 1978), it appears that there are at least five dimensions of economic democracy that would require changes in the educational system. These include: (1) the ability to participate in group decisions; (2) capacity for increased individual decision-making; (3) minimal competencies in basic skills; (4) capacity to receive and give training to colleagues; and (5) cooperative skills.

The ability to participate in group decisions is an obvious prerequisite for the democratized workplace. Educational reforms that might be consonant with this requirement include greater democracy in school organization; more emphasis on group projects and teamwork; greater integration of schools and classrooms by race, ability, and social class; heavier reliance on team teaching; and a focus on group dynamics for improving interactions among student colleagues in problem-solving.

Individual decision making is important in the economic democracy mode because of the increase in decisions that the individual must make in the workplace in comparison with the present situation. That is, a democratized workplace tends to require a greater amount of individual judgment as well as collective decision making. An educational approach that might respond to this need is the construction of a curriculum with greater emphasis on problem solving than that which is found at present.

Minimal competencies for all students become important as workers are presumed to have the aptitudes to rotate jobs and share in decision making. Under existing systems of work, it is expected that workers will have widely different competencies, so that some workers will need very nominal skills and others will need very complex ones. A flattening of job hierarchies, especially through the use of teams and autonomous work groups, would necessitate much greater equality in worker skills and competencies. This requirement suggests that mastery learning types of approaches and criteria-based testing would become more important (see Bloom, 1976).

The emphasis on collegial training, where workers train their fellow workers as members of work teams or groups, would require the ability of most workers to assist others in learning job skills. The fact that workers would need to both train others and receive training themselves suggests that new forms of instruction for the schools might emphasize to a greater extent the use of peer-teaching approaches. We might expect, then, a much greater use of students for assisting other students in learning particular skills.

Finally, most forms of industrial democracy require greater cooperative skills. The movement from a highly competitive form of work organization to a cooperative one will necessitate greater attention to cooperative forms of learning in the schools. Possible educational responses include a greater emphasis on group assignments and problem-solving (Slavin, 1978).

Summary

This paper started with the view that just as democratic participation is a desirable property for our political life, it is also an important goal for other areas of our social and economic existence. Indeed, as Carole Pateman (1970) has suggested, political democracy might not be fully attainable without economic democracy in work organizations. To the degree that considerable pathology in our society is created by the stressful conditions of existing work, a movement toward economic democracy can reduce the incidence of psychopathology.

But one must obviously be wary about predictions of such profound change as the democratization of the workplace. "If wishes were horses, then beggars would ride," is an old saw. Most beggars lack transportation, and in a similar way we find that many of our dreams are delusions at best. Accordingly, one must leap beyond wishes and posit a view of social change that would seem to be useful for predicting the nature of future alterations of those institutions under scrutiny.

In this paper, I proposed a dialectical understanding of the change process in which the structural contradictions of capitalism initiate changes in both the workplace and the educational sector. The dynamics of this dialectic were presented, and specific forms of economic democracy and educational reform that would mediate the contradictions were posited.

The overall conclusion of the paper is the assertion that economic democracy is a very likely prospect for the future, and that it may have the effect of democratizing to a greater extent such other institutions as the school and family. For those of us who abhor the present tyranny of the workplace, our hopes are heightened by this reading of the future. However, we should acknowledge that the forces of domination have been with us for a considerable part of our history as evidenced by the following quote from a secret diary of Marcus Aurelius (c. 100 B.C.), which was said to have guided him in his daily dealings with his fellow man:

TESTES SOURS VIRILITER APPREHENDE, DEINDE COR ET MENS SEQUENTER

Translated liberally, this means "Once you've got them by the testicles, their hearts and minds are sure to follow." This has certainly been an important assumption of the development of capitalist work organizations and state bureaucracies alike. Whether these forms of control are in their twilight years is still to be contested, but the preceding analysis gives substantial cause for optimism.

References

The Annals, Special Issue on "Industrial democracy in International Perspective." Vol. 431, May, 1977.

Baran, P., and Sweezy, P. *Monopoly capital*. New York: Monthly Review Press, 1966.

Becker, G. S. *Human capital*. New York: Columbia University Press, 1964.

Bernstein, P. *Workplace democratization: Its internal dynamics*. Kent, Ohio: Kent State University Press, 1976.

Bloom, B. S. *Human characteristics and school learning*. New York: McGraw-Hill, 1976.

Blumberg, P. *Industrial democracy: The sociology of participation*. New York: Schocken, 1968.

Economic Democracy, Education, and Social Change   183

Bowles, S., and Gintis, H. *Schooling in capitalist America.* New York: Basic Books, 1976.

Braverman, H. *Labor and monopoly capital.* New York: Monthly Review Press, 1974.

Bright, J. The relationship of increasing automation and skill requirements. In *The employment impact of technological change,* Report of the National Commission on Technology, Automation, and Economic Progress, Appendix Volume 2. Washington, D.C.: U.S. Government Printing Office, February 1966, pp. 207–221.

Carnoy, M., and Levin, H. 'Workers' triumph: The Meriden experiment. *Working Papers,* 1976, winter, 47–56. (a)

Carnoy, M., and Levin, H. *The limits of educational reform.* New York: David McKay, 1976. (b)

Carter, M. Contradiction and correspondence: Analysis of the relation of schooling to work. In M. Carnoy and H. Levin (Eds.), *The limits of educational reform.* New York: David McKay, 1976.

Edwards, R. C. *Contested terrain: The transformation of the workplace in the 20th century.* New York: Basic Books, 1978.

Edwards, R., Reich, M., and Gordon, D. M. *Labor market segmentation.* Lexington, Mass.: D. C. Heath, 1975.

Freeman, R. B. *The overeducated American.* New York: Academic Press, 1976.

Gallup, G. H. Ninth annual Gallup Poll of the public's attitudes toward the public schools. *Phi Delta Kappan,* 1977, September, 33–48.

Gintis, H. The nature of labor exchange and the theory of capitalist production. *Review of Radical Political Economics,* 1976, *8,* 36–54.

Grasso, J. *On the declining labor market value of schooling.* Paper prepared for the Annual Meeting of the American Educational Research Association, New York City, April, 1977.

Greenberg, E. S. The consequences of worker participation: A clarification of the theoretical literature. *Social Science Quarterly,* 1975, September, 191–209.

Grubb, W. N., and Lazerson, M. Rally 'round the workplace: Continuities and fallacies in career education. *Harvard Educational Review,* 1975, *45,* 451–474.

Gyllenhammar, P. G. *People at work.* Boston: Addison-Wesley, 1977.

Haber, S. *Efficiency and uplift: Scientific management in the progressive era, 1890–1920.* Chicago: University of Chicago Press, 1964.

House, J. S. The effects of occupational stress on physical health. In J. O'Toole (Ed.), *Work and the quality of life.* Cambridge, Mass.: MIT Press, 1974, pp. 145–170.

Hoyt, K., Evans, R. N., Mackin, E. F., and Mangum, G. L. *Career education: What it is and how to do it.* Salt Lake City: Olympus, 1972.

Jenkins, D. *Job power.* Baltimore: Penguin Books, 1974.

Johnson, A., and Whyte, W. F. The Mondragon System of worker production cooperatives. *Industrial and Labor Relations Review,* 1977, *31,* 18–30.

Kasl, S. V. Work and mental health. In J. O'Toole (Ed.), *Work and the quality of life.* Cambridge, Mass.: MIT Press, 1974.

Katz, M. B. *Class, bureaucracy and schools: The illusion of educational change in America.* New York: Praeger, 1971.

Levin, H. M. A decade of policy developments in improving education and training of low income populations. In R. Haveman (Ed.), *A decade of federal antipoverty programs: Achievements, failures, and lessons.* New York: Academic Press, 1977.

Levin, H. M., and Carnoy, M. *The dialectic of education and work*. Stanford, Calif.: Stanford University Press, in press.

Levin, H. M. Educational reform: Its meaning? In M. Carnoy and H. Levin (Eds.), *The limits of educational reform*. New York: David McKay, 1976.

Levin, H. M. *Workplace democracy and educational planning*. Paris: International Institute of Educational Planning (UNESCO), 1978, in press.

Marglin, S. A. What do bosses do? *The Review of Radical Political Economics*, 1974, *6*, 60–112.

Margolis, B., and Kroes, W. Work and the health of man. In J. O'Toole (Ed.), *Work and the quality of life*. Cambridge, Mass.: MIT Press, 1974.

Mushkin, S. (Ed.). *Recurrent education*. Washington, D.C.: U.S. Government Printing Office, 1974.

Nelson, D. *Managers and workers: Origins of the new factory system in the United States, 1880–1920*. Madison, Wis.: University of Wisconsin Press, 1975.

Ollman, B. *Alienation: Marx's conception of man in capitalist society*. New York: Cambridge University Press, 1971.

Pateman, C. *Participation and democratic theory*. New York: Cambridge University Press, 1970.

Peterson, R. E., Cross, K. P., Valley, J. R., Powell, S. A., Hartle, T. W., Kutner, M. A., and Hirabyashi, J. B. *Lifelong learning in America*. San Francisco, Jossey-Bass, 1979.

Rumberger, R. W. The economic decline of college graduates: Fact or fallacy? *The Journal of Human Resources*, 1980, in press.

Rumberger, R. W. *Overeducation in the U.S. labor market*. Unpublished doctoral dissertation, School of Education, Stanford University, July 1978.

Schiller, B. Industrial democracy in Scandinavia. *The Annals*, 1977, *431*, 63–73.

Slavin, R. E. *Cooperative learning*. Report No. 267, Center for Social Organization of Schools. Baltimore: Johns Hopkins University, 1978.

Susman, G. I. *Autonomy at work: A sociotechnical analysis of participative management*. New York: Praeger, 1976.

Terkel, S. *Working*. New York: Pantheon Books, 1974.

Tawney, R. H. *Inequality*. London: Allen and Unwin, 1931.

Thurow, L. *Generating inequality*. New York: Basic Books, 1975.

Tyack, D. B. *The one best system*. Cambridge, Mass.: Harvard University Press, 1974.

U.S. Department of Health, Education, and Welfare. *Work in America*. Cambridge, Mass.: MIT Press, 1973.

Vanek, J. *The participatory economy*. Ithaca, N.Y.: Cornell University Press, 1971.

Walton, R. E. Criteria for quality of working life. In L. Davis and A. Cherns (Eds.), *The quality of working life*, (Vol. 1). New York: The Free Press, 1975.

Weber, M. Bureaucracy. In H. H. Gerth and C. W. Mills (Eds.), *From Max Weber: Essays in Sociology*. New York: Oxford University Press, 1946.

Wilcox, K. *Schooling and socialization: A structural inquiry into cultural transmission in an urban American community*. Unpublished doctoral dissertation, Department of Anthropology, Harvard University, 1977.

Wirtz, W., et al. *On further examination: Report of the advisory panel on the Scholastic Aptitude Test score decline*. New York: College Entrance Examination Board, 1977.

Zwerdling, D. *Democracy at work*. Washington, D.C.: Association for Self-Management, 1978.

PART IV

Strategies for Social Change

Introductory Notes

The strategies proposed in this section vary in many ways. Some authors are concerned with solving problems within the framework of the present-day social, economic, and political system, others with restructuring the system itself. Some advocate working with small groups of individuals, others with large ones. Some are concerned with the role of mental health professionals, others with a broader range of helpers or change agents. The permutations make for a large array of proposals. To the extent that there is a common theme, it lies in the notion that the emphasis in seeking change should be on "doing things *with* people, rather than to them or for them," as Edward M. Glaser phrases it.

In his paper, Glaser first develops a general framework for the solution of societal problems. He points out that the quality of proposed solutions to specific problems varies greatly, and he stresses the need to evaluate the adequacy of different proposals. He derives two concepts from this: the first concerns the need to approach problems by synthesizing available knowledge in an area; and the second stresses the need for potential users to participate in the planning and implementation of programs. After discussing some examples, Glaser describes areas in need of applications of the general approach. In the process, he provides outlines of some of the "promising developments" in the areas of home and family, schools, and the work place. Glaser's paper thus suggests strategies for solving problems affecting large groups of people by working within the current general framework, although we suspect that achieving the degree of participation in decisions that he describes and advocates might alter the framework itself.

To some extent, the analysis provided by Stanley L. Brodsky and Kent S. Miller of the effect of class action suits on prisons and mental hospitals can be viewed as an expanded illustration of a "promising development" within the current sociopolitical framework. However, Brodsky and Miller's distinction between "system professionals" and "system challenges" makes it clear that in their view "coercing change" through the courts accomplishes more than ministering to the casualties. They argue that court decisions on institutions have led to considerable progress: Harmful aspects of institutionalization have been publicly documented, and there have been specific improvements within institutions and legal recognition of the obligation of institutions to provide services. Their view is that such efforts have been a failure only relative to overly high expectations and that the class action suit remains an effective weapon with which to challenge the system. The courts can continue to be a strong ally to those concerned with equality of institutions, and even paper victories have symbolic significance. Brodsky and Miller point to the effectiveness of ameliorating harm by changing institutions rather than by providing help to inmates after the damage has been done: "The sweeping change by class action suit and court order is a preventive strategy of much value." The strategy they defend falls between dealing with the individual victims and working for extensive structural change in society at large.

Gisela Konopka presents a case for doing both—for helping individuals and working for social change, for being a system professional *and* a system challenger. She rejects the position that views helping individuals as an alternative to changing social structures and illustrates how both kinds of intervention are needed. From direct experience of human suffering the professional comes to understand that its roots are neither exclusively in the individual nor in the social system. Konopka describes various difficulties professionals need to face. In order to work for change they must, at the same time that they display acceptance and understanding, be rejecting. They must insist on ethical values—respect for each individual and the belief in the interdependence of individuals. These values justify attempts to bring about change while avoiding imposing other—secondary—values on people. Not only must professionals be whole persons in the face of these potential conflicts, but they must be aware that the task of helping others and improving society is unending. They must be prepared to put their bodies as well as their beliefs on the line, and they must insure that the means used to achieve change are worthy of the ends. The message might appear discouraging were it not for Konopka's optimism. And her model of what a professional should be like might appear unattainable were it not that her life and work provide an example.

Betty Friedan discusses strategies that she feels have had widespread success in the women's movement. The general attitude toward women 20 or 30 years ago was difficult to fight, principally because women were not seen as people. Once women—or any victims for that matter—begin being seen as people, their demands for the rights and opportunities possessed by other people become compelling. As Friedan writes, "The real ideology of the women's movement was simply the values of democracy applied to women." Emerging as people has not made women's lives easier (indeed the reverse is perhaps the case), but coping with new problems and creating new patterns has been liberating. Friedan feels that this liberation is reflected in improved mental health. The process involves the redistribution of power—in society on the whole and in the family. Friedan is optimistic and this optimism, based on her assessment of how much progress women are making, has drawn fire from many quarters, in particular from those who do not share her assessment of how much progress women have made and who feel that the distribution of power has altered very little. Whatever the case, she is hardly complacent: Women need more than the opportunity to participate in institutions that fail to give anyone a fair deal. Women and men—people—need a new system, and clarifying for us all the humanity of every individual (consciousness raising?) may be an essential part of any strategy to achieve it.

The authors of the next two papers, Kenneth B. Clark and Sharland Trotter, discuss a different kind of strategy. While it may at times involve many of the tactics described by Brodsky and Miller and by Friedan, the essential thrust is to work with the victims themselves to develop strategies and to alleviate their plight. Kenneth Clark's framework for viewing psychopathology is similar to Thomas Hilliard's. Clark, like Hilliard, emphasizes that the individual is part of the social milieu and is shaped by it. As a result, many problems and conflicts have their roots not in individual aberrations or "disease," but in the deviant systems and institutions in which the victim is trapped. This conceptualization is at the basis of the large-scale prevention program Clark founded in Harlem to control juvenile delinquency. The program was, essentially, "an experiment in community psychiatry," operating on the assumption that "emotional problems . . . must be understood in terms of the pervasive pathology which characterizes our society and which makes the ghetto possible." In discussing the complex problem of bringing about desirable social change Clark, like Albee in the keynote address, identifies inequitable distribution and unjust exertion of power as the root of social pathology. He describes the racial ghettos that result from the abuses of the powerful and the powerlessness of the victims. Drug addiction, high infant mortality, high homicide rates, inferior education, unemployment—these are the fruits of institutionalized racism. He concludes that the community action program that he and his collaborators hoped would alleviate Harlem's social pathology failed, perhaps because it attempted to deal with Harlem's problems without fundamentally altering the larger society that produces our Harlems. In this failure one can, however, find the seeds from which more successful strategies may grow, and Clark concludes with suggestions for what has to be done if we are to ameliorate social pathology—and thus prevent psychopathology.

Sharland Trotter describes one outgrowth of the failure of community programs mandated by the federal government, such as that described by Clark: the "indigenous" community programs and natural helping networks. Unromantically, but sympathetically, she examines the power of vital neighborhoods to provide the support that helps people survive crises without enduring damage and to minimize social pathology of the kind in Harlem that Clark so clearly describes. After examining research on factors that influence neighborhood vitality and create a sense of community (whether in a neighborhood or over a greater distance), she discusses the community advocacy organizations that have risen like "antibodies" to counter society's antineighborhood policies and trends. These local, small scale organizations have not only fought successfully in many cases, but in the process have given the people involved and their neighbors a feeling of control over their own lives, and in this way have served a doubly important function. The scale of the operations may seem small compared to the gigantic size of the institutions and systems they oppose, but each success has involved a genuine redistribution of power and even the failures have left people with a greater sense of common purpose and community. These indigenous groups have filled the vacuum left by disillusionment with the "obvious failures of both representative democracy and governmentally mandated citizen participation to meet the needs of the non-rich." They tend, when successful, to grow from single issue protest groups to multi-issue advocacy organizations. Trotter gives examples of successes and analyzes their common threads—the most important being the definition of the problem and the formulation of solutions and strategies by the people directly involved, rather than by bureaucrats, politicians, or professionals. Solving problems together removes threats and strengthens the community and the person. Federal assistance has been valuable, but Trotter makes a strong case that such aid is most effective when it has fewest strings attached. This lesson might be one that could be translated into political action to modify the way in which aid is provided. Nonetheless, it is not clear how we are to keep the power hungry from the federal honey pots, a problem illustrated by the demise, since Trotter's paper was written, of the Orleans County (Vermont) Community Services Agency that she uses as an example of a successful program.

The final paper in this section contains Ned O'Gorman's poignant account of his efforts to help some of the victims. His experience in Harlem documents what so many wish to hide—that oppression does exist in our society. O'Gorman's response to oppression has been characterized as being one of taking care of the victims' wounds rather than preventing them, and indeed the alleviation of pain is a major concern: "Somehow I must heal him, all children, as I teach them." The numbers he can reach with his methods are small, and those he reaches are already wounded, so his strategy is unlike those usually considered to be primary prevention. However, his methods of nursing the children back to psychological health may have in them the seeds of a strategy for altering the system itself. He sees his school as a liberation camp, a place where we can "create within the child the liberated spirit of the conquerer of oppression." Perhaps this liberation is the key to creating individuals who understand the system of oppression well enough to fight it effectively.

There Are No Panaceas— But Let's Look at Some Promising Developments

Edward M. Glaser

If Edward Gibbon were living today, I wonder if he would not be thinking about a companion piece to his classic work, *The Decline and Fall of the Roman Empire*, perhaps titling it the *Decline and Challenge for Renaissance of the American Dream*.

I expect Gibbon would be distressed about our technologically advanced "I want and take" society marred by dramatic increases in crime at all levels, waste, inefficiency, the despoiling of our natural resources, and the disillusionment of our citizenry. Our cities grow ever less safe. Our governments at federal, state, and local levels frequently are wasteful, sometimes corrupt, and too often paternalistically concerned to let us know only news that these gatekeepers feel is good for us—or favorable for their objectives. We seem unable to exercise the severe measures of self-control necessary to reverse today's inflationary trend or to conserve our national resources. Anxiety is rampant, with tolerance for it decreasing, and we are living with a feeling of aimless drifting.

Despite such serious problems, however, perspective may be improved by asking ourselves, "In how many countries on earth would we rather live?" In many instances people and institutions behave responsibly, with constructive concern for each other and their environment. Our challenge is to cultivate and strengthen such behaviors. Our opportunity is to mount a well-planned offensive that can help change the course of American society from downgrading to upgrading the quality of our lives.

Now, how might we proceed to meet this challenge and opportunity? While there are no panaceas for our many societal stresses, or for the more personal ones all of us may experience, there are some promising approaches that perhaps can be made more available. To introduce those approaches, I would like first to offer a hypothesis and two derivative concepts.

The hypothesis, supported by cumulative observation and experience, is: *For almost every problem or need experienced by a large number of organizations, groups, or individuals, the quality or effectiveness of available response to that type of problem seems to fit into a normal probability curve distribution.*

The great majority of the responses appears to fall within the average range (the 68 percent middle portion). In the "very superior" segment—the upper 2 percent of the distribution—we are likely to find outstandingly skillful, efficacious, or ingenious ways of dealing with the given matter. Conversely, in the below average or even middle portion of the distribution, we are likely to find seriously inadequate practices. The difference in results or efficacy between the "upper 2 percent" practices/procedures/products and those that might appropriately be classified in the lower portion of the distribution curve can be enormous—sometimes like the difference between a lightning bug and lightning! Consider, for example, the "standard" diagnosis and treatment of the famed Helen Keller, who in addition to being blind and deaf, was judged feeble-minded and untrainable, and was about to be institutionalized for life. As a last chance, she was put under the tutelage of Anne Sullivan, who helped Ms. Keller unlock her tremendous talents and become a world-renowned example of what can be accomplished by finding ways to bring out an individual's latent abilities rather than overreacting to disabilities (Gibson, 1960).

A need exists for federal agencies to provide research and development assistance in their respective fields to:

1. *Identify* validated, demonstrably efficacious modes of responding to given categories of problems, especially those that have broad societal importance
2. Study the *conditions* or seemingly essential factors required for the *successful application* of those modalities
3. Study the forces that either *inhibit or facilitate* their *adoption/adaptation*
4. *Promote awareness and utilization* of the more efficacious procedures or practices for dealing with given types of problems, and try to do so through processes that help individuals, organizations, and institutions improve their own problem-solving capabilities

To help accomplish the above, let us consider the two concepts referred to earlier that derive from the given hypothesis.

Concept #1: There is a need to develop state-of-the-art knowledge syntheses in various important fields, and to effectively promote wide' utilization of both validated research findings and exemplary practices.

Such documents can link and convert knowledge in a repackaged way that can be accessed more readily by practitioners. Current federal expenditures in support of research and development are about $27 billion annually. A larger percentage of that total might appropriately be allocated to develop knowledge synthesis monographs. Then, by applying systematic strategies to promote broader awareness and utilization of these best-known practices, the quality of our lives may well be upgraded.

It might be helpful to illustrate Concept #1 by an example, and at the same time make clear how the paradigm developed for achieving broad-based consensus on state-of-the-art differs from the usual procedure wherein one or two scholars in a given field prepare a review article.

The process was first tried in the biomedical field in connection with chronic obstructive pulmonary diseases (COPD): emphysema, chronic bronchitis, and bronchial asthma. It focused on bringing together a project team of eminent physician researchers-practitioners in the COPD field. The project director (a psychologist) served mainly as process facilitator and project administrator.

At the initial meeting of the team, agreement was reached on a tentative outline of topics that needed to be addressed in a state-of-the-art paper. Then the group members exchanged ideas on what they thought was, in fact, the best current knowledge and practice with regard to each of the interrelated topics.

The first draft, written primarily by one team member, was sent to the others for review. The same procedure was followed with revised second, third, and fourth drafts, each revision receiving detailed critiquing by the team. It was not until the fifth draft that the team members deemed the paper "fit" for reaction by peers.

By nomination from team members, coupled with a literature survey by the project director, a total of 160 persons outside the project team were identified as well-qualified reviewers. Of these, 120 individuals agreed to read the document. A stratified random sample of 20 from the 120 was sent the fifth draft for review. Upon receipt of their critiques a revised sixth draft was sent to another somewhat smaller "wave," with new criticisms taken into account through further revision. This process was repeated until, by the 13th draft, a point of diminishing returns was reached. That revision was published in the *Journal of the American Medical Association* (Hodgkin, Balchum, Kass, Glaser, Miller, Haas, Shaw, Kimbel, and Petty, 1975). The published article contained an explicit invitation for further critique, and promised acknowledgment of significant responses. The comments received were carefully followed up, debated, and—*when deemed valid*—integrated into the state-of-the-art document, which subsequently was expanded for publication as a monograph.

Through this process the project team learned of research not yet published, and of innovative, seemingly valuable clinical practices or procedures. Thus, new knowledge was "captured" through an expanded network of direct communication with others who were working in the same problem area.

The diffusion and utilization as a result of this innovative development of a state-of-the-art consensus included the following: Over 8,500 reprint requests for the journal article have been received, in addition to permission requests for reprinting about 5,000 more copies. Some of the persons who contacted us described explicit changes in their own practice or in hospital procedures that they were in a position to influence, based upon application of certain material contained in the state-of-the-art document. The paper has been endorsed by the American College of Chest Physicians (ACCP), American Thoracic Society, American Lung Association, Rehabilitation Services Administration, and the National Heart, Lung, and Blood Institute. In addition, the article is being used for continuing medical education. The monograph is being widely disseminated by the ACCP, and a 45-minute documentary of the treatment-in-action has been filmed by Warner-Chilcott Laboratories.

Concept #2: As Gordon Allport stated in "The Psychology of Participation" (1945): "People must have a hand at saving themselves; they cannot and will not be saved from the outside" (p. 123).

Extrapolating from Concept #2, the most favorable condition for promising new knowledge or adoption of change of any kind is to make it possible for potential users to participate in planning and carrying out the implementation. This may seem like an obvious point, yet the usual way of introducing change is from the top down, without inviting those below who will be affected to participate in the planning or decision-making process.

Even when potential users do participate in developing some new procedure to meet a need, it may be necessary to offer resource assistance or technical expertise to help develop skills essential for proper carry-through. It should be clear to the stakeholders, however, that they "own" both the problem and the solutions they have participated in working out. A useful equation to remember in this connection, first offered by the late Dr. Norman Maier, University of Michigan, (1963), is: ED = Q × A. An Effective Decision = its Quality × the Acceptance by those required to implement it.

It may be helpful to illustrate Concept #2 by an example.

In the 1960s Congress funded the Peace Corps and the Teacher Corps. The latter focused on trying to improve the school climate and learning environment in a target sample of inner-city schools through staff development and encouragement of innovative practices. If successful, such programs/practices could (and hopefully would) be disseminated/utilized by other more or less similar schools that could profit from them.

Since its inception in 1965, between $400–$500 million has been spent funding Teacher Corps projects. Congress now is asking, "What has been learned from this project over the years, and to what extent has there been a spread of exemplary practices from the relatively few target schools to the many similar type schools that were not in the Teacher Corps sample?" Various channels can be used to disseminate information. Experience with many such efforts indicates that they are of limited value (Glaser, 1973). In keeping with Concept #2 that "people must have a hand at saving themselves, they . . . will not be saved from the outside," a more likely-to-succeed strategy would be:

1. Identify and evaluate promising innovations developed by Teacher Corps schools, so that there is evidence of unusual efficacy with regard to any practice or program deemed worthy of "export."

2. Identify schools in various sections of the country that are judged to be likely candidates for utilizing some of the validated innovations developed by the Teacher Corps.

3. Approach those schools and ask if they would be interested—with federal funding to defray out-of-pocket expenses—in bringing together representatives of their various stakeholder groups (teachers, students, administrators, parents) to think through any changes *they* might like to experiment with in an effort to further develop the potential of *their* school to become as constructive an educational influence for their constituents as it might become. Part of the incentive would be an offer of free technical assistance from the Teacher Corps, if invited, to help the "candidate" schools achieve their own objectives, arrived at by integrated input from those concerned stakeholders. In that process, relevant approaches or programs from Teacher Corps schools, from educational research and development, from school networks, and from exemplary practices in general would be brought into focus for *consideration* by the schools that opted to participate in the offer. By such a procedure, "not-invented-here" resistance would be avoided, and the power of the participating schools would be enhanced by choosing their own *modus operandi* for moving toward attainment of *their* goals.

To tune in more directly on the theme of this volume, we might ask ourselves, "What are the most fundamental areas of living that have greatest need for the identification and utilization of exemplary practices?" Three key areas that touch all our lives and thus provide significant opportunity for upgrading insight and skill are: (1) the home or family; (2) the school; and (3) the nation's workplaces.

Now let us consider how these two concepts—development of state-of-the-art knowledge syntheses in various fields (including description of verified promising practices) and stakeholder participation in problem identification and resolution—can be applied in the home or family.

Application to Home/Family

What sorts of so-called exemplary practices can be brought to bear on the family? Who decides what is an exemplary practice, or which families need to acquire such learnings, and how such information/training could be provided without invasions of privacy or fostering a government "Big Brother" imposition?

One entry point is in connection with the children of families who have come under jurisdiction of the courts or public social service agencies. Two illustrative categories are (1) children who are termed "at risk" because they have been in repeated difficulty with the law as a consequence of delinquent behavior, or whose parents have appealed for assistance because of alleged socially destructive or seemingly incorrigible behavior; and (2) parents found guilty of child abuse.

Such children and parents are "handled" now in the many thousands of jurisdictions across the country that have responsibility for doing so. Federal agencies such as the National Institute of Mental Health, the Office of Child Development, the Rehabilitation Services Administration, and the National Institute of Law Enforcement and Criminal Justice, have spent billions of dollars over the years supporting research and development on the causes, control, and remediation of maladaptive behavior; that is, human problems or disabilities in need of public remedial assistance. While many of the rehabilitative efforts have not proved efficacious—especially over time—the fact is that some indeed *have* shown very promising results. Those are likely to be classified in the upper two percent of that normal distribution curve mentioned earlier.

For example, Sarason (1978) has reported on a three- and five-year follow-up of 192 male first offenders, ages 15½ to 18, at the Cascadia Juvenile Reception-Diagnostic Center in Tacoma. The total N was equally divided into three groups. The first group went through modeling sessions in which a particular theme was played out on videotape, first by the offenders and then by psychology graduate student models. The second group went through discussion sessions of the same themes, but without role playing. The third group served as a control. Dependent variables (those variables that presumably might be affected or changed as a consequence of the intervention) were self-reports, staff ratings of the inmates on various behavioral dimensions, follow-up interviews, and recidivism rates.

Focusing here only on recidivism rates, three years after their arrival at Cascadia, 22.4 percent of the 192 boys had again become known offenders. However, there were about twice as many recidivists in the Control group as in the Modeling or Discussion groups. In a five-year follow-up, the Control group had slightly more than twice the recidivism rate found in the Modeling and Discussion groups.

Another research and demonstration project now in progress that is showing relatively promising results is being conducted by the Oregon Social Learning Center in Eugene, entitled "Evaluating Agency Treatment of Aggressive Children." The dual purposes of this project are to implement and evaluate a social learning treatment program for aggressive children that involves training the parents in appropriate child-management skills. Results to date indicate a highly significant reduction in deviant behavior over time for the children involved in the social learning treatment program.

But the people across the country who have legitimate responsibility for "handling" such children and parents often are unaware of innovative approaches that have been demonstrated to be more effective than customary practices. Nor are they likely to have the required resources available even if they have heard of such procedures. This brings us to consideration of a proposed prescription through political action and social change.

In brief, the general form of the prescription would be for federal agencies whose mission includes concern with research and development connected with family and children, to ascertain whether there are demonstrably efficacious or highly promising practices, which may not be widely known or utilized, for coping with certain pervasive problems in that field. The next step would be to arrange through grant or contract mechanisms to bring together a research and development team consisting of representatives from institutions or demonstration projects where the innovative practices have been developed or utilized. Then, add to this team several other widely respected experts in the particular field, including some who may be skeptical or questioning of these innovative procedures.

Thus the general paradigm described earlier for achieving knowledge synthesis in the COPD field might be developed, made accessible, and applied to the problems of children and families "at risk." A concomitant task, in a preventive mode, would be to plan appropriate dissemination/utilization strategies, with federal funding to carry out those efforts. This would not necessarily require any additional overall research and development expenditures. Rather, it would require a reexamination of priorities and payoff potential for allocation of available funds.

Another (and simpler to achieve) type of sociopolitical action for amelioration of a serious problem in more families than we may realize is Minnesota's law that addresses domestic violence. Among other things, it gives law enforcement officials increased powers to protect the victim and deal with the abuser.

If the women's movement, political scientists, public administrators, the League of Women Voters, and other interested groups such as the American Psychological Association would join together to study the Minnesota domestic abuse laws, and petition for recommended federal, state, and local statutes and programs, speedier needed progress might be made in coping with this problem. A promising note here is that President Carter recently announced the formation of an Interdepartmental Committee on Domestic Violence, which has been asked to come up with a work plan by June 15, 1979 to guide the government's actions.

Application to Schools

With regard to what I have offered as two derivative concepts from my hypothesis, let me now discuss their potential application to the schools.

In certain schools, some of which are in ghetto or lower socioeconomic neighborhoods, programmatic actions have been taken that have resulted in sustained, substantial decreases in violence and vandalism, and have been documented in the Senate Subcommittee *Hearings on School Violence and Vandalism* (1975), followed by the National Institute of Education's (1978) report to Congress entitled *Violent Schools—Safe Schools*. These findings are not chance. They reflect deliberate, creative programs including involvement of the various stakeholders: teachers, students, school administrators, parents, and, often, appropriate governmental agencies and community groups.

In several such cases there has been training in critical thinking and problem solving about issues of concern to students, coupled with student involvement in attempting to solve the problems they had identified. Such procedures are consistent with our Concept #2, namely: "People must have a hand at saving themselves." Sometimes this has been coupled with a work-through of moral dilemma and citizenship problems. Other ingredients in some cases have been additional teacher training that focuses on child growth and development, along with meaningful new curriculum additions, such as courses on sex, contraception, VD prevention, parent-child relationships, and parenting responsibilities. There has also been training in coping abilities for various kinds of common problems identified by the students, as well as creation of part-time work opportunities for junior and senior high school students, and so forth.

One example of an activity in response to the problem of providing high school students with marketable skill training that could be put to constructive use is a vocational education project developed by the Pasadena Unified Schools, described in a *Los Angeles Times* news story (Barker, 1973). That project invited interested students to participate in the tangible problem of transforming condemned houses (often available from HUD, VA, or FHA foreclosures for as little as $1) into salable property, and in the process acquire building trade skills as well as earn money. Starting from this practical project that served student and community needs, concomitant class discussions were held that led into subjects such as the facilitation of job equity when it is supported by marketable skill development.

Another interesting current example of reportedly effective citizenship education is the Thaler System developed in Gilman, Vermont (Bumstead, 1978). This is a middle-school program for grades 5–8, which sets up a full-fledged microeconomy with a democratic government, including a court system.

A January editorial in *U.S. News & World Report* (Stone, 1979) entitled "Are Ethics on the Way Back?" states: "A school in Indianapolis had suffered deep disciplinary problems and looked like a school in a riot area." Windows had been boarded up because $3,500 worth of glass broken in 8 months could not be replaced. In 5 months of using character education materials, intentional damage was reduced to zero. And 6 years later, student-teacher-community relations were found friendly and cooperative, with the whole atmosphere changed.

A Chula Vista, California, school cut vandalism by more than 80 percent, and others claimed similar successes. Hopes for future benefits in the lives of these students seem reasonable.

In addition to affecting violence and vandalism, some programs such as these have reported significant second-order effects in reduction of alienation and hostility. Those reports warrant verification and analysis. If the alleged benefits of these programs can be validated and appear to have potential for generalization *under certain conditions*, state and federal assistance for dissemination/utilization and for technical assistance where invited would seem well worthwhile. Sociopolitical action might help to make such assistance available.

Some persons feel that the preeminent goal of our educational system is the achievement of literacy for the whole population, and that the schools need to focus their efforts on attainment of that goal. Dr. Patricia Graham, until very recently director of the National Institute of Education, argues for that goal (Graham, 1979). However, in explaining what she means by literacy, she states:

Literacy encompasses much more than the ability to read, write, manipulate symbols, and develop independent means of making judgments and determining actions; it is also preparation for the skills required to function effectively throughout life—the skills that provide access to employment and to greater opportunities for personal fulfillment, both of which are vital. (p. 48)

Such a broad-gauge definition of literacy can sponsor development of knowledge syntheses with regard to various types of needs and encourage participation of all stakeholders in appropriate application of such knowledge.

Application to Workplaces

Now let us turn to application of our two concepts to the arena of work.

In the well-documented Report of a Special Task Force to the Secretary of HEW (*Work in America*, 1972), the authors have a good deal to say about psychopathology connected with work—and strategies for primary prevention. For example:

[There are] no simple solutions to the many social problems discussed in this report, but in locating our analysis in the institution of work, we believe we have found a point where considerable leverage could be exerted to improve the quality of life. . . .

In the third chapter, we review the physical and mental health costs of jobs as they are now designed. Satisfaction with work appears to be the best predictor of longevity—better than known medical or genetic factors—and various aspects of work account for much, if not most, of the factors associated with heart disease. Dull and demeaning work, work over which the worker has little or no control, as well as other poor features of work also contribute to an assortment of mental health problems. But we find that work can be used to alleviate the problems it presently causes or correlates with highly. From the point of view of public policy, workers and society are bearing medical costs that have their genesis in the workplace, and which could be avoided through preventive measures. . . .

The redesign of jobs is the keystone of this report. Not only does it hold out some promise to decrease mental and physical health costs, increase productivity, and improve the quality of life for millions of Americans at all occupational levels, it would give, for the first time, a voice to many workers in an important decision-making process. Citizen participation in the arena where the individual's voice directly affects his immediate environment may do much to reduce political alienation in America. (pp. xv–xviii)

In the last year, there have been several major conferences bearing upon the problem of a reduction in the rate of U.S. productivity growth. To cite one example, on November 14, 1978, in a forum sponsored by the National Academy of Sciences, six representatives of business, government, and academia expressed their concern about the decline in America's productivity and innovative spirit. As evidence they cited the lowered growth rate of our economy, worsening U.S. balance of trade, decreasing number of U.S. patents issued to U.S. inventors, and lessening amount of real dollars being spent by industry on research and development.

The action proposals offered for coping with or overcoming these serious interrelated problems were:

1. Massive reform of federal regulatory practices
2. Greater emphasis on job training particularly of young people
3. Reorientation in tax policy
4. A leveling off of interest rates
5. Incentives for (a) modernizing plant, equipment, and technology; (b) industrial innovation; and (c) basic research and development
6. Curtailment of overall government spending
7. Review of confusing antitrust and red-tape-laden patent laws

These recommendations reflect the issues as perceived by knowledgeable spokesmen. All are relevant. Taken together they probably could stimulate productivity and exports. But as a logician would put it, "Perhaps necessary, but not sufficient." Conspicuous by its absence from the list is the contribution that might be made by managing and structuring work situations in ways likely to motivate employees at all levels to become respected partners in problem identification and problem solving with reference to any aspects of the work situation that were perceived to be in need of review.

One way of facilitating that kind of motivation is to foster, on a broad scale, improvement of the quality of worklife (QWL) in American organizations. A recent promising piece of legislation passed by Congress in the rush before adjournment in October 1978 does attempt to deal with this relatively neglected need. More on this later.

Now, what do we mean by "quality of worklife"? Basically it is a process by which individuals and groups in an organization, through appropriate communication structures that are set up, can have some say about the design and organization of their work. Under that type of participative and responsive organizational climate, problems, suggestions, questions, or criticisms that might lead to improvement of any kind are welcomed. Creative discontent thus is viewed as a manifestation of constructive caring about the organization rather than destructive griping. Management encouragement of such feelings of involvement often leads to ideas and actions for upgrading of organizational effectiveness in various ways, and increased productivity along with higher morale are likely to result as natural byproducts (Glaser, 1976).

One of the subtler benefits that often results from this type of management-work force collaboration is a reduction in needless types of adversary relationships, yet without undermining (in unionized organizations) existing collective bargaining contracts. As individuals and groups come to agree on certain common goals and means for achieving them, they tend to become more self-responsible and thus require less monitoring and controlling. If that evolves, *overhead costs may decrease significantly.* To pursue productivity improvement in comprehensive ways, we need to think of it as more than just output of goods and services divided by hours of work required to produce them. We need as well to explore ways of enhancing *management* effectiveness and efficiency.

The Human Interaction Research Institute (1979) conducted a study (sponsored by the National Science Foundation) entitled "Quality of Worklife Programs: A Preliminary Technology Assessment." One segment of that study has involved interviews with 17 top officials from 15 major labor unions in the United States concerning their attitudes and experience regarding cooperation with management in QWL improvement programs. In a telephone discussion one of these officials described the (unidentified) situation of a midwest equipment manufacturer where there had been a great deal of labor-management friction and poor product quality. As a result, business fell off, the work force was reduced from approximately 800 to 400, and the company soon thereafter was sold to a Japanese firm.

The new owners installed a Japanese chief executive officer who spoke very adequate English. One of his early actions was to call a meeting of the remaining management group and union leaders to share the problems and facts about the existing business situation. He then invited their questions/suggestions. Next, the new manager gave the same information to the balance of the work force. He solicited ideas from all who cared to offer any regarding ways to improve quality and lower costs, thereby making it possible to recapture their lost share of the market. He pointed out that if appreciable sales expansion could be achieved, a happy consequence would be additions to the work force and greater job security for all employees.

A joint labor-management committee was set up to analyze engineering and production problems, receive ideas for operational improvement of any kind, propose problem-solving actions, share in decision making about the design and organization of work, provide feedback of progress to all employees, and so forth. It should be noted that in addition to instituting a responsive, cooperative management-union climate, with joint participation in various types of planning—thus capturing the essence of a QWL process—the new owners showed a very important readiness to adopt modernizing technical changes and a willingness to invest capital in promising new business ventures.

Within 9 months business improved to the point where the company needed to rehire (or hire) approximately 400 more people, bringing the total work force back to its previous peak!

The Japanese do not have a monopoly on managerial practices (such as their well-known quality control circles) that yield sustained favorable results from achieving a relatively high level of worker identification with the legitimate need for cost-effective operation and superior product quality. For example, Donnelly Mirrors, headquartered in Holland, Michigan, has emphasized the redistribution of influence from a top power center to all levels of the organization, the goal being to tap the creativity, resources, and ego-involvement, of all employees. The Donnelly program began in 1952, when the company installed a cost-savings-sharing plan. In conjunction, they added a participative style of management supported by related organization development and training activities. Employee participation in setting goals and in making work-related decisions was encouraged.

Employees have shared in the gains made as a result of their efforts. Reported results over the years include a reduction of the price of its main product by 25 percent between 1972 and 1974, thus expanding Donnelly's share of the market; in 20 years, productivity per person has doubled; employee bonuses have averaged 12 percent over base pay; absenteeism has dropped from 5 percent to 1 percent; quality levels have climbed from 92 percent to 98.5 percent; there has been a marked reduction in returned goods; employee job satisfaction has climbed noticeably.

Donnelly Mirrors happens to be nonunion, but there are a number of organizations with unionized operations that have attempted QWL improvement programs. A few reported examples are the pipe mill at Kaiser Steel in Fontana, California, where productivity was increased 32.1 percent in 3 months after an overall Union-Management Productivity Committee was instituted; the Bolivar, Tennessee, plant of Harman International, that in 1977 became a division of Beatrice Foods; some of the plants in organizations such as General Motors, Eaton, TRW, Midland-Ross, Dana Corporation, Ralston-Purina, and Nabisco. While there are others not mentioned here, the total is very small compared with the number of companies (and unions) in the United States that potentially *could* explore the possibility of adapting to their own situations a method of operating that invites participation in appropriate kinds of planning and decision making by all concerned with regard to ways of enhancing both improved quality of working life *and* productivity gains.

In his excellent book, *Work, Learning and the American Future,* Dr. James O'Toole, former chairman of the 1972 *Work in America* Task Force, points out that such a participative style calls for change in the philosophy and behavior of many managers or officials—both in companies and in unions—with regard to the way human resources are valued and utilized. Such a management style may be viewed by supervisors as an erosion of their authority. And union officials may view such direct contact between workers and management as undermining their role.

From the union's point of view, the major aspect of developing a viable QWL program/process is to create a climate that promotes worker job satisfaction. The key element is not the improvement of productivity or the reduction in labor costs. The key element is the creation of an atmosphere in which workers can take part in the decision-making process on matters that affect them, and to do this in such a way as to expand the opportunities for work satisfaction. From such an operating style, productivity improvement is a likely fallout.

It should be noted that there have been quite a few QWL experiments that have not survived for various reasons. Those cases should be studied for understanding of the *conditions* that seem to be required for success, and the most common reasons for failure.

The type of participative management practice discussed here is entirely consistent with organizational discipline and appropriately controlled operations—controlled, that is, in the interest of efficiency, effectiveness, quality assurance, customer service, profitability, and high employee morale. Managers who evince concern with QWL considerations continue to be accountable for carrying out their responsibilities effectively. If they learn that inviting consultation or "collective wisdom" from persons they supervise is likely to lead to better quality and acceptance of decisions, then they simply become better managers.

Such an approach is not to be confused with some abstract sociopolitical concept of "democratic management." That is, decisions about what is to be done in the work context are not arrived at by "voting." In a psychological rather than a sociopolitical sense, however, the QWL improvement orientation is democratic. It invites employees from all departments at all levels to have a say about their work, which in turn makes for a sense of part ownership of any change(s) that may result because they have had a "piece of the action." Thus, it enhances self-esteem and reduces feelings of powerlessness.

A caveat is needed here, however. While the participative principle offers opportunity for enhancing self-esteem and lessening the feeling of powerlessness, in many situations there needs to be a blending of experts and nonexperts ("the people") from various stakeholder groups. In some situations, what the experts say far outweighs (and correctly so) what "the people" may think/want regarding the matter, and thus participation is not the method of choice in all situations.

Then, too, sometimes a responsible leader or legitimated decision maker is faced with trying to reconcile conflicting special-interest pressures or entrenched opinions/values, or is up against reality time constraints that simply do not permit much participative discussion. In such cases he or she needs to take the position that commensurate authority must accompany responsibility, and mandate a given course of action at the time, accompanied by reasons for that decision. If the consequences are not irrevocable, there can be review/refinement after adequate experience in implementation.

Basically, QWL improvement programs constitute a strategy in the preventive rather than remedial mode.

Now, let us return briefly to the piece of promising legislation referred to earlier. Congressman Stanley N. Lundine was formerly the mayor of Jamestown, New York (population 40,000). In that role he served as the initiator, catalyst, and gadfly for introduction of the Jamestown Labor-Management Committee in 1972, when the city was experiencing a severe economic downturn, unemployment had reached 10 percent, and the city was bedeviled by labor problems. Through the Labor-Management Committee, Lundine was able to get local company managers and union leaders to talk out problems, establish training programs, and in some cases establish cost-savings-sharing arrangements. Significant improvement in the Jamestown scene resulted. In 1976 Lundine was elected to Congress where he sponsored a bill to provide financial incentives for companies and unions to engage in quality of worklife improvement efforts. In the closing session of Congress in October 1978 his proposed bill was passed. It consists of Section 6 added as an amendment to the CETA legislation, and it is cited as the Labor-Management Cooperation Act of 1978. Its stated purposes are:

1. To improve communication between representatives of labor and management
2. To provide workers and employers with opportunities to study and explore new and innovative joint approaches to achieving organizational effectiveness
3. To assist workers and employers in solving problems of mutual con-

cern not susceptible to resolution within the collective bargaining process

4. To study and explore ways of eliminating potential problems which reduce the competitiveness and inhibit the economic development of the plant, area or industry

5. To enhance the involvement of workers in making decisions that affect their working lives

6. To encourage free collective bargaining by establishing continuing mechanisms for communication between employers and their employees through Federal assistance to the formation and operation of labor-management committees

To carry out the provisions of this section, $10,000,000 has been authorized to be appropriated for the fiscal year 1979, and such sums as may be necessary thereafter.

The Federal Mediation and Conciliation Service is authorized to enter into contracts and to make grants under this act only in situations where the employees are unionized. Thus, if funds are in fact provided during 1979 (which now seems very unlikely) to permit implementation of this legislation, companies or segments thereof in which employees are unionized will be able to obtain financial incentives for experimenting with such processes and programs. More important than concern with financial subsidy, however, should be the potential benefits to be gained if this incentive stimulates company managements and employees to explore methods of working together toward certain QWL improvement objectives, and follow through with appropriate action. To be sure, such exploration does not require governmental assistance to initiate; they can do it by themselves.

Concluding Remarks

Let us now restate our two concepts:

Concept #1: There is a need to develop state-of-the-art knowledge syntheses in various important fields, and to effectively promote wide utilization of both validated research and development findings and exemplary practices.

Concept #2: The most favorable condition for improvement programs of any kind to take root and then be sustained is to involve the stakeholders in problem identification, followed by their participation in problem solving. Implicit in Concept #2 is that when people *do* get involved as active participants in a group process to "save themselves," the spirit of caring and of assuming their share of responsibility means working for the general good of all concerned, not *just* for self-benefit. A kindling of our latent potential for helping one another may be the priceless ingredient in the prescription.

It is clear that this concept does not state a new, startling, unusually sophisticated, or esoteric idea. Indeed, the principle of inviting people to participate in decisions on matters affecting them and which they care about appears quite commonplace. Is this just another example of rediscovering the obvious? I think not, because in the hierarchical, bureaucratic organization of much of our society this principle is all too rarely practiced. In the discussion here, there has been an attempt both to reinforce the importance of the principle and indicate how it can be applied profitably for all concerned at the workplace, in our schools, and in our families.

In conclusion, the basic strategies proposed above for identifying, disseminating, and promoting utilization of the most promising knowledge and practices we can find to address serious problems in the broad areas of family relations, schools, and the organization of work are in a preventive orientation. They are proactive, and can be of help to large groups of people not yet beset with the problems or conditions to be prevented. At the same time they serve remedial purposes in specific situations. They represent doing things *with* people rather than to them or for them. Thus, if the stakeholders are partners in planning, and adopt or adapt promising new knowledge or practices to their own settings, they become the ego-involved "owners" of their altered *modus operandi*. Essentially, they will have done it for themselves. By the same token we would be building a more responsible citizenry, in a spirit of greater sharing with each other and less taking from each other. In that process we would be making a forceful response to the challenge for achieving renaissance of the American dream.

References

Allport, G. W. The psychology of participation. *Psychological Review*, 1945, 52, 117–132.
Barker, M. Students work small miracle on condemned house. *Los Angeles Times*, July 12, 1973.
Bumstead, R. The Thaler system: A slice-of-life curriculum. *Phi Delta Kappan*, 1978, 59(10), 659–664.
Gibson, W. *The miracle worker*. New York: French Company, 1960.
Glaser, E. M. Knowledge transfer and institutional change. *Professional Psychology*, 1973, 4, 434–444.
Glaser, E. M. *Productivity gains through worklife improvement*. New York: Harcourt Brace Jovanovich, 1976.
Graham, P. Circuit overload in our schools. *Columbia*, Spring 1979, 4(3), 48.

Hearings on school violence and vandalism. Report of the Senate Subcommittee to Investigate Juvenile Delinquency. Washington, D.C.: U.S. Government Printing Office, 1975.

Hodgkin, J. E., Balchum, O. J., Kass, I., Glaser, E. M., Miller, W. F., Haas, A., Shaw, D. B., Kimbel, P., and Petty, T. L. Chronic obstructive airway diseases: Current concepts in diagnosis and comprehensive care. *Journal of the American Medical Association,* 1975, *232,* 1243–1260.

Human Interaction Research Institute. *Quality of worklife programs: A preliminary technology assessment.* (Final Report to the National Science Foundation, Grant No. ERS 76–16700). Los Angeles, 1979.

Maier, N. R. F. *Problem-solving discussions and conferences.* New York: McGraw-Hill, 1963.

National Institute of Education. *Violent schools—safe schools. The Safe School Study Report to the Congress* (Vol. 1). Washington, D.C.: U.S. Government Printing Office, 1978.

O'Toole, J. *Work, learning and the American future.* San Francisco: Jossey-Bass, 1977.

Sarason, I. A cognitive social learning approach to juvenile delinquency. In R. Hare and D. Schalling (Eds.), *Crime and delinquency: Recent research and theory.* New York: Wiley, 1978.

Stone, M. Are ethics on the way back? *U.S. News & World Report,* January 22, 1979, p. 80.

Work in America. Cambridge, Mass.: The MIT Press, 1972.

Coercing Changes in Prisons and Mental Hospitals

The Social Scientist and the Class Action Suit

Stanley L. Brodsky and Kent S. Miller

The purpose of this paper is to describe a model for social scientists and mental health professionals, a model in which the social scientist becomes an ally of powerful forces seeking to change harmful social systems. One way of conceptualizing this model is to draw a role dichotomy between system professionals and system challengers (Brodsky, 1973). System professionals are individuals who are committed to doing their best to help clients—within the context of the stated goals of the organization. Thus in prison settings, a system professional psychotherapist might well accept as a goal aiding inmates in adjusting to prison rules and policies.

On the other hand, system challengers may be thought of as persons who question the values and policies on which the agencies or social system are based. In the Sanford and Comstock book *Sanctions for Evil* (1971), several descriptions of this role appear, including one under the title of combating institutional evil from within. The system challengers, as we view them, are reluctant to deal with continuing end-products of social inequities, and would rather aim at a mid-range target of social change. The broad-range target would be massive social injustices, problems that are beyond the scope of most governmental bodies to affect. Narrow-range targets include individual day-to-day transactions-transgressions between individuals, the sort of target that is pursued by staff training or direct services. Our system challenger has the mid-range target of the hospital, the mental health system, or the correctional system—or even the hospital building or the training school. The particular vehicle we will emphasize here is the class action suit—although we will also discuss other methods.

We think of the change process occurring in distal or proximate ways.

Distal ways are the ones in which social change is far removed from the actions of the protagonist, by years and by many miles. Surely academic research and theoretical developments may be considered agents of social change. However, there is rarely a one-to-one relationship between any one work and the affects, and the time gap makes causal inferences difficult. Instead we choose to look at proximate change models. The system challenger does something, and electron microscopy is not necessary to see immediate and substantive system change. But as we come to the end of the 1970s, there is considerable doubt in some camps about the prospects for significant social change, and thus before turning to a detailed discussion of the model being proposed, there is a need to place it in a broader context.

The National Mood at the Close of the 1970s

The pessimism and cynicism that characterized the general mood at the end of the 1970s finally spread to include social scientists and mental health professionals. The evidence of a lack of will in grappling with major social problems is close at hand and easily identified, as is the justification for the retreat, although at points the two are hopelessly intertwined. The major themes in prison and mental hospital problems may by now be familiar to the reader, but a few comments on them may prove to be instructive in viewing the role of the social scientist in class action suits and in social change effort generally.

The prison system has retreated from the rehabilitation ideology that has been in effect for 100 years, and a number of people seem to take a perverse kind of pleasure from an "evaluation of evaluations" that reviewed several hundred studies and concluded that efforts at rehabilitation were useless (Lipton, Martinson, & Wilkes, 1975). On the positive side, this movement has been supported by people concerned with controlling the discretion of courts and prison systems, thereby attempting to introduce greater social justice. But the overall effect of the move away from rehabilitation will probably be more people in jail or prison for longer periods of time, and in spite of protests to the contrary, it is likely to serve as an excuse for abandoning the people now in institutions.

The failures of the deinstitutionalization movement have been widely publicized. The dramatic decrease in the population of state mental hospitals has been offset by a corresponding growth in nursing home placement of mental patients. Note that in 1970 we continued to institutionalize the same proportion of the total population—one percent—as we did in 1950 (President's Commission on Mental Health, 1978). Deinstitutionalization is also said to have resulted in the "criminalization of mental illness," with the criminal justice system now managing many patients formerly handled by the mental health system (Abramson, 1972; Forst, 1978; Sosowsky, 1978). Thus the appropriateness of the movement has been called into question, and a backlash is highly visable.

During the 1970s, significant gains were made in understanding the limitations of technology within the mental health field, the role of values, and the need to protect civil rights. There is now a feeling that all of this has come too far, that the rights of individuals may have been inappropriately elevated over family and community rights, and that it is time to move back in the other direction. We seem to be entering a period when many of the people who helped us in seeing the abuse and limitations are now arguing against further reform (Halleck, 1974; Halleck and Witte, 1977; Robitscher, 1977; Stone, 1975, 1977). Paradoxically, in the face of heavy criticism about the abuse of power within the mental health field, and the recognition of the essentially political nature of much of the work, there has been a continued expansion of that power.

Undoubtedly there are other major developments that should be included in the above outline of current perspectives. But this brief description of the pervasive climate provides a backdrop for a more detailed discussion of class action suits and the role of the court in bringing about further change. As we shall see, the pessimism that surrounded attempts at legislative reform has now moved on to envelope the class action suit.

Class Action Suits in Mental Hospitals and Prisons

Over the past few years, public interest lawyers have forced state and federal courts to develop a significant body of mental health law, and have focused attention on the rights of prisoners. The success of various "rights" groups—prisoners, children, mental patients, the disabled—has exceeded the expectations of most observers. Much of this has been as a result of class action suits, frequently involving entire state systems. Probably the best known of such cases occurred in Alabama in *Wyatt* v. *Stickney*. Between 1970 and 1974 the inpatient census in the state system was cut in half, additional staff was hired, and the state budget rose from $26 million to $72 million (Rubin, 1978, p. xiv). Changes of a similar nature, sometimes less grand, occurred in other states as a result of litigation.

In the early stages of this movement the mental health professional within the institution and at the state level frequently welcomed the suits because of a hope that additional resources would be made available, and thus there were friendly stipulations to the charges being made in the courts. As a result of all this action there was talk about a revolution in mental health care and a feeling that significant steps had been taken in correcting the negative aspects of institutionalization that social scientists had documented in detail.

But by 1978, much of this attitude had changed. The themes that began to evolve at conferences and in the professional publications took on a much more reserved and pessimistic quality. It was suggested that the census in Alabama's hospitals was dropping dramatically prior to the *Wyatt* case; that the impact of *Wyatt* was as much a result of changing state policy as it was a cause; that much of the new money was federal money resulting from the switch to desegregated facilities (Brooks, 1978, p. xiv). The orders in class action suits were seldom implemented, and it became the norm for the courts to retain jurisdiction, appoint special masters, and bring the parties back time and again. People began to produce papers with titles like "The Realities of Mental Health Advocacy" (Scallet, 1977), "Paper Victories and Hard Realities" (Bradley and Clarke, 1976), and "Enforcement of Judicial Degrees: Now Comes the Hard Part" (Lottman, 1976). Four years after *Donaldson*, the Florida Hospital from which the case came continued to be in violation on the essential points made by the U.S. Supreme Court.

Significantly, the organization that has probably contributed the most to the success that has been achieved, is beginning to have reservations about the value of litigation. The Mental Health Law Project in Washington, D.C., is beginning to talk about a shift in emphasis to educational efforts rather than litigation (Rosenberg, 1979). Several reasons are given for such a shift: (1) The cost of implementing the court orders is astronomical; (2) reform cannot be "rammed down the throat"; (3) there is an erosion of the previously available support from professional organizations; and (4) class action suits may have a place at the "establishment-of-liability" phase but accomplishments will come only through collective work.

Brooks (1978) has summarized a number of additional questions. Do the changes that have occurred reflect an efficient allocation of scarce resources? Does the shift of resources simply mean that other needs, possibly more important, will go unmet? Does additional staff necessarily mean better treatment? Others (Chayes, 1976; Glazer, 1978) have expressed doubts about the appropriateness of the courts entering the business of administering social services, and the consequences of this trend for judicial systems.

Finally, from the perspective of an economist (Rubin, 1978, p. xviii), the capacity of litigation as a mechanism for the allocation of resources is questioned.

Unless the objectives of litigation coincide with public preferences and until such litigation recognizes the limitations on and alternative uses of society's resources, it is unreasonable to expect that in the long run litigation will successfully achieve the goals set out by the plaintiffs. In the short run, improvements can certainly be attained; the evidence bears this out. But we remain pessimistic as to the capacity of litigation to ensure the attainment of the kind of mental health care system envisioned by those who bring such lawsuits. (p. 18)

Rubin goes on to point out that much of the benefit of public provision of institutional mental health care is due to the "protection" of the public benefits that derive from institutionalization and not from the delivery of adequate care.

SOME REASONS FOR HOPE

There is considerable substance to the problems that have been identified, but there has also been some overestimation of the failures. The troops have tired prematurely, and may be in need of a review of what has been accomplished.

One major consequence has been the documentation of the harmful aspects of institutionalization. In considerable detail, the courts have entertained evidence of the constitutional abuses that have existed for years, and have prescribed for the public and the professions what must be done to put matters right. Even the most hardened prison warden or superintendent of a mental hospital now recognizes that these institutions create more deviance than they cure. There is no going back from this understanding, even though we may not know what to do to correct the problems.

Secondly, there have been specific improvements within institutions. Some of the judicial standards covering the quality of life have been enforced, and for some individual patients there have been dramatic changes. In those instances where there have been "paper victories" only, there has been symbolic value that has had undetermined affects upon practices in other jurisdictions. There is value to publicly affirming what our relations with those at the bottom of the economic and social power ladder *should be*, aside from what they are.

The current tendency to back off from attempts at reform is based at least in part upon expectations that were too high. There is much evidence to the effect that unpopular and expensive decisions of the U.S. Supreme Court are frequently ignored. Take as an example the decision in *Argersinger* v. *Hamlin*, which provided an attorney for any defendant facing a charge that could result in imprisonment. A recent national investigation revealed there has been no real effort in most jurisdictions to apply or even to confront the basic principles of *Argersinger* (Krantz et al., 1976, p. 5). Should we be surprised to discover that many of the complex decisions relating to prison and mental hospitals have not been implemented?

Recent work in the field of program evaluation has highlighted the problems of translating research findings into social policy. One observer has concluded that social science research in general tends to follow, rather than precede, public policy decisions. Henry Aaron comes to this conclusion after reviewing the role of the federal government in its capacity to bring about change in three areas: poverty and discrimination; education and training; and, unemployment and inflation.

The parallel between development of social science and the views of scholars, on the one hand, and developments of public policy during this period, on the other, was striking in each of these three areas. But in many cases, the findings of social science seemed to come after, rather than before, change in policy, which suggests that political events may influence scholars more than research influences policy. (Aaron, 1978, p. 9)

Aaron goes on to suggest that the social science contribution is usually not so much specific information and conclusion as it is a contribution to a general perspective. Much of the research within social science turns out to be flawed, criticized, and rejected. Repeatedly, the function of social science seems to be that of searching out weaknesses and uncovering the failures of programs. Given this reality, policy-makers are prone to ignore research findings when they conflict with deeply held beliefs and predetermined positions.

If Aaron's analysis is correct, then we can take satisfaction in the surprising contribution that social science research has already made to class action suits. We indicated above that there are some who now are inclined to move away from litigation to an educational effort. It may well be that continued efforts through the courts could effectively serve the goals of education and just might accomplish more in "contribution to a general perspective" than would other approaches. This effectiveness might be particularly important, since there is no reason in the short run to expect much reform through legislative action.

Finally, some comfort can be taken from a review of recent court rulings cutting across a number of issues affecting persons in prisons and mental hospitals (Miller, Fein, and Schmidt, 1979). Based upon a review of hundreds of decisions between 1975 and 1977, the authors conclude that with very few exceptions, the courts support the notion that the state has a very direct and continuing responsibility to provide therapeutic services to an ever larger number of its citizens, without regard to setting or type of institution. The current skepticism concerning the failures of rehabilitation has not, it seems, reached the courts, or if it has, the impact has been minimized. Rehabilitative services are being required on both constitutional and statutory grounds, under the exercise of police and *parens patriae* powers.

Along with this general trend to expand therapeutic services, there has been an affirmation of individual rights—the right to refuse treatment, the application of full due process, attempts to tighten the criteria for civil commitment, and the like. But it should be recognized that these rights relate primarily to the question of *how* and *where* the services are to be rendered, not whether they are to be provided in the first place. The role of mental health professionals in addressing troublesome behavior has been affirmed time and time again.

We turn now to two specific examples of recent class action suits.

THE ALABAMA PRISON EXPERIENCE

An elderly Black inmate named Worley James wrote a penciled letter to federal district judge Frank M. Johnson, explaining that in many years in Alabama prisons he, James, had simply become worse and worse in many ways. This letter became transformed into the class action suit of *James* v. *Wallace* against the State of Alabama, and subsequently was combined with two other suits—one for adequate medical treatment and the other for the right to be free from physical harm in the Alabama prisons (*Newman* v. *Alabama* and *Pugh* v. *Locke*).

In January, 1976, Judge Johnson ruled in favor of the plaintiffs in this suit. The rulings severely denounced the conditions in the prisons, criticizing the unacceptable sanitary conditions, the food, the pervasive overcrowding of men into less than 24 square feet of living space, and the untreated and undiagnosed physical and mental illnesses. The court ordered that no more prisoners be admitted to the prison system until the population was reduced to the design capacity of the buildings. Immediate changes in sanitation, food, and living conditions were ordered. Eleven constitutional rights of inmates were identified. And a major effort was begun to change the barbaric, violent, and oppressive circumstances in which Alabama inmates found themselves.

Psychologist participation in this legal action began early. Attorneys for the plaintiffs consulted with many mental health professionals about issues to pursue and minimum standards for maintaining human adjustment. One psychologist, Carl Clements, inspected the prisons repeatedly and testified in court about the effects of these prison living conditions. Following the court order, the Psychology Department of the University of Alabama conducted a prisoner classification project, under the direction of the department chairman, Raymond Fowler. Over a period of four months, 3,191 prisoners were assessed, and approximately 1,000 judged as appropriate for "community custody." The court order had required evaluation to determine which prisoners were fit for noninstitutional living, and most of the 1,000 men and women were transferred to work release centers or other community placements, or released.

The prison classification project was not an unqualified success, and many problems arose in implementation of the court standards and order (Brodsky, 1977; Schuster and Widmer, 1978). Nevertheless, the class action suit and court order present some important lessons in understanding the social change–primary prevention process.

First, no amount of direct service would have been able to ameliorate the emotional harm wrought by the day-to-day living environment. In some prisons, over half of the men were victims of physical or sexual assaults, and carrying a weapon for self-protection was normative behavior. For the men there, as well as for future inmates, the system change allowed the potential for maintaining an emotional status quo. And while the Alabama prison system is worth describing because of the seriousness of the problems, the same process exists in other prisons. In our experience, only a minority, and perhaps a small minority, are not vulnerable to the stresses of prison confinement, and the sweeping change by class action suit and court order is a preventive strategy of much value. The right to avoid cruel and unusual punishment is often abrogated, and the symptoms from such punishment may be severe.

Second, a familiar pattern emerged in the wake of the order. The prison system budget rose, the inmate census and overcrowding dropped dramatically, and attention of citizens at large, newspapers, and legislators became forcibly directed toward prison problems.

Third, much of the evidence in court and the post-order action was based on assessments by social science and mental health professionals. This evidence and these assessments were utilized by the attorneys for the plaintiffs who were suing the system. Thus the social scientists' role could be defined as a system challenger.

Lastly, the resistances to system change persisted even in the presence of the court order. The state is far from being in full compliance. Many of the originally identified constitutional violations continue, although the overcrowding and other violations have been corrected or alleviated.

SOLITARY CONFINEMENT ON DEATH ROW

Long confinement under circumstances of isolation has been studied both in sensory deprivation research and in investigations of solitary confinement in prisons. Several books in the last two decades have considered effects of sensory deprivation (for example, Schutz, 1965; Zubek, 1969). A great range of disturbance has been reported, including cognitive and perceptual disorganization, anxiety, and inappropriate emotional reactions. Within prison settings, so-called isolation sickness occurs with great frequency. The process of developing cabin fever, if one is a solitary explorer wintering over in the Arctic, or going stir crazy in solitary confinement, appears well validated (Lugg, 1977; Taylor, 1961), although a few behavioral scientists have attempted to develop the argument that solitary confinement can be beneficial (for example, Suedfeld, 1975).

The present concern is with *Jacobs* v. *Britton*, C.A., No. 78–309–H, filed in the U.S. District Court for the Southern District of Alabama. This class action suit alleged that the "treatment of death row inmates constitutes cruel and unusual punishment and a denial of equal protection." The alleged violations of state law, and of the Eighth and Fourteenth Amendments to the Constitution, included unsanitary food, improper toilets, physical brutality by the guards, limited visiting, minimal exercise and recreation, and indefinite confinement in these conditions. The plaintiffs' attorneys asked one of us to assess the psychological impact of living on death row. In particular, the issue was raised of whether the conditions themselves had adverse effects on the mental well-being of the inmates. If a substantial hazard to the health of the inmates *was* discovered, this finding would indicate a violation of the inmates' constitutional protection against cruel punishment.

Our investigation centered around the nature of existing psychopathology in the death row inmates—its extent, and whether it was peculiar to these death row conditions. If the disorder existed prior to death row confinement, then no causal inferences could be drawn. A final necessary complication was whether anticipation of execution—that is, having an assigned death penalty—was pathology-producing by itself. If it was, then the effects of the living conditions would be less clear.

Thirty-three prisoners were confined on death row at the time of our study. Initially, the full prison records of each were examined. It was found that these records were generally skimpy and useless for our purposes. Because the prisoners were under the death sentence, and because they were officially under the administrative control of the county jail authorities, no classification testing or assessment process was undertaken.

Interviews were conducted with the two psychologists, the classification officer, and the medical-technical assistant who had some contact with the prisoners. Further discussions were held with the warden and with the correctional officers in charge of the unit.

The medical records were studied, and all doctors' contacts, medical examinations, chart entries, and prescribed medication were abstracted. Two instruments were used in extensive interviewing of a selective sample of the prisoners. The prisoners were seen in interviews lasting from 30 minutes to one hour, and the Omnibus Stress Index and a checklist of solitary confinement related symptoms were administered. The index used is a 12-item schedule for which prisoner norms were available in David Jones's book *The Health Risks of Imprisonment* (1976). The latter checklist was especially constructed from a content analysis of the literature on solitary confinement. While a portion of the results was derived from brief interviews with inmates through their cell doors, the major substance including the present information came from ten detailed interviews.

The Psychological Consequences
Two of the ten men were assessed as seriously disturbed, five as moderately disturbed, and three as mildly disturbed or no maladjustment seen. The medical records of the two most disturbed inmates included items such as "laughs all the time . . . a psychotic depressive . . . hebephrenic schizophrenic diagnosis" and "tears paper up in piles . . . wild-eyed and does not answer." The inmates themselves offered self-reports about the serious emotional consequences of death row confinement. Their statements included:

"If I ever were to get out. I would not be the same person. I just want them to leave me alone."
"They are all out to get you."
"If I am sitting up, I get to shaking, my hands go back and forth."
"I'm confused now. I'm so confused I don't understand. I'm not a killer."
"You just can't sleep . . . you are wide awake."

The reactions reported as characteristic were crying, dejectedness, anger, hostility toward specific persons, confusion, inappropriate giggling, and obsessive ruminations. Headaches were reported as well as anxiety: "The anxiety goes right through you." The milieu was described in negative terms:

"They treat you like an animal here."
"They try to degrade you and break your spirits."
"Respect of the inmate is abused."
"[there are] 23½ hours of [cell] confinement every day."

The physical milieu was described as having bad smells, unsanitary conditions, cold food, limited exercise and visiting, and clothing restrictions beyond those of other prisoners. The general sentiment was that "living conditions here ain't worth a shit." When the inmates were asked if they were aware of sensory deprivation, they agreed and reported that they experienced losses in ability to think clearly, and in recognition capacity, as well as perceptual alterations and hallucinations.

Omnibus Stress Index

In response to the query "Do you experience these symptoms?" eight of the ten intensively interviewed men endorsed the following four items: nervousness, inertia, insomnia, and trembling hands. Seven men reported perspiring hands; six reported a nervous breakdown or feelings of an impending nervous breakdown; and six reported headaches. Five men reported nightmares and dizziness; four reported heart palpitations; and one reported fainting spells. Overall, these patterns were higher than the 50 percent rate reported in the Jones study of the Omnibus Stress Index with Tennessee prisoners.

In the Ferracuti, et al. (1978) study of mental deterioration in prisoners in Ohio and Italy, 21 percent of the older prisoners were found to be susceptible to deterioration, as well as nineteen percent and sixteen percent of two younger prisoner groups. Again, the present prisoners appeared to be suffering more symptoms, more severely. The checklist of solitary confinement symptoms revealed parallel findings. The prisoners tended to report quiet withdrawal, talking to themselves, feeling stir crazy, hostility, confusion, lessened concern about physical appearance, apathy, and memory losses.

The Exceptions

Three of our sample seemed to have adapted reasonably well. They were unhappy about the living conditions, and complained at length, but there were few or no signs of psychopathology. These men generally experienced little current or past anxiety about their lives, and were often flip, and occasionally quite humorous. The interviews were conducted in the one available room, the observation room that adjoined the electric chair chamber. One of these inmates looked through the observation window and quipped, "So that's what old sparky looks like." Another, when offered a Life-saver candy while walking down the corridor replied, "If they really work, I'll take two or three."

Implications of the Death Row Suit

The three interrelated factors—preexisting pathology, effects of being under death sentence, and actual living conditions—could not be fully differentiated. Nevertheless, from the best information available to us, there were many men who had not shown significant earlier disorder and men who reported at least some strongly noxious effects of the living conditions. Our conclusion was that emotionally vulnerable men were very likely to deteriorate, and that the cell confinement, combined with little to do and virtually no positive social contact, represented a substantial stress.

The primary prevention implications concern dealing with such problems. It would be possible to mobilize a team of expert mental health professionals who would treat these men as needed. If prison officers spotted a man acting in bizarre ways or showing signs of psychotic processes, then a prompt referral could be made, and if necessary, the inmate transferred to a hospital or prison treatment unit.

However, the class action suit in this case suggested that a variety of contextual and environmental circumstances caused the emotional problems. If indeed the death sentence was believed to be a causal factor, one preventive strategy might have been to use that factor as a vehicle for changing the law through the legislature or courts. Our own observations of men on death row for years at a time have documented patterns of emotional trouble. Before the death penalty was frozen in the 1960s, we observed men slipping in and out of psychotic episodes as they waited with some uncertainty about their futures. These men, however, were also isolated from other people, prisoners, and staff—and thus precise cause and effect events were not available to us.

The case of *Jacobs* v. *Britton* has been subjected to a series of delays and a trial is pending. If a decision is ordered affirming the positions of the plaintiffs, the long-term effects will extend to future prisoners. As they go through the long wait before a clemency decision (the likely outcome for most death row prisoners in most states) typically commuting the death penalty to life imprisonment without parole, they will be given the opportunity to maintain some sense of personal integrity and worth. The role of the mental health professional in this suit is similar to many other such cases. Clinical knowledge is applied, but not in the interests of direct client service. Rather, the clinical knowledge is directed toward evaluation of an entire living complex and looks at the full range of factors that influence personal equilibrium. These evaluations are in the service of the court, rather than in the service of the immediate individual clients or agencies. It is arguably the court that has the most power to command an immediate change in these environmental factors, and if this is so, then the clinicians' work has a very broad impact.

Hospitals, Prisons, and Primary Prevention

In the face of the considerable attention that has been given to distinctions between primary, secondary, and tertiary prevention, the relationships between institutions and primary prevention may not be readily apparent. By the time the individual is in prison or a mental hospital, the perceived need is not for prevention, but for helping and treatment services. Yet there are a number of ways in which these institutions can be related to concepts of prevention and a number of reasons they should continue to be a focus of reform efforts.

1. The proportion of the population in institutions of one kind or another has not dropped as dramatically as is generally assumed.
2. The institutions consume a disproportionate amount of the resources available for services.
3. The emphasis upon the development of community programming frequently involves institutional populations.
4. The people in institutions represent ultimate powerlessness and these places are the clearest point where the state exercises its coercive powers (frequently in the name of good).
5. Continued support for total institutions as they are now constituted hinders the development of alternative and more effective means of dealing with troublesome behavior.
6. It is in these settings that many mental health professionals have knowingly or unknowingly played a conservative and system-supportive role.

There are a number of basic concepts or practices that could be judged to reflect primary prevention efforts in general. Among these would be included the following: the minimization of dependency; the fostering of a sense of community; maximizing the client's role in decision making; minimizing coercion; and, the reduction of stress. Our prisons and mental hospitals tend to work in directions opposite to each of these concepts. These negative aspects are harmful not only to the clients but also to the staff who work in the institution, and thus in this sense are antithetical to primary prevention. For all of these reasons, a continued effort at reform is important and of consequence to a large number of people.

As an aside, a word should be said about our national commitment to the solving of social problems, particularly those of the poor (who constitute the population of our institutions). The common wisdom is that massive amounts of money were spent for this purpose in the 1960s and early 1970s, and that the federal budget is out of control. The fact is that the federal budget (measured as a proportion of full-employment gross national product) was only slightly larger in 1977 than in 1960, having grown from 18.1 percent to 20.1 percent during this period (Aaron, 1978, p. 5).

Growth in human resource and transfer programs focused on the poor continued during the first Nixon administration, but was reversed after 1973. Despite the concern about the "welfare mess" of growing rolls and rising budgets, cash and in-kind transfers focused on the poor actually declined between 1973 and 1976, from 1.8 percent to 1.5 percent of full-employment GNP and were about where they had been in 1971. (Aaron, 1978, p. 6)

The point is that we may not as yet have made a significant commitment to serving those at the bottom of the ladder, and more specifically, to those in our institutions. There is substance to the argument of some that no amount of money could overcome the inherent abuses in institutions. We tend to endorse this view, but highlight here the fact that such an attempt has not yet been made.

There is a need for system change and system advocacy in the broadest sense, and an approach through the courts by means of class action or public interest suits continues to hold considerable promise. There can be no doubt about the changing role of the judiciary in this country.

Roles that were unacceptable to the courts two or three decades ago are now assumed to be a reasonable responsibility for them (Horowitz, 1977, p. 4–21). We noted above the expansion of judicial responsibility into the administration of public programs, because of the failure of other branches of government to handle problems satisfactorily. The courts now determine entire courses of governmental agency conduct over a period of time, involving changing identities of the named defendants and plaintiffs. There has been a subordination of the significance of individual cases, although these frequently provide a departure point, and the assumption is that the public has an interest in the judicial resolution of important issues.

We are now hearing expressions of concern about the courts having overstepped their bounds, and we can expect the criticism to continue to mount. In the not too distant future, the courts may be a less significant force for change. If or when that occurs, those seeking reform will shift to other avenues. For example, when the American Civil Liberties Union found that under the Nixon courts the percentage of cases it was winning was cut in half, an increased emphasis was placed upon legislative change.

Some Reservations about the Therapeutic State

We have been arguing here the benefits and possibilities stemming from the newly found interests of the courts in the rights of mental patients and prisoners, and the roles that social scientists can play in this process. But there are some problems that need continuing scrutiny.

A part of the common wisdom today is that we are backing away from the "therapeutic state" and the "medical model"—from the notion of providing treatment as opposed to punishment as a means of dealing with troublesome people. This process is associated with the development of a "just deserts" philosophy, mandatory sentencing, an extreme concern for the rights of the individual prisoner and mental patient, and limits on the authority of the state. Without a detailed review of the merits of this perspective, we would like to note that we hold an alternate view. All of the evidence suggests that the social control functions of mental health and criminal justice systems are rapidly becoming interchangeable and amalgamated and that much of the conflict between the two is superficial.

The courts have affirmed with great consistency the states' responsibility to provide therapeutic services. A good example of this can be found in those discussions relating to the right to treatment. Although the Supreme Court in *Donaldson* v. *O'Connor* deliberately avoided dealing with the right to treatment aspects of the case, lower courts have affirmed repeatedly on both statutory and constitutional grounds the right to individualized treatment for a wide range of problems and in a variety of settings. Frequently this right has been placed in the midst of a number of other rights, including the concept of the least restrictive alternative, the right to education and work programs, and protection from harm.

If anything, the courts have tended to be expansive and to integrate the various rights into a general web. For example, the protection from harm concept has been interpreted to include affirmative programming for residents of institutions on the grounds that "harm can result not only from neglect but from conditions which cause regression or which prevent the development of an individual's capability" (*NYSARC & Parisi* v. *Carey*, 1973). It has also been ruled that treatment must be provided not only while the person is a resident of a mental hospital but also upon return to the community (*Patients* v. *Camden Co. Bd.*, 1977).

A further illustration of the tendency to expand the net can be seen in a court's interpretation of a diversion statute for narcotics offenders. Supervisory treatment was deemed to have been intended to include not only those who regularly used narcotics, but also for "prospective users, early stage users or experimenters, even though such persons ought not necessarily require the type of supervisory treatment called for by those who are regular users or addicts" (*State* v. *Alton*, 1976). These last two decisions in particular can be directly related to the concept of prevention.

But there are some potential problems as we attempt to deliver services and particularly with the functional amalgamation of the mental health and criminal justice systems. Until now, much of the attention given to the role of mental health within criminal justice has focused on institutions—specifically upon prisons and mental hospitals. It is important to note that the arena is being shifted away from exclusive concern with institutions, to the community, where operations will be more covert, and due process will be less likely. As the criminal justice system moves to a range of alternatives, the involvement of mental health will increase proportionately.

There are those who argue that sufficient reform has occurred within the mental health system, particularly with respect to legal reform and protections given to those being treated. The fact that we have continuing problems is attributed to the need for reform within the courts and criminal justice system. Certainly there needs to be a renewed concern with applying the law we now have. But reform within criminal justice will not suffice. The mental health system has considerable housecleaning yet to be done.

There are three specific propositions which serve as background for the safeguards and suggestions for reform. Although the real head-banging frequently centers upon procedure rather than substance, one's view of the reality of the criminal justice-mental health confluence is not insignificant, and thus it is appropriate to briefly restate ours.

1. *In their day-to-day operations the social control functions of the criminal justice and mental health systems are quite similar.* The common wisdom holds that the people in the two systems are in heavy conflict and share a mutual distrust. Close examination suggests that there is more smoke than fire, and that in fact there is a mutuality of needs and benefits.

One authority directly states that this is the basis for cooperation between the two systems:

The basis for the collaboration between psychiatry and the law is the fact that they are fundamentally similar institutions that deal with the evaluation and control of human behavior. (Barton and Sanborn, p. 318–319, 1978)

A second authority confirms this reality, but notes some minor differences:

In most of the 50 states, both the police and the mental health authorities are legitimate social control agents. However, the police in all cases have more extensive legal power and can be involved in many more situations of legal intervention than can the mental health worker. Social control via mental health services is real although it is less obvious and circumscribed. (Himmelsbach, p. 2, 1976)

Because it is less obvious and circumscribed, there are a number of mental health professionals who continue to deny this fact, and we have still not shed the fiction that the interests of clients are identical with those of the therapeutic and social service agencies (Gaylin, Glasser, Marcus, and Rothman, 1978).

2. *Punishment and treatment functions, each independently legitimate, can*

rarely be successfully combined. There is considerable agreement that a condition of trust is a necessity between the client and the person offering treatment. This may not apply to the same degree to certain coercive interventions, for example, psychosurgery, drugs, or some behavior modification techniques. But it would apply in the overwhelming majority of situations involving criminal justice and mental health. Treatment under coercion is likely to result in minimal, if any, gain; and regardless of protests to the contrary, in a sense, the mental health professional is always an adversary of the involuntary client. One observer, Ira Glasser, goes so far as to argue that we must begin, at least legally, to mistrust service professionals as well as depend on them, much as we do the police (Gaylin, Glasser, Marcus, and Rothman, 1978).

Most professionals find it difficult indeed to accept this latter point. Those clinicians who feel that decisions made are generally in the best interests of the clients typically fail to appreciate the problems inherent in the benevolence of the state. Evil intent is rare, but conflicting interest, hidden agendas, and a failure to acknowledge the operation of personal values is not. It has been suggested that the most disturbing aspects of these situations is that professionals resist facing these conflicts in the open, so that the hidden agendas have become public only as a result of legal challengers (Bazelon, 1974, p. 22). Many mental health practitioners would not agree with this statement, yet the evidence for its validity is substantial. To begin with, part of what mental health workers are asked to do for the criminal justice system is poorly done: the prediction of dangerousness, the determination of responsibility, and estimates of the probability of successful rehabilitation.

3. *Much of the work of the mental health system involves social and moral rather than scientific issues.* Seemingly technical and scientific solutions are offered to essentially moral, social, and philosophical problems. The designation of a given individual as sick (as opposed to bad) may be viewed as a political act dependent upon assumptions of the observer, not the behavior being observed.

The problems mentioned above are particularly acute with respect to institutionalized populations, but they are also appropriate concerns for a wide range of preventive programs. Some approaches that could be corrective include:

Participation in treatment programs should always be voluntary and based upon informed consent.

Attempts should be made to maximize lay involvement in planning and executing preventive programs.

The prisoner and patient should have a major say in any program that directly affects them.

The courts can be helpful in the continuing attempt to reach these goals, which are relevant to our opening comments about the need for system challengers. The notion of primary prevention is finally beginning to receive some attention. But already there are suggestions that developments are likely to be conservative in nature and focused upon individuals. For example, Goldston has identified seven areas ripe for development: families going through marital disruption; children of severely disordered parents; victims of natural disaster; children at risk for pathological grief following a death in the family; parental competency; children hospitalized for physical conditions; and, people at high risk for suicide (Herbert, 1979, p. 8). This focus on specific populations is in part an understandable attempt to demonstrate that we know enough to mount programs to aid individuals in specific problem areas.

These words have a familiar ring and predictably portend a continuation of old policies. All the more reason for a need to encourage the system challengers.

References

Aaron, H. J. *Politics and the professors.* Washington, D.C.: The Brookings Institution, 1978.
Abramson, M. F. The criminalization of mentally disordered behavior: Possible side-effects of a new mental health law. *Hospital & Community Psychiatry*, 1972, *20*, 13–16.
Barton, W. E., and Sanborn, C. J. *Law and the mental health profession.* New York: International Universities Press, 1978.
Bazelon, D. L. Psychiatrist and the adversary process. *Scientific American*, 1974, *230*, 18–23.
Bradley, V., and Clarke, G. (Eds.). *Paper victories and hard realities: The implementation of the legal and constitutional rights of the mentally disabled.* Washington, D.C.: The Health Policy Center, Georgetown University, 1976.
Brodsky, S. L. *Psychologists in the criminal justice system.* Urbana: University of Illinois Press, 1973.
Brooks, A. D. Foreword to J. Rubin, *Economics, mental health and the law.* Lexington, Mass.: D. C. Heath, 1978.
Chayes, A. The role of the judge in public law litigation. *Harvard Law Review*, 1976, *89*, 1281–1316.
Crouse & McGinnis v. Murray, No. 575–191 (N.D. Ind., filed Nov. 17, 1975).
Davis v. Balson, No. C73–205 (N.D. Ohio, Jan. 21, 1977).
Doe v. Hudspeth, No. J75–36(c) (S.D. Miss., Feb. 17, 1977).
Ferracuti, F., Dinitz, S., and Piperno, A. *Mental deterioration in prison.* Columbus: Program for the Study of Crimes and Delinquency, School of Public Administration, Ohio State University, 1978.
Forst, M. L. *Civil commitment and social control.* Lexington, Mass.: Lexington Books, 1978.
Gaylin, W., Glasser, I., Marcus, S., and Rothman, D. *Doing good: The limits of benevolence.* New York: Pantheon, 1978.

Glazer, N. Should judges administer social services? *Public Interest*, 1978, *50*, 64–80.

Halderman & United States v. Pennhurst, C. A., No. 74–1345 (E.D. Pa., Nov. 30, 1976).

Halleck, S. L. A troubled view of current trends in forensic psychiatry. *Journal of Law and Psychiatry*, 1974, *2*, 135–157.

Halleck, S. L., and Witte, A. D. Is rehabilitation dead? *Crime & Delinquency*, 1977, *23*, 372–382.

Herbert, W. The politics of prevention. *APA Monitor*, May, 1979, *10*, #5, 8.

Himmelsbach, J. T. Consequences of cooperation between police and mental health services: Issues and some solutions. In R. Cohen, R. P. Sprafkin, S. Oglesby, and W. Claiborn (Eds.), *Working with police agencies: The interrelations between law enforcement and the behavioral scientist.* New York: Human Sciences Press, 1976.

Horack v. Exxon, No. 72-L-299 (D. Neb., 1973).

Horowitz, D. L. *The courts and social policy.* Washington, D.C.: Brookings Institution, 1977.

Jacobs v. Britton, C. A., No. 78-309-H (S.D. Ala.).

Jones, D. *The health risks of imprisonment.* Lexington, Mass.: Lexington Books, 1976.

Krantz, S., Smith, C., Rossman, D., Froyd, P., and Hoffman, J. *Right to counsel in criminal cases: The mandate of Argersinger vs. Hamlin.* Cambridge, Mass.: Ballinger, 1976.

Lipton, D., Martinson, R., and Wilkes, J. *The effectiveness of correctional treatment: A survey of treatment evaluation.* New York: Praeger, 1975.

Lottman, M. S. Enforcement of judicial decrees: Now comes the hard part. *Mental Disability Law Reporter*, 1976, *1*, 69–76.

Lugg, D. J. Physiological adaptation and health of an expedition in Antarctica, with comment on behavioral adaptation. Canberra, Australia: Australian National Antarctic Research Expeditions, ANARE Scientific Report, Series B (4) Medical Science, publication No. 126, 1977.

Miller, K. S., Fein, S. B., and Schmidt, W. C. The therapeutic state and current court cases. In K. S. Miller (Ed.), *Conflict and collusion: The criminal justice and mental health systems.* Final Report, LEAA Grant No. 77NI-99-0061, 1979.

Morse, S. J. Law and mental health professionals: The limits of expertise. *Professional Psychology*, 1978, *9*, 389–399.

Navarro v. Hernandez, No. 74–1301 (D.P.R., Apr. 20, 1977).

NYSARC & Parisi v. Carey, 393 F. Supp. 715 (E.D. N.Y., 1973).

NYSARC & Parisi v. Carey, 393 F. Supp. 717 (E.D. N.Y., 1975).

Ohio Assn. for Retarded Citizens v. Moritz, No. C2-76-398 (S.D. Ohio, Apr. 19, 1977).

Patients v. Camden Co. Bd. of Chosen Freeholders, No. L-33417-74-P.W. (N.J. Sup. Ct. Camden Co., filed Oct. 17, 1975).

Patients v. Camden Co. Bd. of Chosen Freeholders, No. L-33417-74-P.W. (N.J. Sup. Ct. Camden, Co., filed April 29, 1977).

President's Commission on Mental Health. Vol. II, Washington, D.C.: U.S. Government Printing Office, 1978.

Robitscher, J. Isaac Ray Award Lectures, George Washington University, Schools of Medicine and Law, in conjunction with the American Psychiatric Association, Washington, D.C., November 6, 7, and 8, 1977.

Rosenberg, N. S. Symposium presented at the annual meeting of the American Society for Public Administration, Baltimore, Md., 1979.

Rubin, J. *Economics, mental health, and the law.* Lexington, Mass.: D. C. Heath, 1978.

Sanford, N., Comstock, C. and associates. *Sanctions for evil: Sources of social destructiveness.* San Francisco: Jossey-Bass, 1971.

Scallet, L. The realities of mental health advocacy: State ex rel. Memmel v. Muncy. In L. E. Kopolow and H. Bloom (Eds.), *Mental health advocacy: An emergency force in consumer rights.* DHEW Publication No. (ADM) 77–455, NIMH, Rockville, Md., 1977.

Schindenwolf v. Klein, No. A-2695-76 (N.J. Sup. Ct. App. Div., filed July 27, 1977).

Schuster, R. L., and Widmer, S. A. Judicial intervention in corrections: A case study. *Federal Probation,* 1978, *42,* 10–17.

Schutz, D. P. *Sensory restriction.* New York: Academic Press, 1965.

Sosowsky, L. Crime and violence among mental health patients: Reconsidered in view of the now legal relationship between the state and the mentally ill. *American Journal of Psychiatry,* 1978, *135,* 33–42.

State v. Alton, 362 A.2d, 545 (N.J., 1976).

Stone, A. A. *Mental health and law: A system in transition.* Washington, D.C.: National Institute of Mental Health, Center for Studies of Crime and Delinquency, DHEW Publication No. (ADM) 75–176, 1975.

Stone, A. A. Recent mental health litigation: A critical perspective. *American Journal of Psychiatry,* 1977, *63,* 273–279.

Suedfeld, P. The benefits of boredom: Sensory deprivation reconsidered. *American Scientist,* 1975, *63,* 60–69.

Taylor, A. J. W. Social isolation and imprisonment. *Psychiatry,* 1961, *27,* 323–326.

Wuori v. Bruns, No. 75–80 (D. Me., filed Oct. 1, 1975).

Wyatt v. Stickney, 344 F. Supp. 373, 387 (M.D. Ala., 1972), aff'd. 503 F2d 1305 (5th Cir. 1974).

Zubek, J. P. *Sensory deprivation: Fifteen years of research.* New York: Meredith, 1969.

Social Change, Social Action as Prevention

The Role of the Professional

Gisela Konopka

The subject, when I heard about it a year ago, made me jump. Here it was, the opportunity to talk about the effort of a lifetime: the combination of concern and work for the well-being of each individual that helps create societies which make possible full development of capacities, which enhance the beauty of interdependence, which help develop whatever it is we call "mental health." I thought it would be easy to express and share with you a lifetime as an old fighter for what I call "Social Justice with a Heart."

But when I sat down to write this paper it became a nightmare—more questions than answers sprang up—a cacophony of voices (was my mental health threatened?). Listen.

A letter from a friend in Germany:

The interrelatedness of social work and politics becomes very clear theoretically, without having an answer for the practical consequences. The more we strive for the betterment of social conditions in our own countries the less we have for the real needy in this world, or is the first the precondition for the latter? Who is your neighbor—in this last part of the twentieth century? (Schiller, 1979)

—A colleague coming from China: "I don't care about 'freedom of choice.' At least people have enough to eat." And another: "Did we ever realize the terror of the group? Nobody in China can be him- or herself. One *must* conform."

—A friend: "Rights of youth, you say? Okay, but what about my daughter spitting at me. What about *me*?"

—"The psychiatrist thought my depression is related to my not caring about clothes. What has that got to do with it?"

—"Poverty makes for unhappiness? I worked my head off to get out of it. My kids who have money now spend theirs on the 'shrinks.'"

—"We spent a lifetime to develop juvenile courts to get young people out of the clutches of the adult court system. Now the 'rights movement' brings them back in."

—"You fought so hard for right for education for everybody. Now we kids are forced to stay in school when we want to get out and work. We are bored."

I have to shut out the voices. Do they just mock or do they say something that makes sense? They do!

I think those partially depressing, confusing voices convey some basic insights we must be aware of:

(1) Mental health concepts are related to value judgments and we must admit this and make them explicit. Maxwell Anderson (1947) said it better than I can say it:

If you live you have to be going somewhere. You have to choose a direction. And science is completely impartial. It doesn't give a damn which way you go. It can invent the atom bomb but it can't tell you whether to use it or not. Science is like—well, it's like a flashlight in a totally dark room measuring two billion light-years across . . . the flash can show you where your feet are on the floor; it can show you the furniture or the people close by; but as for which direction you should take in that endless room it can tell you nothing. (p. 91)

(2) The public health model does not work too well with mental health because cause and effect are a myth. Yet there are factors that show a relationship between certain environmental (human and otherwise) influences and a person's reaction to them. And we must be aware of the infinite variety among people.

(3) In time—historically—a cultural environment changes, and that may change needs and demand new systems. Child labor laws and juvenile courts are recent examples of this.

(4) Perhaps the most important quality of the professional who genuinely wants to be of help to mankind is an inquiring, flexible mind combined with an almost searing honesty and courage to stand up against comfortable dogmas within and fashionable ones without.

With those premises in mind I will trace some of my own attempts at bringing about cultural change, share the underlying philosophy, and draw the lessons the professional may learn from them.

Let me take you back approximately 55 years. I quote from an article about a delinquency institution, called the *Lindenhof*, in the Germany of the 1920s, before the Holocaust:

The Lindenhof was a beginning for the realization of human brotherhood, was a seedling toward a community of human beings, was a cell of a reborn human organism. . . . There was a strong belief that something different was possible, that one could move into a new direction in delinquency treatment which is no more punishment or retribution, a poor substitution for school or a poor substitution for the parents or anything like that, but that it could be: a true school for life; an education that provides an opportunity for development of human potential.

Most significant to us, to my collaborators and myself, was the human being. The mutual relationship of man to man is one of the incredible miracles in the cosmos. (Konopka, 1971, p. 245)

A gaunt young man wrote this as he sat at his desk looking out of his open office door at a corridor freshly painted in bright colors. Sunshine flooded the end of the hallway. There were odd little stubs of iron at the bottom of the window sill, like decorations made by a modern artist. The young man smiled. He knew what those iron remnants were. Not so long ago there had been bars at all the windows. He, his staff, and the delinquents in his charge had sawed them off after several discussions of what it meant to be responsible for one's own limits (Konopka, 1971).

At the time when this happened, I belonged to a youth movement that fought the reactionary forces. Our philosophy clearly demanded a recognition of human dignity. There was never a question in our minds that direct work with individuals (we were influenced by Freud and Adler) and political action were both needed to make this a better world. I never understood the "either-or" positions. Years later, when I studied social work philosophy I again encountered the recurring question, "Is social work a palliative only or is it responsible also for changing institutions?" I found the same answer as in my adolescence and that answer covers all professions, not only social work:

The answer must be that social work is responsible for attempting both: to help individuals in the framework of existing conditions as well as to help change social institutions. When we recognize the multiple causation of problems and realize that the causes lie neither exclusively in the individual nor in the social structure, it becomes clear that a profession which works toward social justice in a wide sense must feel responsible for amelioration and social change. (Konopka, 1958, pp. 194–195)

How did we put this demand for concern for individuals as well as systems into action? Let me answer with examples.

In those times, youth groups consciously included individuals who were on probation or parole. We, 16–17 years old, would get a phone call and—as friends, not "helpers"—would visit the boy or girl, take him or her to our meetings or on adventurous hikes we all loved. They became part of our community.

Or, when brooding summer heat invaded the small stinking courtyards of the Berlin slums, where one overflowing toilet served a block with approximately 200 people, we would go—alone—into such a yard (our parents would have been horrified had they known about this) and start playing with children who sat listlessly and dejected on the stoops. I will never forget the thin arms around me, the white bloodless faces, occasionally rat-bitten or ravaged by illnesses I hardly understood. It was "individual" help to those children, but what it did for us! How we learned about other, painful worlds and how we learned to overcome horror and how it gave us a sense of self and a place in the universe, which is so hard to find as an adolescent. So, consciously, I decided to become a teacher to children who had no advantages.

Directly parallel to those individual approaches went conscious socio-political action. I worked for awhile as a steelworker in a factory, where I saw the plight of women who got up at 4 A.M. to bring their children to daycare centers, worked long hours of hard labor—at lower pay than men—picked up their children and started home for a day's work there. So, I joined labor unions, helped organize women, became part of the social reform movement. Again, individual effort and socio-political group action were not perceived as contrasts.

Then—the advent of the Nazis. We had fought them in debates, in writing literature, but still they came to power. Besides the terror, the killing, the torture, you should know that all the social reforms of human services were destroyed. Women were reduced again to an inferior position. (I heard a Nazi boast that he would have thrown out his wife had she borne a girl!) Homes for children or delinquency institutions returned to authoritarian practices. When I revisited such places after the war under the auspices of the American High Commissioner, I saw only the raw and demeaning treatment that is based on the widespread theory that "badness is inborn, is hereditary" and as a result authorities had to "train" them, beat them into obedience. All this after the efforts of Karl Wilker and August Aichhorn and many others. Nothing was left of mental health concepts.

We learned—the hard way.

Lesson No. 1: Social change cannot be taken for granted.

One has to remember that things have to be done over and over again. The task is never finished. The words on the Supreme Court Building in Washington, "Eternal vigilance is the price of liberty," surely apply to any effort human beings make.

In the years of Nazi terror, I, as most of us, became very conscious of the fact that one cannot do any significant and positive personal service when the total system does not allow for human dignity. Therefore, political action became far more important than anything else. There were underground movements in Germany that tried to fight an inhuman system damaging to young and old. Those who participated could not expect glory, recognition, or even much mutual support. What one could expect was not just death, but painful torture, ridicule, and abandonment.

It is out of such experiences that I totally reject the theory and practice of behavior modification. Not only is the idea of the "all-knowing" treatment person repulsive to me, but I wonder what kind of people we are educating who expect that life will justly distribute punishment and awards. No award could be expected by anybody who got actively involved in political action to destroy the Nazis. I have never forgotten the feeling I had several times when I was in solitary in a cell in the concentration camp. I was sure that I never would leave that place alive. What especially bothered me—and I was young and healthy and ambitious—was that nobody ever would know what wonderful thoughts I had, how much I wanted to love people, how much I had to say. I was very aware of the fact that dying for a cause was not glamorous, as it is so often portrayed in songs and stories and drama, but that it was just dying, just not existing anymore, and that it meant being forgotten. We have to remember that there are thousands who did not come out of this like me, alive, but did die after very courageously fighting the disastrous system. But nobody will ever talk about them, write about them, and thank them. I resented at that time, and still resent deeply today, those people—and they are very often professionals and intellectuals—who shout "social change" and exhort people into action, when they themselves sit in comfortable offices, draw good salaries, gain admiration for what they are doing, but do not face unemployment or persecution as do those whom they exhort to act.

Lesson No. 2: In regard to social action: Do not take the glory if you cannot take the pain.

If there is any danger in the way the political action develops, you have to take the risk of this danger. You must have more than the courage of your convictions, you must back it up with your own possessions, or yourself. If somebody really considers technical development dangerous to human mental health (and I do not) then this person cannot use all the advantages of technical development to spread his or her own ideas. They have to renounce cars and radio and television, and the (to me) extraordinary invention of the telephone, and must live that life they advocate. I say this earnestly because I do think that the greatest temptation for professionals lies in their beautiful gift to reason, to speak, to write, and they can easily fool themselves into believing that they are working for a cause when in reality they only serve themselves. I have struggled with this myself.

Now let me share with you examples of my work toward social change within the United States. The way I see it, the system of this country not only permits, but requires, people to participate in social action. Without it, the Constitution, which is based on an affirmation of the dignity of each individual, cannot be kept alive. This actually imposes a severe demand on every citizen, and especially on those whose professions have as a goal the safeguard of mental health. A professional in our fields—psychology, social work, psychiatry, nursing, education— cannot dispassionately "view" human beings the way scientists do. It is true that with any attempt to change an individual, the first step is a "viewing" or, as we sometimes call it, understanding. This, in itself, is difficult because the total living web of human life is many sided. One must observe, feel with the other person; one must use knowledge derived from other sciences, which describe, probe, and try to explain human behavior.

One must also learn to look at oneself, to learn about one's own biases that may distort or color the "view." The most important point, as I said earlier, is that every practitioner working with people cannot merely "understand"; he or she is always confronted with evaluations of the facts and with active intervention. One is constantly confronted with the dilemma between acceptance of a given situation, people, attitudes, and the demand for a change in them. Every professional effort is pervaded by this consideration. And this makes the whole work of change in an individual or in a society so difficult. Where does one get the right to do this? When we adhered to the medical model and called certain behavior or problems "sick," it made it easier for us. Sickness has to be eliminated. But we do not deal always with problems that we can call simply "sick." We deal with problems of human relationships. For instance, we deal with the problem of what race discrimination does to individuals, communities, and the whole of society. We deal with hostile adolescents who hit out, withdraw, or use drugs because of a variety of problems they face within the family, as, for instance, authoritarian parents, or a noncaring attitude, or perhaps because the school weighs heavily on them. Those are not problems located within that particular individual but derive from systems, or relationships. One does not deal with illness.

For instance, we deal with the deep-seated rejection of the offender by the large majority of the population. We must change public attitudes; otherwise no individual can be helped. I have just come back from Australia where I encountered a society deeply committed to family life. Yet this same society has for decades removed aboriginal children from their families, placed them in large, impersonal institutions, because the families did not follow the Anglo-Saxon pattern. In our country there still exist large institutions for girls, filled with young people whose only offense is premarital sex relations (permissible to boys for centuries but not to girls). All these are examples of our having to work toward change because of reasons beyond "understanding." As I said earlier, there is absolutely no question that we have used value judgments in doing this. The answers will lie more in philosophical, ethical considerations than in scientific inquiry. The effort requires three considerations:

1. A clear distinction between primary and secondary values.
2. An investigation into the sources of value judgment.
3. An acceptance of the interrelatedness of ends and means, of goals and methods.

To enlarge on these three aspects: Eduard C. Lindeman helped make a distinction between primary and secondary values (Konopka, 1958, Chap. 5). The two primary values are the dignity of each human being and the interdependence of individuals. The first one establishes the right of each human being to full development of his or her capacities, while the second makes a demand on each human being to act responsibly toward others in the framework of his or her own capacities. Those are values without which no profession can operate. They are "absolute" in the sense that they become the basic criteria for the practitioner's actions. We may disagree on the origin of those values: the religiously oriented person sees it in divine command, the humanist in ethical law. Both, however, agree on the content.

The recognition of this "absolute" justifies the effort to affect certain cultural changes, if the given culture violates basic human rights—by disparaging individuals because of their origin, race, or religion, for instance, or by an authoritarian, dictatorial way of life, which does not allow for freedom of expression or thought. The code of ethics developed in most "applied" professions is an expression of the binding force of primary values. Standards for professional practice in social work accepted in 1951 by the American Association of Social Workers (then the representative organization of the social work profession) read:

1. Firm faith in the dignity, worth and creative power of the individual.
2. Complete belief in his right to hold and express his own opinions and to act upon them, so long as by so doing he does not infringe upon the rights of others.
3. Unswerving conviction of the inherent, inalienable rights of each human being to choose and achieve his own destiny in the framework of a progressive, yet stable society. (Standards for the Professional Practice of Social Work, 1951)

And the Society of Applied Anthropology (interestingly enough in the same year, 1951) also published its Code of Ethics. It asked for respect for the individual and for human rights and the promotion of human and social well-being. It says: "To advance those forms of human relationships which contribute to the integrity of the individual human being; to respect both human personality and cultural values . . ." (Code of Ethics of the Society for Applied Anthropology, 1951, p. 32).

Both professional groups not only *justified* culture change by the realization of those primary values, they both made it a task of the profession to *promote* them.

But more debatable is practice when it influences secondary values. Those are values in *use*, sometimes related to the moral-ethical realm, often to customs, mode of living, or even aesthetics.

Here work toward change must be exercised with great caution or not at all. We must scrutinize carefully the sources of those values, in ourselves as well as in clients, groups, or community. Only such honest self-insight can help us to determine whether we "impose" our own values arbitrarily or whether they have true importance to the other person or group.

Secondary values are strongly influenced by four factors:

1. Cultural background
2. The precepts and demands of groups that are significant to us (religious organizations, social groups, task groups)
3. Strong personal experiences, such as illness or the death of friends or family
4. Adherence to certain theories regarding human behavior and motivation

Professionals must periodically look at themselves and determine whether their own secondary values enter their work in such a way as to impose their own value system on others. By no means should professionals strip themselves of these values (they would be empty creatures without them) but they must check themselves and examine whether these values are helpful and applicable to others. They have a right to present them or to even promote them, as long as they allow others to take them or leave them—except when primary values are violated.

This means a disciplined and honest insight into oneself.

A final consideration lies in the interrelatedness of means and end. Gandhi said it best: "The means may be likened to a seed, the end to a tree; and there is just the same inviolable connection between the means and the end as there is between the seed and the tree" (in Flesch, 1957, p. 167).

If the goal of our efforts is enhancement of human dignity and mutual responsibility, the means to this end must be in accord with it, otherwise the end is defeated.

Out of these philosophical considerations come *Lessons 3 and 4.*

Lesson 3: Think through your philosophy, and
Lesson 4: Be honest with the means you use even in the political arena.

I had to think a great deal of this during the harsh days of the 1960s when students revolted at universities and when the most neglected minorities, Blacks, Indians, and Chicanos, stood up for their rights. It bothered me that many professionals who had professed their concern for human beings suddenly cringed, became afraid, or yelled twice as loudly as those who had been hurt, perhaps because of their own fear. It seems to me that people in the mental health profession should have learned a great deal about the roots of hostile behavior, should have an understanding of it, and should have stayed calm, though compassionate, in the face of it.

At that time I became involved again in the public arena. I accepted the position of special advisor to the vice president for student affairs at our large state university, to deal with the political movements of the young and the disadvantaged minorities. I felt I had to stand up for mutual respect and not allow any group to think that they could drag down another one. Important new programs grew out of that period: special help for students who had little intellectual stimulation at home; special courses for first year students of all colors and backgrounds, conducted by faculty and community people together to let them learn about the beautiful variety of people existing in our country, and also to gain a sometimes painful look into their own prejudices; university policies were changed in regard to dormitory living, with the acceptance of students as responsible adults instead of the university acting as "parent."

In the wider community new legislation has worked through in regard to employment of minorities. It was exciting to become one of the first faculty members to serve on the newly created Center for Urban and Regional Affairs at the university, and to help make the intellectual resources of the university far more available to the community.

We helped to develop special curricula for women on welfare so that they could get degrees and better opportunities for employment. We worked with housing projects and sent students directly into them to help children with their school work. The university supplied specialists to teach in a Black summer school that had been started by the Black citizens of one of our neighborhoods. I still think with real fondness of the day when I myself went into one of those classes, saw some of the sullen, hostile faces looking at my own not so dark one, and then felt the changed attitude when together we realized the beauty of poetry written by both Blacks and Whites who had been hurt by others. The professional community had not been the one most effective in *starting* the move toward social change, yet it became helpful in implementing it. We had to realize that we were not the "leaders," but that we could contribute to a development most important to general mental health.

Times changed again. The beautiful enthusiasm of the 60s (I call it beautiful though I do not agree with everything that was happening at that time), began to fade and reaction set in. I find this especially in a field I know, in youth services, and particularly among those who deal with delinquents. A harshness and a hardening towards the young is occurring today. Beautiful phrases like "a person must learn to take on responsibility," with which I agree, are turning into "There is absolutely no reason for your bad behavior. You are responsible, and we will punish you for it." I do believe in responsibility, but I also know about the complexity of human motivation.

I find it is time again to swim against the stream. Just recently I talked with a young woman working in probation services, who said to me after one of my talks, "When I am trying to help these young people, I am being made fun of. All they want ("they" being the authorities) is to place them away from the community and preferably in solitary confinement. What can I do?" My only answer continues to be, "You will never be able to stop the good fight. Don't expect this in life. You have to continue standing up for what you do. Do your best with the young people you work with, go on committees, testify before legislatures armed with *knowledge* you gained by working with people, and do this all your life."

I am involved at this time in a nationwide project called the National Youthworker Education Project, started after I published my survey of the needs of adolescent girls (Konopka, 1976). Every month we bring together 20 people who work with youth and who are partially responsible for the policies of their organizations—and we purposely mix professionals from community youth organizations with those from corrections. For about a week we discuss needs, concerns, philosophy of working with young people. We do not brainwash, but we hope to make people think and strengthen their backs so that a basic mental health concern gets translated into practice. We meet the same group again three months later after participants have tried out some new or cooperative work in their communities. We help them to keep in touch with each other.

Almost everywhere adolescents have been neglected and maligned—or ridiculously romanticized. Adolescents still do not have a place in most societies, and those who have offended the mores of a society are frequently treated like concentration camp inmates. I think I have helped to start a nationwide network of people who work with adolescents become a force to help our next generation. This alone will not change everything, but it is a beginning. In the delinquency field there is legislation to remove "the status offender" from institutionalization. It would be all wrong if we now say "we have achieved." Only recently I visited an institution full of girls that I would call "status offenders" but they are placed there under another label. They live with regimentation and with the constant threat of "the hole," the demeaning solitary confinement that everybody seems to think is so necessary to keep "discipline." What can I do? I can only try to speak, to write, to develop more and more people who take mental health seriously. They should not think that their major goal in life is to develop some cheap, quick technique that will change people's behavior and make a lot of money for themselves.

This is really *Lesson No. 5. In any kind of work with individuals or with communities, "empty techniques" do not work.*

We cannot give neat, surefire recipes for work with people which promise "instant" success.

We can only help to develop professionals who deal with humans, who have patience and an inquiring mind, who are flexible, and who have real compassion for others. The professional has a task of developing and using knowledge in addition to feelings of empathy. Out of their vast practice, they can bring to the public the reality of the problems that are often buried under bureaucratic procedures or statistics. They can become advocates, but even beyond advocacy, they have to become co-workers with others in the community. Their knowledge, especially in social action, needs to be fused with the knowledge coming from others. The Messiah complex is just as dangerous as the idea that one has nothing to contribute. Too great assurance easily turns people into dictators. I remember when I was a teenager, a teacher read the following quote by Lessing to us:

If God should hold enclosed in his right hand all truth and in his left hand only the ever active inquiry after truth, although with the condition that I must always and forever err, I would with humility turn on to his left hand and say, "Father, give me this, pure truth is for Thee alone." (Lessing, 1890; *Oxford Dictionary of Quotations*, p. 313)

At the time I was angry with the writer because I would have chosen the hand that held the "whole truth." It took a long life to recognize the wisdom of Lessing, and to accept the fact that there is only the one absolute, namely the recognition of the dignity of every person, and that we always have to live with a kind of uncertainty whether we have translated it into reality best.

To me, the most important quality for anyone involved in the serious business of change, individually or in the community, is to keep integrity and courage, whether one is laughed at, hurt, seems out of step, or perhaps even dies unknown and unrewarded. I would like to quote Morris West:

It costs so much to be a full human being that there are very few who have the enlightenment or the courage, to pay the price. . . . One has to abandon altogether the search for security, and reach out to the risk of living with both arms. One has to embrace the world like a lover, and yet demand no easy return of love. One has to accept pain as a condition of existence. One has to court doubt and darkness as the cost of knowing. One needs a will stubborn in conflict, but apt always to the total acceptance of every consequence of living and dying. (1963, p. 196)

The professional who can approach this kind of demand will help toward social change and better mental health for everyone.

References

Anderson, M. *Joan of Lorraine*. Menasha, Wis.: George Banta Publishing Co., 1947.

Code of ethics of the Society for Applied Anthropology. *Human Organization*, 1951, *10*, 32.

Flesch, R. *The book of unusual quotations*. New York: Harper and Row, 1957.

Konopka, G. *Edward C. Lindeman and social work philosophy*. Minneapolis: University of Minnesota Press, 1958.

Konopka, G. Reform in delinquency institutions in revolutionary times: The 1920's in Germany. *The Social Service Review*, 1971, *45*, 245–258.

Konopka, G. *Young girls: A portrait of adolescence*. Englewood Cliffs, N.J.: Prentice-Hall, 1976.

Lessing, G. E. *Wolfenbüttler Fragmente*, 1890. Quoted in *Oxford Dictionary of Quotations*. New York: Oxford University Press, 1953, p. 313. (Original not seen).

Schiller, H. Letter to the author, December 1979.

Standards for the professional practice of social work. New York: American Association of Social Workers, 1951.

West, M. *The shoes of the fisherman*. New York: Dell Publishing Co., 1963.

Women—New Patterns, Problems, Possibilities

Betty Friedan

Ultimately I am going to hint at new patterns and problems and pleasures and possibilities in the relations of women and men, but having assiduously tried to do some research on your own experience of these phenomena during the five days of this conference, I have decided that we are not there yet. And that I had better spend most of the time giving you concrete proof of primary prevention of psychopathology through social change and political action as it really happened this last twenty years in this country through the Women's Movement. I can bear witness from my original training as a psychologist and from my nearly twenty years as a social change agent, founding and leading that movement to the complex interrelationship between psychology, social change, and pathology that we mutually confront, dealing with the concrete human being in the process of making and surviving the change, and evolving strategies for the next stage of human liberation.

First I want to remind you, because a lot of you here are too young to remember and others would just as soon forget, where we were twenty years ago, when I, as a young housewife-mother guiltily hiding my freelance writing from my suburban neighbors like secret drinking, was starting *The Feminine Mystique*. I want to remind you where we were vis-à-vis psychology, psychopathology, and women. There was, if you will remember, at that time, a single image of woman—the happy housewife-mother—who was always 25 with three children under six, who was fulfilled as a wife and a mother solely through those emotions having to do with her sexuality, her husband, her children, her home: her peak experience, her orgasm, was throwing the powder in the dishwasher. The fact that so many women were already working outside of the home did not affect that image. And it was, above all, in its perniciousness, a psychological image. Remember *Modern Woman, The Lost Sex* (Farnham and Lundberg, 1947)? A whole slew of books had come out using or twisting Freudian psychology to say that the previous century-long battle for women's rights—the vote, careers, higher education—had made modern women terribly neurotic, maladjusted in their proper role as women, which was to live passively, vicariously through men and children, through feminine fulfillment as a life-long housewife-mother. Heeding that message, younger women, 20 years ago, were happily marrying and being told to marry at 17, 18, 19, giving up their own education to put their husbands through, and making a career of three, four, five children—the new happy, happy housewives.

The fact that overwhelming fortunes were being made selling tranquilizer pills mainly to women; the fact that women made up the great majority of the patients in every doctor's office; and, of course, the clients of the burgeoning psychological industry was not supposed to belie that happiness. Further, if you read the magazines, if you listened carefully to the messages in the mass media, no matter how happy, happy, happy she was supposed to be, the woman was also suffused with life-long guilt because she was the culprit of every psychological case history. Something wrong with the children—what was wrong with the mother? Can this marriage be saved—adjust, the wife, adjust! The neurotic, frustrated American "mom" had been discovered as the massive cause of GI malfunction in World War II. But in this new image of woman, she was *fulfilled* as a housewife, totally fulfilled as a wife and mother.

Twenty years ago when I started interviewing suburban housewives, this image, which I called the "feminine mystique," was so pervasive in the mass media, in conventional sophisticated psychological and sociological thought, that there simply was no name for the malaise so many women suffered that did *not* have to do with children or husband. I called it "the problem that has no name," but every woman knew what I was talking about. Anything that had to do with the self of women was more repressed 20 years ago than sexuality had been repressed in the Victorian era.

The modern women's movement, as the history books say, began as a change of consciousness with my book, *The Feminine Mystique*. It made conscious the urgent need of women to break through that obsolete image that had confined their energies and kept them from facing their real problems and possibilities and opportunities in this changing world. You will remember or you will have heard from others, the relief it was to realize that you were not alone, that what you suffered was not necessarily your own personal sin or guilt to be confessed in the confessional, or on the couch, but a general social and political, economic and psychological condition that you shared with other women and that could be changed—that urgently had to be changed.

The modern women's movement had to happen when it did basically because of the evolution of human life. It was not an accident that when I began the change in consciousness I was in my mid-30s with my youngest child off to school . . . and over half of my life left ahead of me. With a life expectancy now of 81 years, there was no way that women could any longer define themselves as life-long mothers. They had to grow beyond the age-old practice of defining women through their child-bearing function. They had to move to a definition of themselves as persons. The post–World War II feminine mystique, misusing Freudian psychology and all the rest, was a last gasp of reaction that temporarily seduced women to evade the risks of personhood. The women's movement was a necessity in evolutionary terms, which I and others put into words. To remind you what happened, once we declared that women are people—no more, no less—then it was simply our American and human birthright—equality of opportunity, freedom, independence, our own voice in society. At first we followed the model of the Black movement, and made some mistakes by assuming too literal an analogy with it and with the labor movement. The modern women's movement began, above all, as an American movement. Its ideology was simply that of American democracy, the respect for the individual, human dignity, human freedom, equal opportunity, the right to fulfill your potential, the right to have a voice in your destiny. They said it was a movement without an ideology, but then I think they mistook what the ideology was.

The real ideology of the women's movement was simply the values of democracy applied to women, not a 10 percent minority, but a 52 percent majority. But when have the values of this, or any revolution been applied in the unique way that came from women's experience, not as an abstract doctrine, but concretely, to the dailiness of human life as it is lived in the home, in the bedroom, in the kitchen, in the office, hospital, classroom, and, therefore, immediately affecting everyone, changing everybody's life. It spread faster than could be believed, faster than any organization could contain. There was never any money. It was a miracle, and perhaps a paradigm of a new kind of human politics. All right. From 1966 to the present, a dozen years or so, there has been this movement, which used laws, which used the methods of the Civil Rights movement and then invented methods of its own, raising the consciousness of women, confronting the barriers of society. We got the laws and imperfectly got them enforced—against sex discrimination in education, employment, and credit. And enormous changes began to happen.

You are witness to these changes. The massive increase in the number of women who for economic reasons have to work outside the home now have a new sense of possibilities. In law schools and medical schools, women are no longer one, two, three percent of the class, but 30 percent and more. Every profession is now open to women. Sports are no longer just for boys, from the Little League up to national basketball. The breakthroughs against sex discrimination in employment are real breakthroughs, not just tokenism. But for many women now going to work as mothers after years at home, the only jobs·they can get are low-paying sales or clerical jobs, which are paid less because they have been held primarily by women. So in average wages, it looks like women are getting paid *less* in comparison with men than before. That obscures the movement of younger women to equal opportunity, and the whole new consciousness of sex discrimination, sexism, in every profession. And the new expectation of equality in marriage and the family.

The psychological effects of all óf this may be quite different, in reality, from the doom and gloom predictions of reactionary social biologists or the simplistic preconceptions of radical feminists. Those who proclaim the natural inevitability of patriarchy are sure that equal opportunity for women will destroy culture itself. Certain sociologists say that the family is a disappearing species because of these selfish women that want to do other things with their lives than stay home all the time with their children. Certain psychologists proclaim widespread male impotence because of the new aggressiveness of women. The rising divorce rate and every other psychologically bad thing that is happening to people today is blamed on the women's movement. But the women who have moved know in their hearts, know in their guts, the rightness, the urgency, the life-opening exhilaration of their own moving.

As I go around this country, lecturing, every year more women of all ages come up and say, "It changed my life, it changed my whole life." (That's the title of my second book; *It Changed My Life: Writings on the Women's Movement.*) When I ask one of these women "What are you doing now?" she starts telling me the new problems: juggling work, her job, and the housework, the children, putting it all together with Band-Aids. New problems of divorce or husbands being threatened, economic problems, time problems; cheerfully, cheerfully, she tells me about all these new problems. "Sometimes it seems like the problems increase geometrically." But I never hear recriminations, regrets. I ask, "Would you go back where it was simpler, more secure?" And she says, "Are you kidding?" No woman would go back, despite the many new problems that women have today. It is better to be a woman today. You feel better being a woman today. You might have *more problems* being a woman today, but you are more alive. And the new problems are much more interesting than the old problems.

I could be accused of being prejudiced, self-serving in this proclamation so, therefore, I want to give you some new national statistics gathered by psychologists that confirm my personal experience and observations. Before I wrote *The Feminine Mystique*, I was in my late 30s and I felt old. I felt like it was all going to be downhill. When I look back, I felt older at 38 than I felt at 48 and a lot older than I feel now at 58. I noticed something interesting when I began looking for women that were moving beyond the feminine mystique. In the mid-60s, right after my book came out, I went around the country, much as I went around this conference, looking for new patterns. It was before we even had a women's movement, and of course, I did not find any new patterns. It was too soon. I did find some individual women who were putting their lives together in new ways, and they had a lot of problems because there were no social patterns, not in this country yet. One thing I did notice about those women—they looked vital, they looked alive. They tended to be a little older than the suburban housewives I had interviewed for *The Feminine Mystique* because this was a time when women in their 20s, in their 30s, were all home with kids. (Only the exceptional one was out there, then, and she might not even have kids.) The few women that had been combining marriage and motherhood and profession were in their menopausal years. But they looked and sounded more vibrant, vital, than the younger trapped housewives I had been interviewing who had all these vague syndromes and symptoms. They might not even wear as much make-up but their skin looked younger!

I started asking them about the menopause and they'd say, "Oh, I don't remember." or "I haven't had it." And I'd say, "What do you mean, you haven't had it?" I would figure out the woman was 50 or whatever. She did not remember when she stopped menstruation because she actually had not experienced the symptoms, traumas, and depression that were supposed to characterize menopause. In other words, menopause was a syndrome that did not exist for such women. What they experienced was a vitality, as if they were growing again.

Then, the women's movement really took off, and women in great numbers began to go back to school, go to work. And even if they continued to write "housewife" on the census blank, they began to feel differently about themselves. It was like a phenomenon you do not even notice because it is so large—that women after 40, after women's life was supposed to be over and downhill, were growing and moving with incredible zest and vitality. Recently, the various fashion magazines showed women now in their 40s and 50s against pictures of themselves in their 30s, and commented that the women really did look younger now. And it was not just a question of the styles that used to make women try to look younger. This was something different.

I began to ask a lot of questions about this "x" that was making some women experience menopause differently, women growing instead of

deteriorating with age. I did not know how pervasive it was. Coinciden-
tally, just in time for this conference, some figures were released that are
really mind boggling. A repeat was done of the classic midtown Manhattan study (Srole, 1975), which in 1954 showed mental health impairment
increasing with successive age groups, and women much worse off than
men. In this and another comparable study by the National Center for
Health Statistics, women were so much worse off than men for every
possible index that could be associated with mental health, from insomnia and fainting to inertia, depression, and feeling about to have a nervous breakdown, that Jessie Bernard wrote a book dooming the future of
marriage because she concluded that while marriage seemed to be okay
for a man, it was driving women crazy.

The men and women originally studied were aged 20 to 59. At each
10-year interval their rate of impairment had increased: mental health deteriorated with age, and more acutely for women. They repeated the
Midtown study in 1975, 20 years later. Instead of finding the expected
increase in impairment, to their utter amazement, it looked as if mental
health had stopped getting worse with age. After 20 years of wear and
tear of living, the deterioration of mental health that had been expected
had not taken place. They could not believe it. Then they began to analyze the statistics more carefully to see what had happened. The impression that mental health no longer deteriorated with age had come completely from *a massive improvement in the last 20 years in the mental health of
women over 40* (Srole, 1975).

Whereas in 1954, 21 percent of women 40–49 had shown what they
called impairment of mental health, compared with 9 percent of men, by
1974 the women who had been 20–29 or 39 in the first study, showed no
worse mental health, or slightly better, at 40–49. Furthermore, the
women now 40–49 showed enormous improvement in mental health
compared with the women 20 years ago aged 40–49. Only 8 percent of
women were now impaired compared with the 21 percent in 1954. In
other words, the women had caught up to the men. They showed, in
fact, less impairment of mental health with age than the men. The psychologists who analyzed these statistics concluded that something really
massive must have been happening to women in the last 20 years that
was not happening to men.

In the other study (Bird, 1979), in which the findings are still being
analyzed, at the National Center for Health Statistics, Harold Dupuy, the
psychologist in charge, compared a national cross-section of 6,672 adults
studied in 1960–62 and then repeated in 1971–75. This study confirmed
the fact that women over 40 were healthier, and did not show the impairment that had been expected with age. The improvement evident at

40–49 was also evident at 50–59. In fact, those years seemed to be the best years of a woman's life, for the National Center for Health Statistics study also revealed a slight, but statistically significant, impression of increased stress for women in the 30–39 year group, and of all age groups under 40, compared with young women in the previous decades. Thirty percent of younger women in the 30–39 age group compared with only 23 percent 12 years earlier admitted to having felt like they were on the verge of a nervous breakdown.

Dupuy and others are trying to figure out what made the difference for women. On the midtown Manhattan study, for instance, 90 percent of the women are now working full-time compared with under 50 percent before. But in the studies of the National Center for Health Statistics, Dupuy told me when they broke the statistics down, working women versus housewives, the working women seemed to be slightly healthier, though the housewives also had benefited. Something had happened in a massive way in the last 15 years that was good for the mental health of women in general.

When I talked to Dupuy about it, he said, "On the one hand, you could say that despite the increased stress you would expect when women have to combine a role as workers *and* housewives, there is this remarkable improvement in mental health. And women who are housewives now also show improved mental health." In the earlier studies, belying the "happy housewife" image of the 1950s, the best educated "career women" with the most prestigious occupations and with no young children showed better mental health than young housewife-mothers. This edge no longer seems true. Young childless career women—a more common pattern today—were also showing signs of increased stress.

All right. What does all this mean? Now I am drawing on my participant-observer knowledge, and from my own interviews of women over the years. It has been good for women to have more self-respect and independence as people, more freedom and options to move on their own in society. It has been good for women to get out the aggression that they used to turn against themselves in self-hate and self-denigration, in masochism, the impotent rage they used to vent on their own minds and bodies. It has been good for women, psychologically, economically— and economics is the bottom line in this. I cannot possibly stress too much the importance of having some independence and ability to support themselves. It has been good for women to come out of those tight, confining masks and be who they really are, to let it all hang out. It has been good for women to be part of a movement, to feel that they are supported by a great movement of other women, even to be able to share feelings without necessarily paying $50 to $100 an hour to do so. It has been good for women not only to be able to assert the self but to be a part, as many have been in one way or another, of a movement beyond the self. It has been good for women, finding the power to change their own lives and recognizing their power to change society.

It is already visibly good for women to have new options, but we are only beginning to know something about the potentials of human growth in females, about the healthy, active, fully grown personhood of women. At this time, certain transitional phenomena can obscure some of this. For instance, you have to be careful to distinguish in your own clinical work, or sociological or psychological analysis, phenomena of reaction, of defensive reaction, and understand that these may be temporary way stations to the real human autonomy and self-definition that women are seeking. Some of the extreme hostility against men that gave a bad image to "women's lib," which is a term I myself do not use, is not liberation, though the rage may be a real and even necessary stage in liberation. Some of that hostility and its acting out or the rhetoric that expresses it came from an ideological mistake, reducing the relationship of woman and man with its complex biological, psychological, social, and sexual dynamic by too literal an analogy to the relationship of worker and boss, or black and white. The separatism that resulted is not synonymous with liberation. To deny the psychological and biological and human interconnectedness of woman and man, to deny all the feelings that women have had about men, love, children, and home is to deny a part of woman's own nature.

It was reaction; women had to get their anger out; better than taking it out on the self. But an excess of that reaction is very similar to machismo. It hides enormous insecurity. Woman's worst problem today is the lack of confidence in herself. Having seen, maybe in your mother or your sister, that powerlessness, that trapped-housewife desperation, being afraid, still, that you might be pinched back into it, being unsure, still of your own ability to move in this complex society, in panicky defense you want to throw out all of the things that characterized woman in the past. Women are afraid of the softness; to hide their own inadmissible need for dependence, now they have to be more independent than any man. Be tough! Tough! Or we risk losing this hard-won autonomy.

But the more the woman moves, the more sure she is of her ability, the more she can afford to also admit her vulnerabilities and her weaknesses. And the more real she becomes. So you must not confuse the reaction, which is another kind of mask, with her real self that is not yet fully liberated. You must look for female machismo, as well as male machismo, and for what is hidden behind that facade.

In the discussions at the conference, I was a little disturbed (as I see that others of my generation are) by the seemingly utter preoccupation with the self, the selfishness, of some of the young women. They are choosing not to have children. They are only concerned with their careers, or they are only concerned with themselves. Now, a certain amount of selfishness is healthy for women. As one of the first woman theologians said, the sin of woman has been selflessness, too much selflessness, evasion of the risks of self by living through others. That can be a sin, you know. In my own origins there is a wonderful saying, "If I am not for myself, who will be for me? But if I am only for myself, what am I?" Woman has to be for herself, or she cannot really be for anyone else. You know from the psychopathology that you used to deal with, and may still be dealing with, what happens to the children when the woman has to use them for her own self-aggrandizement or to fulfill her own needs. She had to be for herself to really be there for her children.

Young women share with the young men today a loss of faith in institutions. When the politics of nation and profession seem irrelevant or utterly cynical and the dollar isn't worth much, when the old religion seems hypocritical, or denies women's reality and the new religion is not yet firm, in what institution can she find meaning? Can we blame the young for the so-called age of narcissism, after the politics of Watergate and Three Mile Island? I hope this is also a transitional stage. Women's rights is not the only issue that has concerned me in my lifetime. But in recent years the only politics where I did not feel like I was wasting my time was the women's movement because this really was changing our lives. And it is confronting the system in subtle ways. Since I do not see any other system giving the answers, I see my responsibility to change my own system. And the women's movement is doing that in ways that are not at first apparent.

Some of you have worried that this negotiating of contracts about who is going to do the housework is taking all the spontaneity out of love and marriage. I will tell you something about this. When you do not negotiate, when the woman is the resentful martyr and feels like a service station as the women that I interviewed 20 years ago used to put it . . . that is really bad for the spontaneity of love and marriage. Why in those years did so many books become best sellers that sold "88 New Ways to Make the Act of Love More Endurable"? Why did the vibrator seem for a while to be more titillating for some women than the human penis? It was not good for love, marriage, spontaneity of sex for women to feel like a service station. The negotiation is an improvement.

I discovered some interesting things in my new interviewing of young women in Vermont and elsewhere. They had been through these knock-down-drag-out fights every time the garbage had to be taken out or dinner cooked: Why should I do it. . . . You've got to do it equally. He won't do his share. Or he wouldn't do it right, and so on and so forth. Until, she tells me, "I suddenly realized that I still was the one really running the house. Maybe I didn't want to give up that power. But in order to do my other work, I simply couldn't be the one that was responsible for it any longer. I couldn't be the only one that everyone would look to. I really had to give up that power. And once I gave it up, then we were able to negotiate." She goes on: "Negotiate, we don't even negotiate any more. It flows. Whoever is able to do it at that time does it, and half the time we don't even bother to negotiate."

In other words, the psychology of power. In recompense for the lack of power in society, women had to have this absolute domination in the home. And that was the American "mom," and you are still dealing with the effects of that in psychopathology. In the last decade, research began to show that when women worked from choice and not from absolute, dire desertion of the husband or whatever, their husbands had more decision-making power in their own homes, compared with the husbands of full-time housewives. In the new families that may evolve as women begin to move to a more equal role in society, carrying a greater share of the economic burden, the power of the woman in the home will be less destructive. As many young men are now finding, sharing the intimate, active life and nurturing of the home and children has its own power and rewards. There may be a virtual disappearance of certain kinds of psychopathology that resulted from the powerlessness (power lust) of women and the absent, passive father. (Incidentally, *Time* magazine a few months ago ran a cover story called the depression of psychiatry. The psychiatry business is evidently down. Most of the patients used to be women. In addition to inflation, the gurus, and disillusionment with the psychological panaceas, have you ever thought that the women's movement itself is helping to put psychiatry out of business?)

I will tell you a new problem I worry about: the conscious or not conscious conflict or choice not to have children at all that may be one cause of the stress for the younger women. "Up Against the Clock," a new study that has come out of the University of California at Santa Cruz (Fabe and Winkler, 1979), shows women, in agonizing conflict over the choice as they approach 35 whether to have a baby or not. I do not want to go back to a mystique, and I do not think that a human being has instincts the same way that animals do, but I do not want to see women choosing not to have children for the wrong reasons. I want them to have the choice. I do not want them to have to have children to justify their existence. But I think there is a powerful generative need or impulse, in women and in men, that is not lightly denied.

I am not even talking now about reproducing the human race or deploring a situation in which the best or the brightest are not having children. I am talking about the woman herself and the woman's total personhood, which surely includes that powerful generativeness. I do not like the discussions in some of the feminist psychotherapy in which the self is defined apart from love, from nurturing, as if the self for woman were only the career, or only the work. As if the self were not also defined in the nurturing of the children, the intimate relationship with the man, whoever. Because if it was denying a part of the personhood of woman when she had to deny those human assertive needs to grow and act and have a voice and use the abilities that she shared with men, it is also perhaps denying a part of the personhood of woman if she denies the powerful needs and abilities and fulfillment of mothering. Motherhood is more than a mystique. But I am not blaming the victim here.

If you believe what you say about primary prevention of psychopathology, if you understand how liberating all that has happened has been for women's mental health, then, for instance, we have to get the Constitutional underpinning so it can not be taken away. We have to get the Equal Rights Amendment ratified. It is your obligation as people concerned with mental health to help do that. It is a mental health question as well as a question of economic and political justice. Then, we have to demand restructuring of institutions, more flexible hours of work, really good child care programs, so that women do not have to make either/or choices.

And we have to have education of men as well as women, not just women's studies, for equality to be livable, and workable, and possible to love in. Unless men change their roles and really begin to do equal parenting, unless we get professions restructured along more human lines by and for men and women (which is the only way it will happen), this will end up with a lot of tired women. Women are getting very tired, the way it is now. To the perfectionist demand on women to be perfect mothers is now added the demand to be perfect career women. Women are now even falling into some traps that men are climbing out of. I was appalled to hear from one of you that young girls are smoking while young boys have stopped smoking.

I am leery of the *mea culpa* kind of men's liberation. I do not think that men are going to do an awful lot to change, just to please the women. They will do some things to please the women. They will have to. But that is patronizing in a way. Let the men change because they need to change, to live their own lives well. Again going back to biological statistics, it is not good that men are dying 10 years younger than women of their age group, that the age discrepancy of men and women at death is widening, that men did not show that great improvement in mental health in this 20-year period. Men have got to make a breakthrough comparable to women's. It is not the same one, it will not have the same confrontational aspects. Men have got to break through the machismo, the competitiveness, the denial of their own real feelings and fears, and they are beginning to do it.

I think you may get shorter and more flexible working hours and less slavery to the corporation—not necessarily because of women moving into corporations, because a lot of women think they have to do it better than the man at this point. But because men, liberated from the whole earning burden and expected to share the parenting, are beginning to say their own "no" to living a whole life just for the corporation. Men's mid-life crisis—there is fire underneath all that smoke. There is a value change taking place among men. The next step of human liberation will be made by men.

Finally, I want to say just one word about feminist psychotherapy. I am a feminist. I was originally trained as a psychologist. I think that any good psychotherapist today must in a certain sense be a feminist, but what that means is simply this: that we listen very, very carefully and sensitively to the woman where she is now. To the woman, herself, whether or not she fits Freudian or feminist book definitions, with respect for her own authenticity or integrity. Taking her seriously, her totality as a person, a woman, and realizing that we do not know all the answers yet, that she is still *evolving*, that we have not even seen yet the limits of women's possibility, but we must respect the reality of her life, here and now.

And if you are a good feminist psychotherapist, you also have to look and listen with the same sensitivity to men, to men where they are now. Realizing that men also have been oppressed, truncated, by sex roles and obsolete definitions of masculinity, that men have all kinds of human potential, similar to women, that they have not been allowed to express or experience. And if you are also committed to the family, as the ground soil, the nutrient for mental health, then you have to realize that your commitment is to the evolving family. That there is no way to go back to the mom-the-housewife, dad-the-breadwinner, Junior-and-Janie-for-ever-children, Good-Housekeeping-seal-of-approval family that only 7 percent of Americans now live in. That we have to look with respect and sensitivity at all the ways that people are moving to live together, to meet their needs for intimacy and mutual support, in all the stages and the new length and complexity of the life span. There are old value judgments having to do with marriage, with divorce, with all sorts of things that were good and that were bad, which we have to hold in abeyance in order to understand where women, men, and the family really are, here and now, and where they are moving. It is going to require every bit of our ability, everything that has been learned in all times to really understand this fast-evolving reality—the changing woman, the changing man, the changing family.

I welcome this community of psychotherapists that were part of the problem 20 years ago, that helped perpetrate the mystique that kept women down. I welcome your embrace of the great human movement of social change, of the women's movement as a primary prevention of psychopathology.

References

Bernard, J. *The future of marriage*. New York: World Publishers, 1972.
Bird, C. The best years of a woman's life. *Psychology Today*, 1979, *13*, 20–26.
Fabe, M., and Winkler, N. *Up against the clock*. New York: Random House, 1979.
Friedan, B. *The feminine mystique*. New York: W. W. Norton & Co., 1963.
Friedan, B. *It changed my life: Writings on the women's movement*. New York: Random House, 1976.
Lundberg, F. G., and Farnham, M. F. *Modern woman: The lost sex*. Philadelphia, Penn.: Richard West, 1947.
Singer, E., Garfinkel, R., Cohen, S. M., and Srole, L. Mortality and mental health: Evidence from the Midtown Manhattan restudy. *Social Sciences and Medicine*, 1977, *10*, 517–525.
Srole, L. Measurement and classification in socio-psychiatric epidemiology: Midtown Manhattan study (1954) and Midtown Manhattan restudy (1974). *Journal of Health and Social Behavior*, 1975, *16*, 347–364.

Community Action Programs— an Appraisal

Kenneth B. Clark

This paper is an attempt to look back on some of my involvements and experiences in the area of minority status, social power, and problems of social therapy or social change. The paper, therefore, is divided into three sections: (1) general rationale, or my conceptual frame of reference; (2) a diagnosis of the social problems and pathology of a particular community in which I have spent a great deal of time living and studying; and (3) a suggested remedy in the form of a proposal for community action that became the prototype for the Johnson administration's War on Poverty. I shall conclude this presentation with a sort of summary epilogue.

Traditionally, mental health has been perceived and approached in terms of individuals. The discipline of psychiatry emerged from the practice of medicine, and this fact probably accounts for the tradition of dealing with personality disturbances in terms of the one-to-one physician/patient relationships that characterize the diagnosis and treatment of physical diseases. Furthermore, mental diseases, or mental problems, like physical disease, inflict pain and discomfort on individuals. It is understandable, therefore, that attempts to deal with emotional, personal, or social instability, which are not essentially medical problems, would imitate the medical model. Up to the present, the psychodynamic theories that have significantly influenced practice in the field of psychiatry and psychotherapy have been concerned primarily with the motivation, the conflicts, and the aberrations of individuals. At times it seems to those of us in the field of social psychology as if this preoccupation with individuals tends to obscure the profound truth that the individual personality is a product of and functions only within a social milieu. So often has this rather simple fact been ignored, that the theory and practice of psychiatry seemed to be predicated upon the assumption that all problems of individual adjustment could be adequately understood by studying and treating the individual. The belief that neurotic conflict was self-generating, and either had its origin within the individual or reflected some peculiar, unique constellation of development forces, or sometimes forces within the family structure, was the prevailing dogma in the therapeutic field. This was probably reinforced by direct observation of the symptoms of psychoses. Psychosis is manifested by individual aberrations, sometimes dramatic behavioral deviance and stark or sudden breaks with reality. The obvious need to diagnose, treat, hospitalize, and protect the psychotic patient certainly contributed to the postponement of the development of a social psychological approach to the understanding and treatment of non-psychotic individuals. The belief that the distinction between neurotic maladjustment and psychotic deviance was merely one of degree led to treatment of both types of problems by the same general methods and interpretations by the same basic theories.

This parallel between the approach to problems in mental health and problems of physical health extends to the recent emphasis on control and prevention of diseases through public health medicine. I believe this is a very positive development. As I understand public health medicine, it is not primarily concerned with the diagnosis and treatment of individuals but is concerned with the general problem of environmental control and public hygiene. The rationale is that this method, if successful, would reduce the incidence of infectious disease, epidemics, and other afflictions of individuals.

I use public health medicine as a model for all attempts to protect individuals by creating a healthier social environment. Understandably, this approach had to take root in the sphere of physical medicine before its rationale and effectiveness could be tested in the area of mental health. I believe that it is now long past time for us to start thinking about mental and emotional problems in terms of a preventive, sociological approach. The basic rationale of the Harlem Youth Opportunities Unlimited (HARYOU) study, which I founded and directed in 1963, was to examine the general problems of minority status and psychopathology as a basis for understanding and controlling juvenile delinquency in the Harlem community at that time. I hoped to test my belief that a high proportion of non-psychotic aberrations of the human personality can be understood and treated in terms of the social power complex and social pathology that affect individual human beings. Most of what is presented in this paper comes from my HARYOU research and some general observations during the past 25 years or more working with my wife, Mamie P. Clark, and as research director at Northside Center for Child Development, which is located in Harlem. The observations and ideas dealing with the relationship among community pathology, personal pathology, and social power come primarily from the study of the Harlem community and the problems of its youth both from the HARYOU study and my research director role at Northside Center.

The final HARYOU report was presented to the President's Committee on Juvenile delinquency in 1964 under the title, *Youth in the Ghetto: A Study of the Consequences of Powerlessness*. The HARYOU document became the prototype for the Johnson Administration's Community Action–War on Poverty program.

Let me tell you a little about the background of the HARYOU study, what was in our minds, and what we tried to accomplish. And I will conclude by telling you of our failures. In its planning stage, HARYOU conducted research on the nature and the dynamics of the community. Before attempting to design a realistic program for Harlem's youths, we simulated and observed the process of community participation and confrontation. The HARYOU staff was directly involved in many of the problems of the community that it was trying to understand. Senior staff members were required to become involved observers. Essentially, HARYOU was an experiment in community psychiatry. It operated on the assumption that the emotional problems of the bulk of the youth in Harlem must be understood in terms of the pervasive pathology that characterizes our society and that makes the ghetto possible.

If individuals were to be helped we would have to remedy the problems of the community in which they lived—and they would have to be involved in seeking the realistic remedies. The unresolved problems of the ghetto spawn human casualties in such great numbers and in such varying forms that one could not hope to increase the effectiveness of the vast number of individuals who need help by any therapeutic procedure that depended upon a one-to-one relationship.

When I looked at the waiting list at the Northside Center and thought of the hundreds and thousands of youngsters who were not even referred to the waiting list, I felt terribly frustrated. One had to work with blinders, to pretend that what was being done within the walls of that and similar clinics was very effective in itself and should not be judged against the tremendous unfulfilled needs outside. It would be impossible within the foreseeable future to train sufficient numbers of clinicians to salvage the number of human beings who are being wasted daily in the Harlems of this nation. The enormity of this problem is staggering for those who refuse to accept the cyclic relationship between social injustices and human degradation as God-given and irremediable.

The fundamental challenge that must be faced and resolved successfully is one of determining the most effective means of bringing about desirable social change. How does one bring about community mental health? How does one persuade a society to develop and maintain social environments that are conducive to health rather than to dehumanization?

Let me make a brief theoretical digression. The problem as I saw it, at that time, was a problem of power. One cannot understand the pathology, the dehumanization, the continued destructiveness of human beings without first understanding something about how those with power use their power to affect the destiny of those who are seen as powerless. Certain aspects of social power are relevant to the problem of providing psychotherapy for oppressed people and depressed humans. As I thought about this, it became more and more clear to me that the problem of power is really not alien to the field of psychology. The psychodynamic theory of Alfred Adler was an early attempt to explain human motivation and problems of social interaction in terms of striving for power. According to Adler, the desire for power comes out of basic feelings of inferiority, which, says he, are inevitable concomitants of childhood impotence and dependence upon adults. Indeed Adler points to interpersonal levels of power when he insists on the universality of various forms of compensation that dominate the ongoing struggle for a sense of personal worth and dignity. The implications of Adlerian theory for the problems of personality development in infancy, childhood, and adolescence, I thought, could or might provide a bridge for understanding and testing the relationship between interpersonal and intrafamilial struggles on the one hand, and social intergroup power conflicts and accommodations on the other.

I am aware of the fact that there is a real risk of overpsychologizing and oversimplifying complex social and political problems. It is all too easy to assume that complex problems of social power, as these are reflected in the perpetuation of social injustices and inequities, can be understood simply by understanding a child's struggle for a positive sense of his or her own worth and his or her conflicts with punitive or overindulgent parents. I therefore had Adler in the back of my mind but tried desperately not to explain what I was observing in Harlem too easily in terms of existing psychological or psychodynamic theory. I went and tried to deal with the problem, by gathering evidence, not ignoring theory totally, but recognizing that theory could only be a starting point or a frame of reference that would enable me to interpret the empirical evidence.

What follows now are the symptoms of social pathology in the form of the data gathered in that study. I present them to you, not as in any way unique, but as indicators of the persistent injustices and inequities tolerated, accepted, justified, perpetuated by people like ourselves in this society.

What are some of the realities of the American racial ghettos? The basic reality in these ghettos is that they are the institutionalization of American racism, racial discrimination, involuntary subjugation, and restriction of freedom of movement; the ghettos reflect and maintain the powerlessness of their victims. Ghettos exist because those with power use their power to perpetuate, not to remedy them. The powerlessness of the victims of the ghettos is reinforced by deteriorated housing, overcrowding, inferior economic status, a high incidence of disease and infant mortality, pervasive physical drabness and ugliness. The HARYOU study revealed the extent to which the physical neglect and mental degradation of the ghetto dehumanizes its victims. A comparative analysis of the indices of social pathology and disorganization in the ghetto revealed that central Harlem ranked high on six of seven indices of social pathology. Its rate of juvenile delinquency was consistently twice, and in recent years, two to three or more times as high as the rate for New York City as a whole. For the past seven, ten, fifteen years the proportion of habitual narcotic users has been from three to eight times that of the city as a whole. Even these figures do not reveal the full extent of the wastage of human potential through narcotics since the accuracy of the statistics seems to be influenced by class and status factors. What is known, however, is that in the Harlem ghetto at the time of the HARYOU studies drug addiction was widespread, and there is no evidence that the situation has improved in the intervening years. The sale of drugs is comparatively blatant; police are obviously accepting this. There seems to be a conspiracy to permit this in Harlem and, I suspect, to make the Harlems a source of whatever economic benefits there are for those who traffic in drugs.

Infant mortality is twice as high in Harlem as in the rest of the city. Proportionately three times as many youths under the age of 18 in Harlem are supported wholly or in part by Aid to Dependent Children Funds as compared with the rest of the city.

The homicide rate of the community is more than six times as high as that of the rest of the city. Only with respect to suicide is the rate in Harlem no higher than the rate for the rest of the city. But contrary to the general belief that suicide rates are lower among low socioeconomic groups, the suicide rate for Harlem is approximately the same as the suicide rate for the city as a whole. And what is even more surprising is the fact that three health areas in the central Harlem community have recorded suicide rates twice as high as the rate for the City as a whole, and these three areas are bounded by Columbia University. I often wonder whether there is a morbid psychological spillover from Columbia University to these parts of Harlem.

In spite of the attempt of Americans, middle class, white and black Americans, to deal with this fundamental problem of morality and conscience by denying it, the social pathology of the American ghetto is real, and it is stark. The new technique for avoiding this reality is containment: nobody can go into Harlem, nobody should go into ghettos because unfortunately these are horrible places. So we wall them off. We try to pretend they do not exist. Yet we cannot wish away the ghettos or the destructive cycle they perpetuate. The powerless victims of American ghettos seem unable to mobilize and sustain their efforts to change the conditions of their lives.

The criminally inferior education provided by the ghetto schools continues to produce hundreds of thousands of functional illiterates each year and makes it impossible for these young people to compete for the types of jobs that would raise their economic status. And do not be misled by pilot programs or special enrollment. These programs are at best palliatives. They address themselves to a comparatively small percentage of the casualties. The majority of the children in ghetto public schools are still victims of educational neglect and in such large numbers that it amounts to educational genocide. Not only must they cope with underemployment and unemployment, but some of the most sensitive of them are doomed to self-destructiveness.

One of these days I would like to write something about suicide in the ghettos; suicide, not in the sense of an absolute, abrupt act of self-destruction, but rather the slow process of prolonged suicide. Self-destruction over a period of time—prolonged symbolic suicide. Like most middle class observers I have often been perplexed by what might seem to be mindless acts of hostility and aggression on the part of some young people in our ghettos. My intuition is that the acts that seem mindless to the middle class are in fact acts of suicidal depression and self-destruction. The individual seeks to destroy himself by destroying others and incurring the wrath of a society which will then retaliate and then become honest enough to destroy him for his aggressiveness.

So much for diagnosis. What did we seek to do about it? It is interesting that after the study and diagnosis, some very realistic individuals suggested that this condition could be a terminal illness and that it was just an act of wishful thinking to think in terms of social therapy. Some "objective" social scientists did not and do not now share our diagnosis. Some observers of American racial problems continue to believe and assert that the pathologies of American ghettos reveal the inherent inferiority of the victims. Others contend that the cycle of cultural deprivation and personal deterioration is difficult if not impossible to remedy. My HARYOU associates and I rejected these perspectives and insisted that our diagnosis was not only self-validating but also remediable. We did have a difficult diagnostic problem in trying to understand the nature of

ization, then by coming together, by organizing, by discussing, by mobilizing their alleged power, they would be able to confront and deal with the realities of their victimization. This did not happen. We did not take into account the fact that these individuals lacked the skills to plan and negotiate for their rights. They were themselves so much the victims, they were easily coopted by more sophisticated political officials and professionals. They imitated the worst characteristics of those who were initially in control. They were manipulated; and they sometimes used the community action apparatus as a vehicle for legitimizing hustles and seeking to justify nonrational actions.

The most disturbing thing I observed was that too often when the indigenous members of the community were placed in decision-making positions, they were no more sensitive than the more privileged to the basic human needs of their brothers and sisters. The human memory is a fragile thing—particularly when human beings are seeking to escape from the traps of degradation.

The failure of community action programs tended to give additional support to the contention that the victims of this society's injustices are themselves responsible for their own predicament.

I conclude by saying to you that if we—and some of us are incorrigible optimists—are going to have effective community action programs in the future, the following conditions will have to be met:

1) Genuine commitment to social, racial, and economic change on the part of the decision makers of our society. There is very little evidence of genuine rather than just verbal commitment to these goals.

2) Social and economic priorities must reflect this commitment. At the moment, defense and balanced budgets determine how this society spends its money.

3) We must train low-status, low-income people in the skills and techniques that will enable them to participate in the process of social change. We must do so while they are actually becoming involved in social-change activities, confrontations and conflicts.

4) We must train a group of professionals in our colleges and universities, in our social work schools, in our urban study programs, in our social science departments, in our public policy and our clinical psychology programs who are able to work with and for those who our society has neglected and rejected and dehumanized. We must train young people to have the empathy and the respect for potential and the humanity of these victims of social inequities. Work with rejected human beings must have the clear objective of providing them with the skills and personal security and psychological strength that are essential for

them to continue the struggle on their own toward the goals of democracy and justice.

These things must be done if we are serious about primary prevention of psychopathology—the theme of this conference. I do not know whether we are able or will do these things that must be done to remedy the problems of our ghettos. But the alternative to effective community action programs is self-perpetuating dehumanization and intensified moral insensitivity. Or, what may be even worse, passive acceptance of and accommodation to injustice, cruelty, and inhumanity as the norms of our "democratic society." This would be a terminal form of moral schizophrenia.

References

Clark, K. B. HARYOU: An experiment. In J. H. Clarke (Ed.), Harlem: A community in transition. New York: Citadel Press, 1965.

Clark, K. B. Dark ghetto: Dilemmas of social power. New York: Harper and Row, 1965. (Reprinted and distributed in paperback ed. by Christianity and Crisis, 1965; Harper and Row Torchbook, 1967.)

Clark, K. B. "No gimmicks, please, Whitey." Training in Business and Industry, 1968, 5, 27–30.

Harlem Youth Opportunities Unlimited, Inc. Youth in the ghetto: A study of the consequences of powerlessness and a blueprint for change. New York: HARYOU, 1964.

Neighborhoods, Politics, and Mental Health

Sharland Trotter

Old neighborhoods are newly fashionable among the young middle-class professionals who grew up in the suburbs. We can debate whether the cause of this trend is economics, changing tastes, or a quest for roots. It is happening—sometimes at the expense of poorer communities which, having withstood waves of urban renewal and highway construction, now find themselves being pushed out—or priced out—by changing fashion.

Old neighborhoods are also newly fashionable among social scientists and policy makers. After more than a decade of ambiguous and often misguided "community" programs mandated by the federal government, there is a new and welcomed focus on self-defined neighborhoods, on voluntarism, and on self-help. Thus, in mental health policy discussions, we hear a lot these days about community support systems and natural helping networks—that is, friends, relatives, spouses, co-workers, and neighbors—and the importance of people's attachments to local, small-scale associations based on mutual aid.

Recommendations abound—from the President's Commission on Mental Health, among others, about how to link professional service providers and programs with these so-called "natural" helpers—by, for example, giving natural helpers more information about formal services, bolstering their helping skills by providing consultation and training, and by capitalizing on the inherent strengths of existing social networks (Warren, 1976).

Without in any way denigrating the importance of these insights or the goodness of these intentions, much of what is being called for by mental health advocates has a disquietingly abstract ring to it. Neighborhoods are clearly in vogue, but there is a latent danger that professionals will be tempted to jump on the neighborhood bandwagon, just as they jumped on the community mental health bandwagon more than a decade ago, romanticizing and idealizing neighborhoods without paying sufficient attention to their social and political dynamics.

In terms of primary prevention, what a good neighborhood provides is a supportive contextual backdrop—not a deliberate or self-conscious helping system. It is important to remember that neighbors are not primarily or necessarily friends, confidants, or surrogate therapists; in fact, they are frequently valued precisely because they mind their own business. Suzanne Keller (1968), who has examined the art of neighboring as thoroughly as anyone, observes that:

The neighbor is one to whom a person turns because of proximity, not because of intimacy, and because he or she provides resources for dealing with "real trouble." Small-scale, transitive, and emergency problems, perhaps—but not therapeutic encounters.

Essentially, the neighbor is the helper in times of need who is expected to step in when other resources fail. These needs range from minor routine problems to major crises, and the help requested may be material or spiritual. Moreover, the help asked for and given is not unlimited. It is called forth in situations that spell danger to a group or community as in times of natural disasters or unforseen calamities, or that routinely afflict any and everyone so that the help you give today you may ask for tomorrow. (p. 58)

There is mounting evidence that those who have adequate social supports tend to be better protected, especially in times of crisis, from a wide variety of pathological states, both mental and physical, than those who lack such supports (Kaplan, Cassell, and Gore, 1977). Gerald Caplan has observed, for example, that often, even the superficial links with neighbors add up to a significant support system which directly affects treatment outcomes for people in crisis (Caplan, 1974).

A vital city neighborhood manages to achieve a remarkable balance between public and private realms, respecting people's demands for privacy while providing endless opportunities for human contact. It is a balance made up of hundreds of "small, sensitively managed details, practiced and accepted so casually that they are normally taken for granted" (Jacobs, 1961, p. 59).

How is such a mixture created? In part, it has to do with the richness and diversity of street life in a city neighborhood, and the gradual accretion of a sense of public respect and trust. On the surface, the public contacts provided in a healthy neighborhood are casual, unplanned, often associated with errands, and usually trivial: people stopping for a moment to chat; admiring or admonishing one another's children or dogs; getting advice from the butcher; giving advice to the druggist on where to get a home improvement loan; trading jokes with the owner of the local dry cleaning establishment. The details are inconsequential, but they add up to an atmosphere of trust that is significant. The absence of public trust is devastating to any neighborhood, and its markers are easy to identify: crime, blight, fear, anonymity, and apathy. Its presence helps fasten people to a social mainstream without implying personal commitments. Read this description by Jane Jacobs (1961), one of our most prophetic urban critics:

. . . Consider the line drawn by Mr. Jaffee at the candy store around the corner— a line so well understood by his customers and by other storekeepers too that they can spend their whole lives in its presence and never think about it consciously. One ordinary morning last winter, Mr. Jaffee, whose formal business name is Bernie, and his wife, whose formal business name is Ann, supervised the small children crossing at the corner on the way to P.S. 41, as Bernie always does because he sees the need; lent an umbrella to one customer and a dollar to another; took custody of two keys; took in some packages for people in the next building who were away; lectured two youngsters who asked for cigarettes; gave street directions; took custody of a watch to give the repair man across the street when he opened later; gave out information on the range of rents in the neighborhood to an apartment seeker; listened to a tale of domestic difficulty and offered reassurance; told some rowdies they could not come in unless they behaved and then defined (and got) good behavior; provided an incidental forum for half a dozen conversations among customers who dropped in for oddments; set aside certain newly arrived papers and magazines for regular customers who would depend on getting them; advised a mother who came for a birthday present not to get the ship-model kit because another child going to the same birthday party was giving that; and got a back copy (this was for me) of the previous day's newspaper out of the deliverer's surplus returns when he came by. (pp. 60–61)

To identify Bernie as an "informal caregiver" or a "natural helper" and attempt to make his role more explicitly therapeutic, to talk about him as some sort of "gatekeeper" to the mental health or social service system is to miss the point utterly. Indeed, Bernie would no doubt be dismayed at such a suggestion—precisely because he understands so well the importance of maintaining that invisible line between public and private lives. A good neighborhood, in other words, encourages casual offers of help without the threat of unwelcome entanglements, and provides a supportive context that can be taken for granted.

The development of a supportive social context depends on a perceived sense of permanence, which in turn requires a core of long-term residents with a shared affection for the place, who have forged neighborhood networks that operate through churches, PTAs, ethnic clubs, civic associations, and the like. A number of recent surveys have demonstrated that the most important factor in an individual's attachment to a neighborhood is length of residence—the capacity to stay put (Kasarda and Janowitz, 1974). To be sure, a good urban neighborhood can tolerate a certain amount of transcience, and can absorb newcomers into its midst with relative ease. But the increments have to be gradual or "community," in the sense of the social, human capital of a neighborhood, is irretrievably lost.

Historically, public policy, in its obsession with buildings and roads, has destroyed countless thousands of once-solid neighborhoods. By now the gross physical assaults are legendary; an $80 billion interstate highway system, acres of expensive and ill-planned subsidized housing, grandiose "urban renewal" schemes that have left havoc, instability, and helplessness in their wake. Harrison Salisbury, in a series of articles for the *New York Times* a few years ago, said it very well.

Even a ghetto [he quoted a pastor as saying] after it has remained a ghetto for a period of time builds up its social structures and this makes for more stability, more leadership, more agencies for helping in the solution of public problems.

But when slum clearance enters an area, it does not merely rip out slatternly houses, it uproots the people. It tears out the churches. It destroys the local businessman. It sends the neighborhood lawyer to new offices downtown and it mangles the tight skein of community friendships and group relationships beyond repair. (p. 137)

In addition to the gross physical assaults, there have been subtler assaults on neighborhoods, including private sector disinvestment, housing policies that have favored single-family suburbs, redlining by banks, credit allocation policies, and, more insidiously, federal tax policies. As our society has become more mobile and fluid, the preconditions for small-scale community life have been increasingly undermined.

Clearly, the price of modernization and mobility has been alienation, a dominant theme in literature and a major concern of social scientists for most of this century. There is disagreement in the scholarly literature about just how seriously neighborhoods as primary communities have been weakened, but the gross indicators suggest that the weakening has been substantial. The classic study of the upwardly mobile organization man of the postwar years, who uprooted family and home to climb the corporate ladder, concluded: "If by roots we mean the complex of geographical and family ties that knitted Americans to local society, these young transients are almost entirely rootless" (Whyte, 1955).

For the sons and daughters of the immigrant generations who made it into the middle class, exchanging the confining if supportive ties of the old neighborhoods for the more anonymous amenities of suburban life may have been a reasonable trade. But with the slowing of the American economy and the apparent hardening of class lines, the new urban immigrants—blacks and Hispanics, primarily—as well as the old white working class, may well face the worst of both worlds: a society more fluid and anonymous but less mobile. They have neither the traditional supports nor the compensating opportunities.

One striking finding of recent research is that poor and working class people tend to be more dependent on informal support systems such as family networks, at the local level than are the more affluent. For example, a Harvard–MIT study found that 15 percent of upper and 19 percent of middle class respondents to a survey indicated that they had relatives in their immediate neighborhood. But 43 percent of the white working class and 61 percent of the white "lower class" lived within easy reach of relatives. For blacks of all classes the figure was 44 percent. For Hispanics it was 59 percent (Coleman, 1978).

A wealthy suburb or an in-town high-rise may score high on all the indicators of alienation: people not knowing their neighbors; few relatives in the area; atomized transportation through the automobile; regional shopping centers rather than neighborhood stores; little if any street life; double-locked doors. But members of the middle class suffer less because they can, after all, afford to purchase some semblance of community.

A car (or two) can overcome the physical isolation. Long distance telephone calls can contact relatives. Housekeepers can be hired to provide child care. Holidays and cultural excursions are taken for granted. The family can join a country club to provide a social life. A buzzer system and security guards can reduce crime and the fear of crime. And if all else fails, a private psychotherapist can be consulted.

But the poor cannot purchase these facsimiles of community. If the neighborhood networks they depend on break down or are destroyed, they simply do without.

Research also indicates that social support networks are somewhat more intact in white working class neighborhoods than in poor black ones. There are many reasons that this might be so. For one thing, the dislocating consequences of urban renewal have been felt almost entirely by poorer neighborhoods. And the housing projects that have taken over streets that once throbbed with casual public life are every bit as alienating as luxury high-rise apartment buildings, and probably more so. When there is little opportunity for natural, public contact, people tend to isolate themselves from one another to a remarkable degree. And when there are the additional burdens of poverty and discrimination, when you cannot be as choosy about who your neighbors are as the upper middle class can be, then suspicion and fear of trouble are likely to far outweigh the need for neighborly advice and help. The irony, of course, is that the people most in need of effective social supports (because they

268   SHARLAND TROTTER

are the most susceptible to the stresses of poverty and racism) often have the least effective supports to fall back on.

But income alone by no means tells the whole story. In a study of the "human ecology" of child abuse and neglect, James Garbarino and Deborah Sherman (1979) did an in-depth analysis of two neighborhoods that were matched on socioeconomic characteristics but which presented dramatically different social environments for child rearing.

Parents in the low-risk area, which was perceived as a stable neighborhood where people had put down roots and where houses were well maintained, were much more inclined to use the neighborhood as a resource for their children. There was more exchanging of child supervision and more parentally sanctioned play among children in the neighborhood. Notably, the parents in this neighborhood, and particularly the mothers themselves, also assumed more exclusive and direct responsibility for child care than did parents in the high-risk area, which had a high percentage of "latchkey" children.

It was found, in other words, that families in the low-risk area were basically able to take care of themselves. It was only in the context of relative self-sufficiency that they could call upon others and make use of informal support networks. That is, they could afford to become involved in neighborly exchanges without fear of exploitation.

In contrast, the picture that emerges from the high-risk area is one of a neighborhood facing disruptive change and deterioration, threatened, among other things, by the imminent construction of an interstate highway through its center. In this neighborhood, the researchers found, there was more transience, less self-sufficiency, less reciprocal exchange, and generally less adequate provision of child care. Instead, very needy families· were clustered together in a setting they considered hostile, where they were forced to compete for scarce social resources.

In such a stressful environment, people are inclined to take advantage of one another whenever possible by "getting all they can from others while giving as little as they can get away with." In short, there is a widespread conviction that the neighborhood exerts a negative influence on families and that a family's own problems are compounded rather than ameliorated by the neighborhood. It would thus seem that socially impoverished families may be particularly vulnerable to socially impoverished environments.

It is terribly important to begin to study families, as these researchers have done, *in context*; that is, to examine the social surroundings that help to shape family life, making the difficult business of child rearing easier or that much more difficult.

Families, of course, are also being rediscovered as a topic of popular debate, scholarly research, and public policy discussion. Long and lively

arguments go on in the pages of academic journals and popular magazines, as well as in living rooms and across kitchen tables about whether
the family is falling apart or continuing to thrive.

Some have voiced a fear that the present concern with families mirrors
a current mood of privatism, a retreat from collective responses to social
problems, and an inclination to look for personal, psychological solutions to problems that are at bottom public and political (Featherstone,
1979). Maybe so. But while they are perhaps less in vogue among intellectuals, neighborhoods represent a growing political force that evokes
precisely the opposite mood—one of collective strengths and social
connectedness.

In cities all over the country, the anti-neighborhood policies and trends
noted above have begun to generate their own antibodies, in the form of
community advocacy organizations, anti-highway coalitions and the
like. Even in some of the hardest hit communities, with the most depressing economic and demographic statistics, there is resurgent energy,
creativity, and ingenuity.

The city of St. Louis offers a striking example. It stands number one
under distressed city criteria (Urban and Regional Policy Group [URPG]—
Carter Urban Policy Document, 1978); number one in per capita vacant
land and building abandonment; number one in absolute population loss;
number one in infant mortality and lead poisoning rates; and number one
in commercial/industrial tax abatement. Pursuing a strategy of downtown development at untold costs to its neighborhoods and their residents, St. Louis is best defined as a downtown commercial district, surrounded by what Martin Mayer (1978) has described as "a zone of
devastation that must be experienced to be believed" (p. 151).

In the middle of this "zone of devastation," in an all-black neighborhood that many had considered beyond restoration,* emerged the
Jeff-Vander-Lou Community Development Corporation. Its immediate
impetus was a city urban renewal plan that would have dislocated many
residents for the second or third time in their lives. With strong local
leadership, a fiercely determined community self-help group, and seed
money from neighborhood churches and a few local businessmen, Jeff-
Vander-Lou not only stopped the city from intervening, but has rehabilitated several hundred housing units, operates an extensive array of
human services, including day care, and has attracted a new Brown Shoe
Company factory into the area, providing more than 400 new jobs.

The St. Louis (or, more properly, the Jeff-Vander-Lou) experience is a

*In fact, a consulting firm retained by the city of St. Louis actually recommended a plan
of radical triage to withdraw services from what were euphemistically termed "depletion
areas." When a public outcry forced city officials to scrap the plan, the experts were be-
wildered and offended (National Commission on Neighborhoods, unpublished paper).

potent reminder of the skills and resources that ordinary people possess and how much can be accomplished through collective action at the neighborhood level.

Local voluntary self-help networks—what people can do for themselves—are of course nothing new. The United States has always been renowned for its multitudes of small, local institutions; indeed, American democracy was founded on the principle of self-determination. There has been an abundance of research and observation, dating from de Tocqueville, that attests to the historical importance of voluntary neighborhood organizations and institutions in the lives of individuals.

For example, an extensive behavioral study of civic participation in five countries showed that in comparison with Britons, Germans, Mexicans, and Italians, Americans were the most likely to belong to local voluntary associations; most likely to rely on those associations to represent their interests in local disputes; and most likely to believe that such associations were important (Almond and Verba, 1965).

The authors of this study concluded that "voluntary associations are the prime means by which the function of mediating between the individual and the state is performed. Through them, the individual is able to relate himself effectively and meaningfully to the political system. . . .

"If the citizen is a member of some voluntary organization, he is involved in the broader social world but less dependent upon and less controlled by his political system" (p. 245).

More recently, local, small-scale organizations have been invoked as a significant means of empowering communities against large, centralizing institutions and insensitive bureaucracies. The major function of such groups is to empower poor people to do the things the more affluent can already do, to spread the power around a bit more, and to do so where it matters—in people's control over their own lives (Berger and Neuhaus, 1976).

In this era of giantism—and privatism—the fact that significant numbers of people are banding together to shape the destinies of their own communities is very hopeful indeed. The community that gave rise to Jeff-Vander-Lou is not so exceptional as it might appear to be. The decade of the seventies has seen the proliferation of a host of local activist groups, whose roots are to be found in the social movements of the 1960s, in the early Alinsky organizations of the 1950s, and in the union struggles of the 1930s and '40s.

Although for the most part they avoid the revolutionary rhetoric of the 1960s, these groups have arisen largely because of the obvious failures of both representative democracy and governmentally mandated citizen participation to meet the needs of the non-rich. Their strategies reflect an increasingly sophisticated blend of confrontation and cooperation woven around such issues as health, housing, schools, public safety, utility rates, and property taxes. If they are initially successful, and as they mature, such groups often evolve from single-issue to multi-issue organizations and move from "protest to program" (Perlman, 1976). For example, Baltimore's Southeast Community Organization (SECO) began as a single-issue (anti-highway) group, gradually became a multi-issue advocacy organization, and has recently branched out into economic and housing development.

Within a neighborhood, each new victory, no matter how small, can feed a sense of possibility that is more important than any specific project, and can be an important force for liberating local energy, pride, and confidence. We need small victories.

In many ways, that is precisely what the new emphasis on neighborhoods is all about—small-scale solutions to problems that are locally defined and collectively implemented.

Let me give a few examples.

Neighborhood Housing Services is a program that identifies a small neighborhood with run-down housing and a lack of confidence in its future, and aims to upgrade every house in the neighborhood, not for middle-class newcomers but for the present residents. While the federal government pays the salaries of a small staff and helps to capitalize a high-risk loan fund, the program is controlled locally, and local residents develop strategies appropriate to their perceived needs. The hallmark of NHS is that in every city where it operates (and there are now about 80), community residents, local bankers, and city officials work together to restore a neighborhood on the edge of decline and to do so before gross deterioration sets in. Besides physically fixing up houses, this approach builds important political alliances and rebuilds neighborhood confidence and pride.

A community poverty agency in the Northeast Kingdom of Vermont (the Orleans County Community Services Agency) has fought a continuing battle with federal and state bureaucracies to use CETA funds not to create make-work, but to help run a locally designed and operated for-profit sawmill. The sawmill is controlled locally, by the people who work in it. It is an instance of a new, local, job-producing industry in an area where most of the employment is provided by absentee-owned companies. The process of creating the sawmill not only created necessary and relevant jobs—it revived community networks.

A community group in Southeast Baltimore (SECO) received NIMH funds to analyze their community's needs and resources and to plan appropriate mental health strategies. People in the neighborhood canvassed other residents, community leaders, doctors, pharmacists, school and human service personnel. When they discovered that families were breaking up, that people were moving out of what had once been a stable neighborhood, and that ethnic pride was often an obstacle to help-seeking, they began to turn obstacles into strengths by developing neighborhood resource directories, family communications workshops, advocacy hotlines, and so forth. The programs themselves are not particularly novel, but the way they were developed is.

The common thread among these programs is that their focus is on every-day, immediate, and immediately recognizable problems *as those problems are defined by the people involved.* Defining the problem means owning it, and that is the first step in taking collective responsibility for dealing with it. Pre-packaged remedies are not dictated by distant bureaucrats; clients are not "serviced" by experts and professionals. Instead, in the process of working through the problem, experts come to be seen not as threatening, disruptive, insensitive meddlers, but as additional valuable community resources, and technical advice is sought when and as it is needed. (This has the added side-effect of improving the self-image of the experts as well.)

More important, the problem-solving process, with its emphasis on local ownership, creates important spillover benefits that are probably more significant than the solution of the ostensible problem. As people learn new skills they acquire competence, confidence, and a sense of mastery. Increasingly, ordinary people in ordinary neighborhoods are coming to grips with the issues and problems that affect them and their families, beginning to see how power and politics operate, and are gaining a new sense of self-esteem.

Because this kind of problem-solving demands communication among neighbors, the fabric of the community is strengthened. Through collective action, alliances are forged, leaders are created, and passivity is sharply challenged. This is prevention in the best sense. The resources and networks that are developed to tackle one problem will be there to tackle the next one.

This approach to social policy suggests a powerful analogy to individual therapy. Clinicians have long known—and their patients have long been impatient with the fact—that psychotherapy requires the patient to do most of the work. Hearing the doctor diagnose the problem does not help. Passively following the doctor's orders does not help. And while drugs are sometimes part of the process, there is no magic pill. The patient must work through the problem in his or her own way, and gain a sense of ownership, both of the problem and its resolution. All successful therapy builds on existing strengths.

So it is with neighborhoods. There are very few communities that do not have some latent strengths on which to build, yet policy makers have largely ignored what good mental health professionals know so well. Instead, they have defined neighborhoods in terms of their defects and weaknesses (a habit that is as destructive to neighborhoods as it is to people). The prevailing model is still one of providing categorical services through massive national programs, and this is frequently both demeaning and futile, because it denies the recipients the experience of working out their own solutions.

This is not to suggest that government should bear all the blame for all of our problems, or that government is totally incompetent to share in the solutions. Each of the small local programs described above was bolstered with federal dollars. But the dollars came with very few strings attached, so that local people were in command from the beginning. And that has much to do with their success.

Moreover, the strings that *were* attached tended to knit various sorts of people together rather than to unravel tenuous relationships as government programs so often do by inspiring political bickering and competition. In a time when public policy seems to reflect a fundamental loss of faith in social sympathies, these programs have deliberatley brokered social empathy and political collaboration by insisting on strategies that require people to work together.

This is a rather remarkable exception to the general rule of federal assistance, to be sure, but it does suggest that aid be sensitively delivered and that government can be effective in helping to provide contexts in which people can help one another.

A successful neighborhood can be defined as one that keeps sufficiently abreast of its problems so that it is not destroyed by them. An unsuccessful neighborhood is one that is overwhelmed by its problems and defects and is progressively more helpless before them.

Once a neighborhood has reached the point of being overwhelmed, once it is beset with a multitude of problems that are beyond the capacity of its residents to deal with, it is clear that preventive action will not make much difference. But if public policy can learn to anticipate trends that are emerging but not yet at the crisis point, carefully targeted government aid can be a powerful inducement to collective action, and that is probably the best preventive medicine there is.

References

Almond, G., and Verba, S. *The civic culture.* Boston: Little, Brown, 1965.
Berger, P. L., and Neuhaus, R. J. *To empower people.* Washington, D.C.: American Enterprise Institute for Public Policy Research, 1977.

Caplan, G. *Support systems and community mental health: Lectures on concept development.* New York: Behavioral Publications, 1974.

"Cities and People in Distress" (Carter Urban Policy Document), Washington, D.C., 1978.

Coleman, R. P. *Attitudes toward neighborhoods: How Americans choose to live.* Working Paper #49. Cambridge, Mass.: Joint Center for Urban Studies of MIT and Harvard University, 1978, 20–21.

Featherstone, J. Family matters. *Harvard Educational Review*, 1979, *49*, 20–52.

Garbarino, J., and Sherman, D. *High-risk neighborhoods and high-risk families: The human ecology of child maltreatment.* Unpublished manuscript, Boys Town Center for the Study of Youth Development, Boys Town, Nebraska, 1979.

Jacobs, J. *The death and life of great American cities.* New York: Random House, 1961.

Kaplan, B. H., Cassell, J. C., and Gore, S. Social support and health. *Medical Care*, 1977, *15*(s) Supplement, 47–58.

Kasarda, J. D., and Janowitz, M. Community attachment in mass society. *American Sociological Review*, 1974, *39*, 328–340.

Keller, S. *The urban neighborhood: A sociological perspective.* New York: Random House, 1968.

Mayer, N. *The builders.* New York: Norton, 1978.

Perlman, J. E. Grassrooting the system. *Social Policy*, 1976, *7*, 4–20.

Salisbury, H. Quoted in J. Jacobs, *The death and life of great American cities.* New York: Random House, 1968.

Warren, D. I. Public policy and the balance between formal and informal problem coping systems in urban communities (USPHS grant 3ROI-MH-24982). Rockville, Md.: Center for the Study of Metropolitan Problems. National Institute of Mental Health, 1976.

Whyte, W. *The organization man.* New York: Doubleday, 1955.

The Education of the Oppressed Child in a Democracy

Ned O'Gorman

I remember, with a considerable chill, one summer I spent at the Aspen Institute of Humanistic Studies. I had been invited there to join in a seminar on the humanities with a rather awesome array of very powerful gentlemen. They were, nearly every one of them, but for a few like myself called to enlighten them in the way of the humanities, in "control" of something—conglomerates, universities, governments—here and abroad. They held certain of the world's secrets in their hands, they knew how to control oil, governments, land, power—physical and corporate—arms, the press. The corridors and plateaus of power were the loci of work for them as my nursery school in Harlem is for me. They lived in those charged and teeming landscapes with complete security but for one intrusion of the serpent.

The seminars in Aspen, for those of you who have not been there—I have been twice and I think I shall not be asked again—are microcosms of what must be the Platonic ideal of that universal gymnasium in the sky, where men meditate on the nature of man in the order of creation. During my visits there I was astonished to find how Aristotle and the Stock Exchange found themselves for moments in an easy, if idiotic, dialogue.

But the serpent intruded and the serpent was a word. The word was oppression. There in Aspen, in that idyllic landscape, the word was avoided, explained away, shunted into the Platonic shadows as if it were an obscenity. I spoke in that seminar and in the seminars that followed of the reality of oppression. But when I mentioned that word it drove my fellow seminarians into fits of rage, the moderators of the seminars into silence, and me into a quite ungentlemanly petulance and at one moment tears. From the most misty-eyed liberal it brought glances of suspicion and hostility. When I asked that the word be studied as we read, say, Machiavelli's *Prince*, it had to be watered down to a mild rhetoric: alienated, marginated, poor, but never, never, never, oppressed peoples. If we agreed that the oppressed did exist, it meant that somewhere out there in the bush hid an army of discontented, angry, repressed creatures who might at any moment spring and destroy all the values the capitalist holds sacred. Somehow the democratic process, our democratic heritage—so ably (but for me simplistically) observed by Mortimer Adler there in Aspen—must have the power to cure whatever ills make a people troublesome, anxious, and marginated. The thought that the very *system itself* oppressed was an affront to the soul of capitalism and democracy.

I trust it will be clear to you now that I am using the word oppression in its most radical, simple sense: It is that process within a society that destroys life, inhibits life, makes growth, joy, celebration, family life, intellectual and spiritual life, physical life, impossible.

Oppression comes from many people, from many established and often trusted organizations: it comes from the churches, from the shopkeepers, from the government, from the courts, from the citizens, from the schools, from the very people oppressed. Oppression is in every society, somewhere in its fabric, a malignant power that must be destroyed. We ought now to reflect, perhaps, those of us for whom the liberation of our brothers and sisters caught in the embrace of death-in-life is the reason for our being, perhaps on those in our society who are the most oppressed of all: the children of the oppressed.

Since 1966 I have been working with those children and in their lives I have observed oppression and its gorgon-like energy establishing the dominion of death, ignorance, hunger, sickness, despair, hopelessness, sexual and imaginative chaos, and the annihilation of creatures of incredible beauty, an annihilation as sure in its mortal, final crushing power as the ovens of the Nazis were for the Jews, the rifle of the settlers in the west for the Indians, the armies of the Colonial powers for the Africans, or the landowners and the generals for the peasants of Brazil.

So, being wiser than my co-seminarians at Aspen, we can agree that oppression of people does exist in our society, and I do not think that anyone would disagree that of all the oppressed those with the least recourse to the law, to healing, are the babes, the very young, those in utero, those whose lives in so many aspects are settled, in style and in development, during the crucial years from birth until 3 or 4.

I came to Harlem with not an idea in my mind. I came to work with God's poor and that was all. I had just returned from a tour of Chile, Argentina, and Brazil for the State Department. During that journey I discovered that my country could not judge the malaise of oppression either in its own land nor in the land of others. It was blind to oppression and nurtured it rather than destroyed it. For me it was a terrible time of the rending apart of illusions. In South America I had the first glimpse of what we are doing now in Harlem. I remember a boy in Valparaíso sucking a gasoline soaked rag to keep the hunger that gnawed at him from driving him mad. That image returns to me rather often in my dreams.

My nursery school (I call it a liberation camp) is in Harlem because I must find a place to receive the children of the oppressed in that part of our democratic society that is called the East Harlem Triangle. Places like that "triangle" exist all over this world. I must insist that you try to understand that I see all people oppressed as people *oppressed*: I do not see the color of their skin; I see their oppression. I am in Harlem because that is where I am. I trust I could work with equal energy in Calcutta, in Belfast, in a village of poor whites in Kansas. But each day into that rather rickety house we call our school come 20 little children from one particular place on this earth. The youngest is 18 months, the oldest 5. My task is to educate them but I am not so naive as to think that the main thing I must do is teach them colors, numbers, letters, shapes and so on. They are very bright children and such learning will come easily to them. I must teach them how to survive, how to understand, reflect, observe, judge, react to the forces around them that are destroying them. It is a difficult task for the world is strong and the powers of oppression powerful beyond telling and the children who come to see me are cowed by oppression, frightened by what they see, but they are powerless to understand what is taking up lodging in them. I am a great admirer of Fernand Braudel, the prodigious historian of the Mediterranean, and a thought of his about the power of individuals on the great process of time and history is one that brings me up often upon the horror of history, its mammoth, tidal energy. Braudel writes:

By stating the narrowness of the limits of action, is one denying the role of the individual in history? I think not. One may have the choice between striking two or three blows: the questions still arise: Will one be able to strike them at all? To strike them effectively? To do so in the knowledge that only this range of choices is open to one? I would conclude with the paradox that the true man of action is he who chooses to remain within them and even to take advantage of the weight of the inevitable, exerting his own pressure in the same direction. All efforts against the prevailing tide of history—which is not always obvious—are doomed to failure.

So when I think of the individual, I am always inclined to see him imprisoned within a destiny in which he himself has little hand, fixed in a landscape in which the infinite perspectives of the long term stretch into the distance both behind him and before. In historical analysis as I see it, rightly or wrongly, the long run always wins in the end. (Braudel, 1973, pp. 1243–1244)

For you see, as I work with the children and try to bring them out of silence into the light of their childhood, I work against the demons and they are powerful. I do not know even if I have any effect on anyone. I wonder if I simply thrust my vision into the darkness and bring no light to that darkness.

As I think about the form that this change must take I know that if I propose too much no one will listen; if I propose too little I do no justice to my children; and if I do not work with what there is I will make no progress at all.

The education of the oppressed child in a democracy is a notion that has not yet been thought much about in American education. Paolo Friere, in the blazing perception of his pedagogy, seems congenial to me, but I know that for the most liberal of educators in this country he is remote and too difficult. The problem is "difficult," quite simply that. The depth of it is troublesome to the most optimistic of teachers. What must be formulated is a language, a science, a method. We are strangers in a landscape teeming with death and incredible forces of life.

How then do I see this problem of educating the oppressed child in a democracy? I can write only about what I have seen. I am not a teacher by training. I am a poet and that gives me perhaps one talent that all teachers ought to have: I have been taught to observe the world closely. The four children I shall describe now, very briefly, are typical of those who come to us. What I have seen is the basis for what I envision our task to be, as teachers of the oppressed.

Monica is 18 months old. When she came to us she could not smile. She could not respond to affection. She could not eat. She screamed and slept. Her parents are alcoholics. She is plagued with a perpetual cold, is in and out of hospitals with severe bronchitis. She is very beautiful and very intelligent. But the life she leads, is *forced* to lead, has damaged the core of her spirit.

Jerry is two. Twice he has come close to death. He is starved by his mother, beaten, abandoned. In his eyes there is the waste spaces of a shattered spirit. He is covered with burns and when he was once admitted to the hospital for an asthma attack he was infested with lice.

Lucy is four. She has been raped once and is now infected with gonorrhea.

John has seen his aunt shoot dope, observed an uncle attempt to murder his wife. He is one of the wisest children I have ever known. His ability, at age six, to hold a coherent conversation, to ask precise questions, and to take instruction is formidable. But already at this early year of his life I see his face change, his spirit wither.

Somehow I must heal him, all the children, as I teach them. So after 13 years of observation and work I began to see the beginnings of a method of healing. I will tell you of it, though it might anger some of you. It has angered my most liberal friends. But it has in it I think the germ of an approach to liberation of our oppressed children, though it must offend our most cherished democratic principles of privacy, individualism, and the sacredness of family, for it begins with the simple, universal premise that in all children if there is no opening to the world during the early years of childhood the future is doomed to tragedy. For the children of the oppressed the opening to the world is, I think, at once political, historical, imaginative, and rooted in the nature of oppression.

When John came to me at three years old he was an enraged child. I could not touch him, hold him, talk to him. I knew as I have suggested that he was a child of startling intelligence. I had to enter into his spirit somehow, so that I could free him into peace and a lucid intercourse with his own life and the life around him. I decided one day that I would talk to him about his life. I began each morning, when the memory of the past night was fresh, to question him about what had happened to him since he left our liberation camp the day before. I asked him what he had eaten, what he had heard. I asked him about his guardians, their friends, and what had occurred during meal time and afterwards. I asked him when he went to sleep, when he got up, what time he had breakfast, what television programs he had watched. I asked him what state his flat was in when he had gotten home. I asked him who stayed with him during the night (often he was left alone with his 2-year-old brother). At first he would say nothing. Then, slowly, he would tell me of beatings, drugs, sexual brutality among his kin, attacks by rats, overflowing toilets, midnight arrivals of police, sudden bizarre trips through the street with his mother in the dark of a storm.

What was happening to him? I was not ever really quite sure. I stood on shaky grounds. I was worried that perhaps I was harming him, forcing him to be disloyal to his family, perhaps forcing him to confront events that he could not properly understand. My coworkers were furious at me as I went about this search for John's response to his life. But I had to continue for I knew that I was on the right track. I knew that the brilliant child had to begin now to face head on the life he led. There was no time to waste. If I stopped what I was doing for fear that I was causing him harm, I would have had to wait until that time that would never come, when he would be "ready" to face the powers of darkness that possessed him and his life. No, I knew, I was certain, that now was the time to begin breaking down the fear, the terror, breaking them down by making him face them no matter how hard it was for him. I knew unless he began then to come up out of the depths of his oppression that he never would survive. He had to begin a process of learning that would bring him knowledge about the state of his life.

He had then, to begin then to understand his oppression. He lived in a world where *nothing was ever questioned, where nothing, no matter how brutal, how inhuman it might be, was ever judged.* No one he knew ever came to his defense, no one ever explained to him that what was happening to him was wrong. No one had ever told him that he was a creature with the right to survive, to grow, to endure, to be happy. He had no way to form a moral stance before evil and oppression. So I had, as I provoked him to talk, to create in him a larger view of the world; that is, I had to teach him to extend his understanding of himself to others. I thought that such an act from a 6-year-old would be impossible. I knew that I did not want him to hate those around him, though probably hating them would have been better than tolerating them. We were undergoing, the two of us, a process of enlightenment that had to transcend mere consciousness; that had to transform itself into an act of charity, self-awareness.

I waited. I had faith in that child. And one morning that faith bore fruit. It was perhaps the happiest day for me in the past year. John walked in and began, as he usually did, to tell me of the events that had happened to him during the night. He was filled that day with grisly tales. As he finished talking to me Lilly brought in her daughter. The child seemed especially still and sad. John looked at her, and after the mother had gone, sat beside her, and with the most extreme gentleness asked her if she were hungry. He asked her what had happened that made her seem sad. He asked her questions that brought him out of himself, into the presence of another.

I account that somehow a triumph. He began to communicate to another a sense of the world that he had gained for himself. He became lucid. He became a judge of what he saw and heard. He speculated. He wondered. He knew that what had happened to him might have happened to another. He entered into the world of other people. I think of Piaget's (1948) warning: "If there were not other people, the disappointments of experience would lead to overcompensation and dementia" (p. 206).

It is that regression into a spiritual and intellectual universe of mute and unintelligible signs and events that render our children at an early age paralyzed in spirit.

What I had worked toward with John was a radicalization of his being at those twin wellsprings of intellect and imagination. I moved him out of the darkness of a blind acceptance of what *was* into the light of a kind of verification of being, his being, at its most profound, at its holiest.

I must move John, and all the children, toward a revolutionary act of life amidst death. We must teach our children, those of us who teach'the oppressed child, that they have not inherited the earth and that there are reasons why they have not inherited the earth. We must establish schools where the oppressed child is liberated. And this next year for John is one of eternal importance for him; his survival depends upon what happens to him next September. If that brilliant and good child enters the public schools he will either be judged unruly and/or retarded, or he will be ignored, or he will manage to rise above it all and triumph, or he will simply decline into sullen despair and fail.

Where then do we begin to change the schools that receive children like John? The challenge is so vast, so terrible in its consequences. I am quite ignorant of where one does begin. I would suggest perhaps we begin with the teachers. The schools do not yet have teachers trained in the psychology, history, and quality of oppression. We have good teachers in the public schools but there are not enough of them for whom liberation and learning is one act in any pedagogy of the oppressed. A teacher of oppressed children must receive them with the knowledge that they *are* oppressed, that each one's *life*, in all its variety, *is* in mortal danger: that liberation is the goal of teaching and that no matter how brilliant, well-intentioned and dedicated a teacher might be, to teach John must be to liberate him. I am not certain how I would train a teacher but I do know that John needs that teacher desperately.

The texts must be revised; the food the children eat in the schools must be prepared with the understanding that the children who come to the schools from the communities of the dispossessed are usually malnourished. The classrooms, the materials used in them, the whole shape and strategy of the day must be reviewed and fundamentally recharged with the goal of healing, radicalizing, and liberating the oppressed child from bondage.

I watch the children and until last spring I despaired of their life but now I think we are ready to take another step to assure them the possibility of survival. So we begin this fall, if all goes well, our own school, certified by the city, with a qualified day care teacher (I do not qualify since I did my studies in 16th century English literature) in a building on 129th Street in Harlem, a building now undergoing a renovation into a simple but beautiful space. I can see nothing else for me to do. If I am serious about the children who come to me, sometimes for four years, I must do more for their survival than cast them out into the public schools. If I do not build this school, this liberation camp, then I betray John and all the others, especially little Juliette who is 19 months.

With the help of our educational consultants, Bettye Caldwell and

Rosmary Lea from St. Bernard's school, we are now beginning the planning of our curriculum, or rather we are beginning our strategy of liberation for that is what we must do—liberate, strengthen, train our children, so that they can "overcome." As we teach them how to read we must do it so that they can read in a real and vibrant way the world around them. We must—as we teach them to spell, add, subtract, play—teach them to go deeply into their own lives and find there the forces that are poised ready to destroy them; go deeply into their lives, into their individual, solitary, private selves and find the strength to fight the oppression around them. I must teach them to believe in themselves, to question what is happening to them, judge what is happening to them often through the despair and oppression of their very kin.

But we are working in the dark for I do not think that what we intend to do has ever been done in quite this way before. To think that Paolo Friere, the phenomenal teacher of the oppressed decade will be of much help to the educational establishment in this land, even to its most liberal membership, is, as I have suggested, a dream. He is far too daring, far too dangerous. But we must talk to our children about the historical moment in which they live, as Friere does to the peasants of Pernambuco. We must talk to them of housing, crime, liquor, dope, anger, violence; we must make them ready to affirm life over death, hope over despair, joy over misery, family over sexuality, love over violence. Everything we do must be focused in an act of liberation. Nothing must be done in secret. Nothing must be done for window dressing to please parents, the government, foundations. Everything must be done to instruct our children in the methodology of survival. We will use what the world had to offer us: Mao, Mozart, Martin Luther King, César Chavez, Camus, Kant, Montessori, flowers, fish, blocks, the ballet, languages, maps, good food, paints. But we will use them all to create within the child the liberated spirit of the conqueror of oppression.

I trust that I have not offended anyone by suggesting that the education of our children must be different from any education given the middle class and by suggesting that in the suffering of the oppressed child is the seed of our methodology of liberation. Their imprisonment in a racist world is the first landscape of their freedom. It is there that they take their first step toward liberation. We must enter, with science and compassion, into the act of oppression in all its simmering horror. Only then will we understand.

I will conclude this meditation, this very tentative meditation, on the education of the oppressed with the stories of two women. They are intended to be parables.

Evelyn worked for me for one year. She was 20 years old then. One day I asked her to quarter and peel a dozen or so apples. I left her to do it and went out into the playground with the children. When I returned I saw that she had not gone far with her work but was struggling with a knife to dislodge something in the apple. I could not understand what she was trying to do. Perhaps I thought, there was a nail in it for I could think of nothing else that made sense. "There's something in there Ned, something hard." I took the apple and cut through it easily, and realized as I was doing it that she had hit the core with her knife and did not know what it was. She had never quartered an apple before, never gotten out the core and pits.

Lillian is a dope addict, a whore, a rotten mother, and all around, a very unpleasant woman. But she is brilliant, cagey and well spoken. I met her once walking down Madison Avenue. She was in bad shape and carried a notebook under her arm. I asked her what the book was and she said it was nothing, just something she had been doing for years. I asked if I could see it. She gave it to me and on the first page she had written: "Lillian's Knowledge Book." She told me that when she could not bear life any longer she would go to the public library and outline articles in the Encyclopedia that interested her. I left her and felt very rudimentary awe in my heart. I was furious at the schools, at the world, at her kin, for allowing that extraordinary desire for knowledge to rot so that all that was left was a notebook: Lillian, on the brink of the abyss and her notebook. Likewise, Evelyn and her muddle with the apple.

The work in our school is a parable, for we observe day in and day out, every season, in every kind of calamity, the holy signs of greatness, smoldering beneath the wrecked spirit. For Lillian and Evelyn, in their youth, the healing and the learning that they sought was denied them. To the world they brought not the power of their humanity, but silence and wasted glory. They were once the children of the oppressed. Now, their children come to me and leave me to enter the schools, the same ones their parents entered. But no, they will not fail for we have determined in our small and weak vision of our life that our children at 57 East 129th Street in Harlem, U.S.A. will be the healing and the healed of the oppressed, the revolutionaries, the heroes, the heroines, the liberated.

References

Braudel, I. *The Mediterranean and the Mediterranean world in the age of Philip II.* Vol. 2. New York: Harper & Row, 1973.

Piaget, J. *Judgment and reasoning in the child.* Totowa, N.J.: Littlefield, Adams & Co., 1948.

PART V

Revolutionary Change

Introductory Notes

It seemed appropriate for a conference on prevention through social change and political action to include reports on developments in societies that have recently undergone massive social and political changes. We were curious about the effects on mental health wrought by the major social changes over the past 30 years in the world's largest nation. Closer to home we wanted to know what was happening in Cuba, where a socialist regime took charge of a Western nation where people were long used to competition, political corruption, religion, gambling and prostitution, and gross inequalities between the sexes and across social classes.

The two papers in this section provide an interesting, tantalizing glimpse of recent events in China and Cuba as they affect changes in human relationships. The spirit of "revolutionary optimism" in China reported by Victor and Ruth Sidel seems less in evidence in Susan Rigdon's report on Cuba. The Sidels explain that throughout their history the Chinese have *not* emphasized individualism and freedom—rather, a feeling of unity with family and village has always been more important. In a land with vast numbers of people living in agrarian villages, the family and clan have been, and are, the major support groups offering protection against hunger and handicap. The Chinese have had only to extend their perception of support groups to the larger society, accepting in the process the intrusion of the revolution's controls over population growth, marriage age, contraception, and so forth.

Mao is quoted as stressing the fact that all knowledge, including knowledge of the revolution, comes through direct experience. It seems unlikely that he had read John Dewey, but clearly learning by doing is a tenet of pragmatists, whatever their political views. Self-reliance, the Sidels explain, is emphasized in matters of health care. Westerners may have difficulty distinguishing self-reliance from individualism, but clearly taking responsibility for one's own health is not incompatible with a concern for the welfare of the group.

Both societies are reported to be organized by committees operating in a sort of pyramidal structure that reaches down into neighborhoods and streets. Community control of China's schools, health, housing, and even more personal matters like contraception, is reported by the Sidels. Local "study groups," somewhat reminiscent of encounter groups, provide an intimate forum for the examination of motivations and attitudes. Clearly this is an attempt to change ways of thinking of a huge population.

One of the difficulties of any social revolution is the resistance created by habits, old ways of thinking and acting, which are embedded in the people who have grown up under a different social order.

As Rigdon points out, some of the Cuban revolutionaries were baffled at the reluctance of the poor and the exploited to commit themselves to the new order. Many poor people were quite willing to live better and to consume more material goods without otherwise changing their life styles or attitudes. The state has undertaken to change the educational system, the mass media, and the arts in efforts to change attitudes, especially of the young. In many ways the task of the revolution in Cuba is more difficult than in China, because the changes in living patterns, life styles, and aspirations are more drastic.

Both of these revolutionary societies appear to view deviance as a result of incorrect social learning. Corrective discussions, lectures, explanations in the form of "heart-to-heart talks" in which the doctor explains to the patient the nature of the illness—all of these imply that the Chinese believe that the person can change as a result of insight and understanding. In Cuba, the rejection and condemnation of homosexuality has led to efforts to isolate homosexuals to keep this behavior from "spreading" to the young. In both societies, we may infer, people can learn to be deviant, and can learn to change their ways, though clearly the latter process is more difficult. Rigdon gives us a detailed account of attempts at prevention, mostly early intervention, with minors who seem at high risk for later criminal behavior. Intervention with the parents of younger children at risk is also a form of prevention used by the Cubans.

The widespread use of "paraprofessionals"—from the barefoot doctors in China to the day care workers and court counselors in Cuba—suggests approaches to prevention and early intervention that are based in social, rather than medical, theory. We learn just enough to be tantalized into wanting to learn more about the effects of the revolution on mental health. Both papers list references that can lead us to further exploration of this question.

The Prevention and Control of "Antisocial Behavior" in Revolutionary Cuba

Susan M. Rigdon

When the Castro Revolution triumphed in 1959, its overriding preoccupation was with land reform, housing, education, unemployment, and health care; discussions of standards of behavior were very broadly and idealistically stated. One should not forget that it was a minimum of two and in some cases as many as 10 years before the Revolution systematically attacked even some of Cuba's most serious social problems, such as vagrancy and absenteeism, truancy, organized prostitution, and juvenile delinquency. Before any government can combat such problems, and certainly before it can attempt value changes that extend, for example, to familial relationships, it is necessary not only to control considerable resources but, in addition, for the leadership to have a reservoir of credibility and trust among the people.

At the outset of the Revolution, behavior control (aside from the normal problems of curtailing criminal behavior) was focused on ending acts of sabotage and other counterrevolutionary activities and in preventing the recruitment of new people to these ends. This was facilitated by the imprisonment or execution of many members of Batista's government (particularly police and army officers), by the mass emigration of potential opponents of the Revolution, by the establishment of the Committees for Defense of the Revolution as a neighborhood vigilance organization, and by the occasional mass "preemptive" detentions of suspected opponents (as at the time of the Bay of Pigs Invasion in April, 1961).

The *Comités de Defensa de la Revolución* were founded September 28, 1960 and later organized, in urban areas, at the city block level. The committees are active in a broad range of programs, including public health,

I would like to thank Ruth Maslow Lewis for her comments on a draft of this paper and for the use of the field materials on which it is based in large part. I also want to express my indebtedness to the late Oscar Lewis, Ruth Lewis, and the 17 other men and women from Cuba, Mexico, and the United States who carried out the original field work.

education, urban reform, sports and recreation, local administration, and surveillance against vandalism and counterrevolutionary activities. Membership in the committees is open to all Cubans 14 and older who are "willing to defend the Revolution."

With their consolidation of power over the state apparatus and over political and economic organization during the past decade, the young men and women who led the Civic Resistance have become middle-aged heads of state, leaders of an established government. As the provisional nature of the government has begun to take on a more permanent, ordered appearance, it has become clear that the leadership wants and expects this change to be reflected in the lives of the general populace. For the past 10 years the Revolution has been attempting, in effect, to transform the politics of opposition into the politics of law and order. This task—the undoing of oppositionist and individualistic mentalities—has turned out to be one of the Revolution's toughest battles.

The triumph of the Revolution came after a century of armed rebellion against colonial and other foreign domination. Opposition was a way of life for Cuba's many highly fractionated, undisciplined, and often impulsive political action groups. Among the larger Cuban population, especially those outside the middle class and segments of the urban working class, there was little tendency to look to the government, its leaders or its institutions, for direction (although of course all Cubans were daily affected by its structure and policies). The government displayed only token responsibility for the urban and rural poor and many responded with attitudes (toward government, not politics) ranging from indifference to hostility.

Fidel Castro's Twenty-sixth of July Movement, as well as other anti-Batista groups, exploited these antigovernment feelings and fostered—as every successful revolution must—a spirit of disrespect for the existing legal and political structure, and in particular for incumbent lawmakers and enforcers. Once in power, however, revolutionaries—especially revolutionaries—cannot govern without law and order. Having no ready alternatives, the new government incorporated into its first revolutionary laws the Constitution of 1940 and the Legal Defense Code of the Batista government, and like the previous regime, proceeded to observe or ignore them when it suited the purposes of the Executive. But the Castro government eventually realized that the atmosphere of disrespect for law, which it had once used to its advantage, could, if left unchallenged, turn against the Revolution. The leadership was faced then with two enormous legal tasks: to write a completely new set of laws, and once written to persuade the Cuban people that these laws were sufficiently just to warrant a rekindling of respect for law and order. This was a minimum prerequisite not only to the achievement of economic goals but to the successful promotion of life styles that would manifest the values of the Revolution and provide the best examples for the acculturation of young people to the new system.

In the late 1960s Cuba did begin a thorough, drastic revision of its civil, penal, and family codes, the writing of a new constitution, and the formalization of the new Communist Party founded in 1965. Reading through this legislation one can easily see that it goes far beyond setting down the institutional framework for the political-economic system. In a socialist society the function of law, says Minister of Justice Armando Torres, is to be "at the service of social development, consolidation of discipline and socialist standards" (*Granma Weekly Review*, 12/30/73, p. 3). According to Francisco Moreno (1970), this purpose is not at odds with Cuban legal tradition, which is characterized by the traditional Roman view of law as "above everything else, a moral interpretation of life—an effort to define those ethical goals that the political community should strive to attain" (p. 374).

In addition to defining the boundaries of legal behavior, therefore, Cuba's new laws establish within those boundaries recommended standards of behavior for almost all aspects of daily life. These are collectively referred to in Article 8 of the 1976 Constitution as "conduct proper to a society free from the exploitation of man by man." A summary description of this conduct is contained in Article 63: "Everyone has the duty of caring for public and social property, accepting work discipline, respecting the rights of others, observing standards of socialist living and fulfilling civic and social duties."

This is, broadly defined, a statement of what is expected from the model socialist citizen now that, by their own estimations, the leadership has delivered on the promises made during the insurrection. The key trait in this model personality—which used to be referred to as the "new man"—is selflessness, or the ability to place the welfare of the community as a whole (as determined by the state) over one's own needs and concerns.

Any conduct that does not reflect acceptance of revolutionary standards can be referred to as "antisocial behavior"; therefore it is difficult to make an inclusive list of antisocial acts. Furthermore, interpretation of these standards is subject to change, depending on how the leadership defines the needs of the country at any given time. Obvious deviations from the proposed norms, such as serious criminal acts and true counterrevolutionary activities (that is, as distinct from those which are labeled by the state as counterrevolutionary) are not the subject of this paper. Here we are concerned with the most common forms of antisocial behavior, many of which could result in misdemeanor or minor civil or criminal charges. Among these are: disorderly conduct, verbal abuse, drunkenness, violations of the Public Health Code, truancy, absenteeism and vagrancy, juvenile delinquency, child neglect and abuse, sorcery and other Afro-Cuban sect activities involving expenditure of money and food. All such behavior is seen as unworthy of the "prestige" of the Revolution.

Every society has some idea of what is considered ideal behavior and of when behavior contravenes generally accepted standards. What distinguishes one society from another is how rigidly these codes are stated and how strictly and by what means they are enforced. But how does a government arrive at a code of conduct as specifically defined as the one Cuba now has? We may assume that if, at the outset, one has an idea of what an ideal society is, one must have some idea, however vague, of how people in that society will behave toward one another and toward the community in general. We know however that mental images and paper constructions of the ideal society do not always hold up well when they meet the truth of the everyday world. They are in some respects at odds with culture and, in their skeletal forms, almost always hopelessly inadequate to the task of transforming economic and political systems. But because the will to transform cultures and political systems is exactly what distinguishes revolutionaries from reformers and the leaders of coups d'etat, they usually do not lack motivation for establishing sets of rules to regulate individual and national behavior in ways deemed essential to the achievement of revolutionary goals. But depending on the individual leaders, how idealistic, and perhaps how young, they are, it may be some time before there is full realization of just how much has to be regulated in order to channel society's human and material resources toward the ultimate goals.

Establishing official codes of correct behavior in any revolutionary society is usually a lengthy process, as the needs of the new socioeconomic order mix with the realities of the old system and with the politics, ideology, and cultural perspectives of the leadership. Clearly some standards evolve from the form of economic organization adopted. For example, in a country with limited resources, which has as a fundamental goal guaranteeing equal access to essential goods and services to all citizens, economic controls are inevitable. In Cuba, where the state owns and controls the means of production and distribution, this has meant mandatory full employment for all able-bodied men, job and educational opportunities determined in part by government-set quotas, wages and prices fixed by the state, elimination of excess consumption by the general populace, and so forth. Other standards seem to originate in broad cultural inclinations; in Cuba, for example, the extraordinarily deep and wide-spread fear of homosexuality has resulted in the arrest and internment in labor camps of many homosexuals. Still other standards have their roots in the individual cultural backgrounds of the leadership, and in the case of Cuban leaders these are fundamentally middle class.

It may be an overstatement to say that what exists between revolution-aries and the poor is a love-hate relationship, but certainly it is one that contains elements of contempt as well as of admiration and sympathy. That is to say that revolutionaries may love the poor in the abstract, but they do not necessarily like the way some live; they may sympathize with the exploited masses, but they will not necessarily tolerate the poor man or woman who continues in a life style considered unbecoming to the Revolution and not befitting a liberated person. Most revolutionaries begin, after all, on the premise that the material aspects of lower-class life are undesirable. Appalled by the distribution of their country's wealth, they vow to extend to every citizen a *modified* version of the middle-class standard of living. With this they also hope to rid the poor of those non-material aspects of their lives which are thought to originate in, and to be manifestations of, exploitative economic conditions. This has less to do with the elimination of the so-called vices of the poor (because most of these are found and tolerated in every class) than with the teaching of middle-class virtues.

If one looks at the model for a socialist citizen, one can see in it a core of idealized Western middle-class values: industry, thrift, social mobility through education, participation in civic and political activities, a stable, rather routinized family life for the rearing of disciplined, educated, work-minded, secularly-oriented children. Like the traditional middle-class person, the ideal socialist citizen engages in few excesses (except perhaps for patriotic zeal), does not "rock the boat," and above all, is "re-spectable," a credit to the system, capable of representing it in the best possible way to the younger generation and to the world. The principal difference between the two modal types is that in the socialist citizen, in-dustry and ambition are harnessed for the community's welfare and not, at least in the first instance, for individual or personal gain.

Looking at some of the Revolution's early efforts one might fairly con-clude that the leadership, having newly liberated the poor, wanted them somehow to look different from the way they looked under the old sys-tem. The new government began in a rather zealous, perhaps self-righ-teous, yet unsystematic way to proselytize poor Cubans to certain mid-dle-class dress styles, work habits, and family patterns. Teams were sent into the countryside to convince couples living in free union to legalize their marriages; some women brought to schools in Havana were taught how to dress differently, to coif their hair, even to shave their legs; prostitutes in rehabilitation schools were taught how not to look like prostitutes; children recruited from poor rural homes to Havana boarding schools were taught, along with their basic education, hygiene and dress habits (above all to keep shoes on their feet).

A number of the more idealistic Cuban revolutionaries were baffled and sometimes impatient when they found that some who had been most exploited under the old system were among the slowest to make a total commitment to the new one. While it is true that few people turned down the opportunity to have the essentials—decent housing, and adequate food and clothing—a certain number did not want all of what the Revolution had to offer. Some rejected not work itself but employment on the terms offered by the state; some were indifferent to matters of hygiene and public health, to their children's truancy, or to the functioning of neighborhood-based mass organizations.

To those people who in the past had no cash in their pockets because there were no employment opportunities, who had been financially unable to keep their children in school, or who had been denied medical treatment for lack of money or insurance, it may have been readily apparent that their difficulties were the result of systemic inequities. However it was probably much more difficult for them to understand that their marital status, familial relationships, recreational habits, speech patterns, and religious beliefs were products of an exploitative situation and in need of change. Many could not understand—perhaps because they could not easily separate themselves from their life styles—why they could not live better materially, without being made over in someone else's eyes. This posed a dilemma for the Revolution: How to change people who had been victimized by the old system without making it appear that they were being victimized by the new one.

It would be impossible to review, let alone discuss, all the means for the prevention and control of antisocial behavior that are at the disposal of a government that controls almost all goods and services, has an extensive system of domestic surveillance, and a penal system that includes a network of labor camps where prisoners can be politically "rehabilitated." Among the field materials collected in Cuba in 1969–70 are interviews with several men who discussed their treatment in prison camps. Because this issue is very complex and needs to be discussed at some length, I have omitted any mention of it in this paper. I have written about it elsewhere (Rigdon, in press). Let us begin by saying that given the Cuban socialist mentality, the policy focus must be on the prevention of the formation of antisocial personalities. Cuban revolutionaries refuse to accept, in theory, the idea that there can be any genetic predisposition

toward criminality or antisocial behavior. Given the right environment
—at minimum, the absence of economic exploitation—a constructive
personality can be formed. (This should not be taken to mean that they
believe behavior or performance can or will be uniform, just that it can
be developed to conform to accepted social norms.)

The first step in prevention therefore must be the removal of exploitative economic conditions, the guaranteeing of all of the most basic material essentials, and the education of the populace to new standards of conduct. Theoretically then, as the environment continues to improve (that
is, as it more nearly approaches true communism), and as the cultural
educational level of the citizenry rises, the fewer instances there will be of
antisocial and criminal behavior. The socialist concept of crime was described by the Minister of the Interior, Sergio del Valle, as meaning "that
crime is not a permanent fact of life but rather something which is overcome gradually in the process of building communism, as the availability
of material goods increases, the culture and education of the masses is
further developed and a community morality is consolidated" (*Granma
Weekly Review*, 1/21/79, p. 4).

The corollary of this belief is that a certain amount of antisocial and
even criminal behavior still can be expected from some of the many people who grew up in the very imperfect environments of the old system.
This has had profound implications for revolutionary concepts of criminal justice in Cuba because it has come to mean in practice that no illegal
or antisocial act committed by an individual can be considered outside of
the socioeconomic background of the defendant or apart from the conditions in the society at large. I will return to this point later.

The government has attempted to hasten the improvement of home
and social environments of children by involving itself in all aspects of
the socialization process. Work centers, day care, the educational system,
the media, the arts, and to a certain extent recreation, are under the state
administration. The state cannot directly intervene in the home but it
does try to contain or control what it considers excesses; representatives
of the local committees can and do speak directly with families or file
complaints with police when they feel child abuse has occurred or where
abusive language or any disorderly or disruptive behavior is persistent.
While it would be extremely rare for state authorities to try to remove
children from their parents' custody, children whose parents have allowed them to drop out of the educational system or to play truant have
been recruited (not coerced) into various boarding school-scholarship
programs and into paramilitary agricultural units. Here, in addition to
their work, they received a rudimentary education, and sometimes training in special work skills.

While parents who live the "old life" can be detrimental to the achievement of economic goals and an embarrassment before world opinion, probably what is most important to the Revolution is the impact of their behavior in shaping the lives of their children. To the Revolution the mind of every infant is a *tabula rasa*; or as Ernesto Guevara said, "malleable clay . . . free of original sin" (Lavan, 1967, pp. 134–135). This comment may have its origins in Marx's description of the "natural fertility" of children's fallow minds that is "destroyed" by contact with modern industry in Western capitalist countries (Marx, 1906, p. 436). Cuban leaders often dispute their obligation to protect children from "old behavior patterns that persist for a long time," and from "family life styles which are in contradiction to the ideals of revolutionary society" (*Granma Weekly Review*, 6/16/74, p. 4). While the government will not forcibly separate children from their parents, it does try to prevent their exposure to other people who are considered negative behavior models. This would be a principal justification, for example, for arresting and attempting to "rehabilitate" homosexuals, an act explained as designed to prevent the "corruption" or "deformation" (the two words most commonly used by officials) of young people. The Declaration of the First National Congress on Education and Culture discusses "the social pathological character of homosexual deviation" and states that it is "to be rejected and prevented from spreading." The Declaration calls for "creative measures . . . including the control and relocation of isolated cases, always with an educative and preventive purpose." It says that homosexuals should be transferred from any position where they might influence children through artistic or cultural activities, and in general that any one whose morals do not "correspond to the prestige of the Revolution" should be barred from any group of performers sent abroad (p. 5).

In its attempts to shape the lives and personalities of Cuban children the state must, of course, rely on the cooperation of parents. It is unlikely that Cubans would ever come to believe that the quality of institutional care could approach that which children receive from their parents. Motherhood has always been nearly sacrosanct in Cuba. Following Spanish tradition, motherhood and childhood have special "protection" under the 1976 Constitution (as they did under the 1940 Constitution). Abandoned or orphaned children were far more likely to be raised by neighbors, friends, relatives, or *compadres* than to be placed in orphanages. These were always considered a last resort and there were never many of them in Cuba. In 1970 there was still fairly widespread prejudice against the system of daycare centers and boarding schools (see for example, Lewis, Lewis, and Rigdon, 1978, pp. 395–396, 437, 496), but one would expect this to be on the decline. A very extreme case of anti-institutional views was expressed by the co-founders of a free-play day care program. These women, who had no professional expertise in this area, were consulting with some of Cuba's leading psychologists and psychiatrists in the construction of their program. They claimed that children left for long periods in child-care centers (by mothers working in harvest campaigns, for example) were "emotionally sick" and "intellectually retarded" by the age of three or four. They said psychiatrists told them that "the symptoms were practically irreversible," and that it was "almost impossible that any of the children could develop a normal personality." (From Ruth Lewis's unpublished study of Cuba's day care system, Lewis and Lewis, 1979).

But today in some ways the home is regarded as one more agent of the state and socialist society, and Cubans are reminded that parental responsibilities are among the most important—if not *the* most important—civic obligations. In the following excerpt from the widely publicized and discussed 1975 Family Code parents are delegated by the state with responsibility for:

1) Keeping the children under their guardianship and care; making every possible effort to provide them with a stable home and adequate nourishment; caring for their health and personal hygiene; providing them with the means of recreation fitting their age which are within their possibilities; giving them the proper protection; seeing to their good behavior and cooperating with the authorities in order to overcome any situation or environmental factor that may have an unfavorable effect on their training and development;

2) Seeing to the education of their children; inculcating them with the love for learning; seeing to it that they attend school; seeing to their adequate technical, scientific and cultural improvement in keeping with their aptitude and vocation and the demands posed by the country's development; and collaborating with the educational authorities in school problems and activities;

3) Training their children to be useful citizens; inculcating them with the love for their country, respect for the country's symbols and their country's values, the spirit of internationalism, the standards of coexistence and socialist morality; respect for social property and the property and personal rights of others; arousing the respect of their children by their attitude toward them; and teaching them to respect the authorities, their teachers and every other person (Article 85).

Prevention of antisocial behavior through improvement of socioeconomic conditions and control of socialization processes are long-term efforts. For the present the fundamental element in prevention is the

296   SUSAN M. RIGDON

basic Leninist principle of organizing everyone and everything (Lenin, 1929, pp. 94–142). To be employed and to be integrated in mass organizations are seen as the best ways to foster healthy social and political attitudes and to prevent crime. "Idleness brings about the worst attitudes, attitudes that are harmful to society and individually deforming," says José Abrantes, First Deputy Minister of the Ministry of Interior (*Granma Weekly Review*, 6/16/74, p. 4).

It is very difficult for any able-bodied man over 16 who is not a soldier or full-time student to get along in Cuba without a worker's identification card; that in itself is a great inducement to full employment of the male labor force. The minority who refuse to work because they are political or religious dissidents, or simply because they were not accustomed to full-time employment and do not like the routine, can be tried under the Anti-Loafing Law of 1971, and may be interned in prison farms if they continue to refuse employment. The government has also used the draft to forcibly incorporate into the system religious dissidents and young men (16 years and over) who have dropped out of the educational system. One Jehovah's Witness who was drafted and imprisoned when he refused induction was interviewed by Oscar Lewis in 1970 (Lewis and Lewis, 1979). There are a few discrepancies between his account and that given by an aunt in Lewis, Lewis, and Rigdon (1977b, p. 417); see also Lewis, Lewis, and Rigdon (1978, p. 549).

Another weapon in the fight against idleness is the effort to bring each Cuban into contact with state organizations at the earliest possible age and to maintain this contact throughout his or her life. Most Cubans join their first formal organization at the age of 7 years by enrolling in the Pioneers chapter at their local elementary school. On leaving the Pioneers, school-age children can enter intermediate and then advanced level student organizations; a select minority are admitted to the Communist Youth at age seventeen, and some later to the Party itself. For all Cubans 14 years and older there is membership in the neighborhood-based Committees for Defense of the Revolution, for state employees, union membership; and for women, the Federation of Cuban Women. (The latter three are in essence mandatory for Cubans employed by the state.) These organizations sponsor countless activities, especially in the areas of neighborhood improvement and vigilance, public health, education and voluntary agricultural labor. In addition, there are the militia and specialized groups such as the Association of Private Farmers.

Once people are employed and integrated in revolutionary organizations, in the nominal sense of having one or two memberships, they can get along and, if they choose, remain more or less aloof from other state organizations and activities. However they cannot do much more than just get along. To move ahead in a career, or in the sense of material acquisitions and better housing, to get scholarships for children to specialized schools and certain institutions of higher education, to travel or study abroad, or to solve any specific problem, one must be at minimum a *fully* integrated, productive worker. The more integrated, the more productive, the greater the access an individual has to nonessential consumer goods, luxury items, and a variety of special opportunities.

To keep track of who are and who are not integrated, productive workers and to report suspected antisocial and criminal behavior, the Department of State Security maintains on each city block (or each Committee in rural areas) agents or contacts recruited through the Committees in Defense of the Revolution. In addition, Committee officers, in particular the Vigilance officer, are obligated to assist the police and the neighborhood courts in law enforcement and adjudication functions by reporting offenses, helping in investigative work, and in submitting depositions to the courts. The Security Department contact, who is supposedly unknown to block residents, is expected to keep a record of any unusual or suspicious behavior in the neighborhood, the presence of any unfamiliar people or vehicles, and so forth.

In 1970 this system did not appear to be as ominous or as effective as it may sound on paper; it depended for its success upon the zeal of the individual contact, how thorough he or she was (it was often a woman because they tended to be home more often than men), and also on the pattern of friendships in a neighborhood. Field workers in two slum relocation communities, for example, found remnants of a "we-they" attitude toward local authorities, if not to the Revolution itself. Many residents expected their neighbors to cover up illicit activities, or at least not to speak against them. In fact cases were reported of officers of the Committee withholding information and/or lying to police about the illegal activities of neighbors, and of individuals ostracized by their neighbors for cooperating with authorities (Lewis, Lewis and Rigdon, 1977a, pp. 261–267, 397–401; Rigdon, in press). The field work uncovered fewer instances of authorities withholding information, but one such case involved a middle-class woman serving as a judge for the People's Court in a middle-class neighborhood. She was assigned to do the investigative work for a trial involving two men of whom she had previous knowledge. One, the relative of a member of the Political Bureau, she knew to be a homosexual, and the second to have been a "hippie" who had been in a "rehabilitation" camp. She deliberately did not introduce this information at the trial and, although perhaps not for this reason, both were acquitted of disorderly conduct charges brought against them by police.

Perhaps the most influential instruments the Revolution has had since the late 1960s for monitoring antisocial behavior, and the one that best embodies the Revolution's holistic approach to the problem, are the People's Courts on which more details, including trial transcripts and interviews with judges and litigants, can be found in Rigdon (in press). These neighborhood-based courts try misdemeanors and minor civil and criminal cases and are presided over by lay judges who, prior to the 1976 Constitution, were elected in public assemblies in the neighborhoods they served. It was in these courts, where men and women with only the sparsest training in legal concepts and practices sat in judgment of their peers, that the state hoped a literal, mechanistic application of the law would be subordinated to the judgment of a defendant in the context of his or her socioeconomic background and of all the circumstances surrounding the acts of which he or she was accused.

It was this concept of justice Fidel Castro (1967) expressed in his 1953 trial for the attack on the Moncada Garrison:

When you judge a defendant for robbery, Your Honors, do you ask him how many children he has, which days of the week he ate and which he didn't, do you concern yourselves with his environment at all? You send him to jail without further thought. (p. 75)

In addition to fulfilling this fundamental purpose, the courts were expected to: (1) educate the people to the letter of the law as well as to the broader moral precepts of socialism; (2) be structured in such a way as to provide maximum popular participation, thereby serving as an instrument for incorporation of the masses in the revolutionary process; (3) make judicial remedies to misdemeanors and minor crimes accessible to every part of the island and to do so in the shortest possible time after the reporting of an offense to the police; and (4) to replace the idea of punishment through monetary fines and incarceration with the idea of rehabilitation through education and/or work for the community and state.

The courts are empowered to assign a variety of sanctions, ranging from a minimum of a formal warning to the maximum of six months loss of liberty on a prison farm. Examples of moderate sentences might include partial loss of liberty, such as being forbidden to frequent specified public places, being required to do agricultural labor on weekends, to attend political study circles one night a week, or to enroll in night school to achieve a specified grade level (usually reserved for persons with less than a sixth grade education). Many of the sentences involving some loss of liberty were conditional, that is, probational. Monetary fines were an option little used in the early days of the courts although today they are in use in at least some of Cuba's courts (*Granma Weekly Review*, 7/9/78, p. 3).

Issuance of a formal warning by the panel of judges was part of every trial because it was seen as essential to the courts' function of educating the public in socialist law. The warning was often issued to both accused and accuser, just as, at times, sentences were assigned to both. This would be most likely to occur in cases involving public scandal, disorderly conduct, or verbal abuse, in which, regardless of who instigated the incident, both parties participated. In these cases the court's opinion is usually that both parties have failed by being involved in a public display of antisocial behavior and setting a bad example.

From a reading of the field materials it is difficult to judge how much success the People's Courts had had in prevention or in rehabilitation during their early, experimental years. While the judges appeared to be conscientious in their work, and gave extraordinary amounts of time to it, and while the courts generally were held in high esteem by Cubans, there still was a failure on the part of some litigants to take the courts seriously. Among the litigants interviewed by field workers, many expressed defiance of sanctions and openly declared they had no intentions of fulfilling them. They were aware that there was a shortage of personnel to follow up all sentences to make certain they were enforced. They also knew that the courts often lacked the facilities and resources to enforce conditional sentences. For example, a woman with small children was unlikely to be forced to serve a sentence on a prison farm if the court could not find someone to care for the children. Some judges were simply reluctant to sentence a pregnant woman or to separate a mother from her children. Therefore it was possible for a woman with young children to be convicted of several offenses without being given, or without being forced to serve, a loss of liberty sentence.

Some litigants understood the special place they had in revolutionary rationale, and knew beforehand the courts were going to attribute much of their behavior to past economic conditions and low educational level. Some took full advantage of this and turned to the courts to help them solve marital and other family problems without fear that strong sanctions might be imposed on them.

Although the nine judges and the other officials interviewed by field workers were very enthusiastic about their work, they also were acutely aware of the problems involved and very frustrated by them. The majority of the judges expressed strong prejudice against a number of the litigants, especially those from the poorest economic backgrounds. These judges were serving an area that had pockets of residents from extremely deprived backgrounds, and they claimed that a disproportionate number of their cases came from these areas. Words and phrases such as "clown," "tramp," person of "low life," or "with no morals," were not at all uncommon in judges' descriptions of litigants (Rigdon, in press). Butter-

300   SUSAN M. RIGDON

worth (1980) also discusses some of the judges' reactions to their cases
(chap. 9). But they took their judicial obligations very seriously and in
general the sanctions they imposed were characterized not by their rigor
but by their leniency. If judges had given vent in their sentencing to the
deep prejudices they expressed during the trials and in the deliberations
prior to sentencing, as well as to field workers in interviews, one might
have expected many litigants to have drawn the maximum sentence. But
in fact this was usually reserved for hopeless recidivists (see Booth, 1973)
or for those convicted of violent crimes. (The courts heard cases of assault with weapons if the wounds inflicted were minor.)

Under the philosophy governing the People's Courts, the end of a trial
ought not to be merely the determination of the accused person's guilt or
innocence in the commission of a specific act. Rather it should be an evaluation of how defendants are measuring up, overall, to the standards set
by the system, and of the extent to which they can rightfully be expected
to measure up given their personal histories. It is a consequence of this
philosophy that, by shifting responsibility for criminal and antisocial behavior to societal causes, individual culpability before the law can be reduced. (It also helps to explain the multiple standards of justice in Cuba,
dependent on one's background and level of politicization; this is discussed in greater detail in my Afterword to Lewis, Lewis, and Rigdon,
1978, pp. 545–554). When finding people guilty, the object of the courts
was not to punish them for failing to obey laws, but rather to assign a
sanction designed to exact from them the kind of behavior state and society defined as constructive. In this way trials were used to instruct the
accused and the public to society's expectations of them.

Prevention of crime through the education of the public to the meaning of antisocial behavior was a primary function of the courts. Therefore whenever a person was found guilty and sentenced, one judge told
interviewers, the court accomplished nothing because the offense had already been committed. Apart from their pretrial and trial duties, judges
were expected to participate in a variety of prevention-oriented work.
This might include service on the Courts' Social Prevention Committees. Each court had one such committee to which it assigned three of its
judges. The committee's other members came from the party, local mass
organizations, and the Ministries of Education and Interior. One of these
committees' many functions was to hold what were called preventive trials. These were private hearings for people whose behavior was considered antisocial and likely to lead to illegal activities. They were a combination of counsel and admonition and often resulted in a rehabilitative
program designed to help the individual alter his or her behavior in a
more "socially conscious" direction.

According to one judge involved in this work, an enormous number of preventive trials during the late 1960s involved minors accused of repeated truancy, dishonesty, poor deportment in school and other public places, and so forth. Parental attendance at the hearings, with legal counsel if desired, was required. Parents were questioned about their life styles, their attitudes toward work, education, family, and the Revolution. If a social worker had been seeing the family, he or she was also questioned at the hearing. A common trial outcome, in the case of truancy, for example, would be the issuance of a warning to the parents and child and a requirement that the child regularly report to a representative of the block committee and present certification from his or her teacher that he or she was attending classes.

"The norm we follow," said one judge, "is that the younger the child, the greater our effort to fix the penal responsibility on the parents rather than the minor because we realize they are responsible for the child's conduct" (Rigdon, in press). However, during the first decade of the Revolution, juveniles were involved in a large number of thefts, perhaps in part because of the very limited liability of minors under the law. It was thought that this encouraged adults to recruit juveniles to their criminal activities and was one of the reasons the age of majority was lowered from 18 to 16 years (which is also the age of eligibility for suffrage and the draft). The government has become progressively less lenient with youth involved in antisocial or illegal activities; in 1966 it established in Havana the first Center for the Assessment, Analysis and Orientation of Minors, and since then has built three more in other parts of Cuba (*Granma Weekly Review*, 1/21/79, p. 4). Juveniles habitually involved in serious crimes were referred by the courts and other authorities to these centers, where their problems were evaluated by staffs of psychologists, educators, and legal experts, among others. Boys aged 14 to 16 years might also be assigned to work-study camps such as Construction City.

The problem of crime among young people becomes increasingly more difficult for the government to rationalize as a whole generation of Cubans has now been born and raised under the revolutionary system. Crime among juveniles is also a particular disappointment to the leadership in whose rhetoric children have always had a very special place, and from whose policies they received preferential treatment. There is a tendency to officially explain a certain amount of the deviations from behavior norms, up to and including serious criminal behavior, as "psychopathic," and to require psychiatric counseling as part of rehabilitation programs. However, the phrase "psychopathic behavior" seems much more likely to be used to describe or to explain criminal acts after they have been committed rather than as a justification for detaining someone who has not yet committed a crime. For a discussion of juvenile delinquency as "part of social pathology" in Cuba see the Declaration of the First National Congress on Education and Culture. The Declaration, in recommending treatment of juveniles guilty of antisocial conduct, distinguishes between those who are "mentally retarded" and those who are "maladjusted" (p. 5). One of the most famous cases of juveniles required to undergo psychiatric counseling was that of the arrest (for property damage among other charges) in 1968 of the so-called hippies who hung out in downtown Vedado (Lewis, Lewis, and Rigdon, 1977b, p. 313). The behavior of some of these young people was described as "psychopathic," and they were required to accept from one to two years of psychiatric counseling in rehabilitation centers.

Whatever the explanation given for specific instances of antisocial or illegal behavior (exclusive of political crimes), the treatment of them will almost certainly be multidirectional. The Revolution strongly believes in a broad, interdisciplinary, integrative approach to the creation of programs of rehabilitation, but two elements in almost any program would be work and study. In assigning a person to such a program authorities are not supposed to focus on setting a punishment suitable to a specific offense, but rather on finding the ways in which they can educate the individual to society's expectations of him or her. In a summary statement of this approach, Minister of Interior Sergio del Valle said, "The battle against crime was conceived as a battle against individual, concrete criminal acts. However, we cannot limit ourselves to this notion of crime since it does not correspond to our conception of the problem" (*Granma Weekly Review*, 1/21/79, p. 4).

It would be very misleading to suggest that the Cuban government expected profound personal transformations in Cubans who had grown up under the old system, especially in people who had lived lives of great material and cultural deprivation. It did however demand a certain number of adjustments from all Cubans in their external behavior, especially in their work habits, and to a lesser extent in their general social conduct. As long as individuals were not ideologically opposed to the Revolution, and most who remained in Cuba were not, they were expected to stay somewhere close to the boundaries of minimally accepted behavior.

Within these boundaries dissent or deviations from the norm are possible. There is a common rule of thumb governing this: "Within the Revolution, everything; outside the Revolution, nothing." Cubans may publicly disagree with any number of individual policies if it is done within the context of support for the Revolution. Cubans fully integrated in the labor force and mass organizations may engage in a certain amount of activity that officially would be labeled antisocial: refusal to participate in any activities sponsored by mass organizations, involvement in minor black market activity, petty gambling, excessive drinking, observance of certain rites of *santería* or of other Afro-Cuban sects, and so forth. The Revolution routinely allows a certain amount of this activity as a kind of safety valve on a population that is under tremendous economic pressures. The government attributes the persistence of some of this behavior in a socialist society, in part, to the current shortages in essential goods and services.

In general it is easier for Cubans of lower-class backgrounds to openly dissent or to engage in antisocial behavior because the Revolution is less threatened by them and because, ideologically, it has a special relationship with them. Much of the refusal to conform is rationalized as a product of their backgrounds, that is, of mentalities that will take a long time to undo. This reasoning is not as freely applied to Cubans from middle-class backgrounds; in part because being better educated, having special skills for operating in the secular, bureaucratic world, and having access to personnel and to resources unknown to the lower classes, they are, from the standpoint of internal security, the more dangerous dissenters.

The Cuban government does not have the resources (as no government has), nor does it have the will, I think, to coerce all Cubans into strict conformity with a rigid code of behavior. In theory, obedience to the state or participation in civic or political activities that is obtained by coercion has no intrinsic value. More important, it goes against Cuban culture; and the leaders of the Revolution, even if they too were not part of that culture, could not deny or be indifferent to its legacy. But, as true revolutionaries they believe that, like Rousseau's philosopher-king, through moral example and the inherent rightness of their position and by embodying some perfect mix of benevolence and discipline, they will be able to define and propagate the general will to the satisfaction of every party to their social contract. What the government counts on and what it deliberately works toward is a confluence of the particular and general wills, until they achieve that perfect harmony that Rousseau thought would exist in the ideal social contract. That this could happen in any real society is at best a dream; for some it is a dream of utopian perfection, for others a nightmare of Orwellian proportions. But philosophically for communists if utopia is to come, it must come in the temporal world. They believe, if not in the perfectability of people and societies, at least in the systematic pursuit of that end.

References

Booth, D. K. *Neighbourhood committees and popular courts in the social transformation of Cuba.* Unpublished Ph.D. thesis, University of Surrey, 1973.

Butterworth, D. *The people of Buena Ventura: Relocation of slum dwellers in postrevo-lutionary Cuba*. Urbana: University of Illinois Press, 1980.

Castro, F. *History will absolve me*. Havana: Book Institute, 1967.

Constitution of the Republic of Cuba. Havana, 1976. (Full text reprinted in a supplement to *Granma Weekly Review*, March 7, 1976.)

Declaration of the 1st National Congress on Education and Culture. Havana, 1971. (Full text reprinted in *Granma Weekly Review*, May 9, 1971, 3–5).

Family Code. Havana, 1975. (Full text reprinted in *Granma Weekly Review*, March 16, 1975, 7–9).

Lavan, G. (Ed.). *Che Guevara speaks: Selected speeches and writings*. New York: Merit, 1967.

Lenin, V. I. *What is to be done?* New York: International Publishers, 1929.

Lewis, O., and Lewis, R. M. *Field notes from Havana, Cuba, 1969–70*. To be added to the restricted collection of Lewis papers in the University of Illinois Library Archives, 1979.

Lewis, O., Lewis, R. M., and Rigdon, S. M. *Four men: Living the revolution*. Urbana: University of Illinois Press, 1977. (a)

Lewis, O., Lewis, R. M., and Rigdon, S. M. *Four women: Living the revolution*. Urbana: University of Illinois Press, 1977. (b)

Lewis, O., Lewis, R. M., and Rigdon, S. M. *Neighbors: Living the revolution*. Urbana: University of Illinois Press, 1978.

Marx, K. *Capital*. New York: Modern Library, 1906.

Moreno, F. J. Justice and law in Latin America: A Cuban example. *Journal of Inter-American Studies and World Affairs*, July, 1970, 367–378.

Rigdon, S. M. *The people's courts and the role of law in revolutionary Cuba, 1963–73*. In press.

Revolutionary Optimism

Models for Commitment to Community from Other Societies

Ruth Sidel and Victor W. Sidel

Visitors to China during the past decade have returned to the West describing a country with a "high pitch of collective spirit" (Terrill, 1971, p. 227), a "sense of purpose, self-confidence, and dignity" (Tuchman, 1972, p. 3), and "a deep sense of mission" (Sidel and Sidel, 1972). Even the liberation of women is seen as a force "able to work and contribute in the building of the new China" (Committee of Concerned Asian Scholars, 1972, p. 292).

In the neighborhood health stations and in schools; in a small neighborhood factory where local workers proudly tell of the recent accomplishments of formerly unskilled workers; on a commune, once barren and brown, and now green and flourishing through the enormously hard work of the peasants; one senses that same feeling of commitment, of working for a cause greater than the self. Oddly, this atmosphere was best described to us in a single phrase, in connection with the only aspect of Chinese life in which it was not readily apparent, the treatment of patients with mental illness. The psychiatric hospitals were the only segments of Chinese life that we saw in which depression rather than exhilaration was the predominant affect (Kagan, 1972; Sidel, 1972). Nevertheless, it was in a description of the techniques of treating mental illness that we first heard the phrase *ko-ming le-kuan-chu-i* ("revolutionary optimism"), a concept that seems to characterize much of Chinese society.

It is virtually impossible to comprehend the meaning of revolutionary optimism in China today without first exploring the role of the individual in Chinese society. This role is a complex one and can be understood only within the Chinese context, not within a Western one. Individualism never occupied the central position in China that it has in the West

The observations described in this paper were made during month-long visits to China in 1971, 1972, and 1977 at the invitation of the Chinese Medical Association. Portions of this material have been previously presented in other contexts (Sidel, 1973a, 1973b; Sidel and Sidel, 1974, 1976).

for the past several hundred years. In prerevolutionary China, the individual was seen as part of a group, part of a family, a clan, a village. Responsibilities to one's living relatives and to one's ancestors were clearly delineated and keenly felt.

Interviewed after a lecture in New York in 1974, the Chinese anthropologist, Francis L. K. Hsu, made some relevant observations that were quoted in *The New Yorker*: "From the Chinese point of view," said Dr. Hsu, "freedom is not the first concern. The importance of personal freedom is a Western premise—it has been from the time of the Greeks. On that premise, people always work for individual aggrandizement, individual sensuality, individual satisfaction. The Chinese have never felt that way. In the old days, the Chinese were supposed to submit themselves to the family and to the kinship group; nowadays they are supposed to submit themselves to a larger group—a political group. In either case, they consider individualism to be selfishness" (p. 34).

But the comparison with the past has also been stated another way: "In the past the Chinese swept only in front of his door post; now he sweeps the whole street." Thus, while in post-Liberation China the individual is no more the center-pin around which all else turns than in the past, his devotion to the collective seems to have broadened and deepened. Not only is there the old devotion to the family or kinship group but now the devotion extends to the group with which the individual works, to those in the neighborhood or commune, and to the people of the country as a whole.

This change has many roots and many facets. Among the roots, certainly, is a socialist revolution, which changed the control of power and of resources in the society. But what has emerged is a special kind of socialism, forged by Mao Zedong and his followers, which makes commitment to the collective good into the highest virtue toward which people can strive.

Wei ren-min fu-wu ("to serve the people"), to work for the good of the society, seems to be the prevailing ethic, expressed in countless signs and posters and in the conversation of all with whom we spoke in China. In order to understand more fully the role of the individual within the context of this ethical framework, it is helpful to distinguish between individuality and individualism as they seem to be viewed in China. Individual talents are carefully nourished and developed. The excellent Ping-Pong player is given extra help and plays on a local or national team; the scientist receives further training and is provided with facilities for research; the dancer and musician have the opportunity to employ their skills; and the person who exhibits special qualities of "caring" is recruited for medical school or into other helping roles. But these individuals are encouraged to utilize their talents not for their own sake, not for the sake of individual development and fulfillment, but for the good of the larger society. Thus individuality is encouraged, particularly when it meets the needs of the larger society; individualism is not.

Health care, for example, has attempted to utilize and promote a commitment both to self-reliance and to the welfare of the group. The focus on mass participation, mass education, mobilizing the masses to engage in sanitation work or in wiping out schistosomiasis, and intense efforts in immunization and birth control programs can all be seen as part of a broader societal view. Within the context of this larger view, issues of privacy, considered an integral part of medical care in the West, take on quite a different character. The number of children a family has, for example, is no longer a private decision; "planned birth" is viewed as a collective problem, one that affects the whole society as well as each family. Whether one's child is immunized against polio becomes the formal concern of the local community, whose stake in the immunization program is emphasized over its importance to the individual. While the Chinese often seem reluctant to deal with traditionally private matters, particularly sexual matters, in a public manner, they nevertheless have developed mechanisms such as small group discussions and the intensive use of paraprofessionals that appear to deal with these issues effectively. They seem able to bridge the gap between the preservation of the family—which has been strengthened and protected in post-Liberation China—and devotion to a broader set of social responsibilities.

This development of course, has historical roots in the Chinese revolution. In his essay *On Practice*, written in 1937, Mao Zedong wrote:

If you want to know the taste of a pear, you must change the pear by eating it yourself. If you want to know the structure and properties of the atom, you must make physical and chemical experiments to change the state of the atom. If you want to know the theory and methods of revolution, you must take part in revolution. All genuine knowledge originates in direct experience. (Mao, 1966, p. 8)

This theme of learning by doing runs through almost all aspects of Chinese life today. A peasant learns the difficulties in determining agricultural priorities by taking part in decision making. The urban doctor learns about the life of the peasants by moving to the countryside for a period of time and laboring with them. The child learns what it is like to be a peasant or worker by growing vegetables or doing a job on consignment from a factory. And, according to this theory, the way to teach over 900 million people the principles of health prevention and health care is to involve them in it.

The mobilization of the masses has been the primary technique by which the Chinese have accomplished their feats of engineering: the construction of dikes, canals, bridges, and large-scale irrigation projects and the damming of rivers. The mobilization of the masses has been the primary mechanism in their feats of human engineering also. Han Suyin has described the process of the education of the masses since 1940 as:

> getting the masses away from the anchored belief that natural calamities are "fixed by heaven" and that therefore nothing can be done to remedy one's lot. . . . To bridge this gap between scientific modern man and feudal man, the prey of superstition, and to do it within the compass of one generation, is a formidable task. (Han, 1966, p. 81)

One of the prime techniques used to accomplish this "formidable task" has been the activating of the "mass." In health care this has meant the broadest involvement of people at every level of society in such campaigns as the Patriotic Health Movement; the training of selected groups of people such as barefoot doctors who are recruited from the population they are to serve; and the exhortation that the individual "fight against his own disease." Individual concern with health reflects the Chinese belief in self-reliance—a virtue as honored today as its converse, mutual help.

This was brought home to us most strikingly while we were observing a kindergarten class for 6-year-olds. They were being taught the life story of Norman Bethune, a Canadian thoracic surgeon, who provided medical services for Mao Zedong's Eighth Route Army in the war against Japan until his death in 1939 from septicemia, secondary to an infection he acquired while performing surgery. Dr. Bethune is a national hero in China, celebrated for his "selflessness," his internationalism, and his self-reliance—all principles that are taught to Chinese children. After the audio-visual presentation, the children were asked what they would do if they came upon a sick person on the street. "I would get water for him," and "I would get medicine for him," were typical replies, all suggesting things the child could do for the sick man rather than going to get help from a doctor or other adult.

In 1952 Mao issued his "Four Main Health Principles," widely quoted in China, one of which is: "Health work should be combined with the mass movement." The Patriotic Health Movement was launched at this time and Joshua Horn (1969, p. 126) states that the Chinese linked the movement to the need to protect the population against the alleged use of germ warfare in Korea by the United States; the Chinese with whom we spoke, however, never mentioned germ warfare. The primary goal of this mass movement in the early fifties, we were told was the elimination of four pests—mosquitoes, flies, rats, and bedbugs—and the people were mobilized to exterminate them under the guidance of health personnel. The Patriotic Health Movement has been maintained and has been expanded to include the sanitary aspects of food, water, and the environment.

Leo Orleans and Richard Suttemeier (1970) emphasize the importance of mobilizing the masses in dealing with the problem of pollution. They describe people organized in the cities to "remove refuse that had accumulated in residential districts" and, more specifically, "the spring patriotic sanitation movement" of 1970, which was organized by local revolutionary committees to mobilize the people to pick up litter and garbage from residences, farms, and factories, to clean up local waters, to eliminate pests, to collect reusable wastes, and to advocate public health measures. They also describe the efforts of the Shanghai Municipal Revolutionary Committee in July 1968 to clean up the Huangpu and Suchow Rivers. The authors quote the New China News Agency as stating that

90,000 persons were mobilized on the industrial and agricultural fronts in Shanghai to form muck-dredging and muck-transporting teams, waging a vehement people's war to dredge muck from the Suchow River. After 100 days of turbulent fighting, more than 403,600 tons of malodorous organic mire had been dug out. (Orleans and Suttemeier, 1970, p. 1176)

The classic example of the use of mass mobilization in health has, of course, been the campaign against schistosomiasis. According to Horn (1969, p. 96), this campaign was based on the concept of the "mass line"—"the conviction that the ordinary people possess great strength and wisdom and that when their initiative is given full play they can accomplish miracles." Before the peasants were mobilized to fight against the snails, Horn states, they were thoroughly educated as to the nature of schistosomiasis by means of lectures, films, posters, and radio talks. They were then mobilized twice a year, in March and in August, and, along with voluntary labor from the People's Liberation Army, students, teachers, and office workers, they drained the rivers and ditches, buried the banks of the rivers, and smoothed down the buried dirt. Horn points out that in the fight against schistosomiasis, the concept was not only to recruit the masses to do the work but to mobilize their enthusiasm and initiative so that they would fight against the disease (Horn, 1969, p. 97).

This method of fighting the enemy is an adaptation by Mao of the methods used so successfully in Yenan during the war to fire the enthusiasm of the population against the Japanese. Mao transferred this ideology into a campaign against such "enemies" as illiteracy, disease, famine, and flood. In this case the enemy is schistosomiasis and the technique used to analyze it is the well-known "paper tiger" theory first used by Mao in 1946 to describe the United States-Kuomintang alliance. It states that there is a dual nature to everything—while one's enemies are real and formidable and must be taken seriously, they are at the same time paper tigers that can be defeated by the will of the people. One has to view one's enemies from this dual point of view, Mao teaches, in order to plan correctly one's strategy and one's tactics.

The individual's commitment to the larger community can be observed perhaps most clearly in China's urban neighborhoods. Cities as a whole are governed by committees that are formal government bodies; the next lower level of urban organization is the "district," which is also governed by a formal committee. Hangchow, a city of 700,000 people, is divided into four districts; the city proper of Peking, with four million people, into nine districts; and the city proper of Shanghai, with six million, into ten districts. Districts are subdivided into "streets" or "neighborhoods," which are the lowest level of formal governmental organization in the city. The neighborhood is governed by a committee composed of cadres and representatives of the people in the area. The committee's responsibilities include the administration of local factories, primary schools, the kindergartens, a neighborhood hospital or health center, repair services, and a housing department, as well as the organization and supervision of "residents" or "lane" committees.

The smallest unit in the urban areas is the "lane," with 1000 to 8000 residents. Some lanes are further divided into "groups," for example, the residents of single large apartment buildings, which are headed by a group or deputy group leader. The lane is governed by a committee chosen by, and from among, the "mass" living in the lane. The committee is, therefore, a "mass organization" rather than a formal governmental body; the elderly play a key role in the organization and administration of these residents' committees.

Each of the nine districts of Peking city proper, to use it as an example, has a population of about 400,000. Among the services provided at the district level are hospitals, sanitation facilities, middle schools (roughly equivalent to our junior and senior high schools), and "prevention stations" for illnesses such as tuberculosis and mental disorders. Within each district there are "neighborhoods" consisting of approximately 50,000 people. The West District of Peking has nine neighborhoods of which the Fengsheng neighborhood, with a population of 53,000, is one. Within the Fengsheng neighborhood's jurisdiction are six factories, eight shops, ten primary schools, four kindergartens, and a neighborhood hospital (Sidel, 1974).

Fengsheng is one of the older neighborhoods of Peking. It consists entirely of one-story dwellings rather than the four- or five-story apartment buildings found in newer neighborhoods. Courtyards, with several families living in each, are entered through doorways in the walls lining Fengsheng's 132 lanes. The people are grouped into 25 residents' committees, each of which encompasses about 2000 people. These committees usually provide a health station and other social services. Within each committee are "groups" of from 50 to 150 people, led by a group leader and a deputy group leader, who organize a number of services under what we might term social or welfare work.

Group and residents' committee leaders, selected by the population to be served, serve as links to higher levels of urban government, mediate disputes among families and between family members, provide social services for those in need, and organize study groups for the elderly and the unemployed. It is through the mechanism of study groups that the attempt is being made to teach the entire population a different way of relating to their world, to "remold their world outlook," as the Chinese say. It is in the study group, surrounded by neighbors and coworkers, that the Chinese are expected to examine honestly their own attitudes and behavior and to attempt to evaluate whether they are still motivated by self-interest and individualism or whether they are attempting to contribute to the common good. These meetings are punctuated by bouts of "criticism and self-criticism" as members struggle to function within their society according to current norms.

These small groups are characterized by a level of intimacy rarely shared in urban America outside of, perhaps, certain therapy groups. One American who has lived in China for several years has observed that study groups are composed of people with whom one works every day or of neighbors whose life is intimately linked to one's own and that everyone is well versed in the others' personalities and traits. This intimacy and interdependence continues outside of study groups and pervades much of Chinese life.

The organization of life in China's neighborhoods and places of work can perhaps best be viewed as a total community support system, one largely fostered and maintained by the residents and workers themselves. This system encourages people to see themselves as part of a total social structure, encourages them to participate actively in that social structure and comes to their aid during times of stress.

As Yi-Chuang Lu (1978) has stated, many of the social values and key innovations observable in Chinese society are also prominent features of contemporary Chinese psychiatric practice: sharing of responsibility between lay people and medical personnel in the identification, prevention, and treatment of mental illness; application of "serving the people" and

subordinating individual interests for the common good; the minimization of elitism in mental hospitals; and the faith in human ability to modify individual behavior and to modify the environment. Much of what
we in the West consider to be mental illness is handled at the "neighborhood" level or at the residents' or lane committee. At these levels, interpersonal disputes and minor diseases, including some psychosomatic
illness, are handled by paraprofessionals ("Red Medical Workers" or
"street doctors") with very short periods of training, elected representatives with no special training for this work, and Communist Party
representatives.

Patients with neurotic disturbances are treated at the district level in
hospital clinics and at psychiatric prevention stations by psychiatrists and
psychiatric nurses using a variety of methods: lectures, help with the "arrangement of the patient's life," Western medicines such as chlordiaze
poxide (Librium) or diazepan (Valium), traditional Chinese herb medicines, acupuncture, physical therapy (electro-stimulation on the skin at
acupuncture points), and individual and/or group psychotherapy. In individual psychotherapy, sometimes described as "heart-to-heart talks,"
the doctor explains the nature of the illness to the patient and tells him
how to "manage the disease." In group psychotherapy, sometimes
known as Mao Zedong Thought Groups, patients study Chairman
Mao's writings, particularly "On Contradiction," "On Practice," and
"Where Do Correct Ideas Come From," in order to learn more functional ways of approaching "objective reality."

In the treatment of psychosis, many of the same techniques are used:
heart-to-heart talks, Mao Zedong Thought Groups, tranquilizers, acupuncture, and work with the patient's family and place of employment.
On the psychiatric wards the patients also help each other to adjust to the
hospital setting and to understand their own problems; a buddy system is
sometimes used, pairing sicker patients with healthier patients.

The primary goal of psychiatric treatment is to enable patients to return to their families and workplaces as quickly as possible. To facilitate
this, psychiatric personnel talk with the patient's family, explaining the
nature of the illness. The doctors or nurses also visit patients' workplaces
to advise their superiors whether the patients should resume their former
work or be given other types of work. During the hospitalization, patients' jobs are kept secure and they receive full salary for six months.

"Mobilizing patients' initiative" and helping them "to analyze the
causes of their disease" are considered key steps in the treatment process.
The patient's active participation is thought to be essential in the treatment of all illness, physical as well as mental (Ho, 1974). *Tsu-li keng-
sheng*, sometimes translated as "self-reliance" but more accurately trans-

lated as "regeneration through one's own efforts," is a central concept; people are felt to have infinite power to remold their environment given sufficient will, so individual patients are thought to be able to remold themselves.

Since the Cultural Revolution, the military model of organization has been taken over by many other segments within the society. This is consonant with the Chinese revolutionary view that without "struggle" there can be no progress. In the Shanghai Mental Hospital, for example, patients on the wards and their doctors were divided into divisions and groups so as to better be able to "fight the enemy," that is, mental illness.

Mental illness is viewed as a paper tiger. It is real and can be damaging; therefore the tactics of fighting the disease include not underestimating it. But mental illness is "not so powerful" and can be overcome; therefore the strategy is to help the patient not to be afraid. In order to facilitate the patient's understanding of his/her disease, the Chinese feel the relationship between doctor and patient must be "correct." Since Liberation in 1949, according to Dr. Wu Chen-i, Professor of Psychiatry of the Peking Medical College, doctors have come to recognize that they and their patients are class brothers, that even though they belong to different working units, they have the same purpose and must "care for each other, must love and help each other" (Mao, 1968, p. 4). If doctors do not have the idea of "serving the people wholeheartedly," they cannot work effectively with the patient. Together the patient and doctor must work to struggle and overcome the disease. It is only within the context of this relationship between doctor and patient that patients can listen to the opinions of their doctors and correctly understand their illnesses. It is only within the context of this relationship that the doctor can "help the patient have the idea of revolutionary optimism which is the basis for all psychotherapy."

It is a part of the concept of revolutionary optimism that the patient is part of the revolution and that the revolution will surely be victorious. Thus, no matter what the difficulties, "the patient will have a bright future." Patients are urged to obtain treatment not only for their own sake but also for the sake of the revolution. They are urged to overcome their illness not only for their own sake but for the revolution. Revolutionary optimism gives patients the encouragement and confidence to conquer their disease. Although the Chinese do not specifically discuss it, nationalism is a key component of revolutionary optimism; working for a better China and being a part of the revolution in China is implicit in the ideology.

Another aspect of revolutionary optimism is the recognition that one's own problems pale in comparison with those of people who have sacrificed themselves for the revolution (Lowinger, 1976). Doctors at the Peking Medical College told of patients suffering from neuroses who are taught that others with even greater hardships are nevertheless struggling to overcome them for the good of the revolution. They are told of members of the People's Liberation Army who have been seriously wounded but still bravely struggle against their wounds, of workers in Shanghai who suffered burns over 90 percent of their body but still try to overcome their illness, of pilots who have lost both legs but work effectively with their prostheses. An old man lost his son during the war of Liberation, and was "very sad." He was told that there were thousands of people who made such sacrifices during the war of Liberation. Even in Chairman Mao's family, he was told, there were many people killed. The patient was in this way encouraged to "handle his feelings correctly"; he "changed his sorrow into strength, his low spirit into high spirit."

Another integral component of revolutionary optimism is the subordination of one's own feelings to the cause of the revolution. As Oksenberg (1970) has written of the Chinese revolutionary view of the New Man: "Losing his old individual identity, he partakes of the greater spirit of the group, and thereby achieves a spiritual transformation."

A 32-year-old male patient in the psychiatric ward of the Third Peking Hospital became suspicious of his wife, was convinced that his wife no longer loved him and that she wanted to divorce him. He only began to recognize the "objective reality" that his wife actually did love him after admission to the hospital. In analyzing his illness, he felt he "was concerned with the individual person, was self-interested." He felt he "hadn't put revolutionary interest in the first place. If I can put the public interest first and my own interest second, I can solve the contradictions which exist in life and my mind will be in the correct way." Mao has termed this submergence of self "Putting public ahead of self."

A woman in her mid-twenties, also a patient at the Third Peking Hospital, was suffering from hallucinations. She heard a voice that said, "What is below your pillow?" "I came to the ridiculous conclusion that there was a biological radio apparatus beneath my pillow." At the same time she heard loud speeches in her mind. In addition to medication and joining a study class in which she investigated her hallucinations through the study of Mao's writings, the patient felt that she must "consider what is happening in the whole world," and that although she was "not completely recovered," she had faith that she "will get better and will continue to struggle" against her illness.

A factory worker was "having difficulties at work, could not sleep well at night, was always getting angry with others, and was not satisfied with anything." He was helped to study Mao's "On Contradictions," and he learned that "contradictions exist everywhere." "Our task" according to the psychiatrist who treated him, "is to solve the contradictions and to contribute to socialist advancement." The patient recovered, was able to work and now helps others who are having similar problems.

Several aspects of Chinese life are made explicit in the concept of revolutionary optimism:

1. The belief in subordinating the feelings of individuals to the needs of the group of which they are a member—the family, the classroom, the commune, the entire society.

2. The belief that individuals are part of something larger than themselves, the revolution, and that this revolution will ultimately be victorious.

3. The belief that participation in an ultimately victorious revolution gives meaning and joy to life, even if the road to revolution is paved with personal sacrifice.

4. The belief in the infinite capacity of people to learn, to modify their thinking, to understand the world around them and to remold themselves through faith in the revolution and for the sake of the revolution.

It is extremely difficult to evaluate the impact of revolutionary optimism on the treatment of mental illness in China. The Chinese psychiatrists with whom we spoke feel that revolutionary optimism is an important part of psychiatric treatment, but they have neither studies nor statistics to support the claim. Given the psychiatric goal of returning patients to functioning within the society as swiftly as possible, the importance of connecting mental patients with the larger society via this central element in the belief system cannot be underestimated. Perhaps Mao has summed it up best: "In times of difficulty we must not lose sight of our achievements, must see the bright future and must pluck up our courage."

While we have concentrated on the experience of China with revolutionary optimism and with commitment to community because it is the example which we have had the greatest opportunity to study, there are of course relevant models in a number of other societies. These include Cuba, with its mass organizations organized at the community level such as the Federation of Cuban Women and the Committees for the Defense of the Revolution (Navarro, 1972; Stein and Susser, 1972; Tejeiro Fernandez, 1975), and Tanzania, with its communal Ujamaa villages and its emphasis on mass education and self-reliance (Nyerere, 1968; Gish, 1975; Chagula and Tarimo, 1975). Examples were also to be found in Chile during the government of Salvador Allende from 1970 to 1973, but these models were immediately dismantled and the leaders executed, imprisoned, or exiled following the military coup in 1973 (Belmar and Sidel, 1975; Navarro, 1976; Belmar et al., 1977).

The Department of Social Medicine at Montefiore Hospital has over the past few years attempted to develop a community health program based in part on these models in the Bronx, New York. Known as the Montefiore Community Health Participation Program, it works with residents in neighborhood apartment buildings to select and train "health coordinators" from among the residents to work with their neighbors on health promotion and health protection. The program, which now has some 50 health coordinators in approximately 30 buildings, has had some limited success. The amount of revolutionary optimism and of commitment to community in the Bronx is limited, however, and the community and we have barely begun to develop it. What sustains us is that there are indeed societies which have.

References

Belmar, R., and Sidel, V. W. An international perspective on strikes and strike threats by physicians: The case of Chile. *International Journal of Health Services,* 1975, 5, 53–64.
Belmar, R., et al. Evaluation of Chile's health system, 1973–1976: A communique from health workers in Chile. *International Journal of Health Services,* 1977, 7, 531–540.
Chagula, W. K., and Tarimo, E. Meeting basic health needs in Tanzania. In K. W. Newell (Ed.), *Health by the people.* Geneva: World Health Organization, 1975, 145–168.
Committee of Concerned Asian Scholars. *China: Inside the People's Republic.* New York: Bantam Books, 1972.
Gish, O. *Planning the health sector: The Tanzanian experience.* London: Croom Helm, Ltd., 1975.
Han, S. Reflections on social change. *Bulletin of the Atomic Scientists,* 1966, 22, 80–83.
Ho, D. Y. F. Prevention and treatment of mental illness in the People's Republic of China. *American Journal of Orthopsychiatry,* 1974, 44, 620–636.
Horn, J. S. *Away with all pests . . . an English surgeon in the People's Republic of China.* New York: Monthly Review Press, 1969.
Hsu, F. L. K. Quoted in "Talk of the Town," *The New Yorker,* 1974, 50(12), 34.
Kagan, L. Report from a visit to the Tientsin psychiatric hospital. *China Notes* (National Council of Churches), 1972, 10, 37–39.
Lowinger, P. Psychiatry in China: A revolutionary optimism. *Medical Dimension,* 1976, 25–31.
Lu, Y. C. The collective approach to psychiatric practice in the People's Republic of China. *Social Problems.* 1978, 26, 2–14.
Mao, Z. On practice. In *Four essays on philosophy.* Peking: Foreign Language Press, 1966.
Mao, Z. Serve the people. In *Five articles.* Peking: Foreign Languages Press, 1968.

Navarro, V. Health service in Cuba: An initial appraisal. *New England Journal of Medicine*, 1972, 287.

Navarro, V. *Medicine under capitalism*. New York: Prodist, 1976.

Nyerere, J. K. *Freedom and socialism*. London: Oxford University Press, 1968.

Oksenberg, M. *China: The convulsive society*. Headline Series, The Foreign Policy Association, 1970, *203*.

Orleans, L. A., and Suttemeier, R. P. The Mao ethic and environmental quality. *Science*, 1970, *170*, 1173–1176.

Sidel, R. Mental diseases and their treatment. In J. Quinn (Ed.), *Medicine and public health in the People's Republic of China*. Bethesda, Maryland: John E. Fogarty International Center for Advanced Study in the Health Sciences, 1972, DHEW Publ. No. (NIH) 72–67, 289–304.

Sidel, R. The role of the community and the patient in health care. In M. E. Wegman, T. Y. Lin, and E. F. Purcell (Eds.), *Public health in the People's Republic of China*. New York: Josiah Macy, Jr. Foundation, 1973, 124–134. (a)

Sidel, R. The role of revolutionary optimism in the treatment of mental illness in the People's Republic of China. *American Journal of Orthopsychiatry*, 1973, 43, 732–736. (b)

Sidel, R. *Families of Fengsheng: Urban life in China*. Baltimore: Penguin Books, 1974.

Sidel, R., and Sidel, V. The human services in China. *Social Policy*, 1972, *2*, 25–34.

Sidel, V. W., and Sidel, R. *Serve the people: Observations on medicine in the People's Republic of China*. Boston: Beacon Press, 1974.

Sidel, V. W., and Sidel, R. Self reliance and the collective good: Medicine in China. In R. M. Veatch and R. Branson (Eds.), *Ethics and health policy*. Cambridge, Mass.: Ballinger Publishing Co., 1976.

Stein, Z., and Susser, M. The Cuban health system: A trial of a comprehensive service in a poor country. *International Journal of Health Services*, 1972, *2*, 551–556.

Tejeiro Fernandez, A. F. The national health system in Cuba. In K. W. Newell (Ed.), *Health by the people*. Geneva: World Health Organization, 1975, 13–29.

Terrill, R. *800,000,000: The real China*. Boston: Little, Brown, 1971.

Tuchman, B. *Notes from China*. New York: Collier Books, 1972.

Overviews

Powerlessness and Psychopathology

Justin M. Joffe and George W. Albee

Why three overviews? It seemed to us that with "so many voices"—the diversity of topics and the range of viewpoints expressed—it might be useful to provide more than one set of reflections to let readers see what stands out in the minds of different listeners after the papers have filtered through these persons' biases, expectations, and experiences. No doubt others will reach still different conclusions from reading this volume, and so, in a sense, there are three overviews in order to validate each reader's personal overview.

What each of us sees in the papers reflects not only our mental sets but, to some extent, the different nature of our involvement in the field of primary prevention, in the conference itself, and in its papers. Brewster Smith and Stephen Goldston are both good friends of the Vermont Conference, having been associated with it in various ways since its inception. At this fifth conference, we invited Brewster Smith to attend and to provide, at the end, an analysis of themes and an overview of the conference. For participants this was an extraordinarily helpful contribution, assisting us all in our effort to make sense of the great load of information to which we had been exposed over the preceding four days. We asked Brewster Smith not to revise his summary too extensively so that we would have on record a fresh and immediate reaction to the gestalt, to the total package of information presented.

Stephen Goldston also attended the conference, but probably his experience of it was different from Brewster Smith's at least insofar as he did not know until afterwards that we would ask him to record his impressions. We are grateful to him for sharing his sensitive and sensible personal response to both the conference itself and the finished papers.

For the two of us, involved in the whole process—the planning, the conference itself, its aftermath—for more than two years, the set of filters must be somewhat different from those of the authors of the other two overviews. In particular, we have probably viewed the papers against a background of sometimes inexplicit expectations that we had in mind when we undertook to put together a conference on prevention through political action and social change. No conference or book ever turns out like one expects it to at the outset, and we have tried to base our summary of what we see as major themes on the product itself, rather than on the ghosts of what we may have expected it to be. Our purpose is not to second-guess either the authors of the papers or the authors of the other overviews, but rather to share our perception of the messages and themes that emerge from the collection as a whole.

There is little in the papers in this volume that makes us feel compelled to alter the view expressed by one of us in the opening chapter that the keystone of the problem is the maldistribution of power. And there is much in these papers that confirms us in this view.

There is a strong tendency in our society to separate and isolate social problems. We have a social problem labeled violence against children in the family, and others labeled battered wives, sexism, racism, abuse of elderly persons, family disruption, poverty and unemployment, the incarceration and decarceration of persons we call mentally ill, the neglect of the mentally retarded, and the isolation of the physically handicapped, to name just a few.

What do all these problems involving different groups have in common? We have suggested, for your consideration, the best answer we can come up with. It is their powerlessness. People without power are commonly exploited by powerful economic groups who explain the resulting psychopathology by pointing to the defectiveness of the victims. The rest of us do not rush to the defense of the victims because we are caught up in the ideology that puts "justice" in the hands of those with power. We join the groups "blaming the victims."

If the foregoing analysis is accurate, it makes little sense to develop separate programs for the prevention of child abuse, spouse abuse, elder abuse, the exploitation of women, minority group members, migrant farmworkers, the handicapped, the mentally ill, and the mentally retarded. If we see all these groups as powerless because of socioeconomic conditions, then a logical approach is to determine whether there might be an equitable redistribution of power. One of the slogans of the 60s was "Power to the people." Another piece of conventional wisdom is that "Money is power." Without meaning to be simplistic, we would like to suggest that we examine the arguments in the papers for a redistribution of power through a redistribution of wealth in our society.

Two further comments on the relationship between power and psychopathology seem to be needed to round out the picture. The first has to do with objective and subjective realities, the second with the complexity of factors that are associated with psychopathology.

When confronted with the issue of powerlessness, many psychologists tend to approach it as a question of individual aberration or misperception of reality. The optimism of such a view is commendable, but the resulting attempt to alter people's perceptions of their ability to affect their own lives is often, we think, not only misguided but counter-productive and ultimately damaging. So much of what the authors in this volume tell us documents the fact that many people in our society, in many situations, are powerless. If they believe that they cannot do much to affect their circumstances, alleviate their misery, or build a better world for their children it is not because they perceive contingencies incorrectly, but because their perceptions are accurate. They see themselves as powerless because they have no power. No doubt this perception itself further exacerbates their feelings of hopelessness and further reduces the likelihood of their making the necessary effort on those few occasions in their lives when they might be able to act effectively. If so, something might be said in favor of "therapy" to make them feel less powerless. But therapists are in short supply and rarely available to those who concern us—and anyway they read a different agenda.

In any case, what do we know about the effects of feeling that one is in control of a world where, in fact, one is not? It seems that either our "therapy" has to create a very powerful delusional system so that the powerless never notice that their actions are not efficacious, or we have to run the risk of those who have *feelings* of control being even more frustrated when they encounter reality. We think that the analyses in this volume suggest that to prevent psychopathology we should not alleviate feelings of powerlessness by altering perceptions but by altering reality. We realize that this is not as straightforward as we may be implying. A key question—to which we have not found an easy answer—is how to make those who feel powerless take action to alter the distribution of power. Perhaps an answer is to be found in the process of helping people understand why they feel powerless and helping them to attribute that feeling to the socioeconomic system rather than to personal inadequacy. This obviously harks back to the condemnation of the defect model of psychopathology and to Ryan's idea of blaming the victim. The problem of powerlessness is exacerbated by the victims, in fact, blaming themselves, as they accept society's assessment of their plight. The rationalization at once excuses the rest of us from working for social change (instead we can do individual therapy with chemicals or couches) and keeps the victims from blaming anyone but themselves. The message we see in all this is that our role is to assure those who feel helpless that their feeling is due to their in fact being powerless—perhaps only then will they attack the system that has made them so.

Binstock suggests that we will not have significant social changes until a national political crisis has been precipitated by "coalitions of the severely deprived." He suggests that we "undertake direct militant action in our local communities." The tactics of Saul Alinsky and of Martin Luther King were effective, he notes, in provoking social change. Indeed, during the early history of social work, effective organizing of rent strikes, sit-ins, and welfare demonstrations by coalitions of have-not groups were effective in bringing about political change.

It is often said that power is not given up voluntarily. Indeed, it often appears that those persons who hold power are protected by laws, by elected officials, by the police, by folkways, and, perhaps most important, by the beliefs and attitudes of the powerless! We are all encouraged to accept the superior wisdom of gurus and leaders, probably transferring our childhood reverence for parental authority onto other parentlike figures. Rebellion against authority does not come easily. But when it does come it often comes with a violence and turbulence shocking in its intensity. Once authority is challenged successfully other potential challengers take courage and continue the pressure.

Our second point about power and psychopathology has to do with the complexity of the relationship. Many of the authors have discussed political action and social change as if they took it for granted that these are the keys to reducing psychopathology and increasing human happiness. There seems to be a danger that this emphasis, appropriate enough for a volume on this topic, might imply that we and the other authors are unaware that this volume represents only one level of analysis of a complex and multi-level system. One can analyze psychopathology at various levels and in terms of various influences. Physiological and cognitive processes within the individual, the individual's interactions with a physical and psychosocial environment—including particularly the family, social institutions like schools and the workplace, political and economic systems, cultural traditions—all of these constitute relevant levels of analysis and, what is more, none is independent of the others. Not only does this imply that one can intervene at various levels to help the individual, but also that any particular intervention, if it is effective, is likely to have a great many effects, not all of which can be anticipated and some of which may be judged undesirable.

Why, then, emphasize the broader variables—neighborhoods, group prejudice, schools and prisons, economic forces, and so on—that are the focus of so much of this book? Such an emphasis seems to us to be not only appropriate but essential to primary prevention. From the field of public health we learn that those diseases that ravaged humankind for so much of its history and that have been conquered were not eliminated by interventions at the level of the individual: the greatest successes have involved approaches that reached groups of people, and often these resulted from nonspecific changes, contingent upon or associated with social, political, and economic change—improved hygiene, less crowded living conditions, safer workplaces, better nutrition. Little of this advance was achieved by intervention in individual chemistry or cognitions. Laws that forced the changes that improved sanitation or provided a living wage were the levers that started the process of eliminating disease. By analogy we argue that intervention at the level of the total socioeconomic system will be the most effective approach to preventing psychopathology, though advances can be made—over less ground and with more danger of impermanence—by intervening at other levels.

Aside from seeing more clearly now that inequities in the distribution of power are at the root of the problem, we also see that the task of producing change is even greater than we imagined. Since those who are deprived of power feel powerless, they are unlikely to act; "the system" is working well, and those with power seem unlikely to want to make changes. We ourselves seem to be somewhere in the middle, neither the most powerful nor entirely powerless, able to see the psychopathogenic characteristics of the system but at the same time with a vested interest in a system that creates the victims to whom we minister. Eventually most of us become overwhelmed by the number of victims produced—they pile up faster than we can treat them—and conclude that some form of prevention is the only way of coping with the situation. Both economically and ethically, prevention has the most acceptable ratio of benefits to costs.

When we reach this point we still have various options as to the level of intervention we attempt. A major parameter of these options is the size of the group we attempt to affect: We can intervene with high-risk groups of various kinds (like pregnant teenagers or physically handicapped children), deal with institutions of many types (schools, mental hospitals, prisons), and with discriminated-against groups (the old, ethnic minorities, women), and so on. It seems that as the groups get larger the likelihood increases that political action and social change will be needed to produce real effects. When we eventually accept that such action is needed we sometimes are unnerved by the magnitude of the task: How can we patch up the casualties, improve the neighborhoods, alter the schools, redistribute power? Konopka gave us an answer, both in her example and in words: We are responsible for "helping individuals in the framework of existing conditions as well as . . . helping change social institutions. When we recognize the multiple causation of problems . . . it becomes clear that a profession which works toward social justice in a wide sense has to be responsible for amelioration and social change."

We hope this volume makes it clear that the question of social change must be faced squarely if we are to prevent psychopathology. It documents not only the horrors of the effects of the present system but shows us the various roads, rocky as they may be, to take toward a better one.

Themes and Variations

M. Brewster Smith

George Albee launched the conference in the proper revivalist spirit with a rousing keynote address that heightened our awareness of polarities of Good and Evil. I agree that the human issues of primary prevention require us to be politically embattled. I think, all the same, that the "medical" and "psychological" models of psychopathology are not quite so polar or mutually exclusive as Albee implies, and that it is hardly fair to identify the perspectives of psychiatry and medicine with hereditary and incurable taint or defect.

Gisela Konopka's moving collation of the wisdom of a full life of helping people amounted to a complementary keynote address. As we heard from her, we need to work collaboratively to help people, whether in primary, secondary, or tertiary ways. We need the commitment and courage to persist in our efforts in spite of uncertain knowledge and in the face of external resistance and difficult times.

Ira Iscoe and Ira Goldenberg provided amplifications and elaborations of the keynote talks, discussing what we ought to mean by primary prevention and its relation to social change. I will return later to Iscoe's stress on *empowering people*—a central theme of the conference. Besides calling for radical change of the system, Goldenberg took a disparaging retrospective look at the "War on Poverty," with which I am compelled to take issue. Common as that view has become in the present conservative swing of the national pendulum, I think it is wrong, and needlessly discouraging of political effort today. The War on Poverty was aborted by the war in Vietnam. And for all its failures, it left substantial new resources of leadership and expectations in its wake. Our social gains are more often side-effects than direct conquests!

In providing an overview of the remaining papers, I will try to pull together some of the strands that we have been dealing with. First, I want to identify what I think is a firm consensus about the objectives of primary prevention in relation to political action and social change. Second, I want to identify our equally firm consensus about the major place where problems of psychopathology exist, where prevention is needed. Third, I saw nearly as firm a consensus about the major obstacles to be confronted and attacked. Fourth, I will review somewhat more briefly the major institutional areas where strategic intervention is needed. Fifth, I will look briefly at some of the strategies we talked about that might be used. Sixth, I will try to bring us briefly to a focus on one issue that came to the fore in the conference, the relative priorities and considerations involved in overall system change versus ameliorative piecemeal change. Seventh, I would like to look very briefly at the concept of power that we have taken for granted, and suggest that we need to deal with differentiated meanings. Eighth, I will call our attention to some risks that need to be made visible that follow from our consensual rejection of paternalistic liberalism. And finally, I will pick up the statement from Dr. Pardes, Director of NIMH, as quoted by Brodsky and Miller, where Pardes was advocating a very narrow, restricted conception of mental health. In his *Monitor* (May, 1979) interview, Pardes was quoted as saying:

Mental health has been too ready to take on the world in past years, and I think we need to be a bit more humble. . . . The prevention program has to be relevant to mental health. There's a difference between broad societal issues and the purview of NIMH . . . and with broad issues of citizen organization and citizens' empowerment, you've got to show me the very strict relationship to mental health.

First, our consensus, then, about the objectives of primary prevention in relation to political action and social change. I think we are very strongly agreed on this point. Slightly different language is used but the ideas seem to be synonymous. We are talking about the objective of *empowering* people, increasing people's options, giving them the potential to live their own lives to a fuller extent. So it is a matter of *quality of life*, but, as Betty Friedan puts it in the context of women's issues, it is not just a matter of *quality*: It is a matter of the extent to which people are really living. This goal is clearly related to how people handle their problems in living, although it may not be so directly related to some of the conventionally conceived mental illnesses. One set of related ideas that we did not talk about at the conference, which is closely related to our goals, is Seligman's increasingly rich conception of learned helplessness and the strategies for dealing with it, initiated in relation to animal models for the study of depression (see Seligman, 1968; Abramson, Seligman, and Teasdale, 1978). He has carried these ideas forward to become much more relevant to the challenge of empowering people to be "unhelpless" in their own lives.

A second consensus concerned the major locus of the problems of psychopathology, the place where prevention is most urgently needed. Here, we clearly agreed with the major thrust of the President's Commission on Mental Health: The problems of psychopathology are heavily concentrated among the poor, the oppressed, the powerless, the dehumanized, the stigmatized. Like the first consensus, this one involves our values but I think the facts here are quite incontrovertible. By whatever criterion of psychopathology you use, the powerless, oppressed segments of the population are where the most problems emerge and where typically the least service has been given.

The third area of consensus concerns the major obstacles in institutions and attitudes. Here we have three familiar labels, plus some parallel matters of concern: *racism*, which we have learned about from various angles in the papers by Hilliard, O'Gorman, and Clark; *sexism*, which Friedan has been calling to our attention; and *ageism*, as evoked in Robert Binstock's paper. But parallel with racism, sexism, and ageism, are, of course, the similar institutional and attitudinal barriers stigmatizing and ostracizing the handicapped, which Blatt has cataloged, and the class exploitation and economic oppression that many of the writers saw as underlying or related to other forms of oppression.

Having identified essential goals and the main locus of problems of psychopathology, and having achieved consensus on the major causes and barriers that have to be attacked, we can turn to the major institutional areas in which strategic intervention might be undertaken. Glaser provides us with the conventional triad of family, school, and work, as contexts in which people live their lives. To these three, one can add, in a slightly different vein, the institutional area of the mass media, which White describes. The mass media provide an environment in which we are constantly bathed. How ought we to deal with these institutional areas? We did not focus on the family as such, although our concern with the relations of the sexes and genders, as analyzed by Friedan, really plants us in that area. School and work emerged, with special clarity and provocativeness, in Levin's dialectical analysis.

Levin's paper strikes me as the most sophisticated, flexible, and wise application of a strictly Marxian economic analysis that I have been exposed to: a Marxian analysis that actually identifies points of leverage where one may expect accessibility to change, that gives us guidance about what to look for next, and what we ought to be working on in schools and in the workplace. Levin's analysis provides hard-nosed guidance to the problems of school and workplace in the light of our recent history.

White's discussion of the mass media seems to me to put the emphasis where it belongs, on the impact of the media in soaking up such an extraordinarily large segment of our lives. This is not just a matter of the "quality of life," but concerns the very constitution of what our lives amount to. As a social psychologist, I lament that these issues regarding the long-term effects of life-time exposure to the tube are beyond the reach of firm, quantitative research. All the same, it seems to me so plausible as to be almost incontrovertible, that the massive proportions of our time that are devoted to alpha-wave-free exposure to the boob tube must surely have some effect upon our attitude toward life—our initiative, our passivity—and must as surely have something to do with feelings of empowerment versus nonempowerment, which we agreed are central to our conception of mental health.

Now as to strategy. What do you do in primary prevention? The writers, for the most part, have implied that if we manage to define the underlying problems explicitly, then at least the major outlines of strategy tend to follow. Looking at kinds of strategies that received some attention at the conference, we heard from Brodsky and Miller about class action suits as a way of correcting dehumanizing institutional conditions and practices. And their report to us was that this is still a useful modality, at least for opening up problems, during this time of generally conservative retrenchment. However, they told us, we need to be ready to move beyond the suit to a more collaborative relationship to follow through and deliver improved service after winning. The whole women's movement, as exemplified and talked about by Friedan, is a set of strategies that the rest of us would be happy to see harnessed on behalf of other kinds of causes.

We have not talked about why the women's movement happened when it did and why it has been so remarkably successful. Of course, there has been much speculation about that. I fear, however, that for most of the issues that we would like to see a social movement deal with, it would be very, very hard to capture the magical ingredient that inspired the women's movement. After all, women are half the population and what they are concerned with involves everybody, whether the men know it or not. We have much to learn from the women's movement. The strategies of neighborhood organization have come up saliently, both in the paper by Trotter and in the special context of the Harlem program in the War on Poverty, as Clark reminds us.

Trotter writes about neighborhood organization efforts that have sprung out of needs and from the initiatives of people themselves. As she suggests, when they have the most impressive mental health consequences, it might be not because they are focused on a mental health issue, but because people are in fact working together in discovering competence and confidence in the identification and solution of their common problems. What is needed, clearly, is the development of new roles for community oriented mental health professionals—as consultant and helper, not necessarily as political leader, and we know more about that now. Hilliard tells us that the *C and E* (Consultation and Education) component of community mental health centers has been very under-developed, usually limited to case consultation. Our great problem, politically and practically, is how to get support for an active, catalyzing, and supportive role for mental health professionals in empowering communities to face their own problems, as Trotter indicates.

My sixth concern is with whether we should worry about overall system change, maybe revolutionary change, or ameliorative change on a smaller and more piecemeal scale. In the Sidels' account of Chinese revolutionary hope, I find an ingredient that we sorely miss in our presently discouraged struggle for justice and primary prevention. "Revolutionary hope" sounds like a gorgeous formula for high morale, a context for commitment to something larger than self that is a critical component of good mental health. But there is a danger here of getting caught in romantic yearning for a situation that simply is not ours, which cannot be helpful to people who are trying to cope with the problems of primary prevention in this country.

I learned much from the papers on the revolutionary countries: First, I think they help us begin to become sensitized to the really inordinate degree to which our own American culture is hypertrophied and over-emphasized on the individualistic and competitive side. This theme emerged in several of the conference papers. Since we are all enmeshed in our culture, it is helpful to look at China and Cuba so as to see what strange creatures we really are. If we are alerted to some of the dysfunctional results of our extreme competitive individualism, we may be able to criticize, and even to begin to change some of our ways of dealing with family, personal relations, school, and work. The China case also gives us a challenge to think about the costs and benefits of the revolutionary models being presented in terms of our own cultural values. As we look at China and Cuba we are at risk with respect to the prime anthropological "disease" of xenophilia: from a xenophilic perspective the Bongo-bongo have better lives than we do, and also the Chinese. We ought to take the revolutionary alternative seriously, but with a strong sense of what is compatible with our own basic values and institutions.

I was much impressed with Trotter's analysis of the delicate balance between publicness and privacy involved in the support systems of our neighborhoods. It seems to me that the invasiveness of the Chinese support system (which seems to be very good for China) might be intolerable for us. So that quite apart from the larger political and ideological context, I think that as we try to learn from interesting and challenging things being done well elsewhere, we should also worry about their translatability to our own cultural and political setting. I found Trotter's paper particularly helpful in updating our consideration of what is happening in neighborhood organization. In regard to some of the less impossible problems that the neighborhood groups that Trotter writes about have been dealing with—problems less intractable than Harlem presents—one gets the impression that the neighborhood organizational strategy is very much alive and very relevant to people on the firing lines in such places as comprehensive community mental health centers.

My seventh point has to do with two meanings of the key concept of power. Here I think I am essentially in tune with what Clark suggests. We can talk about power at the collective, structural, political level, or we can talk about power in the sense of empowerment at the personal level. Obviously, these are closely interrelated concepts, but they are not identical. Politically, we have seen that power has to be assembled and marshaled and used in the tough real world if mental health objectives are going to be achieved. We have to be effective politically if we are to do anything significant toward primary prevention. Clark gives us a powerful illustration of how important that consideration is. On the personal level, empowerment, the possession of options, is a key constituent of mental health, or of being fully human. These two concepts of power are linked, but they are not rigidly linked. It seems to me that in the survival training that O'Gorman writes about for the kids he works with in his storefront operation in Harlem, he was empowering the kids in their personal sphere even though he was not solving the larger political and structural problems of oppression in Harlem as a whole. Political power frequently is conceived of as a zero sum game. I do not think it has to be that way, but it tends to pull that way, and realism requires us to accept that as the way things are. If one group gets more power, then the other group gives some. There is a balance. At the personal level, when we talk of empowerment, increased options, as an important aspect of mental health, no zero sum game is involved at all. We need to recognize this. It is very important to recognize it in relation to genders, love relationships, and marriage. Empowering the ones does not take away the empowerment of the other. Such relationships can be synergic and mutually supportive, and that is why we find it so easy to agree that empowerment is a damn good thing. Nobody loses.

Risks are involved in our consensual rejection of liberal paternalism. We do not like to institutionalize people; we do not like to put people in jails and mental hospitals; we are now in the middle of a large move toward deinstitutionalization, toward mainstreaming the handicapped (Blatt), toward emphasis on natural support systems (Trotter), in contrast with highly professional paternalistic mental health services. These developments are a healthy advance from the former paternalistic approach. They have obvious inherent advantages in empowering people and evoking their participation. On the other hand, these same developments can be turned to very inhumane ends by tax-stingy people, such as proponents of Proposition 13, which is not a blessing to California. You can promote mainstreaming as a way of avoiding giving special education services. You can promote mainstreaming as a way of letting the handicapped child simply sink to the back of the room and be ignored. You can talk about deinstitutionalization and dump the former patients untreated, into socially unacceptable circumstances in the community. Each of these ways of potentially empowering people can be turned to vicious and reactionary ends. Each is very vulnerable at a time of budget tightness and social conservatism.

So here I come back to the point that I was suggesting earlier: We need to keep the message strong—the new message is not a matter of reducing services; it is a matter of remodeling our various mental health service roles to give a stronger priority to the role of consultant, helper and partner, catalyst, trainer, and so forth. The general spirit of this is very nicely exemplified in Leona Tyler's recent book (Tyler, 1978). Out of her background in counseling psychology, Tyler framed this idea of the professional as consultant and helper in a particularly clear way.

In conclusion, I want to attend to the words of Dr. Pardes, the director of NIMH: "Mental health has been too ready to take on the world in the past years, and I think we need to be a bit more humble." Pardes advocated a narrow definition of mental health that by implication is more congruent with the unsatisfactory biomedical model Albee describes. Such an admonition from the director of NIMH is a radical challenge to the consensus of this conference, or, if you will, the consensus of this conference is a radical challenge to Dr. Pardes. I think we do need to attend to the challenge. We are challenged to respond. In the light of the presentations and discussions here, my response would be this:

Everything that we have said about primary prevention as empowerment runs counter to any narrow conception of mental health. All the same, we need to be explicit about the responsibilities we are ready to take on as mental health professionals (a term which includes teachers and researchers as well as those on the front lines.) The whole of HEW, indeed the whole of our entire American citizenry, ought to be involved in primary prevention. Mental health professionals, whether academic or front line, ought to understand and promulgate and keep reiterating this message: Primary prevention is everybody's job. If we understand that message ourselves, we certainly have a responsibility to get the point across as widely as we can, in political discourse and persuasion. We have a responsibility both as mental health professionals and as citizens.

If you are concerned with the primary prevention of psychopathology—if you are concerned with the empowerment of people as an essential part in living a human life—you have to give priority to this wide range of citizen's concerns. We have a special responsibility to promulgate this vision. Some of us also have a more direct role in our communities and our neighborhoods and in the institutions in which we participate. We hope we bring competencies in interpersonal processes and in research, and a distinctive perspective on social and personal problems, without claiming to be universal experts on the perennial problems of mankind. I do not think that we, or NIMH for that matter, need to run away from where human problems really are. If we do run away from where these human problems really are, we will have much more to be humble about.

References

Abramson, L. Y., Seligman, M. E. P., and Teasdale, J. D. Learned helplessness in humans: Critique and reformation. *Journal of Abnormal Psychology*, 1978, *87*, 49–74.

Seligman, M. E. *Helplessness: On depression, development, and death.* San Francisco: W. H. Freeman & Co., 1968.

Tyler, L. *Individuality: Human possibilities and personal choice in the psychological development of men and women.* San Francisco: Jossey-Bass, 1978.

Messages for Preventionists

Stephen E. Goldston

There is a touch of personal irony that I should be writing an overview for this volume. Such irony is on two accounts. First, for most people a conference is but a period in time lasting a few days at maximum; however, my involvement with volume five in the series Primary Prevention of Psychopathology spans a period of a year and a half, beginning in November 1978 and lasting to now as I prepare this material in June 1980, even as I get ready to journey to Burlington once again to participate in the sixth of the Vermont conferences. The second bit of irony relates to a chance encounter on that November evening in 1978 when Justin and Daryll Joffe and I joined George and Connie Albee at their home in Burlington for a home-cooked Chinese meal to be followed by some brainstorming about volume five. But I am getting ahead of my story. About an hour before George was to demonstrate his recently acquired culinary skills, one of the Albee teenagers was in the large country kitchen with a friend preparing their meal while I sat on a bar stool by the counter enjoying a drink. After a few moments the friend, an attractive, dark-eyed youngster of about 16, sat down next to me, and with genuine interest in her voice asked me what I did professionally. I began by talking about primary prevention and my work at NIMH in general terms, and then I began to speak of specific examples of preventive interventions, finally focusing down on the area of marital disruption and its effects on parents and children. Her eyes lit up as she became increasingly involved in what I was saying; I felt that I had rarely had such a rapt audience, and I sensed clinically that what I had been saying was not merely of intellectual interest but also of personal concern. I mentioned how different children respond in different ways to family breakup, but that recent research was providing some information about the commonality of certain behaviors and concerns at specific developmental stages. I went on to talk about how my own two daughters had reacted to their parents'

This Overview is dedicated to the two persons who inspired its content, George W. Albee and Cecile S. Currier.

This paper was written by Dr. Goldston in his private capacity. No official support or endorsement by the Alcohol, Drug Abuse, and Mental Health Administration (ADAMHA) is intended or should be inferred.

separation and subsequent divorce. The more I talked and answered the intermittent questions, the more I felt that I was providing information that some one should have extended to this youngster, but had failed to do so. When the discussion ended and the teenagers, having finished their dinner, had departed from the kitchen, George who had been present and busy in preparation throughout turned to me and said: "You handled that beautifully. Her father ran off with his secretary a few months ago and never gave his kids any explanation."

I relate this incident and label it ironic because it encapsulates succinctly my major approach to primary prevention, that is, dealing with life crises through educational modalities. And here I was in Burlington to take on the mammoth theme of prevention through political action and social change! I wondered then what meaning that theme and the presentations might have for persons on the firing line planning and doing primary prevention interventions, and I continued to wonder through the conference itself as I listened to the papers, participated in discussions and critiques, and overheard passing comments from attendees. Perhaps it all did not fall completely into place for me until I read the manuscripts, reread them, and was able to come to a better understanding of what this collection of papers means for primary prevention 1980.

The basic task of this epilogue is to try to convey, albeit in an idiosyncratic manner, what I believe the messages contained in this volume are for primary preventionists. If my interpretations and inferences are too limited it is because I have taken what is contained in these pages and filtered it through the lenses of my experiences (both personal and professional) in a career focused on legitimizing prevention within the mental health field—the day-to-day frustrations of trying to work within a system, to gain sanction from that system, to achieve a sense of justice and equity toward the viewpoint that the scope of mental health issues extends beyond the psychiatric sphere of mentally troubled/ troublesome/ in trouble persons already labeled with a psychiatric diagnosis.

What I shall attempt to do in the following pages is to move from the macro-societal considerations so forcibly presented in the foregoing chapters to a somewhat more manageable perspective of the community mental health worker charged with developing preventive interventions at the grassroots level. I am mindful of the paradox in this. On the one hand, I recall an agency head telling me early in my career in response to a proposal I had offered which I did not believe to be either unrealistic or grandiose: "It's your job to think big, and my job to think small." At minimum, the lesson communicated to me was to anticipate resistance from those above, particularly if the issues are important. However, on the other hand, I would argue that we need a larger vision, even if it may sometimes be out-of-phase with current realities and swift solutions, to enable us to persevere at our daily tasks and to provide a sense of ultimate mission and purpose. This volume serves that end well and offers approaches consistent with Robert Kennedy's vision: "Some men see things as they are and say why. I dream things that never were and say why not."

From these chapters I have identified seven messages that I hold important to convey to primary preventionists at the community level who attempt to effect some of the systems changes called for in the text:

(1) *A need exists to clearly define the roles, boundaries, and limitations of mental health workers.* Most mental health workers would tend to hold the view that they are powerless and helpless, individually and collectively, to deal in any meaningful manner with the macro-issues presented in this volume. And to some extent that would be an accurate, realistic appraisal. On the other hand, as Goldenberg points out, much depends on how we conceptualize a problem and attempt to have any impact. For example, I would maintain that mental health workers typically have little capacity to affect dramatically the macro-problem of world overpopulation. Yet, mental health workers have a responsibility and an obligation to build bridges and alliances between community mental health agencies and family planning services so that mental health workers are knowledgeable about family planning and can provide options to their clients under appropriate circumstances. The depressed, disadvantaged mother of four, still in her young 20s, may be in greater need of contraceptive information and services to obviate the fear and actuality of another pregnancy than she is for psychotherapy. We tend to view too many problems as either insoluble, requiring massive changes at some other level (preferably necessitating a social revolution), or somehow totally outside of our capacity to manage. I submit that primary preventionists have greater opportunities to have an impact on societal problems having a mental health aspect than has either commonly been assumed or even identified.

(2) *Primary preventionists have the capacity to redress some stressful and damaging environmental conditions, even those which Albee points out are almost invariably linked with excessive imbalances in power.* In this connection I call to the reader's attention a circumstance reported in April 1979 on the front page of the *Washington Post*. The news story detailed the travails of a welfare mother as she made funeral arrangements for her five-year-old daughter who had been killed in a fire. Specifically, this mother was entrapped in the obscure world of "welfare funerals" in Washington, an arena of private grief and public, tax-paid "contract" burials involv-

ing several hundred of the city's poor and costing about a quarter of a million dollars each year. The burial practices to be described are associated with social, racial, and financial conflicts having decided mental health components.

Basically, the contract burials provided for the essentials of a funeral, but not the "extras," such as flowers, a newspaper notice, an extra death certificate, and a guest book for the wake and funeral. The contractor used the occasion of the first meeting with the bereaved to obtain payment for these "extras." After the cash was exchanged, this welfare mother was told that because of the tight schedule of funerals, the service would have to be limited to one-half hour, that the coffin could not be open for viewing since this would cause further delays, and that due to a backlog the funeral could not be held for a week! What stark oppression and extreme insensitivity directed at the helpless at a point of crisis. The article brought to public knowledge the practices of the white-owned funeral business that had a contract from the municipal government of what is a predominately black populated city. At the time, black undertakers asserted that the contract business was insensitive to black funeral tradition, especially open caskets and prolonged emotional grieving. As a result of complaints to the appropriate city agency, as well as of the news story, new legislation was promulgated to permit welfare recipients to choose among a number of funeral homes for city-financed services, thereby closing out the monopoly previously enjoyed by a single firm.

Preventionists reading about this incident would probably observe three factors: (a) the gross insensitivity on the part of the undertaking business having the welfare contract; (b) the mother's grief compounded by this difficult situation; and (c) the fact that at no point, before, during or after, did mental health workers appear to have any involvement whatsoever in either exposing existing procedures or advocating more appropriate practices consistent with the psychological, racial, social, and cultural needs of the bereaved.

This incident deals with a stressful and damaging environmental condition, which certainly seems to be linked with excessive imbalances in power. Moreover, this incident typifies the public health dictum to seek out "foci of infection." But yet, mental health workers played no role in either exposing or changing the oppressive contract burial practices.

(3) *Even when we clearly are on the side of the angels, everyone is not always going to agree.* Perhaps I have stacked the deck with my choice of words, "clearly" and "always," but the message is that what may well appear to make good sense, can be perceived otherwise by some folk. My illustration of this message harks back to an experience I had during the Nixon years. I had proposed, with considerable written justification, and had

secured the necessary funding for a series of short educational films on the theme of helping children to understand death. After reviewing the professional literature on the imperatives of promoting parent-child communications about death in order to sensitize, educate, and de-traumatize children, I concluded that some graphically beautiful films on this subject were needed. As are the ways of a bureaucracy, final clearance on films rested well up in the departmental hierarchy. Consequently, late one afternoon I received a copy of the following memorandum from the Assistant Secretary for Public Affairs:

I have reviewed the initial proposal and summary memorandum to produce several films on "Death and the Child" and concluded that we cannot approve this proposed project in any form.

Films of this nature would be more appropriately developed by theologians and philosophers than HEW.

I drew a black crayoned border around that memo, and to this very day it appears on the bulletin board over my desk, a constant reminder of the message with which I began this segment.

(4) *Systems can be changed both through folkways and stateways.* As a graduate student at Teachers College, Columbia University in the late 1950s, I recall Goodwin Watson, the distinguished social psychologist, stating that stateways make for folkways. His observation was within the context that state-level civil rights legislation providing equal access to housing had demonstrated that blacks and whites not only could reside peacefully together but as a consequence would relate on friendly, human terms. Back in those days, the power of the state was needed to modify unequal access and opportunity as a prelude to changes in folkways.

As preventionists we have the responsibility to change both folkways and stateways. Two illustrations of this message, each dealing with family law legislation in California, emphasize this point. Ten years ago California enacted the first no-fault divorce law in the United States; similar legislation swept across the nation, so that in 1980 there are only three states without no-fault grounds for divorce. Undoubtedly, one effect of such legislation has been to facilitate both the decision to divorce and the accompanying process; to that extent, the stateway modified the folkways about divorce.

On January 1, 1980 a new law went into effect in California that provides a *preference* for joint custody of minor children rather than separate custody to one parent. To a considerable degree, this new law reflects the growing awareness on the part of divorcing parents that parents are forever, in that it is in the best interests of the children to maintain relationships with both parents individually, as well as the increasing phenomenon of custody awarded to fathers and the desire of fathers to have a major role in bringing up their children. To the extent that these considerations influenced legislators, one might conclude that folkways led to stateways. (I do not wish to suggest that these two illustrations are clear-cut instances of the influence of stateways on folkways or the reverse; rather, my intent is to point up the important effects of laws on the mental health of persons involved in their application.)

Beyond testimony at selected hearings, the input from mental health experts prior to the enactment of the two pieces of legislation cited appears minimal or nonexistent. Preventionists should keep themselves aware of how the new custody legislation works and the implications of such laws for their jurisdictions, as well as the role of the mental health professions in collaborating with legislators to promote laws having preventive significance.

(5) *Need exists to maximize the prevention potential in relevant agencies in both the public and private sectors.* We are living in a time of coalitions, special interest groups, and power politics. As Goldenberg, Binstock, and others point out, we must modify both our perceptions of problems as well as the identification of those specific problem areas on which we propose to devote our energies. The Task Panel on Prevention of the President's Commission on Mental Health and the commission in its final report strongly advocated efforts aimed at identifying the prevention components in what may appear to be in basically non-mental health areas, for example, transportation, commerce, justice, housing, labor, and so forth.

(6) *Would that there were less concern about the politics of problems and more emphasis on solving problems.* Hilliard points out the tendency to psychologize problems rather than to deal with their root causes; too often psychologizing is tantamount to dealing with the politics instead of the problem-solving. From my perspective, particularly in a time of scarcity, we no longer can tolerate (as Goldenberg said) "sacrifice of impact on the altar of consensus."

(7) *Prevention demands passion and commitment.* Were I to identify one theme that runs most consistently through the chapters, it would be this message. In different ways, Konopka, Albee, Cottle, O'Gorman, Goldenberg, and virtually all the others have either stated or implied that there can be no change, no justice, without passion and commitment. To be involved in primary prevention is a statement both of one's professional interests as well as one's personal values. Were prevention workers to lose their passion and commitment, the residue would be sterile and valueless.

To summarize, the dilemma mental health workers face in trying to understand and deal with those root causes of psychopathology which are so firmly part of the social fabric was best expressed to me by a young social worker only a year out of professional school who worked in a rural, acute psychiatric hospital:

The system is all fucked. The people we see, besides being severely mentally ill, are poor, uneducated, disadvantaged in every imaginable way, and just plain incompetent to make it. They come here. We labor to bring them back to a reality which is for them an oppression of their very being. We fill them full of drugs and send them out again, knowing full well that they'll be back. I think mental health workers have more than a responsibility to "treat" these people. It seems to me that we also have a responsibility to make it known that these people are victims of a system which is unresponsive and uncaring about their pain.

We seem to have many questions but few answers. These essays have presented a vision of the unfinished work, and an opportunity for a new perspective on the prevention frontier.

Contributors

George W. Albee is professor of psychology at the University of Vermont. In 1977–78 he chaired the Task Group on Prevention for the President's Commission on Mental Health. The commission, whose honorary chair was Rosalynn Carter, prepared a report delivered to President Carter in April, 1978, which stressed the importance of primary prevention. Albee is past-president of the American Psychological Association and of the Division of Clinical Psychology. He served on an earlier national mental health study, the Joint Commission on Mental Illness and Health, which reported to Congress in 1960. He wrote *Mental Health Manpower Trends* for that commission. On the basis of the final report of this earlier commission (a book entitled *Action for Mental Health*) the community mental health centers were established throughout the United States.

Thomas Szasz was born in Budapest in 1920. He earned his undergraduate degree in physics at the University of Cincinnati, where he also completed medical school. He interned at Harvard's program in Boston, did his residency at the University of Chicago Clinics, and completed his psychoanalytic training at the Chicago Institute in 1950. He is currently professor of psychiatry at the State University of New York, Upstate Medical Center, Syracuse, New York. Szasz is widely known for his controversial views expressed in a dozen books, including *The Myth of Mental Illness*; *Law, Liberty and Psychiatry*; and *Ceremonial Chemistry*. He is co-founder of the American Association for the Abolition of Involuntary Mental Hospitalization, Inc. He has been the frequent recipient of awards from civil libertarian, humanist, and public service groups

Burton Blatt is dean of the School of Education and Centennial Professor at Syracuse University. He has been president of the American Association on Mental Deficiency and is widely recognized as a leader in the field of mental retardation. A recipient of numerous awards for distinguished service to handicapped children and adults, he is the author of eighteen books and innumerable chapters and articles. Among his best-known works are *Christmas in Purgatory: A Photographic Essay on Mental Retardation* and *Exodus from Pandemonium: Human Abuse and a Reformation of Public Policy*.

Robert H. Binstock is the Louis Stulbert Professor of Law and Politics at Brandeis University in the Department of Politics and at the Florence Heller Graduate School for Advanced Studies in Social Welfare. He is director of the Brandeis Program in the Economics and Politics of Aging. In 1975 he was elected president of the American Gerontological Society. He has served on a wide variety of national and state advisory boards concerned with aging. He served as the executive director of the White House Task Force on Older Americans and chaired the Adult Development and Aging Research and Training Review Committee of the National Institute of Child Health and Human Development. He has authored, coauthored, and edited a dozen books and monographs in the field of politics and aging including (with Ethel Shanas) the *Handbook of Aging and the Social Sciences.*

Thomas J. Cottle is lecturer in psychology at Harvard Medical School and has been a visiting professor, consultant, and resident scholar in a large number of colleges in the United States and England. But above all else he is a writer—of books, articles, and television documentaries. His prolific output includes some twenty books dealing with the problems of contemporary society and has earned him many national and international awards. Among his best known books are *Children in Jail, Private Lives and Public Accounts,* and *Barred from School.* Cottle is one of the most articulate speakers and intrepid interviewers on the American social science scene today.

I. Ira Goldenberg is director of the Human Services Program at New Hampshire College. He taught psychology at Yale and Harvard for ten years before becoming President of Franconia College. Originally trained in clinical psychology, he has come to be recognized as a leader in the emerging field of community psychology. He has worked extensively with teenagers and has developed residential youth center programs. His involvement with the community is reported in a number of his articles and books, including *Build Me a Mountain* and *Youth, Poverty, and the Creation of New Settings.* He edited *The Helping Professions in the World of Action* and his most recent book is *Oppression and Social Intervention: Essays on the Human Condition and Problems of Change.*

Ira Iscoe is professor of psychology and education at the University of Texas where he is the director of the Graduate Training Program in Community Psychology. For many years he was director of the Counseling-Psychological Services Center at the University of Texas. In 1979 he was a distinguished visiting scholar at the National Institute for Mental Health. Iscoe has been active in the development of community psychology for more than two decades. A list of his offices and consultantships includes nearly every program concerned with the application of psychology to community problems. He is an advisory editor on at least eight journals and has written a number of books, including *Coping Adaptation and Lifestyles* and *Community Psychology: Perspectives and Research.* With Bernard Bloom and Charles Spielberger he edited *Community Psychology in Transition,* a report of a national conference on training in this field.

Thomas O. Hilliard is vice president of the Urban Institute for Human Services in San Francisco. A practicing clinical psychologist, he has taught at the University of California, Berkeley, and has been the director of consultation at the Westside Community Mental Health Center in San Francisco. He was a visiting scientist for the National Science Foundation and has been active in the Association of

Black Psychologists, which he chaired in 1973–74. He was an active participant in the Vail Conference on Graduate Training in Psychology. He has consulted with a variety of national research groups and has written on psychology and law, on prisons, and on the problems of oppressed people.

David Manning White, professor in the Department of Mass Communication, Virginia Commonwealth University, is widely known for his articles, books, and newspaper columns on the effects of the mass media. He coedited a book entitled *Identity and Anxiety*, which had a major national impact, and has written edited, or coedited a dozen books on television, films, and pop culture. He is one of the nation's authorities on how the mass media reflect and instigate psychopathological behavior.

Henry M. Levin is professor in education and professor in the affiliated Faculty of Economics, and director of the Institute for Research on Educational Finance and Governance of the Center for Educational Research at Stanford University, where he has taught since 1969. Before this he was a research associate at the Brookings Institution and a research scientist at the Graduate School of Public Administration at New York University. Levin is widely recognized as a leading theorist in the field of educational change, and he has written extensively about community control of schools and about school effectiveness. His books include the *Limits of Educational Reform* (with M. Carnoy) and *Schools and Inequality*.

Edward M. Glaser heads his own national firm of psychological consultants to management. He is also president of the Human Interaction Research Institute, which is concerned with research approaches to societal problems. He has taught psychology in many institutions and is author of a number of books, including *Productivity Gains through Work Life Improvement* and *An Experiment in the Development of Critical Thinking*. He has received the Myrdal Prize Award for his work in human services.

Stanley L. Brodsky is professor of psychology at the University of Alabama. He has taught at Southern Illinois University and has done research at Jefferson Disciplinary Barracks. During a recent sabbatical visit, he studied British criminal justice. He has written extensively about new approaches to corrections and the applications of community psychology to mental health services. He edited a landmark book, *Psychologists in the Criminal Justice System*, for the American Association of Correctional Psychologists.

Kent S. Miller is professor of psychology and sociology and director of the Community Mental Health Research Center at Florida State University. Miller was visiting fellow at the National Institute of Law Enforcement and Criminal Justice of the United States Department of Justice and has been director of a mental health center and on a number of state and international advisory panels. His writings range across a wide span of community psychology and include the widely-read book, *Managing Madness*. He has also written extensively about half-way houses, mental health centers, and social class variables.

Gisela Konopka was recently appointed professor emerita at the University of Minnesota, where for many years she was director of the Center for Youth Development and Research. Educated in Germany, she fought actively against the Nazis and was incarcerated in a concentration camp. She escaped to Austria, later to France, and then immigrated to the United States, where she did graduate work in social group work and received a doctorate in social welfare from Columbia University. She has occupied a wide range of important positions in the field of social work and has spent the last 30 years as a senior professor and scholar at the University of Minnesota. She has received awards from a score of countries and has lectured almost everywhere in the world. Her service to the community includes the presidency of the American Orthopsychiatric Association. Her books have been translated into many languages. They include *Group Work in the Institution*, *The Adolescent Girl in Conflict*, and *Young Girls: A Portrait of Adolescence*.

Betty Friedan is widely recognized as the person who launched the Women's Movement with her 1963 book, *The Feminine Mystique*. She was the founder and first president of the National Organization for Women, the organizer of Women's Strike for Equality, and the convener of the National Women's Political Caucus. She had wide-ranging graduate training in psychology and she has done extensive freelance writing. She had, and continues to have, a major impact on national and international social thought. A collection of her papers is being cataloged by the Schlesinger Library at Radcliffe College.

Kenneth B. Clark is one of America's best known social psychologists. He recently retired from his position as Distinguished University Professor of Psychology at City University of New York, City College. He is currently president of his own consulting firm, working with industry on problems of intergroup relations. His research with Mamie Clark had a major influence on the 1954 Supreme Court decision leading to the desegregation of schools. He is a member of the New York State Board of Regents and the author of *Dark Ghetto* and *The Pathos of Power*, as well as many other books, monographs, and articles.

Sharland Trotter is a popular and widely known science writer and editor who has worked for the Center for the Study of Responsive Law. She was a consultant for *Trans-Action Magazine* and for four years was editor of the *APA Monitor*, the monthly newspaper of the American Psychological Association. As a member of the Nader organization, she designed, researched, and wrote *The Madness Establishment* (with Franklin Chu), an examination of community mental health problems and the role played by the mental health establishment.

Ned O'Gorman is widely known as an innovative educator and poet. He is the founder and director of the Children's Storefront in Harlem. He has been a Guggenheim Fellow, a Baird Fellow, an Aspen Fellow, and a Rockefeller Fellow, and he has been asked to visit schools in Israel, Tunisia, and elsewhere both in this country and abroad. He has lectured at a number of American and foreign universities and has written *The Blue Butterfly* (a children's book), innumerable poems, and a powerful work about Harlem called *The Children Are Dying*.

Susan Rigdon is research associate at the Center for International Comparative Studies at the University of Illinois. A political scientist, for many years she was associated with the work of Oscar Lewis and Ruth M. Lewis. Together they have published *Living the Revolution: An Oral History of Contemporary Cuba* (in three volumes). Her interest is in comparative politics and especially comparative socialist systems.

Ruth Sidel is associate professor of sociology at Hunter College and **Victor Sidel** is chair of the Department of Social Medicine at Montefiore Hospital and professor of community health at the Albert Einstein College of Medicine. They have visited the People's Republic of China, Chile, Sweden, and Cuba, studying the role of women, child care, and human services. Ruth Sidel has published *Families of Fing Sheng: Urban Life in China* and *Women and Child Care in China: A First-Hand Report*. Victor Sidel has published *Serve the People: Observations on Medicine in China* and *A Healthy State: An International Perspective on the Crisis in U.S. Medical Care*. In 1979 he received the Poilez Award of the New York Academy of Sciences for "outstanding contributions toward the improvement of the health of the population."

Stephen E. Goldston has written extensively in the area of public health, with special focus on mental health training—sixteen articles, three monographs, three books, and six chapters in as many books. He is one of the contributors to *The Issues: An Overview of Primary Prevention*, the first volume in this series. Goldston is coordinator of Primary Prevention Programs for the National Institute of Mental Health.

M. Brewster Smith is widely published, particularly in the humanistically oriented aspects of social psychology. He is author of four books and numerous articles and editor of the *Journal of Social Issues* and the *Journal of Abnormal and Social Psychology*. Smith teaches at the University of California, Santa Cruz, and his current studies focus on personality and social psychology, with emphasis on the theory of the self. He served as president of the American Psychological Association and has acted as an adviser to state and federal governments.

Justin M. Joffe is professor of psychology at the University of Vermont. Author of the book *Prenatal Determinants of Behavior*, he has published numerous papers on developmental effects of early—particularly prenatal—experience, effects of paternal drug ingestion on progeny, and hormone-behavior relationships. Vice president and treasurer of the Vermont Conference on the Primary Prevention of Psychopathology, he edited, with George Albee, *The Issues: An Overview of Primary Prevention*, and is special features editor of the *Journal of Prevention*.

Indexes

Name Index

Subject Index

Social policy, 5
Social psychiatry, 9
Social psychology, 253
Social science, 213
Social Security Act, 71
Social support networks, 263, 264, 267,
   275. *See also* Support systems
Social technicians, 100–102
Social work, 228
Socialism, 21; view of justice, 298–302.
   See also China, Cuba, Marxism
Socialization, 105–106, 162
Society: bureaucratized, 54; free, 28;
   goods-and-power oriented, 105–106;
   just, 20; mobile, 266; professionalized,
   54; reconstruction of, 108; totalitarian,
   28, 29, 231–232
Society of Applied Anthropology, 234, 235
Solitary confinement, 215–216, 238
South America, oppression in, 315–316
Sports: in China, 306; women in, 243
Stanford Conference, 120
Sterilization, 13, 16, 49
Stress, 20, 137, 146
Stressful life events, 146
Suburbs, 267
Suicide, 27, 225, 257
Support systems, 10, 20, 265. *See also* So-
   cial support networks
Surgery. *See* Brain surgery, Psychosurgery
Sweden, 179
Syphilitic brain disease, 10, 27
System challengers, 185, 208, 225
System professionals, 185, 208

Taint theory, 14, 21, 326
Tanzania, 315
Task Group on Prevention, 6, 111, 339
Teacher Corps, 193–195
Teachers, 21. *See also* Schools
Teheran, 30
Television, 95, 159, 160, 161, 163–164,
   328; and Blacks, 148–149; and children,
   162; movies for, 154–155
Tennessee, 218
Thaler system, 198
Therapy, 9, 11, 21–22, 253
Third World peoples, 21, 42, 104, 173
Timidity, 93, 98–99, 100, 103, 232, 327,
   332. *See also* Shyness
Token economies, 102
Training programs, 115, 119–127, 131,
   271. *See also* Education
Truancy, 287
Twenty-sixth of July Movement, 288

Unemployment, 10, 187
Union of Soviet Socialist Republics
   (USSR), 29
United States Department of Agriculture,
   58
United States Marine Corps, 145
United States of America: balance of trade,
   200; freedom in, 42–43; hospital beds in,
   110; hospital census in, 11; medical ser-
   vices in, 118; support for oppression,
   276–277, 315–316
United States Public Health Service, 119
United States Supreme Court, 212, 222
University of Alabama, 214
University of California, 249
University of Michigan, 193
University of Minnesota, 236
University of Pennsylvania, 6
University of Southern California, 160

Vail Conference, 122–123
Value judgments, 234
Values, in human services, 38–39
Vandalism, 197–198, 325
Veteran's Administration (VA), 63, 119,
   198
Vietnam, 102
Violence, 95, 154–155, 197–198, 325
Voluntary associations, 76, 77, 270

War on Poverty, 99–100, 253, 255, 326,
   329. *See also* Poor people, Poverty
Warner-Chilcott Laboratories, 193
WASP males, 18, 21
Wealth, 322
Welfare sit-ins, 72, 324
West Germany, 179
Western religions, 12
White House, 46, 66; crypto-fascist clique
   in, 103
White House Conferences on Aging, 67,
   68
Women: adolescent, 237; and children,
   244, 248, 249–250; consciousness-rais-
   ing, 241; depression, 247; discussions
   with, 243; feminists, 243, 251; image,
   240–241, job-discrimination, 242–243;
   life expectancy, 242; and mass media, 3;
   menopause, 244–246; mental health of,
   245–246; new problems of, 243; and
   power, 249; reactions to marriage, 245;
   selfishness of, 248; and sex, 241, 248,
   292; in sports, 243; subjugation of, 327;
   Third World, 104
Women's liberation, 104, 247

LIBRARY OF CONGRESS CATALOGING IN PUBLICATION DATA (*Revised*)

Vermont Conference on the Primary Prevention of Psychopathology.
Primary prevention of psychopathology.

Proceedings of a series of meetings held 1975– at the University of Vermont.
Includes bibliographies and indexes.
Contents: v. 1. The issues. —v. 3. Social competence in children. —v. 5. Prevention through political action and social change.
1. Psychology, Pathological—Prevention—Congresses.
2. Psychology, Pathological—Social aspects—Congresses.
I. Albee, George W.   II. Joffe, Justin M.   III. University of Vermont.   IV. Title.
RC454.V46   616.89'05   76-53992
ISBN 0-87451-135-6 (v. 1)   AACR2